Praise for *From War to Wonder*

From War to Wonder, Dennis Slattery's new book, not only explicates the beauty and power of the *Odyssey*, Homer's twenty-seven-hundred-year-old marvel-filled epic, it also offers a marvelous way to interact with it on a daily basis. Those who do so will be amply rewarded by finding access to the poem's myriad meanings, as well as their capacity for forging their own personal myths."

~Phil Cousineau, author of *Once and Future Myths*, and editor of *The Hero's Journey: Joseph Campbell on His Life and Work*

What a beautiful invitation this book proffers: to spend a year slowly savoring one of the great masterpieces of world literature and day-by-day discovering how it illumines and deepens your understanding of your own life.

~Christine Downing, author of *The Goddess: Mythological Images of the Feminine* and *Mythopoetic Musings: 2007-2018*

Myth lifts the movement of the invisible world up and into the visible world so that we may become conscious of what drives us, wounds us, separates us, heals us. Slattery's appropriation of the timeless archetype of journey provides all of us a way to reframe our stories, and deal with our own monsters and seductions. Why should we think our journey is different from that of our predecessors, just because we wield different tools? *From War to Wonder* is a fit reminder and a practical instrument for our common human journey, and our common summons to make sense of it.

~James Hollis, Ph.D., Jungian Analyst and author in Washington, D.C.

In the mysterious journey that is our life, there is no better guide to discovering who we are and who we can be than this tremendous book of life: *From War to Wonder: Recovering Your Personal Myth through Homer's* Odyssey. This is something new and necessary that re-storys reading as the most powerful inner journey. Odysseus has imprinted cultures for millennia. Dennis Patrick Slattery enables him to illuminate our own hidden stories and bring us to a rebirth in myth as renewed creativity.

~Susan Rowland, Ph.D., Core Faculty, Pacifica Graduate Institute,
and author of *Jungian Literary Criticism: The Essential Guide*

Great visions deserve great guides. Dennis Slattery is one—a master mentor, teacher, interpreter and servant of the soul, bringing Homer's ancient vision into our modern world desperately in need of renewed spirit. Use *From War to Wonder*, his wise and penetrating guidebook, to follow Homer and Prof. Slattery on your soul's journey to your true inward home, mythos and destiny.

~Edward Tick, Ph.D., author of *The Practice of Dream Healing, War and the Soul,* and *Warrior's Return*

FROM WAR TO WONDER

Recovering Your Personal Myth Through Homer's *Odyssey*

DENNIS PATRICK SLATTERY

Copyright © 2019 by Dennis Patrick Slattery, PhD.
All rights reserved.

ISBN: 978-1-950186-13-6

Cover and interior design by Jennifer Leigh Selig
(www.jenniferleighselig.com)

Photo of Ithaca by Fotis Tasoulis
Copyright: <a href="https://www.123rf.com/profile_ftasoulis">ftasoulis / 123RF Stock Photo</a>

Photo of Odysseus statue by Oleg Kulakov
Copyright: <a href="https://www.123rf.com/profile_mccool">mccool / 123RF Stock Photo</a>

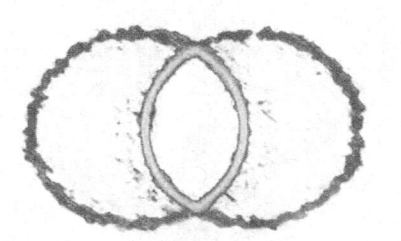

MANDORLA BOOKS
WWW.MANDORLABOOKS.COM

DEDICATION

To Sandy, my Penelope for over fifty years.
We continue to tell our stories to one another.
Some of them are true.

To all of my students who have journeyed with me for decades from Ithaca into the world's far reaches and back again. My gratitude to you for creating the spiral of life through your own mythic insights.

. . . the epic poet accomplishes in his cosmic image the spatialization of time. The poetic cosmos, which, as we have said, comes into being from the act of bringing the myth into consciousness—from shaping the past into memory—contains analogically not only a time-free place (*kleos*) for the deeds that can never die but also a time-bound place for the dead and lost events that cannot go forward (*nekros*).
~Louise Cowan, *The Epic Cosmos,* 16

What would Odysseus have been without his wanderings?
~C.G. Jung, "Liber Primus," *The Red Book: A Reader's Edition,* 182, fn.176

So the sea-journey goes on, and who knows where!
Just to be held by the ocean is the best luck
we could have. It's a total waking up!
~Rumi, "Buoyancy," *The Essential Rumi,* 104-05

In many ways, stories are uncannily similar to living organisms.
They seem to have their own interests.
~Ferris Jabr, "The Story of Storytelling," 36

TABLE OF CONTENTS

ACKNOWLEDGEMENT — i
FOREWORD by Norman Austin, Ph.D. — iii
INTRODUCTION — v

I. Books I-IV. The Birth of Self-Awareness: The Search for Stories. — 1

II. Books V-VIII. From Hiddenness to Community: Wandering Towards Wonder. — 65

III. Books IX-XII. Reclaiming a Coherent Life: The Myth of Remembrance. — 129

IV. Books XIII-XVI. Home to the Unfamiliar: Crafting Revealing and Concealing. — 189

V. Books XVII-XX. Reclaiming One's Self, Cleansing the Household. — 249

VI. Books XXI-XIV. From Reunion to Unity: The Weight of Words Over Weapons of War. — 315

EPILOGUE Four Poems by Edward Tick — 381
WORKS CITED — 385
FURTHER READINGS ON THE *ODYSSEY* — 393
ABOUT THE AUTHOR — 399

ACKNOWLEDGEMENT

I am grateful to Dr. Edward Tick for permission to use four of his poems that appear in the Epilogue.

FOREWORD

The Homeric epics, the *Iliad* and the *Odyssey*, have had a long and remarkable, and indeed a mysterious, history. In antiquity they were venerated by the Greeks almost as sacred scripture, since they were understood as expressing the values of Archaic and Classical Greece. They came into being as written texts sometime in the 8th century BCE, when the Greeks, with a writing system borrowed from the Phoenicians, were able to create their own alphabet, and thus write down the Homeric poems. But the poems themselves were a mystery. Who composed these poems? And when were they written? Did the Trojan War really happen? Was Helen's face really "the face that launched a thousand ships"? The traditional date for the Trojan War is 1200 BCE. Yet the Homeric poems were put into writing centuries after that event was thought to have happened.

In time, the Homeric gods, ageless and deathless, feasting at their leisure and interfering in the most flagrant way in the lives of human beings, came to be a scandal.Philosophy, with its rationalism, slowly pushed the Homeric mythology aside. Then skepticism took another turn when the Greco-Roman world became Christianized. Now the monotheism of the Judaeo-Christian world declared the Olympians gods to be heresies. As Christianity evolved from a local Judaean cult into the universal religion of Europe, the Homeric gods became theologically tabu.

Yet, such was the imaginative reach of the Homeric poems that they themselves could never be eradicated. In monasteries monks, albeit devoted to Christian ideals, continued to transcribe the Homeric poems, generation after generation, though the poems themselves were flagrantly pagan. In time, as the knowledge of Greek virtually disappeared in the Western world, what Western Europe knew of Greek poetry was mostly through Latin. Then came the Renaissance, and Homer was re-discovered in the West when Greek monks, fleeing their Ottoman rulers, escaped to Italy bringing their classical texts with them, and among them the poems of the master poet, Homer. With a shift in consciousness, even though the Homeric world was pagan fantasy, that fantasy was no longer tabu. The Greek language, which had virtually disappeared in the Western world, was revived, first among church leaders, and then slowly introduced into the schools and universities of the West. The Greek language came with the authority of the New Testament, but with Homer tagging along, Homer being both too interesting and too authoritative to ignore. Popes and cardinals were enthusiastic to have the old pagan myths decorate their palaces, whether in paintings or in sculpture.

Then, in the 19th century, there was another renaissance, as scholars discovered comparative religion. Homer, paradoxically, became a hallowed text again, with the Homeric myths being used as the template against which to measure the myths being collected by anthropologists from peoples all around the globe. Then yet another revolution took place under the influence of psychoanalysis, as Westerners awakened to a new consciousness that the mythology of ancient Greece had as much meaning and relevance in our modern secular world as it had in ancient times. Now Homer's *Odyssey* was neither obsolete nor tabu. The *Odyssey* has, in fact, become one of the primary texts in our modern university curriculum. In the past generation or so the *Odyssey* has emerged as not only of antiquarian interest but as a text with significant truths valid at the subliminal levels of human consciousness. Who in ancient Greece would have imagined that Homer's *Odyssey* would be not only interesting but directly relevant in people's lives 3000 years later?

Dennis Patrick Slattery brings to this study of the *Odyssey* a long career dedicated to the exploration of myth and literature as roads into our inner thoughts, fantasies, and dreams. I first met Dr. Slattery when we were participants in a summer institute on Homer at the University of Arizona. We recognized in each other kindred spirits, both of us feeling the deep connection between the Homeric poems and our own lives, both in the outer shape of our lives and in the thoughts and ideals that had given our lives meaning and a progressively greater sense of direction and fulfillment.

Now in this book, *From War to Wonder: Recovering Your Personal Myth through Homer's Odyssey,* Slattery has found a creative method by which readers of the *Odyssey* may explore the riches of the poem in an entirely personal way. After an essay to survey the varieties of psychological theories that have animated our modern interpretations of this famous poem, he takes his readers through the poem by giving short passages as day-by-day readings from the poem, and then inviting the readers to use these passages as an opportunity to meditate on the connections between events and thoughts in their personal life and this ancient epic poem. Those of us who teach ancient Greek literature and mythology recognize that we can sometimes probe more deeply into our personal myths by using a traditional myth than if we were practicing simply self-analysis. Homer's *Odyssey* is a treasure trove of such myths that have bearing on our lives today, because the poem expresses the universals of our human consciousness. I am sure that Dr. Slattery's method of bringing the *Odyssey* into his readers' personal lives will have a profound effect on many of those who will use his book as a guide into the *Odyssey* itself, but, even more important, to gain a better understanding of themselves.

Norman Austin, Ph.D.
Professor of Classics Emeritus
University of Arizona

INTRODUCTION

**Life is *The* Story.
The Story is *The* Journey.
The Journey is *The* Destination.**

Having taught and been taught by many literary classics over a span of fifty years of teaching, I have learned how mythic both reading giants of the literary canon and writing about them is. They serve as well as occasions for deep meditation, contemplation and renewal, including healing wounds we may not have realized we were carrying for years, even decades. It is not so much a therapy that cures as much as it is stories that care, that give back, that speak in conversation for decades and expand to take in where we are as readers in our lives. Many have read Homer's classic and its companion, the *Iliad,* in secondary school, undergraduate and graduate studies while others have read the *Odyssey* on their own or with small groups.

To show specifically the perduring power of Homer's classic, Edith Hall published an extensive study in 2008 called *The Return of Odysseus: A Cultural History of Homer's Odyssey,* which grew organically from an undergraduate course she taught at The University of Durham. One of the course's intentions was to excavate in all media where remnants or larger shards of Homer's epic appeared, including children's books and a wide assortment of films. The epic's shelf life seems never to expire historically or culturally. There is in the simple narrative, really, namely, a Greek king and warrior who has gone to war in Greece "in the late Bronze Age (3) for the sake of Greek honor and who fights fiercely for a decade, spends an equal amount of time returning home and cleansing his household of toxic elements that have poisoned the code of hospitality by those who abused his wife, Penelope, his son Telemachos, and his steadfastly faithful servants.

At the beginning of her study as well, she cites the literary critic Hugh Kenner, who wrote that it is almost impossible to lay hands on the myriad number of "spin-offs from the *Odyssey,* so deeply has it shaped our imagination and cultural values" (Kenner, qtd. in Hall 3). Its traction in the imagination of people globally is hard to pinpoint. Certainly there is the obvious one of an adventure into unknown territory that figures from before Odysseus engaged his struggles, for instance in the Sumerian epics of *Inanna* and *Gilgamesh,* but also down through the Middle Ages in Dante's *Commedia,* into our world of *Huckleberry Finn,* Herman Melville's *Moby-Dick,* J.R.R. Tolkein's *The Hobbit* and Toni Morrison's *Beloved,* then on to Margaret

Atwood's *The Handmaid's Tale* and Neil Gaiman's *American Gods* as well as the film *Wonder Woman*, the eight season series, *Game of Thrones, Patriot Games* as well as so many films loosely termed epic journeys. It also encompasses a recently published work by the analytical psychologist, C.G. Jung, who worked on what has become known as *The Red Book* earlier in the 20th. Century and ultimately made available to us in 2009. It relates, essentially Jung's own comic epic journey into the realms of his own unconscious as well as a stunning assortment of paintings that highlight moments in his descent. Both images painted and text written, then transcribed calligraphically into the shape of a medieval manuscript, give us a rich series of insights into Jung's own personal myth which has as one of its purposes to reclaim something of the medieval imagination.

My own rendering of the *Odyssey* is, however, less a scholarly endeavor; you can read libraries of explications on your own, although I do compile over two hundred sources that bear directly or indirectly on Homer's epic as well as the nature of epic as a literary genre and its expression as both place and power of both collective and personal myths. The latter is a key interest in this study because I intend to explore via the *Odyssey* the mythic dimension of reading literary classics as a way or angle of perception to open the reader up to his/her own mythic presence in the world. *From War to Wonder: Recovering Your Personal Myth Through Homer's Odyssey* follows two previous books that rely on the same patterned interactive format: *Day-to-Day Dante: Exploring Personal Myth Through The Divine Comedy* (2011) and *Our Daily Breach: Exploring Your Personal Myth Through Herman Melville's Moby-Dick* (2015).

Both books have been used by various groups and classes to combine an exploration of the classic itself with a writing meditation at the bottom of each page to encourage further contemplation of one's personal myth. In another publication, *Riting Myth, Mythic Writing: Plotting Your Personal Story*, I concentrated on the nature and dynamics of myth, both personal and collective, through a series of riting meditations to uncover these terrains. The spelling of the word without a "w" highlights the way writing is a ritual enactment of a mythology, a patterned way of seeing and knowing. Again, the intention here was to use cursive writing to access the deeper layers of consciousness and expose patterns and meanings in one's life that comprise one's own mythos. I encouraged my students and participants to set aside their laptops and enter the more embodied act of cursive writing.

More recently published, but in the works for three years is *Deep Creativity: Seven Ways to Spark Your Creative Spirit* coauthored with Deborah Ann Quibell and Jennifer Leigh Selig. There we explored seven regions of creativity by having each of us write a meditation on all categories, followed by questions and invitations to bring the reader into their own creative cosmos. It is currently required reading in a course I teach while my coauthors offer seminars on the book as well.

In all three epics and the book on creativity, however, but not limited to these exclusively, is a continual preoccupation with the nature of story, with the active creative process of the poet to shape a world, indeed an entire galaxy, through his/her fabrication. I like the way that classicist Albert B. Lord puts it in the Foreword to his remarkable study, *The Singer of Tales*: "This is a book about Homer. He is our Singer of Tales. Yet, in a larger sense, he represents all singers of tales from time immemorial and unrecorded to the present" (i). He goes on to suggest some other attributes of epic poets and then circles back to our ancient poet: "Among the singers of modern times there is none to equal Homer. . . . We believe that the epic singers from the dawn of human consciousness have been a deeply significant group and have contributed abundantly to the spiritual and intellectual growth of man" (i).

Lord's statement attests to the sustaining grit of such epics as the *Odyssey*. As I continue to teach it and then craft this book using selections from it to highlight what it has to do with lives today, I recognize that one of the major characters in its composition of twenty-four books is narrative itself. No matter what happens in the time period that the epic traverses and in references to what happened outside its purview, it must be given shape, form and coherence in story. Within the fiction is the multiplicity of parts that comprise its prevailing mythos. So let me add to story's centrality that myth is also a luminous and numinous mucilage that helps to bind the entire work into a coherent narrative and allows room for each reader to set his/her own narrative beside it and notice where the two narratives converse with one another.

I want to offer some insightful reflections by the Humanistic Anthropologist, Robert Plant Armstrong, primarily through his book, *Wellspring: On the Myth and Source of Culture,* for it bends this introduction toward the experience of the reader who journeys through a work of art like Homer's epic and discovers therein rich analogies to his/her own existence. In the title just mentioned, as well as in two others of his, *The Powers of Presence: Consciousness, Myth and Affecting Presence* and *Affecting Presence: An Essay in Humanistic Anthropology*, Armstrong develops what could be called a new discipline stemming from cultural anthropology. Studying his thought, I became more fascinated by what a work of art, and for my purposes, poetry, makes affectively present and what role both myth and symbol play in this felt sense as we read.

As a consequence of this rich imaginal interaction, two events occur: 1. A poem like the *Odyssey,* while finished on the pages, is not completed in the imagination. Each of us as readers participate in completing the work, extending it out to further parameters, offering new meanings, seeing fresh correspondences and analogies that enrich the poem to the degree and intensity that we enter it and yield to its shaped world. If we think of the rich imaginal act of reading as more a pilgrimage than a process, then we sense the veracity of Louise Rosenblatt's insight that "the reader's creation of a poem out of a text must be an active, self-ordering and self-correcting process" (*Reader* 11) in which the narrative line of the reader's life, his/her own myth, finds equivalences in the stories being read. The result is a series of evocations, as Rosenblatt refers to them, and I believe they arise from sensed analogies that now guide both stories in a communion.

Reading poetry is then a form of field work. By that I mean in the relation between reader and the story there is a transfer of psychic or mythic energy, and in that transfer, both are changed, both the text and the reader in an activity that might best be called alchemical. With each reader, another relationship of values is inaugurated such that the reader engages and initiates the text while the text engages and initiates the reader; both share in an exchange of values that occurs in the organic interaction of each. In Homer's *Odyssey*, we are privy through his narrative strategies and what he chooses to expose to us and what remains hidden is a world of values, a cosmos of patterns i.e. an entire and complete mytho-cultural universe, a galaxy of meanings that have the capacity to transform us, as I hope to show through a few of Armstrong's insights.

For Armstrong, value is the medium within which or through which each of us exists as human beings (*Wellsprings* 5). Myths, he further develops, are formative narratives of values' presence. Our own mythic dimension, what I am calling our personal myth, in the act of reading, imagining, remembering, draw inferences in this complex action. These analogies have a substantial role in how we understand a work of art, here of reading a classic text, because the work itself is understood "as an estate of *human consciousness*, a unique binding together in human cognition both of objective phenomena and of subjective values concerning them" (*Powers* 14. My emphasis). Homer's epic, then, assists us in our formation by offering a shaped and aesthetically ordered world of value—a mythic way of seeing, thinking and being aware of the world in a particular and unique way because the text itself is mimetic of human consciousness itself, as Armstrong affirms. My question here is: do we as readers shape the work as well; by that I mean, what we take in, what we leave out or underground is a making or shaping of the work to accommodate our own understanding in *this reading*, so always subject to change.

In this process, which is deeply archetypal and mythic, we are led by means of the poem's details and ordering, so that it achieves a power of affecting presence. We are moved and affected by its design. Armstrong is more pointed: "The work of affecting presence—sharing psychological processes with persons—sometimes seems as much to apprehend its witness as the witness apprehends it" (*Powers* 16). In other words we as readers share in the creation of the work even as it participates in shaping us anew because the deep archetypal patterns being expressed in through Homer's epic, reside in us as well and give our own lives both shape and coherence. That is a good working definition of *mythopoiesis*. From these patterns emerge and grow our life's purpose; these patterns that we inhabit by the powers of analogy comprise our world of meaning that is certainly connected to and feeds the larger purposes that the culture we are enshrouded in designates and cultivates. Said another way, Homer's *Odyssey* (and I am using it as an example of a whole pantheon of great works of literature) is an aesthetic, poetic cultural artifact; by means of it the culture is informed, perhaps reformed, in its own formative principles, those that the culture values most highly and will defend most vigorously if they come under attack.

Susan Rowland's more recent book, *Jungian Literary Criticism: The Essential Guide,* skillfully develops the idea of transdisciplinarity, influenced in large measure by the writer Basrab Nicolescu. Rowland's approach to reading classics of literature through what she terms "ethical close reading" (34) allows the text to exist in its own right while it also encourages us readers "to be morally present, morally in-formed by allowing the text to exist within one's own mental being," citing A. Federico (34). Earlier she expressed C.G. Jung's idea of "the power of words to *provoke* internal archetypes; to produce images in the independently generative power of the imagination" (14). With her insights we draw closer to the way that poetry in the form of literary classics, can activate the psyche of the reader and bring to greater consciousness the similarities in him/her that are the bedrock of their personal myth. So, to read the classics is to enter a deeply enriching mythopoetic construction site, both the text's and the individual's narratives; as such, the act of reading is psycho-mythic in design; it can allow a person, as Rowland suggests, "access to the meaning-making power of archetypal patterning" (69). Within these patterns of psyche, one's personal myth develops and has its shape as well as its relevance for that individual life.

Just as importantly, when we enter the terrain of a literary classic, we find ourselves in a symbolic order of being; nothing in the work is to be taken exclusively literally, for certainly it will reflect the current history in which it was written. But all should be taken concretely in its rich and often mysterious particularity. Through the symbolic order, the soul of the poem reaches out to the soul of the reader; otherwise we may end more fully knowledgeable of Homer's period in history but never touched by the deeper mimetic patterns in the poem that find rich energic resonances with our own symbolic order of being. Angling this way towards the relation of the work and the reader by way of a symbolic intermingling, we grow ever closer to how the work existing in the realm of art inhabits the universe of affecting presence" (*Powers* 45). Such is possible, suggests Armstrong, because "a symbol is a transformer of psychic energy" (45). It has the power and capacity to transform this energy so persuasively that the reader is transformed in the process in this current reading of the work. In a subsequent reading, our angle of interpretation may include a wider and deeper constellation of meanings. Having taught classics of literature on many levels of education for decades and having reread many of them repeatedly, I sense what others have thought: these works, in their richness and complexity, and in their uncanny ability to speak to us when we are very young, in adulthood and in elderhood, must be reread, meditated on repeatedly and imagined at the place and time we now inhabit; they will stretch and deepen to accommodate where we are in our own development psychically, emotionally and mythically. Such a process leaves room for our unconscious life, the terrain below the floorboards, to be contacted repeatedly with varied realizations each time.

Armstrong writes in *The Powers of Presence* that there is a close link between the person and the work of affecting presence, as he alluded to above: "The work of affecting presence is a phenomenon of consciousness, and any theory of the nature of the aesthetic must at base be inextricable from a theory of the nature of the consciousness itself" (16). All this by way of suggesting that the work is not an object but a subject, invoked in the interaction by the reader or the viewer. Armstrong helps us perceive the subject-nature of the work; it is a living organic being in its own right. When we come to read or reread or interpret it, it is "as-if" we are in imaginal dialogue with another person, with its own history, biography and energic psyche. Only then, when it is approached as a living being, does it disclose itself most fully to us as a corresponding organic being with our own consciousness. The text as well exhibits its own consciousness in the manner in which it unfurls before us with its attendant archetypal inflections. Rowland's work helps us to understand such properties in the literary work: "Archetypes are Jung's hypothesis of innate meaning-making and creativity inborn in the human psyche. . . . The creativity of archetypes is inexhaustible, androgynous, equally capable of any and all genders" (*Jungian* 59), she writes, so that archetypes furnish "generative energy that links worlds distant in space, time and culture" (59). They may be the most basic foundation for our creative impulses, insights and productions as well able to assist us as readers in plunging into the depths of the poem's own unconscious field of influence. Reading, then, is a relational enterprise between two mythologies: that of the reader and the text one engages with an intimate imagination that includes both conscious and unconscious levels of both reader and text, as I alluded to above.

Within such a complex, psychologist and mythologist C.G. Jung has written extensively about a process we spend our lives consciously moving through and desiring to achieve: Individuation. He writes that "Individuation is a process by which a person becomes a psychological individual, a separate individual unity or whole" (*CW* 9i par. 490). It is the process by which each of us tries to become as whole and as authentic in our unique being as is possible in our work of crafting the self. It includes the process of composting as part of our compos-ition. What is soiled in us, what matters to us, what is sought for in us is part of the growth pattern, including what is above and what is below, that nourishes us.

The act of reading, as I understand this process, is itself a journey of individuation. The power of a classic like the *Odyssey* rests in its organic form, a form that "incarnates affect. . . . It requires some recognition of this affective power of the analogic" as Armstrong calls it (*Powers* 25). Reading encourages and actually creates the terms for affective presence. What is felt, what is sensed, what is intuited are all part of affecting presence. Both the reader and the work have a myth they each continually give substantial form to. Yes, Homer's world is historically different from our own in many crucial ways; but it is also psychologically similar in universal or archetypal ways, such that we are able to participate in its myth even as it enjoins us to open to our own myth. Perhaps it is in the patterns of each that we most fully coexist through, as Rowland reveals above, "the generative energy that links worlds distant in space, time and culture" (59).

Armstrong suggests that "the myth of a particular people is contained in the pattern according to which the lived world is constituted (48). Through its language, the text resonates "in all its utterance [and]causes the world to be" (48); such is Homer's great achievement: to utter the myth of his people for our own mythic world to connect with it. If Armstrong is right as he continues, that " a myth establishes our range of beliefs and feelings felt" and further, that a myth establishes who a people are and what they believe (49).

What I want to explore off of the above is the way that an energy field is constituted by the connections of energy that I refer to above. I want to call this process of reading Imaginal or Archetypal, for it allows energy fields of both the reader and the work to be inaugurated. The energy of the person and the energy of the work converse through these fields of influence and affluence. The process is enhanced, I have experienced, when the text is brought into the classroom in a ritual ceremony of public reading of specific passages. It is as if in the reading process where the text is performed in reading aloud, we are opened to its energy field, its affecting presence and may find ourselves being "moved" by certain scenes, characters and actions of the plot. Reading then I understand as a field-evoking ritual in which the embodied imagination is in constructive motion.

At the same time, the text itself is exposed to the collective field of the group gathering around it like a Hestian fire, where our focus is on what it means both to us and to the larger cultural matrix in which it is read and interpreted. I would rather say where it is inter-penetrated by the group or the individual reading it. Can it also be, I wonder, if the work itself can also be engaged in its own individuation process as we, who are engaging it and participating in its rich and complex field, are also individuating in the reading/imagining pilgrimage? Is it too much to suggest that a work of art, any art production, is also still unfolding in the world even after the last sentence is written or the artist signs his/her painting after a final brush stroke?

Literary theorist Louise Cowan, has written "On the Nature of Poetic Form" that not only does poetry offer us its own form of knowledge, but that the power of the poetic imagination includes a knowledge of form "which takes us closer to the heart of the work's meaning. Poetry" she goes on to suggest, "offers us paradigms of destiny," namely a concern "with the ends of things, their telos" (Lecture at the University of Dallas on "Poetic Knowledge and Poetic Form" nd).

The energy that gathers and is released in the form of a work has as its corollary our own energy field, inspiriting our own narrative form and finding accords in the work through the mysterious persuasive power of analogy. Part of analogy's force field is comprised of some blending or amalgam of both history and myth; we cannot get to the existence of these analogies by rational explication but more by imaginal contemplation as well as through Armstrong's notion of the power of the analogic which cultivates the work's "affecting presence" (*Powers* 47).

In another context Cowan asserts that "We gain from literature, *by analogy*, a knowledge of the reality of what we nowadays call our 'values'—those intangibles that used to be referred to as 'ideals,' or, classically, as 'virtues'" ("The Literary Mode of Knowing" 18). She adds a formidable insight in another framework that delineates the kind of knowledge afforded by classics of literature: "The knowledge provided by literary works of art frees us from our own limited experience to give us something like 'a second life.' This knowledge, however, is not so much factual and analytical as *analogical*" ("The Literary Mode of Knowing" 17).

I believe she is right, but would underscore the libidinal energy that is transferred from reader to the poem and back again in a dialogical field of mutual individuation through comingling energies. The imagined form in the making may then include the development of the reader in this act of apprehension that points to the reader's own mythic transformation in the process of reading. I say it is mutual because in some important sense, the poem needs us as readers/creators/participants to complete ourselves. Shared is a mutual interpenetration of invocations wherein the reader is invoked in his/her deepest recesses and the poem is invoked in its core mythology.

Reading is then a rite of passage through the written passages that comprise the plot, what Aristotle calls the soul of the poem, as James Hillman reminds us in his own mythopoetic description: "Freud's one plot is named after a myth, Oedipus. With this move, Freud too placed mind on a poetic basis. He understood that the entire narrative of a human life, the characters that we are and the dreams we enter, are structured by the selective logic of a profound *mythos* in the psyche" (*Healing Fiction* 11). Such reciprocity is even possible because as Armstrong writes, in accord with Cowan's sense of analogy, is that the first power that invests the work of affective presence is the power of the analogic, followed by the power of subjectivity, then the power of the mythic and the power of particularity (*Powers* 43). Armstrong further develops this idea by observing that "the definitive power of works of affecting presence is subjectivity, the power of the work's standing in a state of consciousness-of" (*Powers* 43). Two subjectivities are then working in complement with one another: that of the reader and that of the text or work of art; out of that tension "necessitates a third thing" which can arise (*tertium non datur*), "where the opposites can unite," as Jung observes (*CW* 14, par. 705). We may be astonished at what insight reveals that we have not known until now. This complementary confrontation is as Cowan suggested earlier, a form of deep self-knowing with transformative possibilities.

Both the text and the reader bring to the conversation as conversion their own intensity and type of vitality; they exchange these vitalities in the act of reading as a form of interpenetration. Perhaps this idea is not so farfetched when we note Rowland's assertion that "myths are archetypal form-making entities that knit the individual to the collective psyche *on a conscious and unconscious level*. Myths are the engines of psychic rejuvenation" (*Jungian* 63). If the myth of the poem and the myth of an individual interpenetrate, then such vitality, such psychic energy intensifies and creates community between the two through an interactive field of mutual *poiesis*. If the text has its own governing mythology giving it its unique form and shape, its own structure and consciousness of continuity, then we too as readers within our own personal myth find allegiances, alliances and analogies with those giving the text its own unique form. The consequence of such a rich imaginal interaction is transformation, both of the self and of the sentences in the work in a transdisciplinary way.

Already then, in reading the first line of Homer's classic, a communal bond or contact is birthed such that at least for the time of *this* reading, there is no subjectivity reading an objective thing; the text has no more autonomy than do we in the act of reading, which is a rite of migration, a rite of initiation, a rite of passage, and a calling to transformation. No less is the work also engaged in these same steps, so organic and vital is its being. No wonder then, that reading the *Odyssey* in secondary school, later as an adult and still later in elderhood, the same text is not what one rereads in any of these life stations. Rather, the text is in its own formation and accompanies us at whatever stage of life we are in by showing forth analogies for each of them. Such is the mysterious living and organic energy of the poem for us, its powerful and evolving mythos.

From Armstrong's and Rowland's insights and in my own reflections on the mystery of reading, I ask: In reading, what does it do to make me a context in relation to the text; what does my con-textual relation with

Homer's epic, for instance, do to increase my own level of consciousness? Without this crucial moment of transformation, reading becomes little more than an exercise of the intellect and not an experience of a world, a cosmos, a galaxy by the power of analogy. It would be more correct to say "an experience of worlds," since the world of the text is not my world, however much it reaches out in its own invitations to access me in the act of reading. Something is made visible to me that remained obscure or hidden before this moment of reading/revelation. This rich act of the imagination that needs both the text and me as reader, comprises a moment of vision, of a revelation through reading as a mysterious initiation. This inauguration must include some deeper gathering of who I am, essentially.

Some may feel that what I want to forward here may stretch credulity. As I become in the act of reading more conscious not only of the poem's world but of my own through the aperture of the imaginal turf of its plot, I must wonder how the work is becoming increasingly conscious of me; in other words, what does it see of my own ability to be present, to listen deeply, to notice, to contemplate, to discern, to judge, in an engagement that I wish to call a "phenomenology of reading with soul" and not simply with the intellect? Said another way, where does my own ontology meet the work's being? Where do it and I both find rich analogies of being in this reading? For myths too carry energy, create fields of influence and understanding and structure power to free us from fixed, even sclerotic notions of what is real and unreal as well as frozen images of who I am as reader and person. Such a reciprocal imaginal act of understanding carries on both sides the patterns of both individual and culture as well as the deeper layers of experience that Armstrong encapsulates in his term "mythoform." It serves "as a patterning device" (*Wellspring* 95), is prior to reason, and has itself no specific content, as Armstrong extends its description: "It is *ground*--preconcept, prefeeling, prebelief—*ground* pure and simple. It exists as a deep reality which, of itself, lies forever hidden, and its sole 'language' is the totality of our existence. . . as a living myth" (95).

The mythoform's relation to a work of affecting presence is complex and intricate, so I will close with this last observation by Armstrong: "we are to find in the affecting presence the shape of consciousness, the contours of myth, the structure of being" (*Wellspring* 98). We sense that it is ontological as well as mythological and wraps within its contours the psycho-aesthetic. Moreover, like the affecting presence, the mythoform "is a living principle. It is our distinctively human, cultural principle. . ." (100). When we return with these ideas to the reality of Homer's epic, we may ascertain that it too is a cultural artifact, a world within itself that grows organically from the imagination of the age and the craft of the creative poet as it extends itself over millenia into my existence at this moment of engaging it.

Louise Rosenblatt, mentioned earlier, suggests, in keeping with the spirit of Armstrong's insights, that "The reader of a text who evokes a literary work of art is, above all, a performer, in the same sense that a pianist performs a sonata, reading it from the text" (*The Reader* 28). What is evoked is determined or influenced largely through the intensity of the affecting presence *by* the work and perhaps my own affecting presence *on* the work. Here I am interested in how one's personal myth participates in the act of reading to signal reading as an imaginal ritual that allows a transformation of my pilgrimage across the page into an experience that guides me from the plot to my own narrative identity. Rosenblatt observes that the poem is nothing less than the experience shaped by the reader under the guidance of the text (*Reader* 12).

She goes on to assert that "'The poem' comes into being in the live circuit set up between the reader and 'the text'" (14). From her observation we glean that reading is closer to a conversation between two subjectivities than it is a conscious act perpetrated on the helpless, if not passive, text. "The text then is not an object, an entity, but rather an active process lived through during the relationship between a reader and a text" (*Reader* 20-21). Let's call it then an imaginal adventure wherein the point or goal of the journey is the act of reading within an atmosphere of contemplation, not analysis; of meditation, not mastery; and of pilgrimage, not possession.

We hear in Rosenblatt's observation Armstrong's sense of the work of affecting presence as a subjectivity relating to the subjectivity of the reader or viewer of it. Yes, a certain level of tension is to be expected in this relationship, but it is one in which both the text and the reader are offered an opportunity to change, to be altered, and to grow out of old habits of mind and discernment into new and formidable patterns of awareness. From such an intimate confluence a third thing, something new to both the text and the reader, is invited to emerge to convey new understandings for both of them. The philosopher, Hans Vaihinger has extensively developed this idea of "as-if" realities; for our purposes, I limit his discussion to the following quote: He writes of coming on the philosopher Friedrich Schiller's notion of play: "I understood his theory of play as the primary element of artistic creation and enjoyment. . . for later on I recognized in play the 'As if,' as the driving force of aesthetic activity and intuition" (*The Philosophyy of 'As If'* xxv). We read a work like Homer's epic "as if" it were true and thus engage it entirely on its own terms and allow ourselves to be reshaped by it. In such an attitude of "as if," we do indeed as readers complete the finished text even as it leverages our habitual ways of seeing, assessing and understanding. Some of these positions we may give up if we have the courage to question them, even as we question the plot before us.

The point of the above introductory observations is to set you, reader, into a frame of reference, or into a certain receptive attitude in order to be able to risk bringing your own plot into the energy field of Homer's masterpiece. By pausing over some of the passages and honing in on writing meditations that speak directly to you, you will engage processes unfolding into more conscious presence your personal myth. You are invited to enter more deeply, through brief passages from the epic on each page, a more engaged understanding of the myth that propels the *Odyssey* forward and your own mythos into deeper terrains.

    I wish you *bon voyage* on your travels; you will not return home as the person you were when you left the security of your familiar world. Your *nostos* will be one bearing new gifts of understanding, both of Homer's poem as well as the poetics of your own myth-making. The boons will be yours to share.

I

BOOKS I-IV

The Birth of Self-Awareness: The Search for Stories

January 1: Book I

Tell me Muse, about the man of many turns, who many
Ways wandered when he had sacked Troy's holy citadel;
He saw the cities of many men, and he knew their thought;
On the ocean he suffered many pains within his heart,
Striving for his life and his companions' return.
But he did not save his companions, though he wanted to:
They lost their own lives because of their recklessness.
The fools, they devoured the cattle of Hyperion, . . . (I. 1-8).

The poet calls on divine assistance in the form of the daughter of Mnemosyne, goddess of remembrance, so that his creation is not limited to merely his mortal capacity as poet. Lawrence Hatab suggests that "the ancient Greeks experienced creative activity as an arrival from beyond the boundaries of the conscious self" (*Myth and Philosophy* 60). The epic begins with a memory of a fierce and protracted war that Odysseus, a Greek or Achaean, along with many warrior leaders, fought for ten years. Not lack of valor or strength but "recklessness" cost many their lives, both in battle and on their *nostos*, or journey home. They were unable to curb their appetites or control its impulses.

No one reading these lines has escaped combat, strife, or adversaries in their lives. Conflict is one of the many universal conditions we each must contend with, negotiate and finally, survive, often by integrating them into our souls. Exaggerated or reckless responses can end one's life, or one may suffer woundings that can last a lifetime. Something about Odysseus' nature is in each of us. His names means "trouble" or "pain" or "strife." To "odysseus" is to inflict pain or trouble on another, as when Poseidon will "odysseus" Odysseus. To be "odysseused" is to receive pain or strife. (Dimock, "The Name of Odysseus" 409). Right responses to adversity is a wisdom often borne out of one challenge after another in our journey. Learning to navigate adversity and suffering that stems from it is the result of reflective thought as well as an ability to curb one's immediate desire to react and to seek vengeance with mindless violence. Homer's epic calls us to the virtue of restraint, the pause, the moment of holding back so as to reflect on what may be a better way to respond.

Meditation:

Recall when a response to adversity in your life was not measured or appropriate but closer to recklessness. What were the consequences?

January 2: Book I

The father of men and gods began to speak among them.
In his heart he was remembering excellent Aigisthos
Whom Agamemnon's son, far-famed Orestes, had slain.
Thinking of that man, he made his speech to the immortals:
"Well now, how indeed mortal men do blame the gods!
They say it is from us evils come, yet they themselves'
By their own recklessness have pains beyond their lot.
So this Aigisthos married beyond his lot the lawful
Wife of the son of Atreus, and killed him on his return;
Knowing he would be destroyed, since we told him beforehand": (I. 28-37).

Zeus calls his counsel to remember. He recalls the heroism of Agamemnon's son who slays the murderer Aigisthos, who slayed his father. Cousin of the king and lover of Clytemnestra, Aigisthos becomes king of Mycenae until Orestes returns to avenge Agamemnon's death. Zeus sets the moral standard: the gods are not responsible for the recklessness of mortals. This they can easily do on their own. It seems to be in the nature of human beings to inflict suffering on one another, yet they wish at times to pass off the cause conveniently to the gods, circumstances or other individuals. It seems to make little difference for mortals, who will self-destruct, knowing full well that such is their fate if they behave in a particular way; yet they press on with scant thought for long-term consequences.

Accepting our self-inflicted wounds or our wounding others and being afflicted in return, is a difficult task. Let others be the responsible origin, not us. We then often suffer the pain of the affliction as well as the suffering leading to our own culpability. Pain comes from without, suffering from within. Recklessness is excessive thought and behavior that unleashes out-of-control energies. In our recklessness we may abandon all responsibility for our actions. It becomes easier initially when we create a scapegoat for our rash behaviors and thoughts. The gods believe that such a way of rationalizing our conduct is to set up a shadow figure to blame, whether it be an individual, an ethnic group, a religious belief or another who is not able to defend themselves. Such a pattern of behavior can be crippling because it saves one from reflecting on their own culpability.

Meditation:

When have you lost control and lashed out in word or deed toward another or toward yourself? Who did you blame for your outburst?

January 3: Book I

"But the heart within me is torn over skillful Odysseus,
The hard-fated man, who long suffers griefs far from his dear ones
On a flood-circled island where the navel of the sea is.
The island is wooded, a goddess there has her dwelling,
The daughter of destruction-minded Atlas, who knows
The depths of the whole sea, and holds up by himself
The enormous pillars that hold apart earth and heaven.
His daughter has kept back the wretched and grieving man, . . ." (I. 48-55).

The goddess Athene, daughter of Zeus, pleads with her father to assist Odysseus in his homeward journey. He has been trapped now for 7 years with the goddess Calypso with no hope of homecoming. The loss of home does not diminish but actually increases his anguish over time. Calypso's father is he who holds up the pillars of heaven so to keep that divine home in place and separate from earth. Athene's anguish is real and, finally, persuasive as she laments the grief of a mortal she favors. Only Zeus can release Odysseus from his deep wound of loss. Calypso's restraining Odysseus is the source of his suffering and growing despondency, as anyone who has been detained for reasons unworthy of it, knows. Incarceration wars with liberation, with Odysseus wedged between them.

One major theme of Homer's epic is loss—of his men, of the war in Troy, of time itself and of his family most importantly. *Nostos,* the pain of not being able to arrive home secure, intact and joyful, is a universal ache in its paralyzing presence and its impact. Suffering homelessness, the loss of origins and loved ones is one of the greatest afflictions we are often forced to endure. The home, the *oikos,* rightly-ordered, is a refuge, a sanctuary, an island of plentitude in the midst of the world's demands on us. Home in its best placement offers us a respite from risk, uncertainty and turmoil. Being "at home" in the world is a deep and universal yearning. When the home is violated by others, as with Agamemnon, or Odysseus himself, it violates the entire cosmos one seeks to maintain. When the home is in turmoil, the city suffers as well, for the two are so interrelated that the condition of one resonates through the other, like an infection. Odysseus' solitary confinement is easy for us to relate to; we know the yearning of not being at home.

Meditation:

Describe a "flood-circled island" you had to endure at a point in your life until greater forces released you to travel to and regain or rebuild your home.

January 4: Book I

She went down in a rush from the summits of Olympus and stood
In the district of Ithaca before Odysseus' gates
At the courtyard threshold. In her fist she held the bronze spear,
Likening herself to a stranger, the Taphian leader Mentes.
She came upon the bold suitors. They at the moment
Were delighting their hearts with a diceboard before the doors,
Seated on the skins of oxen they had killed themselves (I. 102-08).

Intent on instructing the young Telemachos if he were willing to listen and learn, Athene hurries to Ithaca and in disguise, appears at the threshold of Odysseus's home as Mentes, a king. She holds her spear as she surveys the behavior of the suitors, who essentially ignore her presence. They are distracted by a game and give her no notice, violating the laws of hospitality. Instead, they continue to enjoy the comforts of oxen skin and the animals owned by Odysseus slain for their food and covering. Athene learns much as she notes the self-absorbed recreation of the suitors whose invasion of Odysseus' *oikos* is an invasion by the unbounded energy of human appetites which ignores the stranger as guest.

Disguise and threshold are two universal constants present throughout time. The former fabricates a fiction, a quality that hides one reality by creating another. In an effective disguise, one can see out from it without being seen. The threshold places us between two worlds. Athene in her wisdom knows the effectiveness of both. We use fictions and are met by other fabrications every day. No one can be sure if the other is legitimate or has counterfeited themselves through disguise; so too in what we hear or read can truth be exposed or camouflaged to create an elaborate fiction to reveal a truth or mislead. Thresholds are promises as tentative spaces; they may open out into another world that has little bearing on the one that is on the threshold's other side. Threshold crossings are rich psychological and emotional places of transition and may lead to transformation. In some circumstances a disguise is necessary, even prudent, in order to prepare and execute a transition from one world to another, as Athene's actions reveal dramatically. Now the plot finds its initial motion.

Meditation:

When in your life currently are you at or approaching a threshold in order to journey into a new arena of life with possibilities you may not yet grasp but have decided to risk something new?

January 5: Book I

Godlike Telemachos was by far the first to see her,
For he sat among the suitors, crushed in his own heart,
Seeing his noble father in his mind, if from somewhere
He would come and make those suitors scatter through the halls,
So that he himself might have honor and command his own goods.
Thinking this over while seated with the suitors, he sighted Athene.
He went straight to the gate, and he resented in his heart
That the stranger stood so long at the door (I. 113-20).

Seeming to be at least in appearance one of them, Telemachos sits in isolation surrounded by the greedy bellies of the suitors, sons of the *aristoi* of Ithaca who arrive daily to feast on the possessions of Odysseus without any consciousness of the guest-host relationship whose ritual enactment civilizes. Telemachos entertains fantasies of his father's return to disrupt their daily feasting. He also senses that as the only son he would one day inherit these possessions as well as acquire his own. His wish for honor and fame, *kleos,* is a natural inheritance and proper to him as a young man. But he is suddenly drawn out of his own self-absorbed desires at the sight of Mentes, a guest at the threshold. Knowing what is proper as host, he rushes to the disguised goddess at the same time feeling resentment that the guest was ignored for so long, which he knows reflects poorly on Odysseus' household. His vision of propriety puts him above the suitors.

Civilized customs and behaviors that emanate from them are built in large measure on a sense of mutual respect and hospitable treatment of one another. Such relationships are heightened when it weaves the divine with the human order. The guest-host relation is a code at the heart of hospitality, a quality intimate to the goddess Hestia, keeper of the hearth fire and of warm-heartedness. I have written elsewhere that "She is the presence of restraint, of pause, of holding back. . . "("Hestia: Goddess of the Hearth" 99). If one does not feel this connection to others in respect and care, then each seeks autonomously to satisfy one's own cravings as singular consumers, as the Cyclopes will reveal later in the epic.

Meditation:

Describe one way how you show hospitality to yourself, and by extension, to others. Offer an example of how you have been hospitable to yourself and in social exchanges, to another, without any desire for compensation.

January 6: Book I

Speaking out to her, he uttered winged words:
"Greetings, stranger, you shall be welcomed among us
And when you have eaten dinner, you will tell what it is you need."
When he had said that, he led on, and Pallas Athene followed.
And when they had got inside of the lofty house,
He stood the spear he was carrying against the long pillar
Inside the well-polished spearcase, where many other
Spears of stout-hearted Odysseus were also standing (I. 122-29).

Homer gives due time to the code of hospitality because it is "the long pillar" of Greek civilization and source of generosity and civility. Telemachos is trained in the art of caring for a stranger who comes to his door even though his world is limited. Taught well, he has taken the spear from Mentes and placed it where he can retrieve it if needed. Of course it is Athene's weapon, as she is the goddess of both the warrior in battle and persuasion in speech. Putting Mentes' spear with the others is also a sign of hospitality and community. Athene meanwhile is paying close attention to how she is being acknowledged and treated, and by whom. Distracted by their insatiable appetites, the suitors ignore her. Telemachos does not first ask Mentes: "Who are you?" He first offers him a meal, after which he will learn what it is the stranger needs.

Putting another's needs before one's own is both generous and liberating for both host and guest. A contract of social cohesion is initiated in the ritual of caring for another's needs. At the same time is the care of one's soul in the exchange. In the moment the guest-host social relation is enacted, the civilized life is renewed and strengthened. Those as hosts relinquish some of their power and possessions to the guest, knowing full well that one day the roles may be reversed and one should be able to assume that their treatment of the guest would be reciprocated by a new host. Hospitality, hospital and hospice derive from the same word, but rather than patient, we use the word guest; nonetheless, one's needs in both cases are priority regardless of whether the person is known by the hospitality-givers or not. To show hospitality is to revere the stranger who is out of place and in need of home.

Meditation:

What form of hosting has offered you the greatest satisfaction? Recall an incident that revealed such largesse in you. When were you shown hospitality as a guest?

January 7: Book I

The bold suitors came in. And they themselves
Sat down one after another in seats and in armchairs.
Heralds were pouring water for them over their hands.
And serving maids were heaping bread upon trays.
Young men were filling bowls up to the brim for drinking.
They stretched forth their hands to the food that was spread out ready.
But when the suitors had taken their fill of food and drink,
Other matters came to their minds for attention:
Singing and dancing, which are the graces of a banquet (I. 144-52).

Homer offers us a snapshot of the suitors' daily habits of feasting off of Odysseus' abundance. They violate his household as unwelcome guests only because he is absent and there is no forceful resistance to their greed and impiety. They are bold, meaning not courageous, but brazen in behavior. They are led by appetite only; some servants are complicit with them and others do it because of fear and self-preservation. Their hands are cleansed, preparing them to stretch out towards the nourishment supplied in abundance. They do nothing for such hospitality except to show up daily like freeloaders who feel they are entitled to such treatment. Their appetites move from one satiation to another; when the meal is consumed, they look for further free entertainment, partying without restraint. They are, like so many moderns, distracted by appetite and suffering attention deficit disorder as they gorge themselves excessively and seek further consuming opportunities for continued distraction.

In civil life is a constant rhythm of give-and-take. Giving and taking echo the roles of guest and host when in their right order. But it is understood that these roles should be easily reversed so that the one who hosts is allowed the guest's role as gift-receiving; without such give-and-take hospitality becomes one-sided and locked in so that only one party gives repeatedly while the other takes without ceasing. In the process, the civilized order is violated, continues to deteriorate and feeds only one's baser appetites without mindfulness, courtesy or care. Especially, it is noted, without any piety or offering to the gods. The host is then a victim.

Meditation:

Describe a situation in which you were taken advantage of because of your largesse or when you took without reprieve from another. What happened to either relationship?

January 8: Book I

"All right, then. I will tell you this quite truthfully.
I declare I am Mentes, son of skillful Anchialos,
And I rule over the Taphians, who are fond of rowing.
Just now I have come this way by ship, with companions,
To Temese for bronze, and I carry glittering iron.
My vessel stands here by the fields far off from the city,
In the harbor of Reithron, below wooded Neion.
We declare we are guest friends of one another through our fathers. . ." (I. 179-86).

Athene addresses the grieving Telemachos through the cloth of fabrication. She needs a story to serve him, one persuasive enough that he will choose to be guided by her. Her disguise is of a merchant trading iron for bronze. Innocuous enough. Fabricate, then persuade. Her fiction becomes his reality. Disguise, fabrication, fictionalizing one's self to disarm others occurs throughout the epic. As goddess of language and influence, Athene crafts herself into an acceptable mortal reality so as not to draw suspicion from the suitors. She prefaces her fiction by asserting she will now speak the truth. The divine and human realms wed through story. We read her fiction within the fiction of the epic. This form of expression may actually take us closer to the truth of an event and its meaning than a factual explanation. Here we are in the realm of myth woven into the fabric of history.

The passage can make one wonder if some of the individuals that cross our path are divinities in disguise, or divine in their actions from the sacred within them. Can we ever fully know what stories we are told by others, and even ourselves, may be fabrications that embellish the history of one's life with fictions that are even more credible than the facts of our past and present? Dissembling to persuade is a normal part of life. Do the stories we are told always contain a tincture of coloring to achieve concealed ends? Homer's epic is a *tour de force* on the fragile *and* potent quality of narratives. Fictions can finesse our and others' histories because we are each in our own way expressions of the partially fictional or "as-if" nature of life. Through fictions we can be led to our true destiny.

Meditation:

When have you fabricated your truth for definite ends? When did you discover that another's story was largely a fiction? Did it, finally, matter to you?

January 9: Book I

"He will devise how to return, since he has many resources.
But come now, tell me this, and explain it truthfully,
If, big as you are, you are really the son of Odysseus himself.
You resemble him strangely in your head and your fine eyes,
Since we had contact quite often with one another
Before he embarked for Troy, where the other noblest
Men of the Argives were headed in their hollow ships.
Since then I have not seen Odysseus, nor has he seen me" (I. 205-12).

Speaking as Mentes, the goddess hidden in the folds of a mortal speaks as both a human and divine presence; two worlds collude in her. She points out to Telemachos how his father is polytropic, a man of many devices, and that he will find his way home through his ability to riff on all life situations that present themselves. She asks Telemachos to speak the truth of his identity while she wisely conceals hers. She sees in his likeness to his father a strangeness—Odysseus and yet not him. She in turn speaks the truth in disguise because she has been with him, helping him home since his warring days in Troy. She also offers Telemachos a sense of his own history by linking him to his father. In their connection, Athene and Telemachos dance between truth and fabrication, revealing and concealing, fact and fiction. All are certainly true of language itself, which can camouflage the facts in a fiction, then suddenly burst forth with the truth of something or someone, leaving the audience of such a revelation to wonder what is to be believed.

Sometimes we can sense, on another plane of awareness, when we are being deceived, including self-deception, self-falsehood and when we are hearing clearly the truth of another. All of these point toward the power of stories themselves to persuade us of their legitimacy; fictions can carry a convincing verisimilitude to bring us to think or act in certain ways. Perhaps we are each on a constant odyssey in and with our unique narrative that links us to larger, yet strangely familiar fictions that cluster around us. When we pay attention to just one day in our lives, we notice how many stories come at us to enlighten, persuade, convince, prod or make us question what we thought we knew. We live a good part of our lives and in our dreaming life in a universe of narratives. To be is to be storied.

Meditation:

What pleasure and even pain do you derive from telling your story and on being an audience to others' fables?

January 10: Book I

Then the sound-minded Telemachos answered her:
"All right, stranger, I shall speak quite truthfully.
My mother calls me the son of the man. But I myself
Do not know. No one has ever been certain of his father.
Ah, would that I were the fortunate son of some man
Whom old age came upon with all his possessions!"
. . . .
"Come now, pay attention and take note of my words:
Tomorrow call the Achaian warriors to assembly;
Make a declaration to all. Let the gods witness it.
Order the suitors to disperse to their own affairs" (I. 213-18; 271-74).

Athene is a consummate teacher. First of all, she wishes to learn if Telemachos is interested in being a student, to be instructed at this moment in his life. If so, she insists that he attend to her instructions as Mentes. At the same time she coaxes him into his role as leader, to step into his father's space, as a substitute until he returns home. Looking like his father, he will now begin to behave as Odysseus did. At the same time he is stepping into his own authenticity. We witness his threshold moment as Athene prescribes it: to migrate from invisible young man to visible leader assuming his own voice. It is an inner calling she invites him to respond to, as any hero must who hears and heeds a call, a call to both a difficult context and to an adventure away from the household. She calls him to his own inner authority as a person heroically inflected. She also takes into account his mother Penelope's desires and attends to her fatigue as well.

We listen closely to be called, for it is a desire deep within us to risk ourselves in the world. It is always partly a divine invitation, a moment of vocation, of being called out of ourselves and, paradoxically, into our own natural greatness. Joseph Campbell suggests that "the hero is a man of self-achieved submission" (*Hero* 16); it requires a yielding, a giving of self over to something grander than ourselves. To be deaf to the call, or to many callings, is to be dead in a spiritual sense. To risk is to enact the myth that resides in and resounds in each of us, seeking to be released, to uncoil in the world to add to the world's substance. To refuse the call may be to become a suitor, always taking, never giving back.

Meditation:

When were you called but chose to refuse it for it felt too risky, too uncertain?

January 11: Book I

Having spoken so, bright-eyed Athene went off.
She flew upward like a bird. Into his spirit
She had put strength and courage. She put him in mind
Of his father more than before. When he thought it over,
He was amazed in his spirit; he thought she was a god.
And at once the godlike mortal went toward the suitors.
A renowned singer was singing to them. They were sitting
In silence listening. He sang of the baleful return
Of the Achaians from Troy that Pallas-Athene laid on them (I. 319-26).

Magical and miraculous, Athene flies upward as Telemachos watches her in amazement. He knows now she was not a mere mortal but someone from Olympus, a divine presence that had just entered his life, to call him forth. He has become more mindful of her. The gifts she bequeaths to Odysseus's son are two that the father had also received from her. Without these qualities, Telemachos will never grow into his own authority. He can now, because his father is present in him with a vividness not known before. The mortal absent father congeals with the immortal present goddess that feeds Telemachos' soul and prepares him to step forward in a moment to address the assembled suitors. His initiation is now in motion, his leadership capacity now active, even as the suitors learn through song of the suffering warriors returning home, grieving over their lost brothers.

Stepping into one's own authority, accepting one's own greatness, developing one's own voice—all these are essential for each of us to experience and then acknowledge. It must include as well those who parented us, certainly not limited to our biological parents; their force is enough to change, deflect or confirm our life trajectory. Having self-knowledge and gratitude for those who nurtured us is an essential part of our own mythic certainty, which infuses us with our immortal nature. Without risk, without courage to venture into the unknown, even in our own household, may signal our inability to confront our own nature, complete with its shadows and its sterling promises. "If you have the guts to follow the risk, however," Joseph Campbell believes, "life opens, opens, opens up all along the line" (*An Open Life* 24).

Mediation:

Can you recall when it was that you were led to begin the voyage into your self-definition? What inspired the journey?

January 12: Book I

"Well, come into the house, and apply yourself to work,
To the loom and the distaff, and give order to your servants
To set at the work. This talk will concern all the men,
But me especially. For the power in the house is mine."
She was amazed at him, and back into the house she went.
The sound minded-speech of her son she took to heart.
She entered the upper chamber with her serving women,
And then wept for Odysseus, her dear husband, . . .
The suitors were making a din through the shadowy halls. . . .
Sound-minded Telemachos began speaking to them:
"Suitors of my mother, with your excessive insolence,
Let us now take our pleasure and dine. . ." (I. 356-63; 365; 368-69).

Telemachos steps up and into his new authority to take control of the roustabout suitors in their chaotic behavior. He calls their behavior by name, "excessive insolence," then in a quick reversal invites them to take pleasure in a meal and be entertained by the poet-singer. Something major shifts in the energy of the epic here. The young leader creates a new tone in the household by insisting on silence so the singer can be heard. Persuasion, not force, is his weapon. Language itself spoken with authority, not tyranny, suffices to calm the din and tame the wildness of the crowd devouring his father's home and lusting after his mother, who, amazed at her son's change of demeanor, follows his instructions and departs to the bedroom to weep for her lost husband. The son has awakened in her desire for her husband while Athene has awakened in him his inner authority.

Reclaiming the power of language in shaping a reality before us is a masterful art. Not through the violence of belittling or physical abuse but in the careful deliberation of rhetoric—the art of persuasive utterance that includes song or written expression—can civilize a space where the energy is volatile. Telemachos is our model for how order can be retrieved and maintained through the power of words spoken with authority. Liberal learning can cultivate such an art: to assess a situation, then choose measured speech to correct or amend excess into some moderation. Leadership carries the obligation to think and speak well for a common good. It is one of the major pillars on which rests the entire epic.

Meditation:

Who do you admire for their quality and eloquence in speaking or writing?

January 13: Book I

"And let there be
No noise, since it is lovely to listen to a singer
Of the kind this one is, who resembles the gods in his voice.
And at dawn tomorrow let us all go and take our seats
In council, so that I may tell you something outright;
Get out of the halls and partake of other dinners,
Eating your own goods, visiting each other's homes. . . ."
So he said, and they all set their teeth on their lips
And wondered at Telemachos that he spoke so courageously. . . .
"Well, Telemachos, the gods themselves must be teaching you
To be presumptuous and speak courageously.
May the son of Cronos over sea-circled Ithaca
Not make you king, your paternal right by birth." (I. 369-75; 381-82; 384-87).

Telemachos issues another directive on the behavior of the suitors, to respect the voice of the singer who brings the memories of Troy back into the present. The suitors pause and begin to wonder and fear this new leader suddenly transformed in their midst. They are frightened by his authority and rapid metamorphosis. He seizes the moment of vulnerability to assert his leadership of all the suitors. Antinoos, their leader, breaks his silence and uses language meant to mock the son of Odysseus; his words will ring true at epic's end. The moment is a rare one in which Antinoos addresses Zeus to deny Telemachos his rightful place, in the right order, as successor to his father. Not Telemachos but Antinoos reveals presumption in his fantasy of denying that Odysseus will ever return to Ithaca.

It is not prudent for anyone to think there are free lunches in the world to be taken without yielding something in return. Excess under any conditions seems to invite a contrary swing in the opposite direction. The divine realm as well can be summoned in the spirit of self-gain through power, fame, possessions, and reputation, to name a few. When the soul closes in on itself, as Antinoos makes evident in his words, the larger social order, if not the cosmos itself, suffers a blight. Absent generosity and care for the welfare of others, the baser elements in our spirits are unleashed. Chaos is the immediate consequence of abusing piety.

Meditation:

Have you witnessed, or been part of, a strategy to use the sacred as a pretext for thoughts or actions that stem from another's own self-serving needs?

January 14: Book I

"The stranger is a guest friend of my father's from Taphos.
He declares he is Mentes, son of skillful Anchialos,
And he rules over the Taphians, who are fond of rowing"
So Telemachos said, but in his mind knew the immortal god.
The men turned then to dancing and delightful song
And took their pleasure, and waited for evening to come.
As they took their pleasure black evening came upon them.
Then they went away, each to his own home to sleep.
But Telemachos, where his bedroom was, built aloft . . .
Went to bed pondering many things in his mind (I. 417-25; 427).

Two worlds face off in these lines. One is the world of mind-fulness that grasps the presence of divinity working in the world in disguise. The other is the secular world of distractions and entertainment that can reveal a self-centered and mindless existence. Reflection is set off against consumption. Telemachos is already learning the wisdom and power of disguising reality from those who would use it as a weapon against him. He is wily, like his parents. Learned in *metis*, or craft, he can fabricate reality to achieve higher ends—the restoration of his household. A leader is borne before us, one who learns quickly and enjoys the teachings of an immortal. Telemachos is acquiring the mind-fulness needed to negotiate between worlds as the suitors disperse for the night to their own homes.

Honesty is the best policy, except in those situations when it isn't. Being honest and being naïve are often very close and tightly related. Faced with overwhelming force or odds against one, perhaps the wiser course is to dissemble a bit, to conceal one's hand, when not to do so may destroy any attempts to restore the good. The *Odyssey* is a witness to what strategies might best serve a warring society to recover from the collateral break down of a social order absent its leader. Leadership maintains order, but on occasion it must recover it first. Homer's masterpiece is a political poem, among other categories, for its end is the restoration of the polis. Its end is not just reuniting the family of Odysseus but a wider application: the preservation of the city through language.

Meditation:

When have you chosen to keep the full truth hidden from others in order to preserve or restore an ordered cosmos, or the good, for the sake of a much-valued unity?

January 15: Book I

Going with him, she carried the flaming torches. She loved him
Most of all the servants, and had tended him as a child.
She opened up the doors of the stoutly fashioned bedroom.
He sat down on the bed and took off his soft tunic
And put it in the hands of the shrewd-minded old woman.
She folded up the tunic, put it in smooth order,
And hung it on a peg beside the jointed bed. . . .
There all night long, wrapped up in the sheepskin,
He pondered in his mind the course that Athene had shown (I. 434-40; 452-454).

Like bookends are Eurycleia in old age and Telemachos as a developing young leader. They are joined in love and care for the household, and especially Penelope's well-being. As a figure of the ancient nurturing feminine, Eurycleia serves him as she did his father and the entire stout household with utmost fidelity, order, kindness and selflessness. She is the antidote to the chaotic suitors by bringing order and measure to all she touches, like the young man's tunic. Telemachos too is ordering his life around the goddess Athene's instructions and their implications as he considers them thoughtfully. On the threshold of his life's call to adventure and to the retrieval of his father, he rests now in the well-ordered household absent the suitors' rapacity. This domestic scene gives us an insight into the values the household strives to shelter.

Those in our lives who aid us by their example are priceless gifts. They mentor us too by how they live out values that we breathed in and imitated as we approached moments of departure into what is unfamiliar, unforeseen and beyond being managed. Our memories ponder their wisdom, direction and purpose. A life destined includes both human and divine voices to serve us in keeping our moral compass pointed towards true North. Our life adventures often grow directly from the psychological and spiritual influences we allow in as welcome guests. Joseph Campbell believes the "herald" or guide will appear "in the psyche that is ripe for transformation" (*Hero* 55) to guide the initiate into a zone unknown. The herald may also keep at bay those influences that impede our destiny. Our personal myth is shaped by these and other forces and presences that guide our quest.

Meditation:

Recall a strong model or voice that both directed and nourished your destiny. Or, note whose destiny and life direction you were instrumental in shaping.

January 16: Book II

[Telemachos] went on out of the bedroom, like a god to look at.. . .
He went to the assembly and held his bronze spear in his fist—
Not alone, but the swift-footed dogs went along with him.
Moreover, Athene shed a divine grace around him.
The people all marveled at him as he was coming up.
He sat down in his father's seat, and the old men gave way.
Then the hero Aigyptios began to speak among them,
A man bent with age who knew numberless things (II. 5; 10-16).

Accompanied by his dogs and wrapped in Athene's grace, Telemachos makes his appearance as a leader wearing a mantle of authority. He sits in his father's seat, the wellspring of his heritage and the space of his paternity. Now the older men yield to his light and presence. We imagine what "divine grace" might do to a person's appearance. Is it the light of divine authority melding with this human appearance that gives Telemachos a luster and raises him from his earlier whining frustration at his own impotence? Having yielded to being instructed, he enters the sacred space of leadership guided by the goddess there to chasten them for their behavior. People marvel at his new appearance, which is more a sense of presence than it is of a changed personality. They sense his being chosen for some great deeds in leadership.

We remember those moments when we were thrust into the public realm by circumstances that were and may continue to unfurl our fate. Some divine presence may offer us a vision of our future and inspirit us with the requisite courage and wisdom to lead, to shape the future for ourselves and others. We lead by example, not decrees. Any leading capacity rests on our willingness to learn, to be instructed, to meld our will with powers beyond us and to serve some grander good beyond ourselves. Humility attends such a calling to responsibility for we grasp that we are an instrument in some larger venture. The passage above shows us a young man about to step further into the world guided by divinity who bequeaths to him a mindfulness that is mirrored in his mastery of persuasive language.

Meditation:

Describe when you felt a call to serve something well beyond yourself that you assented to. Has it made a significant difference in your life's trajectory?

January 17: Book II

"And now there is a much greater evil too, that will soon
Fully tear my whole house apart and destroy all my living.
Suitors are assailing my mother against her will,
The dear sons of the men who are the noblest in this place. . . .
But they cluster to our house day after day.
Slaughtering oxen and sheep and fat goats,
They carry on their revels and drink the sparkling wine
Wantonly. Many things are wasted. And there is no man
Of the kind Odysseus was, to ward off harm from the house" (II. 48-51; 55-59).

Telemachos addresses the assembly of elders whose sons are rapaciously gnawing away at Odysseus' household while seeking his mother as their bride and slaughtering the best of the *oikos*' cattle. He speaks sympathetically and courageously for he understands his mother is no longer capable, in her own crafty way, to forestall the inevitable and that she now be forced to choose to marry one of them. Their corruption without boundaries has transformed the household from a state of measured cosmos to a condition of unrestrained chaos. Now the citadel of Ithaca is in peril and Telemachos is quick to acknowledge that "I would ward it off myself if I had the power" (l. 62). Finally, he uses the phrase "no man," which is the name his father gave himself when he confronts the Cyclops, Polyphemos.

A party or celebration that goes on indefinitely is destructive and dispiriting. It debilitates the participants and ignores the crucial virtue of restraint. Celebrations are respites from the ordered behavior that keeps the communal life blood flowing. It is not a substitute for them; when restraints are lifted, anarchy is one terrifying consequence. Appetites are good in themselves but destructive when they force out all other forms of civilized behaviors and assume the throne. Such would include not just appetites of the belly but also of the mind: power, possessions, fame, control, self-serving legislation. Appetites are intimately related to anarchy. When the belly is the tyrant, the mind is discarded as trivial. In *Thou Art That,* Joseph Campbell suggests that one of the functions of a mythology is "to validate and support a specific moral order" (5).

Meditation:

When in your life did you experience appetites out of control, yours or others, and what were the consequences?

January 18: Book II

"Be ashamed toward the other men of our neighborhood
Who live around us. Fear, too, the wrath of the gods,
Lest, aghast at all the evil deeds, they work some change.
I beseech you, both by Olympian Zeus, and by Themis,
Who disbands and also convokes the assembled men,
Leave off, my friends, and let me wear away alone
In my woeful grief, unless my noble father Odysseus
Was ever hostile to the well-greaved Achaians and did them harm;
For this you pay me back, are hostile and do me harm
By urging these men on" (II. 65-74).

Telemachos' words combine rage with self-pity as he moves into his own space to plead to the elders for restraint. He is still easily overwhelmed by the injustice of the suitors, so he pleads for the intervention of masculine Zeus and the "Goddess of Just Order" *(Odyssey*, 14 n.2) and balance, Themis. He also feels his own impotence in being unable to rout them from his home. Yet his words ring true and bring the suitors to silence; many feel pity for his burst of tears that follows the above lines. Perhaps the strength of Telemachos' plea is to arouse shame in the suitors. He admits that his grieving would end if he discovered that his father had ever abused or otherwise alienated his warriors. He points out the Achaians' shin guards used in fighting to give them a protection in battle. Language itself in all its forms is one of the main characters of the *Odyssey*.

Persuasive speech making can signal the emerging power of a new leader or an individual who has found his/her center of power in both speech and mind. Language itself can create a force field of influence wherein the center of authority can shift to a new arena and/or person. The ability to speak the truth well is a rhetorical necessity in public meetings and debates. Having the courage to step up and into such space often requires assistance from the Olympian gods to help one transcend his/her mortal limits. To speak well and convince others can incite wars but also prevent them. Language is so basic to our normal activities that often we give it scant attention, but then we can often let the words of others influence what we feel, believe and act on.

Meditation:

Recall a time when you heard a speech or gave one that affected the thoughts, attitudes or feelings of your audience. What did it evoke in them? In you?

January 19: Book II

"The Achaian suitors are not guilty toward you.
No, it is your dear mother, who knows advantages well.
It is the third year already, and will soon be a fourth,
Since she has slighted the spirit in the Achaians' hearts.
She gives hope to all, and she promises every man,
Sending out messages. But her thought wishes otherwise.
And she has devised in her mind this other deceit.
She set a great loom in the halls and on it she wove
A large and delicate fabric. . . .
Then every day she kept weaving on the great loom.
And in the nights she undid it when she had the torches set up" (II. 87-95; 104-05).

The leader of the suitors, Antinoos—whose names suggests "against mind or mindfulness," is quick to speak up to deflect any blame or responsibility from the suitors by scapegoating Penelope as the cause of their behavior. She has successfully restrained their appetites by a clever ruse that persuaded them to wait until she has finished weaving a funeral robe for her father-in-law, Laertes. She was successful in unweaving at night by torchlight what she crafted during the daylight in the great hall. One unfaithful servant woman exposed her scheme to the suitors. Now, time has narrowed considerably and the suitors now press her to choose one of them in marriage. Antinoos' words are predicated on the assumption that Odysseus will never return to reclaim his *oikos*.

Not always is it force or strength that defeats an adversary. Sometimes it is *metis,* or craft, craftiness, deceit, disguise, or a clever fiction that holds such power. A strong imaginative mind can alter history by creating a fiction, or a fabrication to postpone or ward off a powerful enemy. In this case, it is a clever stall to give Odysseus more time to arrive home to rearrange the household. Such clever feminine energy and resourcefulness is more than a match for the excessive masculine energy of conquest and appetite. The heroic is not always measured in physical strength; it is often the Athenian workings of the creative imagination that reveals more persuasive force. Often it is a combination of masculine and feminine presences that can outmaneuver and conquer a rival.

Meditation:

When have you engaged in or witnessed craftiness that served either a good or a devouring appetite? What did you discover in what you witnessed?

January 20: Book II

So Telemachos spoke, and broad-seeing Zeus sent him
Two eagles from above from the crest of the mountain flying.
They for a time flew down along with the blasts of the wind,
Stretching their wings out close to one another.
But when they came to the midst of the many-voiced assembly,
Then they whirled about and beat their wings rapidly.
They went to the heads of all and destruction was in their look,
As they tore each other's cheeks and throats on both sides with their claws (II. 146-53).

The Homeric world has a porous membrane between divine, natural and human orders, both living and dead. The physical order can carry divine portents, omens and oracles, often pointing to future events through signs and symbols. Zeus affirms the words of aspiring Telemachos by sending his eagles to dramatically render the future violence and suffering of the suitors in the house of Odysseus. When the eagles finish their horrific rendering of one another, they speed off, leaving the suitors in a state of wonder and awe, mingled with fear and dread. The eagles of Zeus carry portents that the suitors may heed, however unlikely. But none can deny the affect these two warring birds have on the souls of their audience.

Prophecies, omens, fortune-tellers, astrological charts, psychic readings, horoscopes, are still with us today. They are remnants of an age where various orders of being conversed with one another in a container of mythical time in which a linear belief of temporality also contained a cyclical, even a spiralic vision where past, present and future mingled with and surrounded one another; divine and human orders of being were materially animated, often by animals, and relationships formed between arenas that today we perceive less holistically. Other forms of knowing reality have been pushed to the margins by the scientific attitude which suggests that only through observation and experimentation can the world be known. Yet Homer's own epic offers a rich avenue into understanding the personal and political orders, and he accomplishes this through myth and fable. "Few poets," writes C. M. Bowra, "have the gift of conveying visible things so clearly as he can" (*Ancient Greek Literature* 39).

Meditation:

Have you experienced a reality, a premonition, a dream or other venues wherein was revealed to you some truth of the future that was borne out in time?

January 21: Book II

"I am much better at prophesying about this than you.
And there are many birds that wander beneath the beams
Of the sun, and not all are in accord with fate. Odysseus
Has perished far off and would that you too had perished
Along with him. You would not say so much in augury,
Nor would you so incite the angered Telemachos,
Expecting a gift for your house, if he provide one. . . .
Let him bid his mother go back to her father's house.
They will work out a marriage and array many bridal gifts,
As many as should go along with a dear daughter" (II. 180-86; 195-97).

Eurymachos, son of Polybos, responds by chastising the old warrior Halitherses, who has just warned all the suitors of Odysseus' imminent return. Eurymachos, claiming to be the better reader of auguries, dismisses the older man's claims. He pushes instead a contrary narrative: Odysseus is dead and will never return. He accuses Halitherses, son of Nestor, of seeking gifts from Telemachos with his "good news" that his father will return. Eurymachos ends his diatribe against Halitherses with his own fantasy: that Penelope return to her parents' home to gather a dowry and prepare soon for her marriage to one of the suitors. Perhaps there is an acceleration of haste in his words?

Foretelling what is to come through the motions of nature is an ancient custom of anticipating a particular future by means of analogies. It is not uncommon to project on to what will or may be our own fantasies or unconscious wishes. We may find ourselves today surrounded by predictions, experts, readers of the current climate—all in the service of perhaps personal agendas. The larger question becomes: what narrative will I accept, adopt, defend and follow? What we choose to believe to be true of the future is very much entwined with our personal myth, including our values and wishes, none of which may actually shape the patterns of history or present inclinations toward an authentic future. "Stories from antiquity provide raw material for personal mythmaking" writes Dan McAdams (*The Stories We Live By* 13).

Meditation:

What standards, beliefs, or attributes do you use to calculate or gauge what may be or might become true? Put another way, what do you assume about the future for yourself and others, perhaps by means of stories you tell?

January 22: Book II

Then sound-minded Telemachos addressed him in answer:
"Eurymachos and all the rest of you noble suitors,
I will not implore you about this or speak out any more. . . .
But come, give me a fast ship and twenty companions
Who can complete a journey with me, thither and back.
I am going to Sparta and also to Sandy Pylos
To learn of the return of my father, who is gone so long,
On the chance some mortal may tell of him, or I hear from Zeus
The voice that most of all brings report to men" (II. 208-11; 212-17).

Done with speeches and scolding, Telemachos tacks his thoughts into action. He asks only for a ship on which to sail first to the land of Nestor, followed by the household of Menelaos and Helen on Pylos. His desire to track his father imitates his resolve to be educated and to learn of the clear trajectory of his own lineage. He is now ready to gain knowledge through narratives, hungry not only for information but for wisdom. Telemachos is open to chance encounters, knows there are no guarantees on his quest and welcomes the voice of the divine father, from whom he may learn of his own. He has heard the call of the hero's adventure and carries an attitude open to any story or event that will give him some final sense of his patrimony and reclaim his own myth in the discovery.

Each of us carries an impulse, a desire, a purpose for our lives in the form of a quest. We are each called to a vocation, to a destiny, but there are no guarantees of success. The adventure invites risk. Chance meetings, instructions from unfamiliar sources, deflections, stalemates, losses, cul-de-sacs—all of these possibilities are part of heroic seeking that calls us. Of course, we can refuse the call and stay put, never heeding or pursuing our destiny. But above all, the journey we assent to must indeed grow from the deepest, most authentic place in us, not handed to us. If we are handed or persuaded of our destiny from a source not deep within us, then perhaps it is someone else's journey, not ours, that we pursue. "Follow your fascination, that is the way to find the myth," Joseph Campbell reminds us ("The Vitality of Myth" tape five of *Mythology and the Individual*).

Meditation:

What quest has been a most consistent voice in your life until now? Do you still believe in it and have a desire to respond to it? If you have responded, what have been the results?

January 23: Book II

"But now I blame the rest of the people, for the way you all
Sit in silence, that you do not address these few suitors
With speeches and restrain them, being yourselves so many."
Leocritos, son of Euenor, addressed him in answer:
Stubborn Mentor, crazed in your mind, what is this you say
Urging them to put us down? But it is disastrous
To fight over a banquet, and with men greater in number.
Yes, even if Ithacan Odysseus himself were to come
Upon the noble suitors banqueting in his house . . .
. . ., he would meet his wretched fate right there,
If he fought against many. You have not spoken properly" (II: 239-47; 250-51).

The debate rages on between the voices of honor who respect Odysseus and were charged with the safety of his home, and the responses of the suitors who want to erase any obstacles that would threaten their handouts. Mentor chastises those who refuse to speak out against the suitors' excessive self-serving behavior. He introduces a key theme in the epic: restraint, holding back, moderation, which the epic will develop subtly and overtly up to the end of Book XXIV. Leocritus then pushes back against Mentor's words, calling him crazy to suggest threatening the suitors whose numbers are in excess; they feel impervious to Odysseus, should he return to claim what belongs to him. He boasts that if Odysseus were to show up now, he would be crushed by their sheer numbers.

The pattern outlined above we see around us today: those whose greed is unchecked and even sanctioned in part, because all those around them are enjoying the same largesse while contributing nothing in return. The belly is boss. They will fight with great ferocity to protect their cushy position as recipients of others' toil. When in charge, the appetites mute and cancel moderation and reciprocity, two of the virtues of the guest-host relationship and a bedrock of civilization. A sense of what is just and ordered is devoured by the wish for more. All forms of justifying such greed, and with it, power, appear one after another to twist the distorted sense of entitlement into a virtue. Power then prohibits any sense of just behavior.

Meditation:

When has your own appetites for something or someone distorted your conventional or normal sense of justice and rightness? When were you taken advantage of by others who showed no interest in what you might need?

January 24: Book II

Telemachos went off apart to the sands of the sea,
Washed his hands in gray salt water, and prayed to Athene:
"Hear me, you who yesterday came as a god to our house
And bade me to go in a ship onto the murky sea
To learn of the return of my father who is gone so long,
But the Achaians delay over all these things
And the wickedly presumptuous suitors most of all."
So he spoke in prayer. Athene came close to him,
Likening herself to Mentor in form and in voice (II. 260-68).

Not unlike a religious ritual, Telemachos goes to the sea, which he will soon sail across, and prays to Athene for the courage to do as she commanded. He tells her he knows who she is behind her disguise. His obstacle is not direction but the necessary will to bypass the prevailing power of the suitors in order to step fully into his own authority. He is restrained, however, by the greed of the status quo, which includes the elders as well as the suitors; he must transcend them both, even if he suffers for his boldness. Delay is the weapon they use against his position and his purpose. It can paralyze his resolve. Athene will immediately appear to him as Odysseus' companion Mentor after his prayer and tell him, "hereafter you will not be a coward or senseless" (l. 270).

Any sea is going to be "murky" when clear paths are not open to us. We must set sail anyway because purpose is more crucial than purity. Prayer, submission, clear vision of obstacles are all a part of our decision. Then we must act; then our courage is truly-tested. Thinking it through is only the journey's genesis. Now it must be incarnated in the ambiguous murky terrain of the world, with its attendant uncertainties and paradoxes, and perhaps against all odds. Then we are given a fuller profile of our level of commitment: to leave a job, a relationship, a way of life that imprisons, or a set of habits that make one feel stuck in life's stickiness, and strike out into an uncertain future. Now we know we are alive and very possibly on the cusp of inventing a new life that is our true self. Joseph Campbell finds that if our world is too denotative, then it literalizes and restricts; if connotative it possibilizes, deepens and expands (*Inner Reaches* 5)

Meditation:

Describe a journey you forged that was murky, mysterious, ambiguous as to its purpose, yet fully necessary for you to feel alive.

January 25: Book II

"Antinoos, there is no way I could dine in silence
With you, insolent men, and enjoy myself securely.
Or is it not enough, you suitors, that beforehand you wasted
Many noble possessions of mine while I was still a child?
And now that I am big and learn about the story,
Hearing it from others, and the spirit does wax within me,
I shall try some way to fling evil fates upon you,
Either by going to Pylos or here in this very district.
I am going, and the journey I speak of will not be fruitless—" (II. 310-18).

Perhaps it is not the wisest move to announce his plans, but Telemachos as a young man carries all the impetuousness of his youth. Yet he stands up to the leader of the suitors and makes it clear that something is soon to change in his household. The suitors have feasted on Odysseus' possessions without restraint for years. Now that he has had history revealed to him through stories, he is courageous enough to take action, even if it means leaving Ithaca to learn more of the narrative of his father's identity and through it, his own. His boasting is met with ridicule and abuse, but it does carry a sense of justice that none of the suitors, let alone their leader, would enjoy hearing,. One hears excitement in his voice as he announces the journey that he is about to embark on to discover both self and origins. Here the terms of the hero's adventure take form.

Not possessing the full story, the part that is way beyond our current temporal place in the world, cultivates impatience. Knowing the full story, by contrast, empowers. Stories can push us out of habituations, stuck places in life by liberating us to seek change, alterations and options to fit our current maturity. Partial motions can nail us to the same trapped timber. Resolve, however, must follow this new form of knowing. Stories can spur us to goodness by helping us shed shackles of servitude. We each carry this Telemachos archetype within. We listen carefully within it to the voice of the divine, which may be in the form of a call to break loose and try creating another narrative, or another set of analogies stimulated by the stories we metabolize into a new myth.

Meditation:

Recall when, at a moment in your life, you were given a full story or a fictitious story when you thought your partial story was complete or the fictitious story true. What changed in you as a result of your new revelation?

January 26: Book II

Then Telemachos spoke to her and called her to the chamber:
"Good mother, come draw wine off for me into jars with handles,
Sweet wine, except for the most savory that you keep,
Thinking of that ill-fated man, in case he comes from somewhere,
Zeus-born Odysseus, and wards off destiny and death.
Fill up twelve of them, and fit them all with lids,
And pour barley for me into well-stitched leather bags. . . .
I am going to Sparta and also to sandy Pylos
To learn of my dear father's return, if I may hear somehow" (II. 348-54; 359-60).

Telemachos continues to prepare for his first enabling journey. It is both a trip out into the world in search of narratives of his father and an inner journey to learn of his own identity. He enlists his favorite servant woman, Eurycleia, who raised his father and was brought to Ithaca by his father, Laertes. His trip is shrouded in secrecy. He has told the suitors of his plans, but now must hide the specifics of it. He is learning to negotiate danger and possible destruction as he launches his quest with Athene's encouragement and guidance. His education is about to begin in greater earnest within a much larger world and world view. It will begin when he steps off the land and onto his own ship to command.

We each can come to know from an inner sense or calling when it is time to shift our life's direction. The call of the heroic necessitates a break or a breakdown of the familiar when life is frozen, deadly, unsatisfying, paralyzed or perhaps just too "safe." Something now must intrude to crack open the stale chrysalis of habits, well-worn grooves and perhaps deadening routines. One's myth needs a radical overhaul. Like Telemachos, we acknowledge the right time, the advantageous moment, to hear and then heed the world's calling us to a new myth-way more than simply a path-way. The alternative, if one chooses to refuse the call to the world, is a form of living that is sterile and life-sapping. Not acquiring a new job, but acquiring a new style of living, more attuned to who we are becoming, is the deeper purpose here. Risk-taking becomes a form of myth-making. If we refuse the call, then his/her world "becomes a wasteland of dry stones and his life feels meaningless. . ." (*Hero* 59), Joseph Campbell reminds us.

Meditation:

Reflect on a crucial juncture when you heard a call and responded to its provocative and perhaps unsettling voice, or a call you were too busy to hear.

January 27: Book II

"Take cheer, nurse; this plan is not without a god.
But swear you will tell nothing of this to my dear mother
Before the eleventh or twelfth day has come,
Unless she misses me and hears that I am gone off,
So that she might not weep and injure her lovely skin."
So he spoke; and the old woman swore by the gods she would not,
A great oath, and then when she swore and completed the oath,
Right away she drew off wine for him in the jars with handles
And poured barley for him into well-stitched leather bags.
Telemachos went into the house and joined the suitors (II. 372-381).

Towards the end of Book II is a tender moment when Telemachos brings into his confidence the old servant, Eurycleia. He is also very solicitous towards his mother in not wanting to upset her and cause her further suffering. He also acknowledges in humility the forceful presence of divinity in the order of things. He does not act alone as he goes undercover of the surface of life to forge a new path for himself. All of his plans revolve around an act that will grow in stature as the epic continues: oath-taking. Language is in service of a pact of restraint, of what must remain hidden if it is to retain its force in crafting a richer reality, one that realizes the essential nature of hospitality and courage when it is denied.

Fidelity to life, trust in others and a stout heart all encourage civilization to flourish. At times we each must exercise restraint or keep things hidden and shape consciousness for a greater good. Oaths hold disparate elements in a healthy tension so life itself can unfold in secret. Telemachos is gaining his emotional and political hold on life's circumstances by engaging craft in planning under cover of conventional reality. *Bie,* or force may eventually be needed, but at this moment, *metis,* craftiness, must rule. An oath may hold a reality in abeyance and can be used to find agreement between two opposing forces who might otherwise inflict violence on one another. Oath-breaking occurs when trust itself is held hostage after a period of freedom and mutual hospitality. An implicit oath that assumes certain behaviors from guest and host is at the core of civilized generosity. The suitors may be understood as those energies in the soul that self-serve only.

Meditation:

Think of when, to accomplish something important, you had to create a pact or oath to keep your intentions hidden, for it was not the right time to reveal it.

January 28: Book II

Then the bright-eyed goddess Athene had another thought.
And she went on to the halls of godlike Odysseus.
There she diffused sweet slumber down on the suitors,
And confused them as they drank. The goblets fell from their hands.
They rose up to go sleep through the city. And not long
Did they sit, when once slumber fell on their eyelids.
Then the bright-eyed goddess Athene spoke to Telemachos,
Calling him out of the well-situated halls,
Likening herself to Mentor in form and in voice: (II. 393-98).

It is too early in the narrative to fight the suitors directly, so Athene is content in subduing them temporarily. Drinking wine makes them sleepy, to which she adds the potion of confusion to their excessive imbibing. She buys time (*Kronos*) in order to prepare for the right time (*Kairos*). This incident is the first of many situations in the epic when characters succumb to sleep. It is a signal of becoming fully unconscious, giving up all vigilance and mindfulness and an awareness of what is happening. It is also another illustration of the power of camouflage; she uses wine's natural seductive qualities to hide her potion that breeds confusion. It is no less than altering consciousness to promote mindlessness, distraction and perpetual confusion, all excellent forms of becoming unconscious.

Being confused, disoriented from what is, losing presence of what is taking place, drifting off, being easily distracted—all these are the symptoms of mindlessness. Next to bright-eyed Athene, the god of divine confusion is Dionysus; his association with wine is fitting. Confused, we wander, with no clear purpose or design for our lives. Now here, now there, we are left in a trackless void without intention. So consuming is a default condition. In addition, one is powerless, easily conquered and slain. Athene's brilliance is focused not on changing their external conditions alone but the mind's interior authority.

Carl Kerenyi tells us that Athene was the first of the children of Metis and Zeus; she was "called the owl-eyed maiden Tritogeneia. . . ..equal to Zeus in courage and wise counsel. . . ." She is one "who rejoices in tumult" (*Gods of the Greeks* 118-19).

Meditation:

When confused, what do you employ to bring your mind back into focus and recover your purpose? What was the source of this confusion?

January 29: Book II

"Telemachos, already your well-greaved companions
Are seated at the oars awaiting your urging.
Let us go, so that we may not long delay from the journey."
So did Pallas Athene speak, and she led on
Speedily. He went along in the god's footsteps.
But when they had got down to the ship and the sea,
They found the long-haired companions there on the sand.
And Telemachos addressed them in his holy might:
"Over here, friends. Let us load on provisions. Already
All are gathered in the chamber" (II. 402-11).

Disguised as Mentor, Athene speaks to Telemachos with an urgency in her voice. In one of her many attributes she is the goddess of *Kairos*, of the right time, or of excellent timing, as well as more generally time's sacred dimension. Being in accord with time itself comprises part of her wisdom. Her new student has no desire to argue with her; on the contrary, he places his mortal feet into the impressions made by his divine Mentor. Her pace becomes his pace; he is in perfect accord with her footing. He is willing to be led, instructed and guided by her wisdom as well as her power. His first journey away from home enjoys the tutelage of divine presence. From it he is able to step into a commanding persona with his men and begin the journey not just to Pylos and Sparta, but interiorly into his own authority as a leader of men.

Some of us are more fortunate than others in being gifted a mentor to whom we can confide and from whom we may gain confidence in decision making. Mentors are gifts, blessings on the path of our life adventures. Without them, we may easily expend huge amounts of time reinventing what another with more experience already knows. Our guides in life can keep us moving on our path, caution us where there is danger and ensure that we don't remain open to being instructed by less reliable voices of authority so we might avoid seeking answers to the wrong questions. How fortunate is Odysseus and his family, for they have been favored by Athene, whose mother, Metis, is an ancient goddess of Mind, Measure, and Order," as Leonard Shlain writes (*The Alphabet Versus the Goddess* 130).

Meditation:

In mentoring another or in being mentored, what was the greatest gain for you personally? Was there also a price tag for such instruction?

January 30: Book II

So he spoke, and led them, and they went along with him.
When they had brought everything to the well-timbered ship,
They stowed it away as Odysseus' dear son ordered them.
Telemachos then boarded the ship, but Athene went first
And sat down in the stern of the ship. Close beside her
Telemachos sat. They let the stern cables loose,
And themselves boarded and sat down at the oarlocks.
Bright-eyed Athene sent them a driving breeze,
A driving West Wind roaring on the wine-faced sea (II. 413-21).

Order and arrangement, even a certain protocol, attends moments when the divine and human engage a cooperative enterprise. Given divine inspiration or being inspirited by the divine goddess, Telemachos displays a quiet leadership. He speaks from an inner knowing whose seeds have been planted by the divine goddess, which he has willingly assented to. When she and Telemachos board the ship, he stays close to her; her presence carries power and authority as well as a fondness for "Odysseus' dear son." All of these qualities nourish the young man as he begins his heroic adventure, blessed by the presence of his most faithful mentor. The natural order, the human order and the divine order all conspire around the young leader and his crew to launch them on the sea of history.

Such an initiation it is for the soul when we first set sail into life's uncertainties. We say to our children, "make something of yourself and your life," in hopes it will encourage them to think about their own vision of life that is in formation. It is a poetic endeavor. To be blessed with divine instruction or guidance is a great gift we must be open to hearing from at-times the most surprising sources; oracles may use the most commonplace circumstances to speak their wisdom. To yield control to the divine or the transcendent is itself an act of faith and courage. It blesses the undertaking and helps shape the appropriate attitude towards the quest. Our pursuits are often in the form of a question we put to life as we seek a home in a wider context. A guide seems indispensable at first, for our own compass is not yet calibrated to go it alone.

Meditation:

Think of when you truly launched yourself into the world, whether you had a sense of your destiny or not. Were you given a guide, or even several, on the journey? What form did one of them assume?

January 31: Book II

Telemachos, as he urged his companions on, told them
To grasp the tackle. And they hearkened to his urging. . . .
Then they hauled up the white sails with well-plaited oxhide ropes. . . .
When they had tied down the tackle on the swift black ship,
They set up mixing bowls filled to the brim with wine,
And poured libations to the deathless, ever-living gods,
And of all especially to the bright-eyed daughter of Zeus.
All night the ship pierced her course, and at morning too. (II. 422-23; 426; 430-34).

The journey has begun. All is in order, measured and arranged. Telemachos and his men are favored by Athene as she creates a strong wind to advance them to Pylos, the home of the old warrior Nestor. After setting sails and securing the tackle, they turn, not to their bellies as the suitors might do, but to honoring the goddess through libations. The narrator underscores the immortal quality of the gods who remain constant amidst the flux of life. Athene especially, far and clear seeing, carries a wisdom about her that she freely shares with Telemachos, then he with his men. They in turn are eager to follow her lead because they trust her to carry them toward what they must learn on their adventure. Telemachos is now following as well in the footsteps of his father who ventured forth with his ships some twenty years earlier in defense of Greece's honor. Telemachos' adventure carries something of that same legacy within him.

Much comfort emanates from a world view that includes the tangible presence of a supernatural reality infusing, influencing and informing the natural order of the world. Even while the human order is ephemeral, that does not preclude our participating in another level of being. By paying close attention to divinity as our model for right thinking and measured, controlled action, we participate in a higher order of being even as we continue to become. The gods are within us as well as without. Their mandate for order and measure informs the world of many, allowing them a peace and tranquility that may be difficult for others.

Meditation:

How do you understand the presence of a higher order working its way through the patterns in your daily life? Said another way, how does spirit infuse the matter of your life?

February 1: Book III

They came to Pylos, the well-established city
Of Neleus. On the sands of the sea those men were sacrificing
Bulls all of black to the earth-shaker with blue locks.
There were nine groups, and in each one five hundred men
Were sitting. And for each group they put forward nine bulls.
While these were eating the entrails and burning the thighs to the god,
The others sailed straight in, furling into place the sails
Of the balanced ship; they pulled her up, and got out themselves.
Telemachos got out of the ship, and Athene went ahead (III. 4-12).

The first territory for Telemachos to learn of his father, which will aid him in locating his place in history, is the land of Neleus, its founder, son of Poseidon and father of Nestor. Nestor's is the most trusted long memory of the Greeks; his knowledge is the most complete and detailed as it reaches further back in time than his younger colleagues. Sacrifice to the gods, not uninterrupted consumption, is the first event Telemachos witnesses, accompanied as he is by one of the great divinities. By sacrificing to Poseidon, those at Pylos remember and hold sacred their origins through ritual enactment. They are a pious people whose largesse to the gods is authentic worship, abundantly given. Order, arrangement and symmetry are all ingredients of their mythology. Placing the sails correctly on the balanced ship reveals to us a world view of right order, due measure and balance.

When we travel, we inevitably meet different customs, rituals and behaviors that may conflict with or complement our own. Since the traveler in another's land is a guest to their hosts, generosity of spirit rather than judging their differences, the guest simply accepts these rituals as dissimilar, not better or worse than her own. We can learn as much about our own ways of doing things as we can in observing others that appear like us, but with different thought patterns, actions and beliefs. Being open and porous to new and unfamiliar ways are positive occasions for increasing our own knowledge of the world and perhaps reflecting on the values that comprise our own myths, both personal and collective. "Mythology is a system of images that endows the mind and the sentiments with a sense of participation in a field of meaning," writes Joseph Campbell (*Thou Art That* 8).

Meditation:

When has travel to new lands shown you your own customs, thoughts and behaviors in a new light? Did you change in any way that has stayed with you?

February 2: Book III

Telemachos got out of the ship, and Athene went ahead.
The bright-eyed goddess Athene addressed him first:
"Telemachos, there is no longer the least need for you to be modest,
For just this did you sail on the ocean to learn about your father,
Where the earth has hidden him and what fate he has met.
But come now, go straight to Nestor, breaker of horses.
We will see what advice he has hidden in his breast.
Entreat him yourself to speak unerringly.
He will not speak falsely. For he is very sound of mind" (III. 13-21).

Athene reveals her brilliant psychology here, not through information as much as cultivating in Telemachos a disposition toward learning. Modesty can be a virtue and a hindrance for the student. She encourages him to be bold in pursuing knowledge of his origin; she has brought him to the shores of wise Nestor, a patriarch of the Greeks and a fountain of knowledge of Troy, war and the grief of loss. He is as well a vessel of wisdom, willing to share his knowledge, if petitioned to do so. Athene also reminds Telemachos why he has set off in his ship. He has a destiny she encourages him to re-collect as way of reclaiming his courage. Athene also makes two references to being hidden: in the earth and in Nestor's breast. This important theme of concealing and revealing is one of the many heart beats of the epic. Insulation and revelation form a perfect marriage in the *Odyssey*.

Learning has at least two impulses: holding back and listening to one's teachers as well as forging ahead with the right questions to unlock the knowledge of another. Not so much challenging the teacher as probing for what information will advance one's own understanding and self-identity. Learning to become a good student is also to cultivate being a proper guest in the house of another's knowledge and history. By learning what one is ignorant of, one advances one's own self-knowledge because now it is placed in a wider and deeper context. New content brings with it new contexts for understanding within a mind that continues to grow sound and supple. Part of learning's mystery is the relation between new content within old contexts and old knowledge that requires a refreshed context.

Meditation:

Recall a time in learning when you pushed yourself out of familiar and safe territory to venture into unknown contexts. What was revealed to you?

February 3: Book III

Then sound-minded Telemachos addressed her in answer:
"Mentor, how then shall I go? How shall I approach him?
For in quick responses I have no experience.
Modesty becomes a young man addressing an elder."
Then the bright-eyed goddess Athene spoke to him:
"Telemachos, some thoughts you will have in your mind,
And a god will suggest others. For I do not think
You were born and raised without the favor of the gods."
So did Pallas Athene speak, and she led the way speedily.
He went along in the god's footsteps (III. 21-30).

Mentoring another can take a multitude of shapes and directions. For Telemachos, uncertainty and anxiety about how to address an elder publicly is daunting; Athene assures him of two points: one, that he is capable of having his own thoughts emanate from his own nature; two, that he will be visited by other thoughts from his divine nature. She predicates both of these observations on the belief that he is favored by divinities, a form of grace we might say, that allows him an openness to divine intercession. Athene indirectly praises the young man's parents as good guides in his life. For the time being, she is content to lead him into the public sphere of strangers where he will learn to speak publicly within his own authority. As a devoted student, he continues to follow in her footsteps.

Public speaking can be a terror for many. With language, we expose ourselves in our deepest nature. All attention is riveted on us; we are evaluated immediately and may be judged wanting. But silence can be a worse offense as we grow, even haltingly, into our public voice. In public discourse we are challenged to think on our feet, keep our wits about us, and express ourselves authentically. Through public discourse we further define ourselves in both our limitations and our attributes. It is a major step in entering the world's conversation with our own insights and vocal inflections. Realizing that there may be a divine impetus for our assuming a place of leadership, even in a modest way, can tease us out of ourselves and connect us with a realm beyond our own needs and self-absorptions.

Meditation:

Recall when you were coaxed or pushed into a public arena. What were the consequences of such an exposure as you learned something about yourself in public speech and conversation?

February 4: Book III

. . . Pledging her, he addressed
Pallas Athene, daughter of aegis-bearing Zeus:
"Say a prayer now, stranger, to Lord Poseidon,
Whose feast you have come upon in arriving hither.
But when you have poured a libation and prayed, which is fitting,
Then give this man also a cup of honey-sweet wine
To pour a libation, since I believe he too says prayers
To the immortals. All men have need of the gods.
But he is younger, and equal in age to myself.
Therefore I will first give you the gold cup of libation" (III. 41-50).

As a host, Peisistratos, son of Nestor, cares for the goddess and her mortal student by inviting them to participate in a ritual to honor the gods, a necessity for all mortals, whether they know it or not. Their timely arrival finds them at the feast in honor of the god Poseidon, Odysseus' main adversary to arriving home. Peisastratos also honors Athene, disguised as Mentor, first, then recognizes in Telemachos another who is pious toward the gods and who prays to them. Odysseus' son is being initiated into *pietas,* honoring divinities over and above the belly's needs. The ritual is one that offers honor and respect to the immortals in part by enacting the roles of the proper host serving the new guests, as Telemachos is honored by being served a gold cup of libation first.

Religious rituals are acts of remembrance towards powerful presences that often guide and instruct us into the deeper mysteries of being. These rituals are incarnated reminders that we are not independent beings but rely on and must cultivate relationships with the invisibles, especially when they reveal themselves and wish to be remembered. Behind the visible phenomena are guiding forces, like destiny and chance, grace and benevolence, as well as destructive forces, that we should acknowledge as part of the world's larger mythology. The gods are not a luxury but a necessity. Through them we mortals can find a measure and order in our daily lives that both ground us and encourage our vision to go beyond our often limited and opaque sense of the world.

Meditation:

To what or who do you pay homage and offer prayers, perhaps in your own form of ritual? What does such recognition add to your life's meaning?

February 5: Book III

Then sound-minded Telemachos addressed him in answer,
Taking courage, for Athene herself had put in his mind
Courage to ask him about the father who had gone away,
And so that a noble renown among men might belong to him:
"Nestor, son of Neleus, great pride of the Achaians,
You ask where we are from. And I will inform you.
We have come from Ithaca, which is under Mount Neion.
It is a private affair, not a public one, that I speak of.
I seek widespread report of my father, if somehow I may hear,
Of the stout-hearted, godly Odysseus, who once, they say,
Sacked the city of the Trojans, fighting at your side" (III. 75-85).

Having seen to his guests' needs and comfort, Nestor asks Telemachos and his comrades to identify who they are and from whence they came. Hospitality first, interrogation of identity comes second, as befitting the code of welcome. Telemachos musters the courage offered by Athene to publicly declare who he is and what he seeks from the wise Nestor who harbors the longest history of his people and of Troy. In a way, his story goes public for the first time to an accepting audience, something he has not experienced in his own home. He is candid and forthright in identifying himself in place and intention as a modest guest as he enters the ancient ritual of the guest-host relationship. Here he crosses the crucial threshold into public life and exercises his voice of authority as a public person.

We are our narratives in large measure. Others want to know our story in order to identify our notions, desires, ambitions and hardships. Few things in life connect us to one another with such a unifying power than does our shared narratives. Through words we craft ourselves into being through a well-told story. Our narratives arise from the deepest places of our authentic selves. What we choose to say and what we choose to exclude is a craft as we judge who our audience is and what we should and should not disclose to them. Marcel Proust has written that "the reader's recognition in himself of what the book says is the proof of the book's truth" David R. Loy reminds us. (qtd. in *The World* 63). When we read stories, we place a mirror in front of our deepest nature.

Meditation:

When you tell another your story, what do you begin with? What order or arrangement do you specify in the telling? Do you think it matters?

February 6: Book III

Then Nestor, the Gerenian horseman, answered him:
"Ah friend, since you have reminded me of the woe we suffered
In that land, we sons of the Achaians, unchecked in our anger;
How much both in the ships upon the murky sea,
Wandering for booty wherever Achilles led,
And how much, too, we fought around the great city
Of Lord Priam. There at that time all the best were slain!
There lies warlike Ajax, there lies Achilles,
There Patroclos, a counselor equal in weight to the gods:
There lies my dear son, at once mighty and excellent, . . ." (III. 102-11).

Telemachos' plea to Nestor to tell him the true story of his father's fate is met with a memory of extreme suffering and loss by the Greeks at Troy. The past is suddenly made present through an anguished narrative in Nestor's recollection. His speech has a confessional, even cathartic tone to it, for their anger was excessive, as was their search for booty and perhaps their lust for killing. His story gathers force as he laments the excess the Greeks succumbed to; his recollection is a key moment of recognizing and mourning for the dead, including his own son. It is also a moment in Telemachos' life where he learns the history of the war that has kept his father out of reach for twenty years. The feeling of loss and sorrow in Nestor's speech is extraordinary. One senses the war has not yet ended.

The nature of a story is in part the retrieval of a painful past by grasping it again through the changed atmosphere of the present. Recollection and reflection often change the past's meaning as it fits into a current narrative. Remembering and telling one's story has both a pastness about it as well as a forceful presence to it. "The resuscitative function of memory—bringing the dead back to life—takes many, often unrecognized forms. Intractable guilt, rage, or grief, sometimes serves this honorable purpose of keeping faith with the dead," writes Jonathan Shay of figures in Homer's *Odyssey* who recollect and tell stories of the past (*Odysseus in America* 80). May it also be true that those who hear stories of loss, in war or in life generally, with its attendant suffering, are also traumatized in the hearing? The power of stories is that they can make past wounds immediately present.

Meditation:

When you relate a story of your past, especially when it involves painful loss, does it alter that history in any significant way?

February 7: Book III

"And no one there ever wanted to be compared to him openly
For craftiness, since godly Odysseus far surpassed
In all sorts of wiles—your father, if it is true
You are that man's offspring. Awe holds me to look upon you.
Yes, indeed, your speech is like his. You would not think
A man so young could speak in such a likely way. . . .
And when we had sacked the lofty city of Priam
And gone off in the ships, and a god had scattered the Achaians,
Then Zeus plotted out in his mind a woeful return
For the Argives, since they were not all prudent or just" (III. 120-25; 130-33).

As host and patriarch, Nestor continues to narrate for Telemachos the history of Troy, the nine years of suffering in combat and the unique character of the young man's father, a man of wily ways and clever ruses. He then scrutinizes Telemachos' physical appearance and manner of speech and wonders at the similarities to his father. Telemachos in turn is gaining a sense of his own historical lineage through narrative; Nestor reveals to him his father's traits that Telemachos approximates but does not copy or imitate, for he knows not his father's personality and habits. Nestor also marvels at how well the young man speaks, not knowing Telemachos' tutor is Athene. It is a moment of public awakening for Telemachos, who can now understand himself within a historical/narrative context.

We cannot really know ourselves in a historical context until someone who has known our parents and/or siblings meets us and discovers in our uniqueness patterns and traits of our lineage and heritage. Seeing from a historical perspective, whether individuals or nations, provides a context for understanding on a much deeper level. We in turn begin to know ourselves as both a figure in history and a person with both a personal and collective myth—original and derivative at once. One may wonder when one speaks of his/her parents that they are also speaking of themselves, as in a rhetorical mirror. Such a point of view establishes one in a historical context as they see how they share a similar mythos with one's parents, siblings, cousins, aunts, uncles and/or grandparents.

Meditation:

Recall a moment when you learned something about yourself through traits of one or both parents or siblings. What did that recognition do for your own sense of identity and context in the world?

February 8: Book III

"Mentor, let us speak of this no more, though we care for him.
There is no longer a real return for that man. Already
The immortal gods have devised for him death and black fate.
But now I want to ask and inquire about another story
From Nestor, since he knows justice and prudence beyond
Others. . . .
O Nestor, son of Neleus, do utter the truth:
How did Atreus' son, broad-ruling Agamemnon die?
Where was Menelaos? What sort of destruction did cunning
Aigisthos plot for him, when he killed a far better man?" (III. 240-45; 247-50).

The signs of resigning himself to his father's death descend on Telemachos. If his father is not to return, then his story seems no longer important. Presumptuous in his declaration, trapped in his despair, Telemachos gives up on ever seeing his father. Instead, he wishes to take full advantage of Nestor's tutorial on his right "sense of justice and prudence" by asking him of other Greek warriors and the conniving Aigisthos, who slays Agamemnon, Orestes' father, when he returns home with Cassandra as his possession from Troy. His is the story of a naïve and fatal homecoming. Telemachos wishes to fill in the gaps to give himself a much larger context in which to imagine his father.

We may all be guilty of writing histories whose accuracy we don't really know but making certain assumptions nonetheless of the future we can only dimly calculate. Such is the power of myth: to create an "as-if" reality to help us cope with the environment we are ensconced within. Myth in this sense helps us to adapt to it, writes D. Stephenson Bond (*Living Myth* 42-43). Through stories Telemachos constructs a life for himself that does not include his father's homecoming. We each can and do create multiple stories that assign meanings to our present lived realities; often their foundation is little more than a series of assumptions, wishes, desires, hopes as our shaky but needed scaffolding. Thus, we can use the power of stories to deflect the pain and sorrow that may accrue if we wait until we know the truth, or we can use that power to know the truth.

Meditation:

Recall an assumption or series of assumptions that you molded into a story to accommodate the reality you were in as you understood it. Were you able to let go of that narrative when the facts surfaced, or did the facts confirm the fiction?

February 9: Book III

"Meanwhile Aigisthos plotted these woeful things at home.
For seven years he ruled Mycenae, the rich in gold
When he killed Atreus' son, and the people were subdued under him.
In the eighth year, an evil for him, godly Orestes
Came back from Athens and killed his father's murderer,
The cunning Aigisthos, who had killed his renowned father.
When he had killed him, he gave the Argives a funeral feast
Both for his hateful mother and for cowardly Aigisthos" (III. 303-10).

Nestor agrees to Telemachos' request to tell the story of Agamemnon's deadly homecoming. The Greek king was naïve to suppose all would be as he had left it when he sailed to Troy as leader of the Achaians and then home again. With the king's murder, the people capitulated to the new leader of Mycenae and lover of Clytemnestra. Then the slain king's son, Orestes, returns to avenge his father's murder by killing his mother and her lover. The heroic, passed from father to son, returns for justice. The story certainly affects Telemachos' outlook on his own destiny as he sees himself in the heroic mirror of Orestes. There is honor in Orestes as well since he follows the killings with a ritual funeral for both his mother and her lover. Telemachos needs to hear this story especially.

How often we may have seen and felt our own destiny through the story of another. This is what the Greeks understood as *mimesis*, in which we feel as if through a mirror some aspect of our own plot is stimulated by a similar story of another. It is a basis for both individual and community-formation. Perhaps our destiny was put in motion by a narrative that we felt as our story that happened to another. Our own mythic consciousness may have awakened for the first time through a story told to us. We sense our future through this narrative set in the past but vitally alive in the present. Some qualities or essences of another rouses in us a similar archetypal template. Our psychic energy begins to gather around this plot and we are in-spired to follow its pattern or to recognize that we are already within this patterned way of thought or behavior, even of its destiny. Like Telemachos, we listen with a full presence to see where our own story resonates within the grand plot of another's life.

Meditation:

Has a significant portion of your life's purpose been offered to you through a story that "rang true" for you?

February 10: Book III

"But I exhort you and urge you to proceed on
To Menelaos. For he has come recently from elsewhere,
From men from whom no one would expect in his heart
To return, whom storm winds had once led astray
Into a sea so great that not even the birds
Could get through in a year, it is so great and dire.
But go on now with your ship and your companions.
If you wish to go by land, a chariot and horses are here;
My own sons are here also, who will be your guides. . ." (III. 317-25).

Nestor has given the young son of Odysseus all that he has about his father—the long view. Now he needs additional stories and this time from one who has returned from Troy after suffering great hardships. Menelaos will serve Telemachos as a protégé of his own father's homecoming, one that took almost as long as Odysseus' journey. Nestor grasps that Telemachos needs memories of his father to build his past from, as a cornerstone serves an architectural structure. Through these accumulated stories, metaphors for the reality they shape and embody, he will slowly construct his own myth based on his father's history storied to him by many sources as well as by divine guidance. He then must travel not to the site of a war but to the site of narratives, their own form of historical presence. They are crucial to his developing consciousness based on a much broader context than he had available to him at home.

There is something profound about a guest to get as close to the head waters of a story as is possible. We also have a deep yearning to be told the story from eye witnesses or those who had direct involvement with the one we search and yearn for. Eyewitness accounts carry a certain numinous energy with them. It places us close to the origin of a person, an event, or a historical moment of great import. It is a far different experience than reading about it wherein questions cannot be asked with the same directness that intimate contact with someone who knew the person or event. Finding the right source is often accomplished by chance, or design, or by good guides both mortal and divine.

Meditation:

Describe an experience wherein you were guided or led to the right source to help you with a major life decision. Was it chance, good fortune, luck or design, for example? Was it through prayer, petition or a chance encounter?

February 11: Book III

Nestor restrained them and addressed them with a speech:
"May Zeus and the other immortal gods prevent
Your going away from my house to the swift ship
As from someone wholly without raiment, or destitute,
Who does not have coverlets and many rugs in his house
Either for himself or for his guests to sleep in softly . . . .
Not indeed will the dear son of this man Odysseus
Lie down on his ship's deck so long as I am alive
And so long as children are left to me in the halls
To entertain guests, whoever comes to my house" (III. 345-50; 352-55).

Telemachos' desire to ship out to Sparta and Menelaos' tutelage about his father strikes a chord in Nestor's sense of hospitality. This civilized gesture is both a virtue and a necessity. He insists that Telemachos and his men restrain from leaving so quickly to sleep on their ship's deck when his accommodations are so much more comfortable and inviting. A tension is created between Telemachos' desire to hurry to Sparta and Nestor's desire to treat him as a guest by offering a comfortable bed. Out of respect for his father and for Nestor's generosity, Odysseus' son and his men stay in his palace and follow the edicts of restraint instead of haste and even a bit of recklessness, two major themes the epic addresses throughout. The code of hospitality must be revered and preserved.

Every journey has its own timing and rhythm. Life calls us repeatedly to adventures while another impulse, namely, to dwell, is also part of journeying. Wisdom enters when one discerns a balance between these opposing forces—each of which is part of the archetypal constructs: journeying and dwelling, motion and stasis, ignorance and knowledge. Journeying requires periods of rest and recovery. Our own voice of restraint may serve us out on the road or seas every bit as much as the purpose of our quest. Listening is crucial, as is responding in our own voice.

In the experience of reading a classic like Homer' epic, Donald Cowan suggests "this ability to distance oneself from actuality and so gain a broader perspective is a crucially important skill to be gained from a literary work" ("The Uses of Defeat" 50).

Meditation:

Have you to date in your life journey relinquished the voice of restraint and rest? How has it helped you to heed it in certain circumstances?

February 12: Book III

"Dear children, fulfill my wish very speedily,
So that first of the gods I may propitiate Athene,
Who came in clear form to the lavish feast of the god...."
So he said, and they all got busy. The heifer came
From the plain, and there came from the swift, balanced ship
The companions of great-hearted Telemachos....
                  And Athene came to take part
In the sacrifice. The old charioteer Nestor gave gold,
And then the other gilded it round and decked the heifer's horns,
So that the goddess would be pleased to see the decoration (III. 418-20; 430-32; 435-38).

Now that Telemachos has been persuaded to postpone his journey for a day, Nestor puts in accelerated motion an abundant ritual of celebrating the young journeyer and by extension, his father's memory as the warrior whose journey from Troy was the longest. Telemachos has revealed yet another trait of his father. Nestor singles out Athene to be honored in the feast. He recognizes her presence from the beginning, so to honor her divinity is a driving desire of the feast. How different all this must appear to Telemachos, who has witnessed constant feasting of the suitors without the piety and regard of acknowledging divinity or the desire to create something aesthetic to please one of them. Not appetite but aesthetic presentation leads the household of Nestor. Telemachos brings all of his ship's crew to the feast and Athene appears to sanctify the sacrifice.

In a civil society, banquets, feasts, and celebrations are crucial bulwarks against barbarism and merely satisfying appetites. Rituals remember and bless key values held within the myth of a people. Rituals ennoble human actions like nourishing the body through remembrance and here, through a sacrifice. Something of worth is given over so that important values may enter the ceremony of nourishment, which now takes place on several levels: divine, mortal and a sacrificial animal from the natural order all congeal in the ritual to offer a sense of wholeness and proper measure to the festivities. Civility is celebrated.

Meditation:

When does ritual play an important role in your own nourishment? Where do you see a need for a ritual that does not exist presently?

February 13: Book III

Perseus held the blood-bowl. The old charioteer Nestor led off
By washing his hands and sprinkling barley. As he started,
He prayed much to Athene, throwing hairs of its head in the fire.
And when they had prayed and tossed the barley offering on,
At once Nestor's son, high-spirited Thrasymedes,
Stood close and struck it. The ax slit the tendons
Of the neck. The heifer's strength was loosed; the women shrieked,
His daughters and daughter-in-law and the respected wife
Of Nestor, Eurydice, eldest of Clymenos' daughters (III. 444-52).

Telemachos witnesses this ritual sacrifice which honors the heifer, Athene and civilization itself in its bonding of the mortal and immortal realms. Odysseus' son may not have seen such a measured and respectful killing before: "When black blood flowed from it and the spirit left the bones" (l. 455). The ritual is a sign of order, measure and communal involvement in a shared worship. The violent killing is given a measured context. It brings on death; in the feast of the heifer it also renews life and the ancient cycle of birth, death, birth. The barley is the grain of the fields to be mixed with the animal sacrifice. The moment of striking a fatal blow has a hallowed and numinous quality to it. In the moment of death and the women's shrieking, the poet gives us a sense of the relationship between various members witnessing the death of the animal as well as all those who will enjoy the fruits of its body.

Deeply ingrained in us is the yearning for ritual sacrifice which is as ancient as humanity itself. It seems a part of all religious traditions. Life's precious quality resides in part in one's ability to take an ax to it. In death, the one sacrifice sustains life, so a paradox rests at the heart of ritual sacrifice. It also reminds us of life's fragile continuation. But the violence is modified and contained by the ritual enactment. The heifer's death—quick and skillfully brought about, is an affirmation of the life principle itself. It is also the basis of an individual's or a people's mythology. Violence is part of life. Sandra Easter writes that "Ritual opens us to an expanded awareness of the existence of reality beyond the sensible, everyday world. . .and provides a structure for containment of intense emotions . . . (*Jung and the Ancestors* 149).

Meditation:

When do you engage a ritual that sustains and affirms life for you?

February 14: Book III

Meanwhile, the lovely Polykaste, youngest daughter
Of Nestor, the son of Neleus, washed Telemachos.
And when she had washed him and anointed him richly with oil,
She put a lovely mantle on him and a tunic.
And he left the bathtub in body like the immortals;
He went and sat down by Nestor, shepherd of the people.
When they had roasted the outer flesh and pulled it off,
They sat feasting. Noble men did watchful service
Pouring out the wine into the golden goblets (III. 464-72).

First, in a general way, Telemachos is being initiated into a larger culture through stories and ritual enactments, each of which contains their own narrative power. He is bathed and anointed in an initiation that ends with his being honored by being seated next to Nestor. His appearance now is aligned with that of a divinity. He is bathed, then dressed anew and honored both for himself and for who his father is. It is a form of birth into a new life. Nestor's education of Telemachos is almost complete. The young man learns so much of what comprises civilized society by being given an opportunity for intimate participation in it. He has been received into and renewed by these ritual encounters that highlight nobility and beauty; he is prepared for the next chapter of his journey.

Rituals are meant to transform the participants and perhaps the witnesses of these rites. A people's myth is incarnated in ritual activities they have created to remember and to honor certain aspects or moments of their communal lives. The bath here cleanses one of one's old self and renews one through the donning of a new self. One is changed in the process. Here an individual's stature is elevated, acknowledged, and celebrated. The performance or enactment of ritual renews core values a people live by and by means of. It is a religious experience that is sacred as well as secular, communal as well as private and memorial as well as future-oriented. Victor Turner observes that "The wisdom (*mana*) that is imparted in sacred liminality is not just an aggregation of words and sentences; it has ontological value, it refashions the very being of the neophyte" (*The Ritual Process* 103). Such is Telemachos' rite of passage.

Meditation:

Where in your current life is ritual lacking? Could you inaugurate a ritual for something or someone that has had deep value for you?

February 15: Book III

Telemachos got into the beautiful chariot.
Nestor's son, Peisistratos, chief of the men, along with him
Got into the chariot and took the reins in his hands.
He whipped to start up. Not against their will the pair flew
To the plain, and they left the sheer citadel of Pylos.
All day they shook the yoke, holding it up on either side.
The sun went down and all the ways were shadowed. . . .
They reached the wheat-bearing plain. From then on they strove
To finish their journey. So the swift horses bore onward.
The sun went down and all the ways were shadowed (III. 481-85; 495-97).

Having been lovingly restrained to enjoy Nestor's largesse and the ritual of sacrifice, as well as his own ritual cleansing, Telemachos and Nestor's son reveal an urgency in their travels to Sparta, home of Menelaos and Helen. The two horses seemingly inexhaustible pulling the chariot, appear to fly across their route. All day they travel hard, spending one night at Pharei (l. 488), then push on early the next morning. There is an urgency in their journey to gather information of Odysseus and return to Ithaca. Telemachos' view of the world continues to broaden and deepen in many directions as his own myth enlarges to accommodate his new enlarged reality. As the sun departs, shadows cover the atmosphere and their travels, offering another dimension to the journey—its darkness.

Travel stretches and challenges us. What is our daily familiar life is dismantled or overhauled as new customs, beliefs, histories, foods, schedules intrude into our familiar ground to shake it up. The world becomes more vital, wondrous, even painful, as we see how elastic we can be when assaulted by so much newness. In the process we may be transformed in the deepest part of ourselves as old beliefs and assumptions fall away like dead skin to make room for new ways of adaptation. The journey is double: out to the world and deep into ourselves. In the tension of the two we are remythologized on both levels. Travel offers its own form of rites of passage where adaptation, not rigid fixity, is our strongest virtue. By remaining pliable and not imposing our familiar order on an unfamiliar world, we can enjoy the exhilaration of the new without threat.

Meditation:

Explore for a moment two ways that travel to foreign parts shook up your normal life and expanded or deepened it.

February 16: Book IV

Then they led the men to the godly house. When they saw
The hall of the Zeus-nourished king, they wondered at it.
There was a gleam like that of the sun or of the moon
Beneath the high-roofed hall of glorious Menelaos.
But when they had taken their joy of looking with their eyes,
They went out and got washed in the well-polished bathtubs. . . .
A handmaid poured water from a pitcher she was carrying,
A lovely golden one, over into a silver basin
For washing the hands. She set up a polished table alongside (IV. 43-48;52-54).

Contrary to the hospitality shown at Nestor's palace, here with Menelaos all of Telemachos' men enjoy the full luxury of his and Helen's hospitality. Here also is a house that inspires wonder because of its luxurious beauty. A numinous light permeates it. Menelaos himself is described as glorious. The beauty of the household elicits joy from the men; their souls and bodies bask in the astonishing beauty of place. Their cleansing is communal. Of course they are learning what a rightly measured and ordered household looks like as well as what rituals make it heart-warming. Guests are pampered by the host, the opposite condition reigning in Odysseus' home. Telemachos and his men will return with these newly-discovered images of hospitality.

Something more than efficiency is attached to the home of others. Being guested also includes the surroundings, the beauty, the elegance of both people and possessions. Aesthetics is an integral part of the world of civilized life. A sense of wonder should be part of our experience when we enter the domicile of another. In *All Things Shining,* Dreyful and Kelly affirm that in the *Odyssey* "the word that is translated 'wonder' here—*sebas* in the Greek—literally implies the sacred phenomena of reverence, worship, and honor, as well" (85). Artifacts, possessions from travel, a measured aesthetic surrounding should also be part of the experience of another's home. Care for the body is not incidental. Being immersed in a bounty of food, drink, conversation in a space of safety absent all violence and discord, is part of the guest-host relationship. Friendship rests deeply at its core—and below that, the stirrings of culture itself.

Meditation:

What can you recall that struck you with wonder, in sight, sound or in another format?

February 17: Book IV

"Would I might dwell in my halls with just a third share
Of those things, and the men were safe who perished then
In broad Troy, far away from horse-nourishing Argos!
But nevertheless I frequently sit in our halls
Mourning and grieving over all of them; sometimes
I please my mind with lamentation and sometimes
I cease from it. For quick is the glut of cold lamentation" (IV. 97-103).

Menelaos' lament is in response to his overhearing Telemachos tell Nestor's son of all the bronze, gold, amber, ivory and silver objects of beauty that make him wonder all the more and compare this opulence to what Zeus' halls might look like. Menelaos confesses that he wandered for eight years acquiring possessions from many cities before arriving home, but while he gained these possessions, his brother Agamemnon was slain by Aigisthos and Clytemnestra. He feels guilt for all these treasures and would gladly part with many if it meant the men he lost at Troy could be alive today. His laments for the dead bring him little consolation, however, for the pain of loss he lives with because so many were unable to return home with him. He seems to gain some solace over the act of lamenting their loss, but he knows as well that such laments can be a trap if indulged too long.

Appearances can deceive any of us. Telemachos sees wealth while Menelaos sees and feels grief over loss. Amassing treasures and booty in one's travels will not satisfy the suffering grief brings in its wake. Outward beauty cannot erase the sting of a heart that mourns the loss of others, especially of those fellow warriors lost in battle. At some point the glory of war fades in the face of overwhelming loss that marks the true cost of war's violence. The more valuable treasures and gifts are those souls who did not return home. Even lamenting their loss after a time proves modest consolation. In addition, with so many of war's veterans, even speaking of the losses of friends in battle proves too much, so they remain silent in their own suffering. In *Warrior's Return*, Edward Tick writes that such suffering often leads to substance abuse and violence in the vet's own home (43-45). Warriors may return from war, but war's horrors remain in their backpacks.

Meditation:

When have you experienced a dramatic loss that no amount of wealth or possessions could ever make up for or fill in that loss?

February 18: Book IV

". . . When I think of him, since none of the Achaians suffered as much
As Odysseus suffered and bore. For him there were destined
To be troubles, and for me a perpetually ceaseless grief
Over him, since he has long been gone, and we do not know
If he lives or is dead. I suppose they are mourning him now,
The old Laertes and constant Penelope,
And Telemachos, whom he left as a newborn child in his house."
So he spoke, and roused in him a longing to mourn his father.
A tear fell on the ground from his eyelids as he heard of his father
And he held the purple mantle up before his eyes. . . (IV. 106-15).

Menelaos' account of Odysseus is more current and more emotional and more intimate than was Nestor's recounting of him. When Menelaos states that for Odysseus there were to be "troubles," he has just named the lost warrior in that word. Odysseus' name means to inflict and to receive troubles in the form of pain and afflictions, writes G.E. Dimock ("The Name of Odysseus" 413). Menelaos also acknowledges that a great deal of the pain surrounding Odysseus is that no one knows if he lives or has perished. The grief felt is heightened through this uncertainty. The story's effect on Telemachos is palpable; he weeps for his loss because the story Menelaos tells slices into him. He tries to hide his weeping, but Menelaos sees it.

Stories have an extraordinary power to make what is absent immediately present. A story's effect on one's emotional reality can be all-consuming. It depicts a reality that for the moment overwhelms the presentness of one's situation and replaces it with a formed and shaped genuineness that can be more potent than the current event. The *Odyssey* is an epic whose focus is continually on the making of narratives—fictions or facts—with a potency to render both the truth of matters or their deceptions powerful and lasting. Each of us knows how transformative a story well-told can be in our life to convey a deeper truth in a felt way. "The trauma field" of war can "cause transgenerational trauma. . . " (*Warrior's Return* 49), so one avenue to healing can be through narratives like Homer's epic that can allow a reimagining of the original traumatic events.

Meditation:

Can you depict the most prominent story line of your life, one that measures most fully your actions and achievements to date?

February 19: Book IV

While he pondered these matters in his mind and in his heart,
Helen came out of the high-roofed fragrant bedroom,
She who resembled Artemis of the golden shafts. . . .
Right away she asked her husband in words for the details:
"Menelaos, nourished by Zeus, do we know who these people
Who have come to our home claim to be among men?
Shall I dissemble or speak the truth? My heart bids me to.
I think I have never yet seen anyone so like him,
A man or a woman; wonder holds me as I see this man, . . ." (IV. 120-22; 137-42).

While Helen appears in only a few scenes in the epic, her seduction and transport to Troy by Paris set the Trojan War in motion. Now, back with her husband and a god-like beauty, she steps into public view to ask who these guests are that have appeared in their home. Following quickly on this question, she asks if her own words should be truthful or deceptive. Fiction or fact is what she wonders would be best to speak. Like stories themselves, she understands, words are double-edged, capable of concealing or revealing what is true. This theme drives the action of the *Odyssey* from first to last. "So like him" refers to Odysseus and she is held in awe or wonder by Telemachos' presence, as if Odysseus himself might be standing before her.

The *Odyssey* will continue throughout to entertain the power of words to camouflage the truth of events and individuals or expose them to the light of what is true. Words can be understood as enactments of realities, either true or fictional, which makes *us* wonder if the fictional has the capacity to carry more of the truth than the mere facts of a person or events. So much of what we hear or read is based on a fundamental trust that what we accept is associated with the truth. Every expression conveys an act of trust. But in most cases we really don't know if we are hearing or reading what is the actual reality of what we perceive. If Homer's *Iliad* focusses on war, the *Odyssey*'s emphasis is on the power of words to make us wonder. Dreyfus and Kelly add that wonder "is used in Homer to indicate that one cannot help but to stand in awe before something sacred" (85).

Meditation:

What standard or gauge do you use to measure or assess the truth or falsity of what words convey?

February 20: Book IV

"But let us cease the lamentation that was made before,
And let us once more think about dinner; let them pour
Water on our hands. There will be stories after dawn
For Telemachos and me to talk out with one another. . . ."
Then Helen, who was born of Zeus, had another thought.
Right away she dropped a drug in the wine they were drinking,
A soothing pain-killer, that made one forget all his ills,
And whoever swallowed it down when it was mixed in the bowl
Would not shed a tear down his cheeks the whole day long
Not if his mother and his father were both to die, . . . (IV. 212-15; 219-24).

Suffering the past in memories is central to this scene in which the gore and glory of Troy's war threatens to devour the community in grief. Acknowledging loss may soon turn to losing all festive enjoyment over the presence of Telemachos and his comrades. Menelaos is right to call a halt to the stories that gather around Odysseus' loss as well as his almost fictional presence in the figure of his son. Helen steps forward to ease the afflictions of memory by altering the consciousness of each sufferer—those who actually fought in Troy and those who through remembered narratives have suffered a similar trauma.

Grief over loss can rock an individual, a family or a nation. War's trauma can last for decades if untreated. Revisiting certain key moments from the litany of afflictions and horrors in battle and in the loss of family and friends adds to the loss. Finding ways to speak of the loss can be a major step to even being in the presence of that initial suffering. Jonathan Shay observes" "I believe that every veteran who returns to civilian life after a long time in combat has moments in which he is afraid he is losing his mind" (*Odysseus in America* 108). Ken Burns and Lyn Novick's series on the Viet Nam war (2017) derives a great deal of its power from the interviews of veterans from both sides of that protracted battle; without their presence and their voices, the war's history would remain largely statistical. In their stories we who had not been directly part of it, but who suffered the psychic wounds caused by it, experience it nonetheless on a visceral level.

Meditation:

Reflect on a traumatic experience that changed you and perhaps made you question your identity. Were you able, over time, to relate that story of such an affliction? Is it important to you in your life now to tell it or have it told?

February 21: Book IV

> "But come, sit and dine now in the hall,
> And enjoy the tales. I shall tell an appropriate one.
> Now I shall not be able to tell or enumerate all
> Of the many trials there were for stout-hearted Odysseus;
> But what a deed this one was the mighty man did and dared
> In the land of the Trojans where you Achaians suffered troubles
> When he had submitted himself to disfiguring blows, ...
> He likened himself in his concealment to another mortal,
> To a beggar, he who by the Achaians' ships was nothing like that.
> In that guise he entered the city of the Trojans. They all
> Overlooked him. I alone recognized him as he was" (IV. 238-44; 247-50).

Helen now shifts the narrative in order to tell of Odysseus' sacrifice, his cunning, his idea of creating the Trojan horse that will carry several Achaians in its hollow belly inside the gates of the city, as well as his disguise to fictionalize his identity. She admits to not being able to recall all of his sufferings, but she can nonetheless give a good portrait from a strategic angle, of his character for the sake especially of his son. He sacrificed himself to beatings at the hands of the Trojans; in disguise, he concealed his real identity for a larger intention. He fabricated himself, like a good story, to achieve a certain effect or goal. Helen's intent here is to portray him as true through a fiction. She alone saw through his disguise as she was held by the Trojans, but, she goes on, "he eluded me cunningly" (l. 251).

We fabricate ourselves to some degree through the stories we spin about ourselves and the clothes we garnish ourselves with. Fashion itself is a lucrative business promoting fictions through fabrics and fabrications. Others too can spin a reality of us through their stories of who we are, from their point of view. In an age of social media this avenue can be destructive and debilitating. Others may enhance, embellish or even fall far short of our true design. What we learn from telling stories of ourselves and others is that a gap may always exist in who we are and who we story ourselves into being. We have both a narrative truth as well as historical truth, argues psychologist Donald Spence (*Narrative Truth and Historical Truth: Meaning and Interpretation in Psychoanalysis* 15)

Meditation:

When might you or have you embellished your identity in story telling or left out elements to create a particular effect of who you are?

February 22: Book IV

"I and the son of Tydeus and godlike Odysseus,
As we sat in their midst, heard you as you shouted.
And the two of us were eager to make a start,
Either to get outside or to reply at once from within.
But Odysseus held us back and restrained us though we wanted to.
Then all the other sons of the Achaians were silent
And Antilochos alone wished to give you answer
With a speech. But Odysseus steadily pressed the man's mouth
With his powerful hands, and he saved all the Achaians.
He held him until Pallas Athene led you away" (IV. 280-89).

Menelaos now takes up storytelling to praise both Helen and Odysseus. He tells of being in the hollow belly of the Trojan horse while Helen circled it, calling out the names of the best Danaan fighters, using the voice of their wives. Those Argives within felt compelled to respond to Helen's naming, but Odysseus knew better and restrained them from revealing their presence inside the horse's belly. One especially wished to shout out but Odysseus physically restrained him. If they were discovered prematurely, the Argives would probably lose the war. Silence over speech becomes a more lethal weapon than anything one could possibly say in this circumstance. A valid response to a story may also be silence.

Restraint, patience, tolerating the tension between desiring to attack vs. holding back, are constant motifs in the *Odyssey's* major actions. It is a signal of wisdom in life to know when to surge forward and when to exercise silent restraint. A sense of timing is crucial as a strategy. In certain instances, restraint can be a powerful weapon because it allows for time to pause, to hesitate, until the right time—*kairos* in Greek. Odysseus' craftiness includes his ability to pause and let the right time ripen before taking action. Much of Buddhist thought gathers around holding back, allowing for gaps, rather than charging forth. We may in the West say "count to ten before speaking." That breach opened through restraint can allow other options to form, perhaps to defuse a situation from becoming more volatile. Homer's stories often highlight restraint as a form that wisdom may take in life.

Meditation:

Think back to a situation where your capacity to pause, to refrain what you want to say or do, was shown to be your wisest action.

February 23: Book IV

Sound-minded Telemachos addressed him in answer:
"Menelaos, Zeus-nourished son of Atreus, chief of the people,
I came to see if you might tell me some news of my father.
My house is being eaten up, my fertile lands are ruined,
My home is full of enemy men who perpetually slay
My throngs of sheep and my shamble-footed, crumple-horned cattle,. . . .
So now I embrace your knees to ask if you are willing
To tell me about that man's woeful death, if you saw it
With your own eyes, perhaps, or heard the tale from another
Wanderer. For excessive sorrow did his mother bear him!
Sweeten nothing out of pity or respect for me,
But tell me straight out how you encountered the sight, . . ." (IV. 315-20; 322-27).

A singular urgency slips into Telemachos' voice because of an unbearable tension between a home being devoured and an ambiguous future fueled by the question of his father's being alive or dead. What he yearns for is knowledge that will help him calibrate himself in the world. He is convinced his father is dead; he seeks confirmation of it, perhaps through a witness or a story, so he can return home with certain knowledge and take on the suitors through that reality. He also seeks the truth unvarnished, unsoftened or unchanged because of his host's desire not to injure him. His is a mighty courage here: to listen to the truth undisguised or fragmented. Hearing the story of Odysseus' death will allow him a new context to think and act within. In the process he is developing into a formidable warrior.

What is hardest and best, we wonder in moments of crisis: to hear the raw truth of matters or be deceived so as to be spared from suffering? Sometimes we do not want to know the truth; the narrative is too destructive. Such is the power of stories. But we often realize that living within deceit or half-truths will be more painful still, once discovered. Not knowing is a horrific way to suffer. We are caught between a reality we may not want to confront and one that leaves us in the dark. The tension between them can elicit a parade of fantasies and what-ifs that can arrest us in knots of uncertainty.

Meditation:

Reflect on how you handled receiving unbearable news that applied to you or to a loved one. Do you recall what your initial response was to it? How did it change over time?

February 24: Book IV

"But what the unerring old man of the sea told me,
Not a word of that shall I hide from you or conceal.
The gods were still holding me in Egypt, though I was striving
To return here, as I had not sacrificed full hecatombs for them.
The gods have always wished their injunctions to be kept in mind.
Well, there is a certain island in the much surging ocean,
Over the Nile, and they call it Pharos, ...
There the gods held me twenty days. No breezes ever
Came blowing upon the sea, the ones that become
Escorts for ships over the broad back of the sea" (IV. 349-55; 360-62).

Menelaos' narrative continues to expose a major theme of the epic: concealing and revealing, hiding and uncovering, which is Odysseus' major method for successfully arriving home and subduing the suitors, always with the goddess Athene's approval and complicity. Menelaos promises Telemachos he will reveal all of the story and leave nothing out. He too is restrained, held back from returning home; his being held back for twenty days matches in a lower key Odysseus' twenty years of restraint. Menelaos had failed to appease the divine presences; he had held back in his sacrifices so they held him from returning home. Like Odysseus, he is held on an island away from all other social territories. Telemachos does not know it, but he is hearing his father's story through Menelaos' narrative. By analogy Telemachos is hearing two stories at once.

What or who restrains us on our life journey is an important question to consider. What god or goddess might we have invited or created as a restraint? When is the right time to push forward? What small island may we have banished ourselves on? Holding back from life, being restrained, can serve us; it can also lock us in servitude to what we may be better off relinquishing. Only we, in retrospect, can gauge the help or hindrance our being held back has had on us. For some, greater patience and tolerance can grow from such restrictions. Wisdom seems to include the sense of knowing when to hold back and when to push forward with gusto, tempered however, with a recognition of caution.

Meditation:

Reflect on a time or circumstance when life restrained you from moving to something new or back to something familiar. From the present, assess that restraint now.

February 25: Book IV

"The daughter of mighty Proteus, old man of the sea,
Eidothee; her heart I aroused especially,
When she met me walking alone apart from my companions,
For they were always roaming around the island fishing
With bent fishhooks, and hunger wore on their stomachs.
She stood close to me, spoke and uttered a speech:
'Are you a fool, stranger? Are you too slack of mind?
Do you willingly let go and enjoy suffering pain?. . .
If somehow you could hide in an ambush and catch him,
He will tell you your course and the measures of your way,
About a return, how you may go on the fish-laden ocean, . . .'" (IV. 365-72; 388-90).

Attracted to the warrior Menelaos, Proteus' daughter first berates him concerning his desire to suffer because of a low intensity of mind, then instructs him on how to persuade her father to guide them home. Menelaos tells his story publicly so that Telemachos may learn of the way that guides are crucial, as he has experienced directly since Athene appeared to him and he is being guided now by Menelaos' narrative. Now he is given an added option through story's power. Love too is essential here: that perhaps one cannot fully instruct another without love being present in some form, as it will be for Odysseus who will be guided by Nausikaa, daughter of King Alcinoos. "The measures of your way" suggests a mindfulness and careful instruction in order to find home.

Stories are among our best guides to help us see the underlying form of our life; we tell stories often to entertain but also to instruct others. With our stories we create a field for the other to dwell in so that insights may appear often in abundance. That same story may also be self-instructive. Poetry itself, Northrop Frye suggests, "is primitive in the sense of expressing a fundamental and persisting link with reality" (*The Great Code* 37). Poetry is a form of knowing and deepening in that knowledge so we grasp more of life's complex, ordinary principles. Without narratives like Homer's epic to guide us, we can become fixed in place, as Menelaos' story reveals. Then "being at home" always eludes us.

Meditation:

What does the act of telling or hearing a story do to your understanding of the person and the situation described?

February 26: Book IV

"She bedded us down in a row and threw a skin over each;
There the ambush would have been most dreadful. The dire smell
Of the sea-nourished seals oppressed us dreadfully.
For who would lie down to sleep with a monster of the sea?
But she saved us herself and thought up a great remedy;
She brought and put under each one's nostrils, ambrosia
That has a sweet aroma, and it destroyed the smell of seal,
And we waited with enduring heart the whole morning" (IV. 440-47).

Ambush, waiting, restraint, foul smells, disguise in the form of a skin of another seeking home: all these themes and more gather in Menelaos' rich story of his struggle to arrive home, not always by action but also by being still and concealed. Perhaps most important is the guiding role of the brilliant Eidothee in assisting the weary warriors to return home. Not force but craftiness is operative here—restraint and disguise as two central elements, as two ways of being that pervade the epic. Force or might has a counterweight: wiliness and illusion as two creative forces in the soul. Finally, the act of enduring with heart rather than responding by instinct, or of needing to do something, is what the warriors learn under Proteus' daughter's tutelage. How different from the appetite-driven suitors.

Being able to play, to improvise, to use what is at hand to one's advantage, to imagine in a new way, to see the possibilities in situations that seem hopeless, to be open to yielding to the presence of another as guide, to rely on more than oneself—all these are virtues in achieving a desired end. Love and compassion may appear as formidable forces to gain a longed-for goal. Creativity, seeing outside the membrane of convention, tacking into a new breeze--all highlight the power of imagination to see what others may gaze right past. To be measured and to be willing to endure, to prevail by non-action is also a part of wisdom: the ability to see what measured response is called for in a given situation. At times we need guidance to help us see by means of the correct frame rather than the one that while effective in past events, may be a hindrance in the present. Being mindful is an attitude as well as a state of consciousness; we may be best protected by pausing.

Meditation:

Remember a time when you were helped or you helped another improvise to achieve an end that was in sight. What was the consequence of this aid?

February 27: Book IV

Right away, Aigisthos thought up a crafty design.
He picked out the twenty best men in the district and set
An ambush, and bid them make dinner on the other side.
And he went to call Agamemnon, shepherd of the people
With horses and chariot, planning his horrid plans.
He led him in unaware of his destruction,
And after feasting him, slew him, as one kills an ox at the crib.
None of the comrades was left who followed the son of Atreus,
And none of Aigisthos' but they were killed in the halls" (IV: 529-37).

In this flashback Homer offers another form of craftiness and deceit. This time to slay the king who has been away fighting for ten years. Craft is in the service of murder, not mending through restoration . Agamemnon is far from blameless, yet his butchered body is not a just way to treat the warrior who has returned home with his own concubine, Cassandra. The great disguise is food and the feast to keep him in a naïve state and blind to what rests beneath it. Aigisthos is a figure of small consequence who, when he slinks into a position of power, can be extremely destructive. Like an animal, the king is sacrificed to the selfish ends of his attacker, but not before Aigisthos, in deceit, calls upon the code of hospitality by setting a feast before the king, like the last meal provided one before an execution. Knowing the terms of a destructive homecoming gives Telemachos further knowledge for his own trip home.

We cannot often be sure of the appearances of situations or conditions and people who seem to be what they reveal but may in fact be concealing an opposite reality cloaked by pretentious or fictional language and behavior. Lacking any degree of discernment or led unwittingly by a deceiver, any of us can be seduced by the dissembling tactics of others. Motive is at the heart of an authentic or duplicitous presentation of self. Because we have the capacity to conceal our true intentions does not mean we live continually in distrust. Such an existence breeds cynicism and fear. But without trust, can we even have a civil society? The *Odyssey* reveals throughout how trust is a force and a quality that allows culture to develop and flourish; its absence is devastation and a free reign of appetites.

Meditation:

When were you taken completely off-guard by a revelation that what you trusted was not deserving of it? When did you dissemble for a desired end?

February 28: Book IV

They sat the suitors down together and stopped their contests.
Antinoos, son of Eupeithes, spoke out to them,
Troubled. For his heart, black all round, was greatly filled
With rage. And his eyes resembled a shining fire:
"Well now, this voyage is a great deed carried out very boldly
By Telemachos. We thought he would not carry it out.
In spite of us all, he went off, the young child, just like that,
When he had dragged down the ship and chosen the best in the district.
He will begin to be a trouble even more. Yet may Zeus
Destroy his power before he gains the measure of manhood" (IV. 659-68).

The poem shifts back to Ithaca and the banqueting suitors. Antinoos, their leader, is clearly shaken by their miscalculation that Telemachos would never sail from home on his own; they underestimated his boldness and are unaware that he was encouraged by the goddess Athene. His black heart is wounded by this new "trouble," naming his father Odysseus without any consciousness of saying it. The mindlessness of the suitors in their familiar roles as invaders of Odysseus' home blinds them to the possibilities of others. So busy and distracted are they by entertaining their appetites, that only now do they begin to realize the maturity of Telemachos that occurred just beneath their quenchless appetites. Antinoos now plans to "lie in ambush and watch for him as he comes/in the channel between Ithaca and rugged Samos" (ll. 670-71). Homecoming is as treacherous now for him as it is for his father. But he has the homecoming story of Agamemnon to guide him.

A black heart devises evil to quash any threat to its power. The success and growing strength of an adversary can foster rage, bad judgement and fury to annihilate such an unsettling presence. Calling on a higher power to destroy one's adversary may prove to be an impotent prayer. It is an ancient urge, once in power, to remain there and to suffocate any counter presences that threaten. Power seems intent on perpetuating itself, often in the service of making the mediocre and incompetent appear to be better than they are. Power may not corrupt so much as expose a "blackened heart."

Meditation:

Describe when you have witnessed someone cling to power for its own sake and perhaps to satisfy one's most basic appetites.

February 29: Book IV

Then Medon, sound-minded in knowledge, answered her:
"I do not know whether some god incited him
Or his own spirit roused him to go to Pylos to learn
If his father will return or has met his fate."
When he had said this, he went into the house of Odysseus.
But heartbreaking anguish poured over her. No longer
Could she bear sitting on a chair and many were in the house.
But she sat down on the threshold of the richly adorned bedroom
Lamenting piteously, and the serving maids moaned about her,
All the many that were in the halls, young and old (IV. 711-20).

The focus shifts away from the suitors and their plot to ambush and slay Telemachos on his return. Penelope laments his departure now that she knows the truth of his absence from Medon; both of his speculations are true in Telemachos' yearning for his father. Grieving his loss, Penelope, who often prefers threshold places to inhabit, rests between her and her husband's bedroom, occupying both the household in its public space and the bedroom, a private sphere, and unites the two—both her son and her husband. She has reached her limits of tolerating loss since her husband and now her son are away from the household, leaving her more vulnerable to the suitors' desires than ever. Her servants join her in supporting her loss by participating through their own sounds of grief, expressed communally.

Grieving the loss of family members is strong enough to dismember those suffering that absence. Critical anchors in the world are pulled from one, leaving those in grief groundless and adrift at sea. One could say the myth that gave their life grounding has been pulled from them. One's own identity may hang by a thread as grief melts one down. The future may begin to dissolve in the face of such loss; a hole in one's heart grows larger, more jagged and without boundaries. At this moment Penelope, like any mother, is at her lowest point as she suffers her own journey, which oblivion threatens to end. Feeling the possible permanent loss of family may be the deepest anguish. Grief loosens who we are and can disband parts of our identity, perhaps permanently. We need a functioning myth to give our lives a sense of coherence.

Meditation:

When you lost a companion, family member or close friend, was there a loss in you that has not yet returned or been recovered? Describe it.

March 1: Book IV

As much as a lion deliberates in a crowd of men,
Fearing when they draw the stealthy circle about him;
So much did she ponder, and balmy sleep came upon her.
She sank back, and slept, and her limbs were all slackened.
Then the bright-eyed goddess Athene had another thought.
She made an image and likened it in form to a woman, . . .
She sent her to the halls of the godly Odysseus,
So that she could make the grieving and wailing Penelope
Cease from her tearful wailing and lamentation. (IV. 791-96; 799-801).

Benevolent and compassionate, the goddess creates an image of the young Ipthime to visit and soothe Penelope in her deepening grief over the possible loss of her son. Athene engages in an act of *poiesis,* or a making, in order to foster another reality, as Homer is doing as well in his crafting the epic we are reading. Healing is a part of both creative enterprises. Penelope is compared through a rich analogy to a lion, not a lioness, as Odysseus will later be compared to a female beast. These gender crossovers build an image of a conjunction of masculine and feminine elements united in one, both in the imagination as well as when Odysseus arrives home. The end result is that Penelope experiences a relief from her agony of loss through the healing fiction of Athene.

Sleep is another opportunity for creative play, now in dreams, reveries and fantasies. The night opens new fields of creative play. Penelope is the energy of feminine presence that ignites another and equally rich form of knowing, a knowing by analogy, indirectly but more mysteriously and richly than is allowed through a literal perception. Knowing is then a creative process that informs us on both a conscious and unconscious level of awareness. The consequence is a deeper and even timeless form of knowledge, the kind that poetry and the arts afford, by creating a new context and a fuller perception to see by means of. James Hillman has "spoken of images as animals. Now I am carrying these feelings further to show operationally how we can meet the soul in the image and understand it" ("Inquiry into Image" 81). The image, we see in the passage above, is its own life form, a manifestation of soul and a rich opening to deepening our understanding.

Meditation:

What kind of knowledge have you gained through an artifice like a poem, a novel, a film, that somehow deepened your understanding of your own life?

March 2: Book IV

The shadowy image answered her and addressed her:
"About that man I shall not tell you in full detail
Whether he is dead or alive. It is bad to utter windy things."
When it had said this, it slipped through the bolt of the doorpost
Into the blasts of the wind. The daughter of Icarios
Rose up out of sleep. And her own heart was gladdened,
So clear had the dream rushed upon her in the gloom of the night.
The suitors had boarded and were sailing on the watery ways,
Devising in their minds sheer murder for Telemachos (IV. 835-43).

The image has its own life form and way of presentation. It opens us to another form of knowledge: the place of the dream and its shadowy reality. Iphthime is Penelope's sister, another daughter of her father Icarios; she brings Penelope a healing story that gladdens her heart. The figure refrains from easing her sister's yearning to know the fate (*moira*) of her husband, but just her presence as a shadowy image heals or modifies her sister's wound of grief over loss. She then, like a figure in a fairy tale, slips through an impossible narrow space into the fierce winds. Penelope is refreshed and liberated from the gloom engulfing her. But pressing right up against her lightened heart is the description of the suitors who have launched a determined plan to murder her son when he returns home.

Dreams, visions, reveries and revelations can crush us; they can also lighten the burdens of our lives with a fantasy or premonition of the future or even a new attitude toward the present. One could call such "visitations" oracular, miraculous, or even moments of grace. Such a presence can act like a salve applied to a wound, or a therapy to ease a traumatized life as Penelope's. From the order of the divine such a visitation/annunciation offers us a balm so we can feel uplifted by it, if only temporarily. Within or next to the sufferings of life are moments when a reprieve visits us in the form of another person, an event or circumstances out of our control that cares for our well-being. We must remain open to recognize these gifts. Dianne Skafte's excellent *Listening to the Oracle* shows just how often we are visited by such voices of guidance in our dreaming or waking everyday life (47). Such presences reveal another layer of reality that often remains hidden to us.

Meditation:

Recall a dream figure or other benevolent presence that helped you through a difficult time in your life. Did you learn to trust such visitations?

II

BOOKS V–VIII

From Hiddenness to Community: Wandering Towards Wonder

March 3: Book V

The gods took their seats in assembly. And in their midst
Was high-thundering Zeus who has the greatest might.
Athene spoke to them, reminding them of the many cares
Of Odysseus. His being in the nymph's home concerned her. . . .
"He is staying on an island suffering strong pains
In the halls of the nymph Calypso, who by compulsion
Is holding him back, and he cannot reach his fatherland,
For he has no ships there with oars and no companions
Who might convey him over the broad back of the sea" (V. 3-6; 13-17).

The epic focuses on the clear reality of the divine realm in which the goddess Athene pleads to the other gods to remember the warrior of Troy and to allow him safe passage home. In this realm there is no question of who rules this divine sanctuary. *Bie*, or might, is Zeus' domain above all others. Pedro Lain Entralgo writes that "in the Homeric world there is no gap between those movements of the cosmos that seem spontaneous and those that the will of the gods directly causes. . . (*The Therapy of the Word* 14). Zeus is praised by the divinely-inspired poet as his daughter reminds them all of Odysseus' arrest under the control of the goddess Calypso. Her name means "hidden" or "oblivion" (Dimock 414). But her restraining him has grown to excess and Athene knows that without her intervention he may die on her island.

Being stuck, grounded in stasis, unable to help oneself, is a familiar condition we have all experienced. How one found one's self in such a predicament can be difficult to trace, but one point is clear: we often cannot change our arrested condition by ourselves. It is a humbling and frustrating dilemma; it can, however, open us to a new reality of our limits, boundaries and finite options. Illness, divorce, death of a loved one, loss of employment, loss of savings—each can bring us to a place of grief where we can only sit and wait, perhaps for divine or human intervention. Living with hopelessness may become our biggest challenge. We may recall the lament of Dante at the beginning of his *Commedia* remembering how he was stuck in a dark wood with no sign of an exit or assistance. Often an act of grace brings us a helper, a guide, to get us moving.

Meditation:

Describe the feeling of having experienced being stuck, paralyzed and uncertain of what to do next. What was the outcome of that condition?

March 4: Book V

Like one of these, Hermes bore himself over many waves.
But when he arrived at the island that was far away,
He stepped from the violetlike ocean onto the dry land,
And went on till he came to the great cave wherein the nymph
Of the fair braids was dwelling. He came upon her within.
On the hearth a big fire was burning, and the smell from afar
Of cedar and easy-split citron was exhaled through the island
As it blazed. She within, singing in a lovely voice,
Moved to and fro at the loom and wove with a gold shuttle (V. 54-62).

Having successfully convinced her father to liberate Odysseus from Calypso's island, Athene commissions Hermes, messenger of the gods, to fly to the island to instruct the goddess on Zeus' wishes. The setting is primal and elegant, a balanced blend of nature, with the cultural act of weaving and the use of a gold shuttle. Calypso's cave is a natural home with a large fire burning and the sweet aromas of various woods blending their smoke and suffusing the island with a welcome fragrance. Her island resides at the margins of the world, yet within itself has a homey center. Calypso sings as she weaves like an artist in performance. It is an idyllic place at first glance, yet an impossible obstacle to the man held there yearning for home. Lawrence Hatab observes that "Myth simply displays the various and varying forms of the existential field in all their profusion" (*Myth* 33).

We may yearn for Calypso's solitude and contented condition. Hers is a place of reprieve from our full and busy life. She is the source of many individual's yearnings, but we don't want such enchanted stays to be permanent. Its beauty relies on it being temporary, as well as a place from which we may freely leave. Part of its charm is that it carries an other-worldly air about it, both mortal and immortal, akin to a spiritual retreat or a temenos of repose. Its wonder resides in its temporary duration. The texture of place, with its weaving and song, can from another angle of vision, be a seductive arena wherein one loses one's freedom. Her island is akin to that occasion in life when we seek shelter in a grove only to realize that what we sought can restrain us from returning home.

Meditation:

Recall a time when you yearned for and stayed in a Calypso-inspired place, full of wonder and novelty. What was the experience like and what impulse or plan promoted your exit?

March 5: Book V

And right on the spot round the hollow cave had been drawn
A trained vine in bloom that was blossoming with clusters.
Four springs, one after another flowed with white water
All close together; one turned one way, one another.
All around soft meadows of violet and wild parsley
Were blooming. And even an immortal who might come there
Would wonder to look and be delighted in his mind.
As he stood there, the Runner, the slayer of Argos, wondered,… (V. 68-75).

Calypso's space has the sights and smells of a paradisal island full of fresh water turned this way and that, vines cared for, various wild plants, all giving in the imagination of anyone gazing on it a sense of wonder, mentioned twice above. Within such a space the goddess works at her loom with her golden shuttle, making something new. Hermes pauses, takes a breath and wonders in delight at this scene of tranquility and artifice as the two intertwine one another. The scene is the opposite of war's violence. Not war but wonder is the effect that Calypso's creative space has on immortals like Hermes. But within this place of imagination and craft is Odysseus yearning for home. He has been incubating in this place of wonder for seven years.

We dream of tropical islands, a river cruise, a magical new place that can be used for respite and for healing of body and soul. It may finally exist nowhere but in our imaginations, but that does not diminish, but actually refines and strengthens, our vision. Nonetheless, it is a salvific image, a promise of escape from life's tensions, uncertainties, conflicts and wounds. We might think of it as a temporary vessel of gestation and restoration, where one may renew oneself in the beauty of the natural and creative world of soothing images that can allow us to purge temporarily the dross of a frantic, even traumatic life. It is a magical place where mortals and immortals can cohabitate. Philip Fisher writes that wonder "is the pleasure of amazement, that is, wonder taken in the aesthetic sense of admiration, delight in the qualities of a thing. Admiration in its root *mira* is, of course, the Latin word for wonder and also the root word for miracle"(*Wonder* 11). Wonder is at the other side of War.

Meditation:

Have you spent time in a place, real or imagined, where you have or wish to retreat for a period of renewal? Capture it by drawing or writing about it.

March 6: Book V

And he did not come upon the great-hearted Odysseus within;
The man was weeping, seated on the beach where he had been before,
Shattering his heart with tears and laments and groans.
He was looking out on the barren sea shedding tears. . . .
"Hermes of the golden wand, my respected friend,
Why have you come to me? You have not come often before.
Say what you have in mind. My spirit bids me to do it
If I am able to do it and if it can be done;
But follow me, so I may entertain you as a guest" (V. 81-84; 87-91).

For the first time in the epic Odysseus is present in person rather than in stories. In the midst of the beauty around him he is check-mated, isolated and suffering in lamentation. His suffering is complex, including missing and yearning for home and suffering the trauma of war's wounds. Calypso greets the god Hermes and wishes first to ritualize his presence through acts of hospitality, a way to bestow respect and praise on her guest while keeping her other guest restrained. At first she wishes to oblige her friend from Olympus for visiting her, even as Odysseus is imprisoned by the goddess's appetites. As he looks out to sea, Odysseus lingers between two worlds: the devastating and violent world of war in Troy and the yearned for nostos or homecoming that will allow him to restore himself and his city.

Grief as a powerful and arresting emotion can paralyze us and engender a death in life. Loss of what we had and continue to yearn for replaces our life and shapes us into one who can only wait and endure in pain. Odysseus here is a broken man, as we have felt when what gives our life value is stripped from us, leaving us dismembered and between worlds. When our fate raises our suffering to a more intense level, we are transformed in a wounding initiation that takes us to the core of who we are. It can change our identity. But enduring in the face of suffering can prove to be a boon in memory when we have succeeded in modifying that sorrow. Carol Pearson helps our perspective here in writing of the Warrior archetype: "Their ability to endure pain without flinching demonstrated the highest Warrior virtues—courage, fortitude and endurance (*The Hero Within* 101).

Meditation:

What loss have you suffered that altered your sense of who you are and/or wish to become? What did grieving teach you?

March 7: Book V

"Zeus now orders you to send him off as fast as you can.
For it is not right he should waste here far from his dear ones.
No, his fate is still to see his dear ones and come
To his high-roofed home and his own fatherland."
So he said, and Calypso, the divine goddess, went cold; . . .
"You are cruel, you gods, jealous above all others,
Who begrudge it to goddesses when they sleep with men
Openly, if one wants to make a man her dear husband. . . .
I myself saved him as he was bestriding his keel
All alone, when Zeus with a dazzling thunderbolt
Crushed his swift ship. . ." (V. 112-16; 118-20; 130-32)).

Only moments before acting as a good host to her divine guest, Calypso quickly becomes enraged by Hermes' directive from Zeus that after seven years, Odysseus is to be freed so he can fulfill his fate—to return home. She strikes back at all the gods, accusing them of jealousy over the love she as an immortal feels towards a mortal. She seems certain that Odysseus is being pulled from her because the gods begrudge her happiness with a mortal. The tension develops between the fate of a mortal to be fulfilled and the yearning of an immortal to violate his fatedness because of *her* appetites. Without Zeus' intervention, Odysseus will die on Ogygia. She is wounded by this request and feels that because she saved him when he was exhausted and near death, that she can claim him for herself. Her appetite tempts her to override Zeus' and fate's directives.

Many feel this mysterious energy or impulse in us called fate (*moira*) and its insistent quest to be realized in one's life. Many die without fully acknowledging it or incarnating it. Forces like Calypso enter to disrupt fate's flow and flowering in one's life. Coming to a recognition late in life or at the time of death that one suffocated one's particular "call to adventure," as Joseph Campbell refers to it (*The Hero With a Thousand Faces* 49), can be a terrible moment of awakening. It signals a life not fully lived along lines beyond our personal likes and wishes: "The myths and folk tales of the whole world make clear that the refusal is essentially a refusal to give up what one takes to be one's own interest" (59-60).

Meditation:

What is it you are fated to do or be in your life as you both understand and feel your destiny at this stage of your adventure?

March 8: Book V

"I would not for my part board the raft against your will.
Unless you will put up with swearing me a great oath, goddess,
That you will not plot some other bad trouble against me."
So he said, and the divine goddess Calypso smiled,
She caressed him with one hand, and spoke out to him directly:
"Ah, you are a real rogue, skilled in tricks that are not futile,
To have conceived and uttered a speech of this sort.
May the earth and broad heaven above witness this oath,
And the flowing water of Styx, which is the greatest
And most dreadful oath there is for the blessed gods:
I will not plot any other bad trouble against you, . . ." (V. 177-87).

One of Odysseus' great gifts is speech's power to persuade, to enchant others with words and create elaborate fictions through language. Like his patron guardian, Athene, he has the power of persuasion, which the goddess Calypso sees through with delight. Here he furthers one of the epic's great themes: oath-taking. An oath bonds in mutual or even "sweet agreement" (*homophrosyne*), two opposing forces or differing opinions or beliefs by means of an agreement fashioned in words. He seeks her cooperation in the oath for self-preservation so he can freely craft his raft, his home on the seas of Poseidon, to take him to Ithaca. But first he must craft the safe conditions in which to build it. Calypso delights in his ingenuity and assents to his oath by helping him construct his raft.

Our lives are structured and supported by oaths, mutual agreements, shared understandings, promises, concessions, give-and-take contracts, promissory notes, agreements to show up, tasks to complete, and vows to one another. Oaths may be informal agreements or official "oaths of office" to carry out in action what words unconditionally bind us to. Oaths are the mucilage that allows cultures and civilizations to flourish. Cease fire oaths can staunch mass killings. Order and measure are often the positive results of laws and oaths formed. Marilyn Stewart shows that the word *homophrosyne* comes from *phroneo*, to think, be wise or sound in mind and *omois*, to be of the same rank, equal; common, mutual, agreeing and coming together ("Imagination and Mapping in *The Odyssey*" 79).

Meditation:

When did you feel betrayed by a violated oath or agreement with another or others? When have you participated in an oath that changed lives?

March 9: Book V

Odysseus of many devices addressed her in answer:
"Lady goddess, be not angry at me this way. I myself know
All this, that beside you the prudent Penelope
Seen face to face is less striking in form and size.
For she is a mortal and you are immortal and ageless.
Yet even so I am wishing and longing all my days
To go home and to see the day of my return. . . ."
Then she took thought about sending great-hearted Odysseus away;
She gave him a great ax fitted to the palms, . . .
A beautiful olive wood handle, well fitted in place (V. 214-20; 233-34; 236).

Continuing to perfect his craft of persuasion, Odysseus once again enlists his rhetorical skills when he compares the beauty of Calypso to his long-sought for wife Penelope. He speaks of their most essential differences as he ends seven years with the goddess. Yet his desire is not to be rewarded with immortality if he were to stay with the goddess, but to return to his mortal world of home and family. Alone with the goddess, Odysseus has ceased living in many respects; he is checkmated from his life and hovers on the brink of despair. He chooses human life with all of its imperfections over the unnatural existence of immortality. Calypso equips him with the tools that will allow him to build his conveyance home. She gives herself over to his well-being and to the wishes of Zeus.

It is easy to think that our lives are filled with immortal constructs that will last forever. We find that word "forever" in our vocabulary as an illusion that parts of our life will go on into eternity. We may say "I wish this moment would last forever" without a real sense of what that might mean. More awakened, we acknowledge that our life is packed with impermanence, transitions, aging, limitations, illnesses and finally, death. Wisdom seems to be an ability to enter the present impermanent moment as an eternal "now," while recognizing its fleeting nature. Living in this tension dispels all illusions of *forever* while we savor in the instant what will soon dissolve. But for Odysseus in this moment, he is driven by desire towards *poiesis*, to making or crafting a transport vehicle for home and for insisting that Calypso craft an oath that she will no longer impede his journey.

Meditation:

What do you savor and appreciate most in any given day of your life? Are you able to live with each moment's constant impermanence?

March 10: Book V

But he cut beams, and the work went quickly for him.
He felled twenty in all and hewed them with the bronze ax,
Planed them skillfully, and set a straight line upon them.
Meanwhile, the divine goddess Calypso brought along augers,
And he then bored them all and fitted them to one another.
Then he made it fast with pegs and fastenings;
And just the way a man who is a well-skilled craftsman
Rounds off the hull of a broad ship for carrying freight,
The same measure did Odysseus make for his own broad raft (V. 243-51).

Homer reveals the skills of Odysseus as a builder, one who is self-reliant yet still needs a helper to achieve homecoming. His labor is measured, combining force with craft to convey him home. His voyage is divinely sanctioned and divinely assisted. Like a well-crafted story, the raft is an expression of his ability to order matter into a practical form. In his making the raft, he imitates other craftsmen who would build an entire ship for moving freight. In his own manner of making his raft for one man, he imitates the task of ship-building in miniature. He calls on his memory and on his history to provide a way home. From the natural elements that are home to divinity, he forms an artifact for practical use. Such crafting already begins his pilgrimage back into society as his fate prescribes.

Creating order and measure to incarnate these qualities in the world is a primal human need. We each have an impulse for *poiesis*, for making out of raw elements a formative product or idea or story that is different from the initial elements used. Sometimes such a creative impulse arises out of necessity, at times out of an aesthetic desire or a need to give pleasure and joy. Inherent in our basic nature is a need to construct in due measure an order in reality that was not present before, or if so, not quite in the creative form we choose to give it. We complete ourselves in acts of creation and deployment. In their book, *Deep Creativity: Seven Ways to Spark Your Creative Spirit,* the authors list a series of qualities of Deep Creativity, including how it is embodied, ensouled and alchemical (Quibell 321-25).

Meditation:

Think back on something you created that perhaps even surprised you in the making. What might it have completed or extended or deepened in you in the process? What might it have healed in you as well?

March 11: Book V

But Cadmos' daughter saw him, Ino of the lovely ankles,
Leucothea, who earlier had a mortal voice
And now in the sea swells gets honor from the gods.
She took pity on Odysseus as he was driven about in his pains.
Like a shearwater she rose in flight from the sea,
Perched on the raft, and addressed a speech to him: . . .
"But do as follows; you do not seem foolish to me:
Take off these clothes and leave the raft for the winds
To carry; and swim with your hands, and strive for reaching
The Phaeacians' land where it is your fate to escape.
And here now, stretch this veil out across your chest" (V. 333-38; 342-46).

Once more, Odysseus, his raft destroyed by the enraged god Poseidon who seeks revenge because Odysseus blinded his son, the Cyclops Polyphemous, receives aid from another divine goddess Ino, daughter of Cadmos, who founded the city of Thebes. If he is willing to be guided, he will survive to fulfill his fate. She is the honored feminine who pities the solitary warrior and coaches him to shed his clothing and replace it with the immortal veil and to swim to Scheria, the island home of the Phaeacian people. He must help his own cause by being willing to be aided again by the compassion of a feminine presence. After the fierce masculine energy of war, the warrior continues to absorb the divine feminine energy and wise counsel he needs to succeed in his striving for home.

All of us have been saved or aided or given succor by life's presences when our own limitations excluded us from advancing ourselves. A willingness to yield to other powers for assistance is a sign of wisdom, not weakness. Thinking we can always accomplish what we desire on our own has the markings of a fool. Odyssean wisdom insists that we keep our goals in mind and be willing to give over control to achieve our ends, for life itself is a place of trouble and triumph. Perhaps our aid will arrive in the form of a divinity, a mortal or in some combination whose aim is to rescue us to continue our lives. If one believes that his/her life is destined, that a plan is in place that one must recognize and pursue, then it may be easier to accept assistance when we confront our limits.

Meditation:

When have you out of compassion aided another in need or been aided by a benevolent source? What did you learn about yourself in accepting this help?

March 12: Book V

But Athene, daughter of Zeus, had another thought.
She bound up the courses of all the other winds
And bade them die down and all go to sleep. . . .
Then for two nights and two days upon the thick wave
He wandered, and his heart many times saw destruction ahead.
But when the fair-braided Dawn finished the third day,
Then at that point the wind died down and there was
A windless calm, and he sighted land nearby,
Scanning sharply, as he raised himself from the great wave (V. 382-84; 388-94).

The passage reveals a rich congealing of divinity, mortality and the natural order all conspiring to create resistance followed by assistance to Odysseus as he troubles his way home. Athene puts the destructive winds to sleep in an act that reminds us of a fairy tale or folk tale, with its magical assistance. Then Odysseus is able to survive his wandering, which is his fatedness, in another format; just below the water's surface is a divine purpose: to arrive at an island where he will remember his history and re-collect himself before being taken home. But he must first suffer the rage of Poseidon's turmoil before gaining solid ground under his feet. Here his heart, not his mind is a way of seeing and experiencing moments of possible annihilation. Then, his suffering is abated. He suffers his way to serenity in knowing he will survive.

Suffering through those moments in our lives when we are unmoored by forces beyond our control, when we are forced to wander, or to float aimlessly, seemingly without any direction or goal, in complete unknowing, can be terrifying. All familiar grounding is torn out from under us. We are "cast adrift" from all certainty in a personal or collective crisis that can bring panic and loss of identity with it. But they can also be moments of giving over, yielding, going with the flow of another power, energy or agency that we can choose to trust to guide us. We stay flexible with our fate. Yielding is not giving up so much as it is giving over and in to something that transcends us. In recovery groups it is called "a higher power." We can relax into such unsettledness and watch for land on the horizon.

Meditation:

When life circumstances cast you adrift, what landfall did you encounter and who assisted you in getting ground under your feet again? Or did you continue to wander, to float on the surface and see where you are being taken?

March 13. Book V

There his skin would all have been stripped off and his bones broken
If the bright-eyed goddess Athene had not put a thought in his mind;
He caught at the rock with both hands as he dashed upon it,
And held on to it moaning, till a great wave came along. . . .
As when an octopus is pulled out of its den,
Numerous pebbles are caught in its suckers,
So against the rocks the skin from his stout hands
Was stripped off. And the great wave covered him over.
Then surely wretched Odysseus would have died in excess of fate
If bright-eyed Athene had not given him presence of mind (V. 426-29; 432-37).

Survival would have been impossible without the goddess' assistance. As the presence of thought, of awareness, coupled with an effective strategy, she offers Odysseus mindfulness in the face of panic and desperation. Again, restraint, patience and persevering are the end products of thoughtfulness—this and force or strength *(bia)*. Craft and force together save him in his suffering. Poseidon will not easily be appeased; he represents that force or presence in life that wants to unseat us in turbulence. In the simile, Odysseus is compared to the tenacious quality of nature's creature as he loses even his skin in a moment of painful shedding of the Trojan conflict. His exposure to the elements is complete when the wave devours him fully, a signal of fate's excess against the counter forces of mindfulness.

The force of our own character, combined with the mentoring of a divine power, often conspire in our survival; even when we are flayed by life, we need not succumb to its hostility or natural supremacy if we practice mindfulness. The rocks and waves that flog us also offer a place to sink our tentacles around. Life itself in even the most painful form is preferable to death. At times, the memories of what we love and wish to regain can help us survive. The depth psychologist C.G. Jung has suggested that the Greek word "*daimonion* that came upon man from without" … was originally a spirit in human or animal form that expressed itself as fate or providence. . . (*CW* $9_{,1}$ par. 454). Our fate is in the world but our decision to accept it or not comes from within. Homer suggests that divinities inhabit both realms, both thought and external phenomena.

Meditation:

When your life situation has stripped your skin from you, what allowed you to survive? Were you able to see this situation as a path in your fatedness?

March 14: Book V

But when he caught his breath and the spirit in his mind
Awakened, he unbound the god's veil from himself
And he let it go into the sea-mingling river.
A great wave bore it back down the stream. Ino quickly
Took it in her own hands. He slipped out of the river,
Lay down on a rush bed, and kissed the grain-giving earth.
Then, grieving, he spoke to his own great-hearted spirit:
"Ah, what do I suffer; what will happen to me at last?" (V. 458-65).

Once again, Odysseus is aided in his suffering to survive by feminine assistance who extends divine aid to him. He follows her instructions and returns her gift at the juncture where the salt sea and fresh water mingle. In his mind resides a spirit that awakens to what his instructions are. Grateful to be on dry land, but encircled by unknown conditions, Odysseus nonetheless gathers himself in his grief where he has no remnants of Troy or Calypso's island to support him. His condition is liminal, in-between sea and land, known and unknown, life and death, trouble and peace, mortal and divine, gratitude and grief, masculine and feminine. Jaffa Frank reminds us that the poet Hesiod in his *Theogony* believed the briny ocean water is masculine and fresh water is feminine (qtd. in *Eyes of the Gorgon* 81), His future is uncertain, his fate in question. Still far from home, he contemplates in grief his ambiguous future.

We may remember when we were saved and helped to survive on any number of levels by a guide or saving element that suddenly appeared to aid us past our mortal limits. Some other force or presence may have our sustained our survival in mind. Death is cheated and we are allowed to continue living while still suffering uncertainty, the absence of a clear path, and the exhaustion of life bearing down on us, reshaping who and what we are. We may feel both blessed and cursed and begin to wonder if we can continue to survive the ambiguity, even hostility of a hazy tomorrow. But the sound-minded goddess, for Odysseus, or any guide for us, can gift us the courage to persevere.

Meditation:

Recall how you survived a painful part of your history wherein all your familiar supports were dissolved or dismantled, leaving you in an uncertain world. How did you survive this crisis?

March 15: Book V

So, as he thought, this seemed to him to be better.
He went on into the wood; he found it near the water
In the clearing around, and came upon two bushes growing
From the same place, one of wild olive, one of tame. . . .
Nor did rain even reach through to them, so thick
Did they grow over and under each other. Odysseus
Went in beneath them. He quickly gathered a broad bed
With his own hands. Leaf-shedding had been quite plentiful,
Enough to give shelter for two or three men
In the winter season, even if it were especially hard (V. 474-77; 480-85).

In this rich moment Odysseus is stripped of all remnants of the past: the chaos of war, and his prolonged entrapment with Calypso, which may have incubated him in his grief; but his desire to return home is never keener than now. His healing must continue by reconnecting with the natural order that he freely chooses. His "home" here is primal and mythic. The natural order reflects his two natures—wild and tame—warring and domestic that cannot be separated, so entangled are they growing over and under each other. They must be in conjunction for Odysseus to arrive home. He enters the womb of mother earth—a bed and a burial place—so he may be reborn, naked, at dawn. His bed is alive between the two olive trees, yet shrouded in dead leaves.

Psychologically and emotionally, the wombs in our life can take many forms. We can spend our lives dying and awakening in an endless cycle of becoming fully conscious to what we at one time were dead to. Any valuable renewal requires some form of dying—to old habits of thought, attitudes, behaviors, resistances that comprise a former destructive life. A life truly lived is one wherein expiration dates on many items in it abound. If we cannot die to ourselves and to life's patterns that arrest us, we may not be able to claim we have ever authentically lived, or lived rightly, according to the organic patterns of our own nature and to the force of our personal myth. Louise Cowan suggests "epics show us. . . the pattern of moving from the old myth to a new, carrying everything of value with it as it goes" ("Epic as Cosmopoesis" 25)

Meditation:

What is dying or trying to die in your life right now? Do you at the same time feel somethings stirring to be reborn? Are these impulses entangled irreparably?

March 16: Book V

Godly Odysseus, who had borne much, rejoiced to see it.
He lay down in the middle, heaping the fallen leaves over him,
As a man may cover a torch with black embers
At the edge of a field, where no neighbors may be by,
And save the fire's seed, so he need not light it from elsewhere.
So Odysseus covered himself with leaves. Athene
Shed sleep on his eyes, so it might release him quite soon
From toilsome fatigue, and she covered his eyelids over (V. 486-93).

The naked wanderer feels joy because what he has discovered and created is his home, like the home in Ithaca. He finds his balance between his wild and tame natures, the world of war and the world of domestic tranquility. The dead leaves hold in his body heat to preserve his life that was almost extinguished by Poseidon's wild wrath that covered Odysseus over with waves. The extended simile is rich on several levels. He is at one moment self-sufficient and in another dependent on the benevolent care of Athene, who nurtures him. Sleep itself is a form of death that renews. Odysseus heals, buried in the earth, and his energy is banked like smoldering ashes for safe keeping. Athene banks his eyes to secure for him a deep sleep that rejuvenates and restores his basic life energies. Only then will he have the stamina and mindfulness he will need next morning. James Hillman reveals how Athene invented instances of limitation and containment" ("On the Necessity of Abnormal Psychology" 19) which includes pottery, sanctuary, cave and altar. Odysseus' containment in the earth under the leaves is Athene's realm.

At various intervals we may find ourselves reduced to basics in life, where a stripping away or a paring down is a necessity for an authentic renewal, where parts of our old myth need to be shed, leaving us less encumbered by elements that staunch our psychic blood flow. Some find this in solitude, or in retreats, or in favorite places of renewal, others in taking a day off periodically or heading out in solitude, or in illness, separation or a painful loss. These events can distance us from our daily routines so we can see them with a new clarity. Such aloneness can help us disentangle what is crucial and what can be let go of in our lives.

Meditation:

What do you do on occasion to reclaim and renew your life, perhaps by reducing it to basic necessities? Or, when has life reduced you, where complexities were cut away in some form that eventually renewed you?

March 17: Book VI

When she had said this, the bright-eyed Athene went off
To Olympos, where they say the gods' seat is forever
Secure. It is not shaken with winds and is never wet
With rain, nor does snow fall there, but a cloudless clarity
Spreads far upon it, and white gleam runs over it.
In that place the blessed gods enjoy themselves day after day.
The bright-eyed one went off there when she had prompted the girl.
And right away the fair-throned Dawn came and awakened
The fair-gowned Nausicaa. At once she wondered at her dream,
And went through the halls to announce it to her parents, . . . (VI. 41-50).

This interlude in human action allows the poet to contrast the sense of balance and harmony of the gods in their celestial home with the uncertainties, ambiguities and sufferings of mortal existence. The terms of the divine world include: security, solidity, a mild climate that is constant, clarity, gleaming whiteness, daily enjoyment in a permanent profusion of mildness and joy. The life of mortals, by contrast, is laced with suffering, loss, longing, yearning, appetites, excess, deficits, pain, confusion and eventual death. The epic vision includes both realms and divine figures like Zeus, Athene, Hermes and Poseidon move between both terrains.

World religions have as one of their many attributes a reminder of a world lost that may be regained as each of us pilgrimages home to our true nature and to a realm both transcendent and welcoming—a lost paradise. They carry a promise of redemption and renewal, of harmony and balance through grace given as a gift to aid us, and a loving divinity that supports us in our turmoil and confusions. Olympus and Heaven are territories of the imagination, archetypal constants that our soul yearns for in some specific form; they are interior landscapes residing in all people that can offer us hope when life's uneven and unforeseen elements descend on us with little warning. They can also intrude themselves in dreams, which have a knowledge all their own, as both Penelope and Nausicaa learn. The latter will be led by her dream to Odysseus as he was led to her island by the goddess. Both will conspire to move Odysseus closer to his own feminine power.

Meditation:

What image or belief sustains you in times of crisis and uncertainty? Where do you turn for guidance and solace?

March 18: Book VI

And she took hold of the whip and the glistening reins
And whipped them to go; there was clatter of the two mules . . . .
And when they came to the beautiful stream of the river
Where there were plentiful places to wash and much
Lovely water flowed forth to clean what had got very dirty,
There they unharnessed the mules from the chariot
And shooed them out along the eddying river
To graze on honey-sweet field grass. From the chariot
They took the clothes in their hands, carried them to the black water,
And trod them in pits, swiftly vying with one another (VI. 81-82; 85-92).

The young maiden Nausicaa, aroused by a dream sent by Athene, asks her father to have a chariot harnessed so she and her waiting servants can take their clothing to the stream to be washed. She confidently leads the chariot to the clear waters in an idyllic setting, almost rivaling the serenity of Olympus, while her parents King Alcinoos and Queen Arete await her return. She and her handmaidens wash the clothes in a competition close to where Odysseus sleeps, exhausted from his surviving the rough seas and Poseidon's wrath. The scene is a simple domestic one engineered by the goddess to further the warrior's travel home. It will also be Odysseus' first contact with a domestic world rich in wealth and hospitality. As goddess of containment, James Hillman affirms, Athene is also goddess of the reins and harness, things which control, limit and protect ("On the Necessity of Abnormal Psychology" 19).

This passage reveals how even the simplest human situation may have a deeper intuition and shape than its appearance conveys. The simple task of washing clothes hides in its folds a divine design; one cannot know when and how a divine or invisible presence, often through the most ordinary of tasks, may guide and assist the needs of mortals. Gods, goddesses and other transhuman forces can be present and active in our daily lives, orchestrating situations and conditions that have another level of meaning and intention which we may discern over time. Our own level of awareness and openness may be the most effective means of recognizing such guides and following their direction and wisdom.

Meditation:

When have you detected another hand or presence guiding you in the simplest matters? What was your initial response to such a discovery?

March 19: Book VI

"Ah, me, to what land of mortals have I come this time?
Are these men proud and savage and without justice,
Or are they friendly to strangers and have a god-fearing mind?...
Or am I somewhere near men who are of clear speech?
Well, come, I shall make a trial myself and see."
When he had said this, godly Odysseus came from under the bushes.
From the thick wood he broke off in his stout hand a branch
With leaves, that it might cover the skin round a man's loins,
And he went like a mountain-bred lion, who, relying
On his strength, goes rained on and blown on, but his eyes
Within are burning, and he chases after oxen or sheep... (VI. 119-21; 125-32).

Life's uncertainty once more descends on Odysseus as he contemplates the unknown land he has been hurled into. He thinks of two possible opposites of what he has stepped into and slept within: savages or people with clear speech and a healthy fear of divinity. With fortitude and forbearance he risks revealing himself, covered only by nature's leaves when he steps into public life again after seven years quarantined by the goddess Calypso. This threshold is a dramatic one as he forages into uncertainty and possible destruction. In a gesture of modesty and restraint, he covers his loins with a branch so as not to frighten the young women playing ball outside his natural shelter. The suggestion is that he has been reborn from the earth, naked like an infant, unknowing, with Athene his faithful midwife.

Only when life creates such ambiguity in us and before us do we feel the extent of our courage or its absence. We may feel that we stand naked and alone, vulnerable and isolated, in the face of life's uncertain fate. But such moments may be the signal of a rebirth into a new consciousness. Some may stay in the bush-created home, below the dead leaves, content to die there psychologically or spiritually rather than confront the dragon of ambiguity. "Too risky," we might persuade ourselves, "so best to remain anonymous in oblivion," so we fail to venture forth to face our more vital destiny. A large and perhaps essential part of our unlived life remains buried in leaves of familiarity.

Meditation:

Think of a time you stepped into the unknown, naked and alone, armed only with your courage and choice to live in uncertainty rather than die a slow death in the warm snare of security.

March 20: Book VI

Frightfully begrimed with brine did he appear to them.
One ran one way, one another, on the jutting shores.
The daughter of Alcinoos alone stayed; Athene
Had put courage in her mind and taken fear from her limbs.
She stood in one place, facing him. Odysseus wondered
Whether he should grasp the fair-faced girl's knees in prayer
Or supplicate her where he was at a distance, with soothing words,
To show him the city and also to give him clothes (VI. 137-44).

With Odysseus' appearance Nausicaa's servant women scatter at his sight, as if a wild beast had made its threat known. Only the princess remains steadfast, for Athene gifted her with courage and took fear from her. Now Odysseus must choose wisely and creatively at this moment so as to gain further assistance in journeying home. He chooses words over physical action, persuasion over violence, moderation over might. Greek scholar Norman Austin writes that at this moment "the suppliant's aggressive posture must be translated into poetry" ("Nausikaa and the Word" 22). As language, and especially poetic utterance continues to be a proven treasure in the epic, and with it a supple creative mind, war begins to be subdued by words. The power of persuasion, Athene's domain, is here brought forward as the best action to preserve Odysseus's continued voyage. Words can create worlds, as the epic repeatedly reveals.

The ability to use persuasive speech is both a gift and a learned asset. It can, however, lead to wars or shape a peace. Behind persuasive speech are intentions to do good or to further selfish causes. Odysseus's speech is as persuasive as Athene's. We know how careful one must be in making a case for a certain belief or action; the wrong choice of words can dismantle one's goals and intentions, no matter how noble. Words can conceal one's motives or expose them to view. Words carry emotions and tones of being, so their precision in matching one's intentions is vital. We can actually further our destiny by the words we choose to assist our journey, either on our own, or, as with Nausikaa, with another's aid.

Meditation:

Recall a time when the value of the gift of words was crucial in your life. What were the circumstances that brought you to use persuasive speech that made an effective difference in the outcome?

March 21: Book VI

Right at once he made a soothing and wily speech:
"I am at your knees, mistress. Are you some god or a mortal?
If you are one of the gods who possess broad heaven,
I myself would liken you in look and size and form
Most closely to Artemis, the daughter of great Zeus. . . .
Never before have I seen with my eyes such a person,
Either man or woman. Awe holds me as I look. . . .
May the gods grant you as much as you wish in your mind.
May they provide you a husband and also a home,
And noble sympathy. Nothing is better or higher than that,
When a man and wife have a home who are sympathetic
In their thoughts" (VI. 148-52; 160-62; 180-84).

Odysseus has been known historically as a trickster, a rogue, an artist, a poet and a craftsman. Graced by Athene, he is a man of many turns and wily words. He wins over the confidence of the young curious Nausicaa with words by praising her beauty and comparing her to the divine huntress in nature, Artemis, another of Zeus' daughters. His feeling in her presence is that of awe as a form of wonder. He wishes her a strong union with a husband in the form of a blessing or a wish for her good fortune; of course he is thinking of his own yearning for his wife Penelope. When in harmony, they will enjoy a bond of *homophrosyne*, or a sweet agreement or accord with one another. In such a union they imitate the order of the cosmos and the harmony that most often exists in Olympus. Nausikaa, of course, is wishing the same for herself; this man in front of her may be a strong candidate.

Persuasion through speech is a divinely-inspired art form. When Odysseus addresses the soul of Nausicaa and her fierce yearning for a husband, he establishes the power of prose to persuade by making the other feel seen and valued. Words charm, which is another form of persuasion; words can go to the heart of the other in a style and manner that elicits from them a desire to help one in need. Storytelling, we have seen, is another form words can assume to entertain and transform, even heal, oneself and others. This softening of the other that words have the capacity to achieve, is Homer's constant counter to violence and war.

Meditation:

When have your words softened and permeated another, or when have you been transformed by the influential power of another's words?

March 22: Book VI

So she poured grace upon his head and his shoulders.
Then he sat off apart, when he had gone along the beach of the sea,
Gleaming with beauty and graces. And the girl marveled.
And then she spoke out to her fair-braided serving maids:. . . .
"Beforehand he appeared to me to be unseemly,
And now he seems like the gods who possess broad heaven.
Would that a man of this sort might be called my husband
And be dwelling here, and it might please him to stay
In this place. But, maidens, give the stranger food and drink" (VI. 235-38; 242-47).

Odysseus finds himself between worlds, between the grace-giving charm of Athene and the growing wondering desire of Nausicaa. Athene transforms him after he has washed the brine and dirt from his body and donned the clothes the young maiden offers him. He now appears to her as a god, as earlier he had said she appears like a goddess. A form of courtship is unfolding here, but for Odysseus it is a means of getting home, while for Nausicaa its purpose is to persuade him to stay and marry her. His appearance seduces the young princess; he has become a form of the divine in human form. Her fantasy grows that this is exactly the image of the man she wishes to wed. Norman Austin claims that "Nausikaa has transformed a wild brute into a man of beauty, courtesy, and charm" ("Nausikaa and the Word" 29). Their living in two worlds and speaking from them entertains us.

One of many wonders of human beings is that they can change right in front of us, either by what they say or with a change in the lighting or a different angle of our vision. We all have some dust of divinity in us and it may surface in a smile, a laugh, a gesture or a look of wonder or a touch; we feel smitten or overpowered by their matchless beauty or the stature of their presence. Grace is the word Homer uses above. Grace is an attribute of divinity; when it is shared with us, we are miraculously transformed in the other's eyes. A different imagination is at work, revising and renewing the other's presence in a mysterious way. The person we find transformed may never be able to retreat to his/her former person. Underneath this incident above is the suggestion that poetry itself, its choice of words and incidents, can create a world that has transformative, if not healing powers, on us.

Meditation:

Recall a moment when another was transformed before your eyes, or you felt transformed by the way another began to see and relate to you.

March 23: Book VI

"Stranger, understand quickly what I say, so you may
Very soon get an escort and a return from my father.
Near the road you will find a shining grove of Athene,
One of poplars; a spring flows in it, a meadow is about it.
There is my father's preserve and his fruitful vineyard, . . .
Sit there a while and wait till the time that we
Come to the town and arrive at the house of my father.
But when you consider that we have arrived at the house,
Then go to the city of the Phaeacians and ask
For the house of my father, great-hearted Alcinoos" (VI. 289-93; 295-99).

Nausicaa has shown the greatest hospitality to this stranger who arrived naked into his life from out of the earth. She has clothed and fed him; now she offers him instruction on how to continue his journey home. Her explicit directions are clear. At the site of Athene's grove is her father's vineyard where Odysseus is to wait until Nausicaa and her servants have reached home. Then, at the right time (*Kairos*), he is to walk alone through the town to her father's palace, asking directions as he finds his way. Her description gathers up a place of worship of Athene; her father's cultivated vineyard at the edge of town is a rich image of culture. Nausicaa is forceful, clear, a leader, a mature woman who both instructs and directs the warrior-wanderer. She bridges for him the territories of nature and culture, like the wild and tame olive trees growing from the same root that he slept within, perhaps realigning his own natures, wild and domestic, finding a balance between them. From such a balance regained, he will step out toward home.

Mentors, guides, instructors are peppered through our lives, especially when we venture into strange territory or find ourselves beginning over or renewing a dimension or a direction of our destiny or desires. We have also guided, instructed and aided others in need. As a human family we are obligated to assist others when we can. We can't know how we may be used or when we become an instrument to promote another's well-being, safety or longevity. Open to helping others, we know that tomorrow we may be on the need-end of life and pray for assistance. Perhaps the divine dimension in life watches over us and aids us when needed.

Meditation:

When has a situation arisen wherein you were instrumental in aiding another or were aided by another in a time of hardship? What did either event reveal to you?

March 24: Book VI

". . . . But when the house and courtyard enclose you,
Go very swiftly through the hall until you reach
My mother. She sits at the hearth in the fire's gleam,
And turns sea purple yarn on the distaff, a wonder to see,
Propped against a pillar. And serving maids sit behind her.
And there the chair of my father is propped up against hers,
Where, seated like an immortal, he drinks his wine.
Pass him by and throw your hands around the knees
Of my mother, so you may speedily rejoice and see
The day of your return, even if you are from very far away" (VI. 303-12).

Nausicaa's instructions push Odysseus into the role of a student, a learner ready to know the proper protocol by which to approach the Phaeacian King and Queen. The king appears to be passive; his chair is supported by that of the queen, who is actively engaged in the creative process of making. Her daughter tells Odysseus her mother is a wonder to see, as she weaves threads into a beautiful object. Both the queen and her daughter are feminine forces leading the way, assisting the lost masculine warrior home to his wife and son. Their strength reveals that the constant thrust of the *Odyssey's* plot is engineered by feminine powers, "which must be recognized to make possible a proper relationship—what I call an androgynous relationship—in which the male and female meet as co-equals"(*Goddesses* 161), writes Joseph Campbell on this epic.

Being open and willing to be advised or instructed is a signal of an authentic leader. The dangerous ones are those who prefer to hear nothing that does not agree with their narrow opinions and ideas. Gaining or retrieving the ability to listen is crucial to solid leadership. It constitutes a large part of remaking a shattered leader or person. To be instructed by a woman is difficult for many men, but the ability to be guided by feminine wisdom and clear-sightedness, an Athene trait, is its own reward. In the scene above, the real agent of change is the queen and her daughter, not the king. Knowing in any situation or organization where the power resides comes from a discerning mind and/or wise counsel.

Meditation:

When have you been helped or guided by a source that surprised you? Ask yourself what was surprising about your accepting this particular source as a guide.

March 25: Book VI

She managed the reins so that the servants and Odysseus
Might follow on foot. And she skillfully applied the lash.
The sun went down and they came to the famous grove
Sacred to Athene, and there godly Odysseus sat down.
Then at once he prayed to the daughter of great Zeus:
"Hear me, unwearied one, child of aegis-bearing Zeus,
Hear me now, since you did not hear me before
When I was smitten and the famous earth-shaker smote me. . . ."
So he said in prayer; and Pallas Athene heard him,
But she did not appear to him face to face. For she feared
Her father's brother (VI. 319-26; 328-29).

While Odysseus places his trust in the beautiful Nausicaa, the young maiden seeking a husband, he prays to the goddess in a plaintive and frustrated tone, feeling abandoned by her when the sufferings of Poseidon were visited on him and will continue to haunt him. He feels his isolation from her; he does not know that she was instrumental in his rescue. The piety he exhibits even in a tone of being let down reveals why Athene respects and assists not only him but also Penelope and Telemachos. Athene too has her own limits and fears towards Poseidon's uncontrolled power and rage. He is as real a force in the world and in human life as she. So Athene prudently hides from Odysseus so as not to threaten his journey home. She may not realize Zeus has instructed his brother that Odysseus' fate is to return home, but not unbloodied by Poseidon, a god of affliction and pain.

Prayer may not have the same meaning in ancient Greece as it does for us today. Yet common qualities are apparent. We may address as a suppliant a higher power when we feel abandoned and afflicted or when we require counsel or help in directing us anew. Or when we feel the necessity of a blessing to encourage us. We may also find it liberating to step out of our central control office or bunker and yield to some presence beyond our capacities. Prayer can decenter our self-determined base and place us in a willing attitude of acceptance when in extreme need. There is something important too in where we pray. Here Odysseus opens to his divinity in her sacred grove, a place of worship in nature, a rich temenos.

Meditation

What life conditions bring you to pray, either for yourself or others? Is there any specific place or time that brings you to pray?

March 26: Book VII

> Athene,
> With kind thoughts for Odysseus, shed a thick mist about him,
> Lest some great-hearted Phaeacian should confront him,
> Taunt him with a speech, and ask him who he might be.
> But when he was ready to enter the charming city,
> Then the bright-eyed goddess Athene confronted him.
> Likening herself to a virginal young girl with a pitcher.
> She stood in front of him, and godly Odysseus asked:
> "My child, would you lead me to the home of Alcinoos,
> The man who is the ruler over these people?
> For I have come here as a long-suffering stranger
> From afar, from a distant land; so I know no one
> Of the men who possess this city and its fields" (VII. 14-26).

Homer dwells on Odysseus's transition from nature to the city, important because it is pivotal to his homecoming journey. He enters not as a leader but as lowly supplicant. His guide is to be Athene, disguised as a virgin carrying a pitcher performing a menial but necessary task. Odysseus is humble as he asks her to lead him to the home of the king and queen. Athene assumes such a common role to see how Odysseus responds to the lowly and ordinary, and then to supplicate himself to its terms. It's as if he is starting his life again, first through a rebirth out of the earth, and now as a lowly wanderer. As a common person in his present condition, he seeks not his other roles as warrior and king of Ithaca but bends to the conditions he faces.

Yielding to life's condition when our own identity has been stripped to its essentials is difficult for many. When we lose our place in society through a reduction in our stature and reputation, we are left with just the essential core of who we are. Campbell is helpful here: "If you do not dare the adventure, you will enjoy a respectable…life. If you do opt for the adventure, you experience an interesting life. It will be full of danger, full of surprises, full of shocks. . ." (*Correspondence: 1927-1987* 297). We must persevere, keep going, rely on the goodness of others until we "get back on our feet."

Meditation:

Recall a situation when of necessity you had to ask for help and to trust who stepped forward to aid you. What effect did this have on you?

March 27: Book VII

Odysseus wondered at the harbors and the balanced ships,
The meeting places of the heroes themselves, and the walls,
Long and lofty, fitted with stakes, a wonder to behold. . . .
"Father stranger, this is the house that you requested me
To point out to you. You will find kings nourished by Zeus
Eating dinner there. Go in and do not be frightened
In your heart. . . .
You will first come upon the mistress in the halls.
Arete is the name she is called, and her ancestors
Are the same who begot King Alcinoos" (VII. 43-45; 48-51; 53-55).

An artist and artisan himself, Odysseus wonders at the balance and order he sees on his journey to the palace. He admires the supreme craftsmanship of the city's walls conveying symmetry and order and due measure. Not envy but wonder is his response as the place changes and restores him. Athene relays that this grand setting is closely related to her own home on Olympus, perhaps a place midway between divine and human settings. Arete is the central figure to whom he must supplicate and plead for his return home. The queen's name means "excellence," and this quality is what the wanderer must seek in order to arrive home restored and reordered.

Wonder is a healing attribute toward things and others. Philip Fisher suggests that "with wonder, above all else, there is the address to delight, to the bold and beautiful stroke, to pleasure in the unexpected. . ." (*Wonder, the Rainbow and the Aesthetics of Rare Experience* 6). Wonder opens us up; it allows us to appreciate the aesthetics of things as well as their underlying patterns, order and symmetry, all fulfilling their unique design. Wonder may also open us to instruction, to change, to further and deeper truths. Perhaps wonder calls us to what is excellent in our experiences. Wonder beckons the best in us and may be the antithetical impulse to war and violence in all its forms. What we wonder about, what we are drawn to, is another indicator of our personal myth. It is what we wish to pursue as a necessary part of our journey to wholeness. Wonder makes us curious. In wonder and curiosity we care about what draws us to it.

Meditation:

What is it now in your life that calls you to wonder about it? Can you describe the felt sense of such an experience?

March 28: Book VII

Odysseus went to the famous house of Alcinoos. His heart
Pondered much as he stood there before reaching the bronze threshold.
There was a gleam like that of the sun or of the moon
Beneath the high-roofed hall of great-hearted Alcinoos.
Bronze walls were run round it on every side to the corner
From the threshold, and there was a frieze of dark blue about it. . . .
And on either side there were gold and silver dogs
That Hephaistos with his skillful faculties had formed
To watch over the great-hearted Alcinoos;
They were immortal, and ageless for all their days (VII. 82-87; 91-94).

Every detail of the royal palace has been shaped exquisitely and all was to provoke wonder and awe as well as enjoyment. Their world is both aesthetic and functional, dressing some of its artifacts from the hard work of the crippled artisan, Hephaistos, son of Zeus and Hera, but he was rejected by her because of his malformed body. Odysseus is transformed by these riches of culture; they speak to his own deep and now activated creative spirit, swelling him with pleasure. Through these crafted images Odysseus is brought closer to home and further away from war's violence. Karl Kerenyi tells us that Hephaistos was "only a crippled craftsman dwarf; he had the skill to create young virgins made of gold, who moved as if they were alive. . ." (*Gods of the Greeks* 71).

Within a full, busy and at times frenzied life, we can easily lose the sense in us that delights in the beautiful through its particulars. An aesthetic blindness can dim our appreciation of a world full of objects of beauty that soothe and heal us in ways often difficult to describe. We can be buoyed up by objects and words that attract us because of their quality, craft and charm that penetrates the heart. Viewing them without possessing them recovers part of our humanness; our civilized selves respond in delight to their subtle powers. Philip Fisher believes that the ordinary is what makes the unexpected such a provocation, "when the *extra* ordinary can take place and evoke wonder" (*Wonder* 57).

Meditation:

Remember when you were aesthetically arrested and stilled by a crafted object, a book you read, a piece of music you heard—anything that aroused your aesthetic sense of the world through this attraction and pulled you from the mundane to the marvelous. Describe the experience.

March 29: Book VII

And there the leaders of the Phaeacians were seated
When they ate and drank. They possessed unfailing abundance.
And there were golden youths on well-built pedestals
That stood there holding in their hands flowing torches. . . .
And there were fifty serving maids through the hall, women
Who grind up in a mill grain of an apple hue,
And who do weaving on looms and turn the distaff
Seated, the way the leaves of the tall poplar turn;
And from the close-woven linen the moist oil drops off (VII. 98-101; 103-07).

The story is full of abundance, balance, order, skill and craft, as well as a certain opulence and a high degree of thoughtful arrangement, delight, and joy. Lacking is what dominates Odysseus' home now: reckless excess expressed through mindless consuming. The Phaeacians' images permeate Odysseus' imagination to restore the wounded, traumatized warrior with images of wholeness as well as a harmony between masculine and feminine energies, human and divine correspondences. These and other images, as well as his treatment by his hosts, heal his soul as he learns to enjoy their hospitality. Edward Whitmont helps us here in observing, "Life is characterized by its ability to create, maintain and recreate new processes and patterns of form and order" (*Alchemy of Healing* 28), suggesting that before Odysseus is capable of remembering and telling his story shortly, that his frame of reference must be altered for such a creative act.

Being in the midst of order orders us anew. Being in plenitude within a serene atmosphere cultivates these states in our souls. In a calm surrounding we feel more calm. We become our surroundings; they shape and form our emotional and psychological lives as well as feed our bodies. After a major trauma, if we have any hope of reaching a place where we feel secure enough to tell our stories in order to put the pieces of our scattered lives together, we need to be immersed in a safe, if not abundant, setting to allow it to occur. Fisher, cited above, goes on to state that his purpose in his book is to create an argument "that will work along the path that runs at the border between an aesthetics of wonder and a poetics of thought," (7) that will help us appreciate Odysseus narrating his history.

Meditation:

When has a setting or surrounding helped you heal? What were some of the qualities that promoted this renewal? Has it continued to deepen?

March 30: Book VII

As the Phaeacians are knowing beyond all other men
To drive a swift ship in the ocean, so their women
Are skilled in weaving. Athene has endowed them highly
With skill in beautiful tasks and with noble minds.
Outside the courtyard is a great garden before the portals,
One of four measures. A fence runs around it on both sides.
And in that place tall blossoming trees are growing.
Pears and pomegranates, apple trees with shiny fruit,
And sweet fig trees and blossoming olive trees.
Of these the fruit never perishes and never leaves off
In winter or summertime, all the year round (VII. 107-17).

Images of abundance, plenitude and bounty pervade the atmosphere of Scheria. Nature and culture are in harmony. Nobility of mind meshes with blossoming nature in perpetual largesse. Order, balance and measure define their world. There exists as well an equality and equanimity between men and women; each provides their own skills to further the enterprise of the whole. The social structure is horizontal as well as vertical. Competition yields to cooperation that promotes a general sense of well-being among them. No matter the seasons the fruit is always present year round. Athene's bestowing on them skill in tasks done by noble minds reveals her continual presence in advancing cultures.

Perhaps Scheria is a place of an ordered and abundant imagination. It is an ideal state or condition not just to be wished for but to strive for. It sets a high standard of sweet judgment and cooperation, aesthetically delighting all its people. A goddess helps organize all the skills she endows them with. A general serenity and balance is the norm. One might call it a utopia in contrast to the dystopic world of Ithaca as it suffers disharmony and disorder. The epic claims that this benevolent condition could indeed exist somewhere and where it is not present, it could be a goal to aspire toward. The Phaeacian world is as close, perhaps to the Olympic domicile of the gods as mortals can reach. It is as well a serene place in the soul that can be imagined and thus envisioned as a golden mean. From within such a safe refuge, Odysseus will unfold his history in stories that reclaim him.

Meditation:

Describe your own reaction to the above lines of the epic. What has been your experience, if even temporarily, of such a balanced and lush world?

March 31: Book VII

As he stood there, godly Odysseus, who had endured much, marveled.
And when he had marveled in his heart at everything,
He went speedily over the threshold into the hall.
He found the leaders and counselors of the Phaeacians pouring
Libations to the far-sighted god, the slayer of Argos. . . .
Odysseus threw his hands about the knees of Arete,
And then the divine mist poured away from him.
They grew silent through the hall when they saw the man
And wondered to behold him (VII. 133-37; 142-45).

One senses a change in Odysseus' spirit as he pauses to marvel at the world Homer has so richly described. As a man of many thresholds, Odysseus absorbs this new marvelous world, then steps across the boundary into the thick of its atmosphere. The Phaeacians are, as is often the case, pouring libations and celebrating one god or another, this time the slayer of Agamemnon's kingdom. Dutifully instructed, Odysseus makes his way directly to the knees of Queen Arete as Athene lifts the mist enshrouding his presence. They immediately wonder at his figure who appears abruptly as a god among them, seemingly from nowhere. Richard Onians describes how "the knees played a part in the spinning process is clear (*The Origins of European Thought* 306) and relates the knees to the three sisters of Fate. Perhaps we see Nausicaa's brilliance in sending Odysseus to the knees of her mother, in whose weaving hands rests the weary warrior's fate.

We may recall a time when we were in the presence of a new, abundant world that brought us to wonder or to marvel at its particulars. Given a new context, we might have felt a transformation begin in us over its beauty and power. Then our familiar world view, our habitual ways of thinking and believing, would alter. Our new context shifts the way we had previously patterned our life's content. Such is the change in our mythic consciousness. We see anew by means of this change of place. One of the gifts of travel is that it often evokes in us a sense of the marvelous at the world's riches and its sufferings, its treasures and its trials. At its basis is the power of the world to shift our mythology, our way of perceiving and the categories that govern our method of interpreting the events in our lives.

Meditation:

Describe a time when you were suddenly arrested by a sense of wonder over something seen, heard, tasted, smelled or touched.

April 1: Book VII

Odysseus pleaded with her:
"Arete, daughter of Phrexenor, who was equal to a god,
I, who have suffered much, fall at your knees and your husband's
And all those dining here: may the gods grant them to live
With blessings; and may each one turn his possessions over
To his children in his halls, and any prize the people have given.
But call up an escort for me to reach my fatherland
Soon, as I have long suffered woes apart from my dear ones."
When he had said this, he sat down on the hearth in the ashes
By the fire. And they all became silent in stillness (VII. 145-54).

Odysseus' speech is so powerful and his actions following his plea so dramatic that all fall into silent stillness. Odysseus supplicates himself by sitting in the ashes of the hearth. His speech, motivated by Athene, is persuasive and moving as he praises all there in measured order. He unites the world of mortals with the noble qualities of the Phaeacians. He references the generosity of the heads of families who hand their possessions down to their children in acts of generosity. Lastly, he pleads for himself to be returned to his origins. His plea is both humble and potent, befitting his skill with words as he is skilled in crafts. Now his other gift, besides being a skilled warrior, as a man skilled in crafting speech, surfaces. This shift from warring to wording marks a shift in his development.

Speaking with soul, with heart and with skill is a fading art today. Homer's epic returns us often to the craft of speech as a way to conjure or instigate a reality through the actions of others affected by another's words. Our lives are soaked in rivers of words, assaulting us from every direction. Odysseus as wordsmith reveals the power in brevity, in being frugal but mindful with words that move others to action or to a similar point of view. The Greek word is "peitho," meaning persuasion and signals Athene's presence. James Hillman asserts that "In the mouth of Athene speech becomes a curative hymn, a word which etymologically means "spun" or "woven" words" ("On the Necessity of Abnormal Psychology" 20). Homer's epic is among other things a sustained study in words' efficacy and potency. In the scene above his pleas silence the room in wonder.

Meditation:

When have you been moved or persuaded by the words of others, or have yourself moved others by language that was forceful but not violent?

April 2: Book VII

"Let us welcome the stranger in the halls and offer
Fine sacrifices to the gods; then let us take thought
For a convoy, so this stranger without pain or distress
Under our convoy may arrive at his fatherland,
And speedily rejoice, even if he is from very far away.
May he undergo no evil or suffering in mid-passage
Before coming upon his land; but then he will suffer
Whatever his fate and the grave Spinners have spun for him
With his birth thread at the time when his mother bore him" (VII. 190-99).

An entire philosophy of life is offered in the King's instructions. Nous is the cause of ideas and images, or from where thought emanates, writes Bruno Snell (*The Discovery of the Mind* 9). The host wishes for his yet-named guest a passage free of discord and strife to rejoice in his homecoming. He wishes Odysseus be free of discord, but fate itself may advance other troubles. Fate is beyond the control even of the gods, as Zeus informed Poseidon earlier. The three Spinners, Clotho, Lachesis and Atropos, are the sisters who comprise one's fatedness from thread to fabric, or clothing. Odysseus' birth thread points back to his origin, the place and woman through whom his life began. King Alcinoos' speech highlights one of the most popular themes of the epic: weaving, fabricating, and making something coherent out of the chaos of threads that must be given an order.

We cannot know our fate but we can recall our origins, a place where our fate may be hiding-in-waiting. Origins and destiny are closely interwoven, and Athene is the most prominent goddess of weaving, plaiting and bringing strands together ("On the Necessity of Abnormal Psychology" 28-29). We each have some control over the threads of our life, but beyond that limit, life has its own story for us to live and then to narrate in recollection. Perhaps our life is not fully lived until partially or fully recollected, so to allow its meaning to emerge. It would be of great value if each of us decided to write a memoir of the most memorable and meaningful moments in our plot. It would be another way of hosting our heritage. As guests in the world we often rely on the help of others; as hosts we can make the lives of others more welcoming and stress-free. Our lives are a continual journey as guest and host, with fate, the great unknown, hosting it at every moment.

Meditation:

When you imagine your life, what moments feel most fated, what most chosen?

April 3: Book VII

Odysseus of many devices spoke to him in answer:
"Alcinoos, concern yourself with something else. As for me,
I am not like the immortals who possess broad heaven
Either in body or form, but am like mortal men. . . .
But permit me to eat dinner, burdened as I am with cares,
For there is nothing at all more shameless than the hateful belly
Which bids a man to remember it by compulsion,
Even one who is much worn down and has sorrow in his mind
As I now have sorrow in my mind. . . .
But arouse yourselves at the appearance of dawn
And bring me, wretched as I am, to my fatherland" (VII. 207-10; 215-19; 222-23).

The king has been speculating on whether this man, who is still nameless, is a god come down from Olympus to mingle with him and his people. Odysseus responds that he is not beyond being a mere mortal, one suffering and anxious for home. He is as well burdened with all the urgencies and desires of other mortals, including his appetites, which he suffers by necessity. He observes of his own bodily desires that his belly is shameless and that it will growl to be satisfied no matter how dire the situation he finds himself in is. Like an animal within, it craves satisfaction. Odysseus calls this reality to mind publicly; his thoughts about his belly reveal to his audience his virtue, his mindfulness and his embarrassment at needing to feed his belly, precisely what the suitors in his home make their central task daily back in Ithaca. Lacking mindfulness, they consume without end.

Belly and mind can war with one another if not integrated on some level of compatibility; otherwise they are antagonistic, remaining at odds with one another. Belly and mind can also be in sweet agreement (*sophrosyne*) with one another if both are moderate and balanced. Both are necessary to a person's unity and identity, but they can in times of trauma and stress, war against one another. Appetite signals the animal side of our nature, while mind (*mens*), thought, reason can connect us more fully to the divine part of ourselves and others in reciprocal respect. We can also thirst and hunger for knowledge, which unites these elements in our quest for wholeness and coherence.

Meditation:

When have you experienced a split and dissension between belly and mind? What have you been able to achieve in uniting them in a healthy and balanced marriage?

April 4: Book VII

She recognized the mantle, tunic, and clothes when she saw them,
Lovely ones, that she made herself with her serving women.
And she spoke out to him and uttered winged words:
"Stranger, I should first like to ask you a question myself:
Who are you? What men are you from? Who gave you these clothes?
Did you not say you got here wandering on the ocean?"
Odysseus of many wiles addressed her in answer:
"It is difficult, queen, to speak out in full detail
About troubles, when the celestial gods have given me so many.
But this I will tell you that you ask and question me of" (VII. 234-43).

We watch the rules and codes of hospitality unfold in Odysseus' time on Scheria, which exists far from other peoples. The time is now ripe (*Kairos*) to discover the identity of the stranger, to know his name and his origins. Queen Arete is the one who questions him directly to reveal himself. A stranger becomes familiar through one's name and story. Her questions are pointed as openings to Odysseus' identity lying beneath the clothing she recognizes as spun from her and her servants' hands. He is both familiar and unknown. He is to repay the labors of hospitality by revealing what has been heretofore concealed. Less self-pity than a weary, fatigued and worn out disposition prompts the wanderer to speak of his "troubles," which is to utter the meaning of his name—to give and to receive strife and pain, from when his grandfather Autolycus named him when he was a youth.

Odysseus' name is that of every one of us who tells his or her story and reveals both pain caused and pain received from the world. But the setting for one's narrative unfolding must be right and the audience both expectant and receptive. Blurting out our story without discerning carefully both audience and setting or context is meager manners and meager questing. It is also in many cases foolish and self-serving. When others "host" our story they should be trustworthy and safe for us to expose who and what we are. Telling our story to the wrong audience can recoil on us later, if we were not initially mindful of our vulnerability. One of the rules of rhetoric is to pay attention to who the audience is and to inflect one's story to their interests and expectations, as Odysseus knows.

Meditation:

When have you told your narrative to an audience of one or of many that you later regretted? What did you learn from such an error?

April 5: Book VII

"But I alone took in my hands the keel of the bobbing ship
And was carried nine days. And on the tenth black night
The gods brought me near the island Ogygia, where Calypso
Of the fair braids dwells, dread goddess. She took me in
And kindly befriended me, nourished me, and said
She would make me immortal and ageless all my days,
But she did not persuade the heart within my breast.
I waited there steadily seven years. And always I moistened
With my tears the ambrosial clothes that Calypso gave me.
But when the eighth year in its cycle came around,
Then she urged me and bid me to go away, . . ." (VII. 252-62).

As he initiates his narrative, beginning from the most recent adventure, Odysseus weaves his identity into his audience's curiosity; here begins his craft as a story teller, which will become fully developed in Books IX through XII. These books will further enchant and arrest the minds of his audience and further seal his passage home. But in this segment he reveals his lengthy hiatus with the divine feminine, who promised him immortality if he agrees to abide with her. Odysseus' fidelity is to Penelope. His son and Ithaca and more broadly, to human life itself with all its troubles and joys and not to the realm of the immortals. Calypso clothes the man who now has nothing left from Troy; she holds him captive until an order from Zeus delivered by his messenger Hermes liberates him to once again pursue his fatherland. Now he wears the clothing of the Phaeacians as he transits home.

Forbearance, the ability to wait, to endure, to spend precious time on hold is a challenge for all of us. Waiting passively, unable to engage one's own will or agency, is a difficult lesson to integrate. When our life is disrupted by circumstances—illness, loss of employment, fortune, freedom, or death of loved ones—we may call on our faith, our memories, our times of freedom, all in the service of allowing us to imagine a time of liberty and safe passage. It is a forced or chosen time of gestation to allow new growth, even while in the moment it feels like a waste of time and energy. Knowing the right time to speak is wisdom.

Meditation:

Recall a time when your disrupted life forced you to wait, to endure, and to rest in the stasis the disruption forced on you. Now, how do you remember that period in your life?

April 6: Book VII

>"And yet I was to have still more to do
With the great distress earth-shaker Poseidon raised against me.
He stirred up winds and hindered me from the voyage
And he raised an indescribable sea so the wave did not
Allow me, heavily groaning, to be borne on the raft.
Then a tempest scattered it, and I myself
Cleft this gulf as I swam on through, until the wind
And water carried me and brought me near your land. . . .
I stepped out and went to sleep in the bushes and heaped
Leaves about me. A god poured down boundless sleep" (VII. 270-77; 285-86).

Odysseus relates just how he came to wash ashore on the island of Scheria, a place on the edge of the world, isolated, yet full of abundance. Now we have two versions of his adventures—Homer's and his. He acknowledges his adversary who wishes to punish him for wounding his son, the Cyclops Polyphemos. This wounding happened in the past from the current moment of Odysseus' storytelling, but it is in the future as part of his narrative yet to be related. He is here between his historical life and his narrative life. His identity—his myth—continues to unfold in the plot of his story. Of course he is selecting those elements in his story to win the support of the Phaeacians. But more, his narrative is his way of putting the pieces of his life into a coherent form by pulling on what has already happened in history to be narrated in the future through the present.

What happens within us as we relate our history to a sympathetic audience? There is the literal history of a series of events that happened to us; there is also a "narrative truth," as Donald Spence calls it (*Narrative Truth and Historical Truth* 27) that organizes our life from the inside out. What events we acknowledge in story we transform into experiences through our narrative imagination. James Hillman suggests that the word "soul" "makes meaning possible, turns events into experiences" (*Revisioning Psychology* xvi). Our soul is engaged in a narrative creation more than the events lived but not formatted into an intelligible meaning. Our stories and the way or style in which we tell them, speak as much about our personal myth as the events we relate.

Meditation:

Reflect for a moment on what shifts or changes when you craft your story? When you then share it with others? Do the events you relate become transformed?

April 7: Book VII

"This is the truth I have told you, though I am distressed."
Then Alcinoos spoke out and answered him:
"Stranger, of this at least my daughter did not properly
Take thought, in that she did not lead you to our house,
With her serving women. For you besought her first. . . ."
"She bade me to follow along with the serving women,
But I did not want to, as I was afraid and ashamed
Lest somehow your heart be offended at seeing me.
Very suspicious are we tribes of men on the earth" (VII. 297-301; 304-07).

Etiquette, right behavior, a proper measure between the code of the host and that of the guest is under scrutiny here. Odysseus admits that he recalls his narrative both in distress and feeling the distress again in his remembering. He appears to be retraumatized in relating his long story with Calypso. Alcinoos, sensing his dismay, acknowledges how his daughter failed to personally lead him to their palace. Odysseus quietly comes to her support in admitting that his own fear and shame held him back, for the nature of man, he offers, is to be suspicious of one another. His humility touches the king in its authenticity. In his responses Odysseus hopes to supplicate himself to the king, as he did earlier with Arete.

Fear and shame can stop us from venturing forward in life. We may easily be arrested by these formidable emotions and succumb to their demeaning power. But in a civilized encounter and within a safe vessel, we are encouraged to speak the truth of our emotional life rather than bury these feelings under the rubble of presenting a false sense of what we are experiencing. Our candor can be an effective way of owning our feelings in the moment in order to integrate ourselves more fully, especially when we may have been shattered by a life event that left us fractured. James Hillman reminds us of Karl Kerenyi's writings on Athene; her name "refers to a containing receptacle, 'a kind of vessel, a dish, a beaker, or pan'" (qtd. in "On the Necessity of Abnormal Psychology" 27).

Meditation:

Recall a situation when you felt drawn to denying and hiding your feelings about how an experience affected you. Were you able to push against that impulse to withdraw and to lean forward in giving your experience the language it deserved and required?

April 8: Book VII

"Would that by father Zeus, Athene, and Apollo,
Being such as you are, and of a mind like my own,
You might have my daughter and be called my son-in-law,
And stay here. I would give you a home and property
If you willingly stayed. No Phaeacian would hold you back
Against your will. May that not be pleasing to father Zeus,
I appoint your convoy for a day, so you may know it well,
That is, tomorrow. Then you may lie overcome in sleep.
And they will row on a calm sea until you arrive
At fatherland, home and whatever is dear to you, . . ." (VII. 311-20).

King Alcinoos first places in front of Odysseus what he would wish the stranger choose to do: marry his daughter, for which he would be very generous to the wanderer. He reveals that if Zeus himself did not sanction such an arrangement, then the king would provide Odysseus a transport home to all that he loves and yearns for. He places the desires of the god over his own in a generous act of piety. Not his appetites and wants, nor even Odysseus' own, would be placed above the desire of the god. Alcinoos discerns in Odysseus a like-mindedness, another form of *sophrosyne*, of a sweet accord or agreement with another; he would welcome such a person into his family. Alcinoos reveals that yielding to the wishes of the gods is far more prudent than insisting on his own template for the future. This show of piety for the gods is not lost on Odysseus. By the king's actions Odysseus is reminded of what a home is like that reveres divine presences in life.

An indicator of our own growth and wisdom is apparent by what force or presence we are willing to bow to when our own desires for a certain reality are strong and persistent. Do we restrain ourselves, pause and reflect, or do we follow the urge to simply push through to a desired result or achievement? What we yield to and what we resist are important indicators of our own personal myth. We each struggle and commit great energy to selflessness and to selfishness. Wisdom would seem to insist in knowing when to yield to another's wishes and when to remain faithful to our own. It also implicates what we wish to pursue with the feeling that it is our authentic destiny, our life to live, and not another's.

Meditation:

To what forces or presences or limitations do you yield to in your life currently? What in the past were you able to let go of, to cease pursuing?

April 9: Book VII

They went from the hall with torches in their hands.
And when they had spread down the thick bed busily,
They stood beside Odysseus and urged him with speeches:
"Come rise up, stranger, the bed is made for you."
So they said. It seemed welcome to him to lie down.
So godly Odysseus, who had endured much, slept there
In the jointed bed under the resounding portico.
Alcinoos slept in a nook of the lofty house;
His lady wife beside him prepared a bed and a resting place (VII. 339-47).

Book VII ends with a generous scene of domestic bliss. First the stranger guest is made comfortable, as if he were in his own home. The warrior is only too happy to be given a clean and welcoming space to sleep in, with much more comfort than the leafy mattress in nature he enjoyed earlier. Now he is gifted the luxury of a made bed which he swiftly lies on to restore himself. Alcinoos and his queen lie in a bed she has made up for the two of them, perhaps in a remote corner, a nook intimate and proper for the majestic couple. It is an image that Odysseus longs for, to have Penelope by his side again. This domestic scene offers an inside look at the culture of the time and the generosity that can attend a stranger in need. The virtue of hospitality is evident here as a basis of civilization, of assisting others in need and of providing for what they are incapable of giving to themselves currently. All of this setting contrasts the inhospitable suitors.

The need for rest, for restoration, can be an area in our life we do not honor enough when we feel exhausted and even dizzy from our multiple pursuits. We long to "get away," to breathe more easily. We may need to be reminded of this need more when we are "not at home," but out in the world, where our good fortune may place us among others who gently persuade us to rest, to sleep and to rejuvenate ourselves. The proper host serves all the needs of his/her guest, including an insistence that they rest without responsibilities or concerns for payment in kind. When the setting is one of safety, harmony and calm, the worn out guest may decide that rest is a gift given by others; it is a time of soul restoration before one pushes into the unknown.

Meditation:

When have you served others or been served by others with the gift of rest, ease, and renewal? What else was renewed in you through such generosity?

April 10: Book VIII

"This I command the young men. And as for you others,
You scepter-bearing kings, come to my lovely home,
So that we may entertain the stranger in the halls.
Let no one refuse. Summon the godlike singer
Demodocos. The gods have granted him to please beyond others. . . ."
The two and fifty young men were selected
And went, as he bade them, to the strand of the barren sea.
But when they got down to the ship and to the sea
They dragged the black ship in to a depth of salt water
And set up a mast and sails upon the black ship (VIII. 40-44; 48-52).

King Alcinoos sends out an edict for the kings of other parts of Scheria to join him in honoring the guest, whose identity he still does not fully know. Most importantly perhaps, the blind bard Demodocos is also to be present to entertain all guests with his song. As a descendant of Orpheus, Demodocos is to play the lyre to accompany his story. At the same time as Alcinoos' summons, the king has also ordered a ship to be prepared to take Odysseus home soon and swiftly after the rituals of hospitality have been observed. We may sense with some anticipation the end of Odysseus' two decades away from home, first as a warrior, then as a wanderer and soon to be an extended story teller. The ship is prepared and ready to sail, but not before Odysseus identifies himself and further assimilates his narration.

When we are pulled out of our familiar lives by chance, necessity, or other uncontrollable circumstances, the return, especially after the lapse of months or years, cannot be too abrupt. Scheria is the image of a place of re-entry, a median territory between mortals and divinities, a land of enchantment and a vessel of the poetic imagination. It is a portal by which we enter our past lives. Certain psychic and emotional preparations are essential so that one does not return, yet remains a stranger in his/her own land and household. A gradual return allows a slower, more complete assimilation, with many rituals enacted to ease the return. As one has changed from their adventures, so will home appear different when they return.

Meditation:

Remember a time when you left home for an extended period. What did you do to prepare yourself for a successful homecoming? What might your family and friends do to prepare for you? Or, have you witnessed the homecoming of another and his/her effect on family and friends?

April 11: Book VIII

And when they had taken their fill of food and drink
The Muse bade the singer to sing famous deeds of men
From the lay whose fame had by then reached broad heaven,
The quarrel of Odysseus and Achilles, son of Peleus,
How once they wrangled at an abundant feast of the gods
With terrible words. . . .
This did the far-famed singer sing. But Odysseus
Took his great purple mantle in his stout hands,
Pulled it over his head, and concealed his handsome face;
He was ashamed before the Phaeacians for shedding tears
Under his eyebrows (VIII. 72-77; 83-86).

After all the guests have eaten and drunk wine, they settle in as Demodocos, inspired by the Muse of poetry, begins to sing of and further immortalize the deeds of heroes. Up to this moment Odysseus has yet to reveal his identity. The singer's words open up the warrior's wounds and the trauma of Troy. The pain is too great for him as the poet's story returns Odysseus to the horrors of war and his bitter strife with the great fighter, Achilles, the central heroic figure of the *Iliad*. Odysseus' grief overwhelms him. He conceals himself, as he does throughout the epic, for a series of reasons. He is ashamed to grieve openly among his hosts. His wounds are still too raw after all this time; he does not yet wish to identify himself to his hosts. The song the singer offers has evoked a re-wounding in the warrior listening and weeping. The trauma is reignited through song, through poetry.

No one's life journey is trauma-free. We each suffer from what our life sets before us. The events of our suffering are the first line of traumatic experience. Others' recollecting our wound is the second. Our own recollections and expression of such pain is a third. Listening to another recount our afflictions can gather as much, if not more, intensity than the original condition. We experience old wounds suppurating when we are thrown off our life's course. Yet, as I have written elsewhere, "our wounds have the capacity to advance our consciousness to new levels of awareness" (*The Wounded Body* 16). Our defects and afflictions can be occasions for deeper forms of insight and self-understanding of our identity.

Meditation:

Have you experienced another recount your misfortunes and afflictions? What was that experience like compared to the original event when it was storied?

April 12: Book VIII

Odysseus again covered his head over and moaned.
Now, as he shed tears, he escaped the notice of all the others.
But Alcinoos alone took note of him and perceived him,
While seated near him, and heard him as he deeply groaned. . . .
"Now let us go out and make trial in all sorts
Of contests, so that the stranger may tell his friends
When he returns home how much we surpass others
In boxing and wrestling, in jumping and also in running"   (VIII. 92-95; 100-03).

The Phaeacian audience, delighted by the stories of the singer, fail to notice their guest growing more deeply dispirited and withdrawn by the narratives that push him deeper into remembrances of pain and loss. His relation to the narrative is too raw for him; he groans in travail. Jonathan Shay suggests that Odysseus is "ambushed by his own emotional reaction" (*Odysseus in America* 15) as a test of his endurance. The power of past events, when converted into narrative form, can cripple Odysseus in the present. As a warrior and a wanderer, his suffering intensifies through memories given a poetic and aesthetic form and publicly witnessed. Odysseus continues to conceal his identity from the audience, but Alcinoos, perceiving his grief, interrupts the singing by suggesting sport contests.

Only we know the limits of our grieving for what has marred us and what we yearn to retrieve: home. Few archetypal situations can rival in intensity our need for home, for family, for the ordinary and familiar and the security it brings. There exists a positive side to be able to feel safe enough to grieve without ridicule or judgment. Part of returning home necessitates recollecting what has interrupted our being-at-home, as well as adjusting to any trauma suffered when one was homeless. I have explored how when our wounds are put into words, then healing advances ("The Narrative Play of Memory in Epic" 337). Words can rescue us from our woundedness as well as cultivate a deeper relation to them. Words in story form can be a life preserving vessel in which to contain our suffering and that of others. The entire *Odyssey* explores the therapy of words in story form as well as other healing expressions.

Meditation:

When were you pushed by necessity to remember a period in your life that was traumatic? Or, when did you choose, finally, after perhaps many years, to confront and to give voice to a deep affliction?

April 13: Book VIII

"Come, friends, let us ask the stranger if there is any contest
That he knows and is skilled in. He is not bad in form,
In his thighs and in his calves and both hands above them,
And his neck is stout, and his strength great, nor does he lack
His prime; but he is broken down by many evils.
I think for my part there is nothing worse than the sea
To shatter a man, even though he be very strong."
Then Euryalos answered him and addressed him:
"Laodamas, indeed you have said this properly.
Go challenge him now yourself and say what you said" (VIII. 133-42).

To ease Odysseus' suffering in remembrance, the Phaeacians begin a series of athletic contests to divert the warrior's attention. Laodamas, son of Alcinoos and Arete and winner of the boxing match, seeks out Odysseus' strengths and skills so he may participate with the young men. His assessment of their guest's physical strength is favorable, yet he sees in Odysseus the turmoil and suffering he has endured. But the king's son cannot discern beyond Odysseus' own story related earlier of how the god Poseidon afflicted trials on him as he sailed from Calypso's island. He does not know the longer story of Troy and all the subsequent losses Odysseus suffered before his seven years with the goddess.

Our physical appearance tells only a fragment of our larger narrative. We can see the physique of another and assess it with some accuracy. But the deeper identity is indoors, invisible and concealed, but highly influential of who we are in our being and scars, memories, desires and intentions. Can we ever truly reveal our longer, more complex story to others? We can only go by what we are told by another or others and make our interpretation from that. That is what is revealed; the rest remains concealed. Jerome Bruner reflects on restoring memory in our stories: "our capacity to turn around on the past and alter the present in its light, or to alter the past in the light of the present" (qtd. in *The Wounded Storyteller* 65). In one way, our identity is enmeshed in both what we tell and what we restrain from exposing. It is one of Homer's major themes that he explores throughout the epic: knowing what to conceal and what to reveal in our narrative tellings.

Meditation:

What influences are at work in your selecting what you wish others to know of you and what you prefer to conceal?

April 14: Book VIII

"Father stranger, come here too, and try the contests,
If you have ever learned any—you seem to know about contests.
Yes, there is no greater glory for a man as long as he lives
Than what he achieves by his feet or by his hands.
Come now, have a try; scatter the cares from your heart.
Your journey is not far off, and already the ship
Is drawn down for you, and the companions are ready." . . .
"Laodamas, why do you taunt me in calling me to this?
Troubles are more in my mind than contests are" (VIII. 145-51; 153-54).

Two worlds clash here: the domestic and insulated realm of the Phaeacians and the post-war traumatic island of Odysseus' soul as it continues to rehabilitate from battle. The contests in the games is a safer more civilized, and less destructive version of war with winners and losers; prowess is revealed but without the terror of dying. From Laodamas' perspective Odysseus should feel secure and happy because the plans are in place, and the ship is ready to carry him home, whatever the distance. From Odysseus' point of view, the games seem a superfluous distraction that delays the warrior from reaching his home as well as his impatience with this display of skills that feels constricting, not constructive. Odysseus has been in the military and has suffered moral injury, "a uniquely and significantly unaddressed war zone harm" (*What Have We Done?* 20), that becomes part of his narrative, as David Wood explores in his book.

We live our lives each day through a hierarchy of priorities. When our hierarchy is violated or disrupted by something far less important that muscles its way on to our list, we can suffer the sting of impatience and perhaps even feel victimized. Our time is so precious that wasting any of it on distractions or entertainments when larger tasks or developments cry out to be attended to, we may feel trapped by life's circumstances and suffer a moral dissonance between our values and our life circumstances. We might want to keep one eye open to the disruption for what it wants us to notice and act on. What looks like a mundane interruption may blossom into something of far greater urgency.

Meditation:

When have you felt arrested in life by trivia when to your mind more urgent matters clamor for attention? Did it ever occur that the trivial over time became more monumental than first realized?

April 15: Book VIII

Odysseus of many wiles answered, glowering at him:
"You have spoken not well, stranger; you are like a fool,
And so the gods do not grant delightful gifts
To all men, in shape or in mind or in speaking.
One man is rather insignificant in look;
But a god crowns his speech with grace, and men behold him
And are pleased. And he speaks without faltering . . . ."
And another man will be like the immortals in look,
But there is no gracefulness to crown his speech;
And so you are striking in look, and not even a god
Could make you otherwise. But you are of futile mind" (VIII. 165-71; 174-77).

Odysseus responds to the impudent Euryalos who has just demeaned his guest in front of others, including the king. The insolent young man breaks the code of hospitality in insulting the war-weary visitor, who utters a distinction between two kinds of men in their overt and hidden natures: one is not particularly handsome but speaks with grace and eloquence, while another appears as handsome as a god but speaks without measure or mindfulness. Euryalos is an example of the latter. The battle here is rhetorical, highlighting one who speaks eloquently and the other basely. Odysseus speaks directly from the wounds of war he has embodied and from the intense longing for home after battle.

Our language yields us to the world with a clarity and depth that appearance alone fails to capture. Our physical appearance may be more a given, but our speech is what we cultivate or curtail. Our interior appearance emerges in how we raise up or demean others with our words. They mark us much more distinctly than our appearance ever can. Our looks are more passive, our talk or writing more active. The latter captures something of our deepest nature and our closeness or distance from the gods. Walter Otto suggests that "even language was, without a doubt, created in the commerce with the transcendent power which moves the world . . . it emerged with primal force in the form of glorification and prayer" (*Dionysus: Myth and Cult* 26).

Meditation:

What is your calculus of judgment of a person: how one looks or how one speaks? We could also include: how one behaves. In your mind, what is the most accurate measure of who the person is?

April 16: Book VIII

"But even though I have felt many ills, I will try the contests,
For your speech gnaws my heart. What you say urges me on."
So he said. Springing up with cloak and all, he took a weight,
A broad one, not by a trifle larger and stouter
Than the ones the Phaeacians threw among themselves.
He whirled it around and shot it from his stout hand. . . .
                It flew past the marks of all,
Speeding quickly from his hand. Athene set the distance,
Likened in body to a man; she spoke out directly:
"Even a blind man, stranger, could make out this mark
By feeling it, since it is not mingled at all with the throng, . . ." (VIII. 184-89; 192-96).

From speech to action is Odysseus' trademark, his way of being in and relating to situations and conditions in life. It is his myth. As one learning to exercise the role of a proper host, which can include restraint, as well as experiencing his wounding by the words of another, he channels his energy, with Athene's guidance, into hurling the shotput. It lands so far from the indentions of others that Athene observes: "But is first by far" (l. 197) since it stood apart, ahead of all the others. His prowess, controlled and ordered by the vessel of the contest, reveals his superior abilities. Athene aids this containment, she who as goddess blends persuasive words with decisive action. Once again Athene serves as mediator, using sport contests to defuse what might destroy the guest-host relation.

Insults from others can be an occasion for retaliation through violence. From here, chaos opens out to destruction of both the guilty and the innocent. Patience, a certain balance, and a constructive response will lead to a different result. Being guided by a divine presence, or a belief in the palpable force of a god or goddess, saves order from descending into disorder. Violence unchecked can undo what has been constructed; anger without boundaries can dissolve a situation of order into chaos. In that move, culture is weakened, civil life diminished or dismantled. Walter Otto writes that "This excellence of 'intelligence' or 'counsel' constitutes an essential trait in the Homeric picture of Athena" (*The Homeric Gods* 50).

Meditation:

When have you been in a situation where restraint and tolerance saved a confrontation from dissolving into irreversible violence?

April 17: Book VIII

Alcinoos alone addressed him in answer:
"Stranger, you have said this to us not ungracefully,
But you would like to show the excellence that belongs to you,
Angry that this man has stood up to you in the games
And blamed you, as no man would reproach your excellence
Who knew in his mind how to speak sensibly.
But come now, give heed to my word, so you may tell it
To another hero when you are in your halls
Dining beside your wife and your own children,
And remember our excellence in such deeds as Zeus
Bestows on us steadily since the time of our fathers" (VIII. 235-45).

Odysseus finishes his assessment of his own excellence in skills as well as where he is deficient. His story holds all his listeners in awe. Alcinoos steps in to praise the kingliness in Odysseus by praising his excellence in speech to complement his prowess in action. He agrees with Odysseus' reprimand of the young man, Euryalos, who verbally abused him, thus weakening the guest-host relationship. When he says that "no man would reproach your excellence," he repeats the fictional name Odysseus will use to the Cyclops, Polyphemos to deflect his true identity from him. Finally, Alcinoos wishes that his guest would carry stories of excellence of his people back to Odysseus' own home to immortalize in memory the sterling qualities of the Phaeacians in sport, feasting, dancing and piety towards the gods. By his words he will create the Phaeacians in the minds of others. Such is how traditions and history itself remain alive and vibrant.

First impressions are powerful and lasting. We seek to be remembered fondly for the totality of who we are, not one incident or character trait our immortality is dependent in part on; our mythic presence is entangled in the words others use to describe us from their memories. Memory is a myth-making organ that transcends time. Our glory's existence is a memorial act of imagination. The narrative identity others' share about us comprises our reality for those who hear the stories. Our identities are always imaginal acts of creative construction.

Meditation:

Think of someone you remember unfavorably. Time to revise your description? Think of a person your remember favorably. What qualities of that person do you hold in high regard?

April 18: Book VIII

"Let someone go at once and bring for Demodocos
The clear-toned lyre which is lying somewhere in our halls."
So said the godlike Alcinoos, and a herald rose
To bring the hollow lyre from the home of the king.. . .
They smoothed a dancing place and broadened a lovely ring;
The herald came near, carrying the clear-toned lyre
For Demodocos. He went to the middle then. Young men
In their first youth stood round him, skillful in the dancing,
And beat the godly floor with their feet. Odysseus
Gazed at their flashing feet and wondered in his heart (VIII. 254-57; 260-65).

Odysseus' initiation back into the cosmos of an ordered culture through elegant rituals continues as he marvels over the preparation for song and dance led by the next generation of Phaeacians. Emerging from almost two decades of warring, then wandering and wondering if he will ever arrive home, here he can enjoy through that same wonder over the ritual of dance. At the center is not a warrior but the poet of words and music, the story teller and bard. Going to the middle witnesses the honor and importance of the people's poet who emphasizes what is vital to be remembered and to integrate into their collective history. The social activity is joyful, cheerful, playful and uniting. Around the bard's musical expressions the Phaeacians gather in dance and merry making—all are enlivened, including Odysseus as he recovers some of the joys of life from war's trauma.

Play, playfulness, communal celebrating in dance and song is such an integral ingredient in a people's on-going creation and renewal. It invites in the presence and energy of Dionysus, god of festival, wine, intoxication and ecstatic abundance. When he is disbarred from our lives, existence flattens out, loses joy, dampens wonder and revelry. Celebrating rituals renews the spirit of individuals, tribes, even civilizations. Casting off cares temporarily invites renewed energy and joy back into the souls of participants. Coherence is restored and renewed in the festive energy of "flashing feet." Otto reminds us that "A number of gods are expressly called 'giver of joy' (*charidotes*), as for example Dionysus and Aphrodite" (*The Homeric Gods* 109).

Meditation:

Do you make room in your life for times of festival, music and dance? If not, when did these activities die out?

April 19: Book VIII

Then playing the lyre, the man struck up a beautiful song
Of the love of Ares and fine-crowned Aphrodite,
How they first had lain together in the home of Hephaistos,
Secretly. He gave her many gifts and shamed the marriage bed
Of her lord Hephaistos. A messenger came at once to him,
Helios, who perceived them lying together in love.
Hephaistos, when he heard the spirit-hurting story,
Went into his bronze works plotting evil in his mind
And put a great anvil on the anvil block, and hammered bonds
Unbreakable and indissoluble, that would hold them there fast (VIII. 266-75).

Demodocos sings the story of infidelity and excessive appetite unrestrained that shatters the boundaries of the marriage oath. The tale tells of the violated oath that two agree to in the marriage bond. The broken oath shames the marriage and the bed, the space of intimacy where sharing stories congeals further the bonds of marriage. Wounded in his spirit, the great club-footed artificer Hephaistos plots vengeance against those who violated the oath, and with it, the former love for the goddess of Love and daughter of Zeus. Hephaistos does not use violence but artifice to exact justice, transforming his wrath into a creation that fosters justice. Rather than slaughtering them, he chooses to bind them with invisible webbing to hold them fast in their infidelity. He is to bind love with war or violence.

We have been told, wrongly, that " all is fair in love and war" until Aphrodite and Ares violate us when love and war conspire to wound us in one of our most vulnerable conditions: the unqualified love and trust for and in the other based on mutual fidelity. Human appetite may convince itself to step over these boundaries to satisfy personal and mutual impulses. The result is a breakdown in one of the pillars that sustains a civilization: love's trusting nature. Its violation ripples through the entire range of a people and weakens all its members. James Hillman reminds us that "Athene shares limiting, harnessing attributes with Ananke" ("Necessity" 26), the latter term meaning constriction, what is necessary and "what cannot be otherwise." We are reminded of Hephaistos' club foot that slows his pace; he makes up for it with a quick and agile imagination.

Meditation:

Describe a situation in which you violated a trust or were violated by the acts or words of another. Describe the consequences of either one.

April 20: Book VIII

And when in his anger he had fashioned a snare for Ares,
He went into his bedroom where his own precious bedstead stood.
He spread bonds all around the bedposts in a circle
And he spread many out from the rafters up above,
Subtle as spider web, that no one would ever see,
Even of the blessed gods, so well for deceit did he make them.
And when he had put the whole snare around in the bedding,
He made as if to go to Lemnos, the well-built citadel
That is the dearest by far to him of all the lands (VII. 276-84).

Deceit follows deceit. Hephaistos turns to his gift as a great artificer in order to right the scales of infidelity by creating such a fine filament of a net that even the other gods cannot perceive its presence. Now the bonds between him and Aphrodite that have been broken will be met with stronger bonds, equally invisible, that will contain and restrain the two gods in the act of love making. His artifice will make the invisible visible for all to see, like a news flash to the gods that reveals the unfaithfulness of a famous person. Snagging infidelity in process imitates or matches the violation itself. We know from the conditions that Odysseus is journeying home to face, that the suitors have been unfaithful to the code of hospitality in both their excessive appetites and in the servant women who have begun sleeping with some of them. He will construct his own net to punish their infidelity to the code of guest-host relations.

Unfaithfulness in any form is a violation of the individuals involved as well as a principle of an oath or sacred agreement. Larry Kent Graham understands such violation as a "moral injury, and injury to the soul" (*Moral Injury* 15). Infidelity is a spiritual violation as well as a physical and emotional one. In it all parties involved are diminished; because the bond is both fragile and strong, its violation can easily lead to an Ares response so that not infrequently violence is the consequence and death its final result. Some presence of Athene is necessary, for she is known as a reconciler and a peace maker when possible; she can also make war if necessary. As a presence in our mental and emotional lives, Athene can also create a pact or agreement for both opposing parties, which we will see at the end.

Meditation:

When has infidelity led to violence in your life or in the life of someone you know? How did it end? Was there any reconciliation?

April 21: Book VIII

"Come, darling, let us enjoy the couch and the bed ourselves.
Hephaistos is no longer in the district. Already
He is gone off to Lemnos among the wild-speaking Sintians."
So he said. It struck her as delightful to go to bed.
The two of them went to sleep in the bed clothes. And the bonds
Fashioned by various-minded Hephaistos were spread about them,
So they could not move or raise their limbs at all.
And then they knew it when they could no longer escape (VII. 292-99).

The delight anticipated by Ares and Aphrodite is brought up short by the strong filaments of the invisible net that drops around them to hold them fast in an embarrassing restraint. Now they are both fixed together and immobile. The artificer has revealed their infidelity by both cunning and force by making their hidden tryst visible for all to see, like the plot of a story that exposes what is invisible to the visible order. Blinded by lust, both god and goddess misjudge the craft and craftiness of the deformed, betrayed god. Appetite blinds the ones entranced by desire once again. The story exposes to Odysseus one possibility when he returns home. Albert Cook observes that "Odysseus discovers himself on his way home" ("The Man of Many Turns" 450). Through this story of infidelity, Odysseus is mentored by the betrayal of the gods to consider that betrayal may also be awaiting him on his arrival home.

Forces, presences, behaviors in the world we can't see may exert their impact on us when we are caught unawares. Perhaps there are always invisible presences enacting their force of justice and equilibrium against excesses and broken oaths that restore order and balance to a world thrown off balance when one or another appetite takes the captain's chair and assumes command. A sense of justice may, but not always, right wrongs, balancing out the world's order and reestablishing a sense of justice, which may include a dismal fate for those who were responsible for upsetting an innate order through their own blind greed or lust for power and authority. Recklessness is then replaced with some reconciling presence, as Athene offers repeatedly in Homer's epic. Larry Kent Graham suggests that renewal, repair and reconciliation are essential to heal a soul wound (*Moral Injury* 15).

Meditation:

Recall when you have witnessed justice served by some intervening artifice, technology or presence.

April 22: Book VIII

He stood in the doorway, and a wild anger seized him.
Terribly he shouted and cried out to the gods:
"Father Zeus and you other blessed ever-living gods,
Come see deeds to laugh at that are not to be endured,
How Aphrodite, the daughter of Zeus, dishonors me always,
Lame as I am, and loves the destructive Ares
Because he is handsome and nimble of foot, while I
Was born feeble. . . .
But you shall see how the two of them have gone into my bed
And are making love there. It grieves me to see it" (VIII. 304-11; 313-14).

Hephaistos' rage and feelings of violation are palpable through the vehicle of his "wild anger." Betrayal of trust, breaking one's word and one's vow or oath and codes of conduct run throughout the *Odyssey*. When driven to excess, appetites can violate all boundaries of what has been agreed upon as right behavior; oaths and codes can restrain them, like invisible nets cast over individuals and entire people. Hephaistos in his anger and woundedness invites all the divinities to have a good laugh at the expense of his being cuckolded. Zeus' own daughter has brought dishonor on him and on the vows of marriage. He calls her a few lines down "the bitch-faced maiden" because though a beauty, she has no restraints on her heart (1. 320). He also contrasts his lame condition with the more nimble-footed Ares. Yet his skills as artificer to restrain wins out and points us toward how oaths themselves, when well-crafted, can dissolve destructive behavior, even wars.

Hephaistos uses his talent, *metis,* rather than force, *bia,* he does not possess directly, but only through artifice. He successfully constrains and paralyzes infidelity. By means of artifice, of a making of something fitting for the occasion, he brings the truth to the surface, as will a well-crafted story or narrative that develops conflict in order to show a possible solution to a universal human condition. One wonders if Hephaistos' woundedness, his club foot, is not his gift and his strength, for he becomes an artificer of beautiful things for the pleasure of others. Does this suggest that we might look at where we have incapacities as a place of development of talents that might never have been solicited without it?

Meditation:

Consider where you have an incapacity, a flaw or imperfection, that has been life- long or temporary, and how that limitation might be turned to an asset.

April 23: Book VIII

Unquenchable laughter rose up among the blessed gods
To see the devices of many-minded Hephaistos. . . .
The son of Zeus, Lord Apollo, addressed Hermes:
"Hermes, son of Zeus, runner and giver of good things,
How would you like to be constrained in strong bonds
And sleep in a bed alongside golden Aphrodite?"
Then the Runner, the slayer of Argos, answered him:
"Far-darting Lord Apollo, I wish that might come about!
Three times as many endless bonds might hold me fast
And all you gods and all the goddesses might look at me,
But I should be sleeping alongside golden Aphrodite" (VIII. 326-27; 334-42).

One of the only instances of laughter in the entire epic occurs here over the infidelity of Aphrodite. In tragedy, this event could lead to murder, but in comedy it is treated more lightly, with less gravitas, by the gods. They do not laugh at Hephaistos being cuckolded but for his clever strategy as artist practicing his craft and his craftiness. As artificer he entertains them. He creates something almost invisible but which has a tensile strength to restrain divinities; he holds infidelity captive so it can be publicly witnessed. Hermes has no qualms admitting he would love to find himself in that same bed with Aphrodite. He would not balk at being constrained with her in such intimate quarters. His levity about such fortunate circumstances suggests he would not actually do it.

While not diminishing Hephaistos' pain at his wife's infidelity, in the world of the *Odyssey* the attitude is comic. The gods' responses reveal a world in which such a transgression creates in Hephaistos a desire to bring artifice, not violence, to bear on the circumstance of the marriage oath's violation. Attitude is everything here; there is pleasure in creation, in cleverness and mindfulness. It carries its own Eros within it. There is delight in creation, both for the creator and for those who enjoy its fruits. It points to the resilience of the imagination to use artifice, not bloodshed, as a means of coping with transgression. Odysseus as a warrior full of bloodshed's memories, witnesses this response as he moves from the lore of warrior to one of a mindful leader.

Meditation:

When in being wounded or shamed or violated by the mistrust of another, did you turn to a creative outlet to promote your own healing?

April 24: Book VIII

When he had said this, Hephaistos in his force undid the bond.
When the two were released from the bond, strong as it was,
They rushed off right at once. He went away to Thrace,
And Aphrodite of the lovely smile got to Cyprus,
To Paphos, where she had a sacred grove and fragrant altar . . . .
This was what the widely renowned singer sang. Odysseus
Was delighted in mind as he listened, and so were the others,
The Phaeacians, who have long oars, men famous for ships (VIII. 359-63; 367-69).

The power and delight of the story acts like a healing balm on the warrior, still a stranger to the Phaeacians, who hungers for his own bed and bond with Penelope. Hephaistos releases the two sporting in infidelity and Aphrodite, seemingly unruffled by the base witness of the amused gods and goddesses present, returns to her sacred grove and sweet-smelling altar. The bard Demodocos offers this song to unite the divine and human orders and perhaps to reveal how fidelity and its abuse occurs in both realms. The song raises no suspicions of his wife Penelope's faithfulness, so sure is he of her constant fidelity to their marriage oath. He delights in the story as a well-crafted narrative and where bonds hold in suspension the violation of the two, not unlike the power of an oath to hold two contraries in tension, so that a third element—peace—can prevail.

Stories, even when their subject matter can be painful, offer the audience entertainment and delight. They can also underscore a precious value, a belief, a code of conduct in need of reinforcement. They are also persuasive in their own fictional force. Tim O'Brien writes that "what stories can do, I guess, is makes things present. I can look at things I never looked at" (*The Things They Carried* 225). Stories also allow and invite reflection, contemplation, so their narrative may find a corresponding reality in us by directing us to some value we may have forgotten or grown dull about. This form of correspondence the Greeks called *mimesis,* a knowing by analogy and relationship between the external plot of the story and the reader's or listener's own internal narrative, one's personal myth.

Meditation:

Recall a story you heard or read that delighted and informed you through its subject matter, the language that conveyed it and the images that informed it. Did this same story "ring true" for you?

April 25: Book VIII

Then godly Odysseus spoke to Alcinoos:
"Lordly Alcinoos, illustrious among all peoples,
You did claim that these dancers were most excellent,
And it has been shown true. Awe holds me as I look."
So he said, and Alcinoos in his sacred strength rejoiced. . . .
"Listen, leaders and counselors of the Phaeacians,
The stranger seems to me to be very prudent.
Come, let us give him a guest's gift, as is seemly. . . .
Each of you give him a well-washed mantle and tunic
And bring him a talent of precious gold" (VIII. 381-85; 387-89; 392-93).

Odysseus' return to an ordered world of measure and social graces as well as piety towards the gods continues as he compliments his host on the quality of entertainment in his honor he has just witnessed. Alcinoos is pleased by Odysseus' judgment and his courtesy in lauding the fine artifice just completed. The narrative has fed his injured soul. Prudence is the virtue the king senses in his guest's action. He is to be rewarded with a host of gifts to take home with him to enhance his joy at the prospect of his arrival in Ithaca. Gift-giving comprises an important part of the ritual of establishing the guest-host relationship. It is a tangible emblem that a host can use to bless his guest. Soon Odysseus will return the favor by offering the Phaeacians the gift of his own narrative.

Being treated with value as a guest is one of the highest forms of recognizing the worth and integrity of another. One is hosted and received as a guest of honor, truly an enduring gift in itself. To do so before one even knows the identity of the guest is particularly noble and generous. One is given value as a person in his own right, not as one known through his/her achievements or status. Generosity lies behind the host's treatment; gifts freely offered with no expectations of a return is a high mark of an ordered, civilized world and world view. Such generous attention is enough to restore a battered soul living in the chaos of battle and incubated for seven long years by a goddess. Being blessed through gifts is a way of restoring the soul from its battered condition in chaos.

Meditation:

Describe when you were treated generously as someone's guest or when you hosted another with lavish attention and generosity.

April 26: Book VIII

At the same moment a housekeeper called him to go
To the bathtub to be washed. He saw the hot water
With gladdened heart, as he had received no such treatment
Since he had left the home of Calypso with the lovely locks.
The care he got all that while was as it would be for a god. . . .
And out of the bathtub he stepped and he went amid the men
As they were drinking wine. Nausicaa, who had her beauty
From the gods, stood by the column of the stoutly made roof
And wondered at Odysseus as she took him in with her eyes (VIII. 449-53; 456-59).

In small steps Odysseus is ushered back into the cosmic order of culture and of civilized life after decades of war's destruction and after visiting so many deformed and delightful versions of the *oikos* in his travels, which he will narrate in the next book. Wounded in heart by what he has sacrificed for the Greek cause, he is soothed by the hot bath water to mollify his wounds and cleanse him as preparation to narrate his history. The generous treatment gladdens his heart and washes from him more of the horrific experiences of combat. Norman Austin, writing perceptively of this scene, reveals: "Before Nausikaa sits the man of her dream, a *kouros,* fit to be her bridegroom, a splendid sight indeed. . ." ("Nausikaa and the Word" 29). In his treatment he is fashioning a new narrative. His reordering of himself is a slow and sustained therapy of the soul. Nausicaa, who stands where Penelope will stand in her own home, sees him in his glory now, and yearns for him in wonder and sorrow that she will soon lose him to his journey home.

What heals us, especially when we are exiled for a time from our family, friends and familiar surroundings, can often be simple gestures of generosity from others to make us feel valued, that we have an identity and can express gratitude for kindnesses that makes the strange more bearable, even welcomed. A hot bath or shower, a fine meal, a talk with a friend, can restore us to ourselves and to those surrounding us. Travel in most any form wearies us; kindness restores us.

Meditation:

When have you been assisted in your travels that restored you in times of fatigue and stress, or when someone came to your aid when you were stranded in some way? Did it alter your thinking or your own behavior in any way?

April 27: Book VIII

When he had cut some off the back—but more was left on it—
Of a shining tusked boar; and swelling fat was about it.
"Herald, take this portion over to Demodocos
So he may eat, and I will embrace him, grieved as I am,
For among all the men on the earth singers are sharers
In honor and respect because the Muse has taught them
Poems, and she cherishes the tribe of singers."
So he said; the herald brought the meat and put it in the hands
Of the hero Demodocos. He took it and rejoiced in his heart (VIII. 475-83).

Immediately after Nausicaa pleads with Odysseus to remember her when he arrives home, the herald leads Demodocos the singer into the midst of all who are dining. Now Odysseus assumes the role of host as he cuts a large portion of meat and orders the herald to give the bard a choice portion of boar meat to honor him in his role as singer of stories. The Phaeacians honor him as a pillar of their cultural life. Odysseus is learning to host excellence even in another's home. He knows Demodocos has been singled out by the Muse, daughter of Zeus and Mnemosyne, goddess of memory. The narrator describes Demodocos as a hero. The poet is heroic because he brings people stories to nourish and heal them. His is another form of heroism whose role Odysseus is about to step into.

Perhaps our stories are the real heroes of our lives. When we tell them, we connect with others on a deep living level because we share what binds us as one, yet remains separate. They deepen our sense of ourselves. David Loy claims that "we cannot understand anything without storying it. So to understand is to story" (*The World is Made of Stories* 6). If we can tell them well, sing them in attunement, we place ourselves at one with others. Stories are our identities. They con-text-ualize us in a larger field than our finite lives can encompass. Every day of our lives we can observe our unfolding narrative. By so doing, we bond with all other people on a much deeper and inclusive imaginal level. When the Muses are present in our story telling, we reach a deep level of *communitas*, namely, "giving recognition to an essential and general human bond, without which there could be *no* society, writes Victor Turner (*The Ritual Process* 97).

Meditation:

Describe a time, when a stranger became instantly familiar to you through stories, either you or the stranger narrating it.

April 28: Book VIII

"Demodocos, I give you praise above all mortal men,
Either a Muse, a child of Zeus, has taught you, or Apollo.
Very becomingly did you sing the fate of the Achaians,
All they acted and endured, all the Achaians suffered,
As though you had somehow been there yourself or heard one who was.
Come, change your subject and sing of the stratagem
Of the wooden horse Epeios made with Athene's help,
the trap that godly Odysseus once led to the citadel
when he had filled it up with the men who sacked Ilion" (VIII. 487-95).

Assuming the role of the host, Odysseus continues to praise the poet singer because of his skill in ordering, arranging and singing his story. He renders the story of Troy with such fine verisimilitude that listeners are transported back in time to the original event. In his praise Odysseus wonders at the power of language to transport the audience from where they are "now" to the story's "then." They exist in two worlds simultaneously. Odysseus then suggests he change his topic to today's artistry with the hollow Trojan horse that will trick their enemy and bring down the walls of Troy in defeat. He speaks of himself in the third person just before shifting to first person when he reveals his identity and narrates his story in Books IX through XII. The power of the poet is to create a world of "as-if" so that the story's efficacy rests on its power to persuade the audience through crafting an analogy of the original event. The poet offers an analogy of being itself.

We all realize how a story effectively told can enchant and transport others to another realm by the imagination's ability to create a formed experience in words, music, drama or other art form, and to see by means of that medium. Our stories carry our values, our beliefs and our perceptions—all of those elements that comprise our personal myth, our way of being aware and in tune with the world. Stories also have the capacity to render the myth of an entire people. They convey knowledge but in a storied structure of being. Stories can delight and instruct by interpreting historical events along certain imaginal trajectories. Wisdom resides in the narratives that bring us to wonder at their content and their meaning.

Meditation:

Name an insight you have had in your relation to narratives, your own or one you have heard or read. What is the value of that insight for you now?

April 29: Book VIII

"If you do tell me these matters in proper form,
Then at once I will proclaim among all men
How a propitious god endowed a divine singer."
So he said. Inspired by the god, he began and showed forth his song,
Starting from where some of the Argives on the well-timbered ships
Boarded and sailed off, when they had set fire to the huts,
And the others who were round the famous Odysseus already
Were seated in the assembly of the Trojans concealed within the horse,
For the Trojans themselves dragged it to their citadel (VIII. 496-504).

Odysseus continues to encourage Demodocos on, to tell the stories persuasively by relating the incidents "in proper form." He suggests that divinity enters the singer to inspire his skills as a story teller beyond his normal talents. All of this, orchestrated by Odysseus entering Demodocos' space to relate his own adventures and to assume that he is to be transported home. In the plot resides the pattern of his life's arch, which he will hear in part when Demodocos begins to relate the events that follow Odysseus conceiving and helping to build the hollow horse wherein they lie in its stomach awaiting the Trojans conveying it into their city. Odysseus uses his suggestions to Demodocos to introduce himself to the audience now before he reveals his identity in Book IX.

Fame (*kleos*) through narrative is a desire we all harbor. Being recognized for our deeds is part of why we tell stories of others and ourselves. Stories identity us, give us a place and a name in the world. But stories must expose a form, an organic form, according to literary theorist Louise Cowan, who writes that the "act of *poiesis* sees meaning in life, gathers it up and gives it a form" Form, she continues, "is embodied insight" ("The Joy of Learning"). At times we hear of stories others have told of us; now we exist in the memory of others in a novel way. Our true identity may or may not be present in the fictions that become part of the legend that we continue to unfurl. By our stories others will know us, most especially when a well-wrought story carries the kind of embodied insight Cowan alludes to as "*poiesis,*" a making or crafting the narrative into a coherent form.

Meditation:

When have you been surprised to learn something true through a story told about you? When, in telling a story of another, did you become aware of something not known before?

April 30: Book VIII

There he said the man dared fight his most dreadful battle
And won, that time too, through great-hearted Athene.
This did the renowned singer sing. And Odysseus
 Melted, and a tear from under his eyelids wet his cheeks,
As a woman weeps embracing her beloved husband
Who has fallen before his own city and his own people. . . .
Just so did Odysseus shed a piteous tear under his eyebrows.
Then, as he shed tears, he escaped the notice of all the others
But Alcinoos alone took note of him and perceived him
While seated near him, and heard him as he deeply groaned (VIII. 519-24; 531-34).

Demodocos sings of the particulars of the Trojan conflict when, by cunning and artifice, the Greeks led by Odysseus, hide in the belly of the wooden horse and subsequently defeat the Trojans. He sings of Odysseus gaining more *kleos* in his toughest battles inside the walls of Troy. Listening, the warrior is overcome with emotion as he hears the skillfully-told story such that he is carried back in memory to the grief felt at the loss of so many Greeks and the horrors of war itself. His wounded memories bring him to tears; it also connects him through a simile to the feminine and to Penelope specifically, who has wept for years at her husband's loss and may be losing hope of his ever returning. Alcinoos again intervenes and orders the poet to halt his song, and to turn his attention now to Odysseus' identity and his own narrative. Doing so relieves the hero from his anguish.

Stories can transport us back to an original wounding in memory, to a moment of bliss, to a turning point in our lives. Tim O'Brien, writing on the Vietnam war, believes "Stories are for joining the past to the future. . . . Stories are for eternity, when memory is erased, where there is nothing to remember except the story" (*The Things They Carried* 38). We are on-going narratives who invest so much of our emotional lives in our stories. David Loy suggests "the world is made of our accounts of it because we never grasp the world as it is in itself, apart from the stories about it" (*The World* 4). Thus, narratives, told or heard or read, have the power to reframe us, reform us, refresh us and rewound us. Narratives can serve as our moral compass.

Meditation:

Is there one story from your past that most potently defines you?

May 1: Book VIII

"And so in your cunning notions do not yourself now conceal
What I ask you about. It is better for you to speak.
Tell the name which your mother and father called you there,
For no one among men is wholly without a name,
Neither a worthless man nor a noble, from the time he was born. . . .
Tell me your land and your district and your city,
So that the ships that are steered by thought may convey you there,
For there exist no pilots among the Phaeacians,
And there are no rudders at all such as other ships have,
But the ships themselves know the intentions and minds of men" (VIII. 548-53; 555-59).

The king has asked the singer Demodocos to hold off on further narrations; he then tells Odysseus it is time to reveal himself and to tell his own story. Demodocos' singing has prepared both Odysseus and his audience for the warrior to narrate his own story. First he suffered the events in Troy and his travels to the Phaeacians; he then heard part of the Trojan narrative; now he moves into his own telling. Alcinoos asks his guest to begin with his name--for most of us our origin—and then to identify his homeland, so that the king's ships can return him to his proper place. Odysseus is given instructions as guest to reveal what has been concealed. The protocol of hospitality is to comfort the guest who in turn reveals his own story as he now hosts those who have been so hospitable to him. Alcinoos also tells him of the ships steered by thought alone, who have their own consciousness, their own magic abilities and intentions, needing no guidance.

When we tell and retell our origin story, we reclaim ourselves always on another level of awareness. Our memory shifts to accommodate our audience and to reveal who we are at this telling. Each remembered event, when retold, shifts to include certain details omitted earlier and to mute others. Such is imagination's way with memory; we may choose a different voice and language in telling or retelling our narratives. Reclaiming our narrative self is crucial in understanding who we are in a larger context and what our prevailing myth is. We reestablish ourselves in the world when we tell our story orally or in writing.

Meditation:

When you publicly relate your narrative from memory or from writing, what effect does doing so have on you? Does it deepen your sense of who you are?

May 2: Book VIII

"Tell also why you lament and grieve in your heart
When you hear the fate of Ilion and the Danaan Argives.
That did the gods fashion, and they spun the thread of death
For men, so that it would be a song for those to come.
Did some kinsman of yours perish before Ilion,
A nobleman, son-in-law, or father-in-law,
Those who are dearest, next to one's blood and family,
Or perhaps some companion of sympathetic mind,
A noble one? Since not inferior to a brother
Is a companion who possesses a prudent mind" (VIII. 577-86).

Alcinoos has a keen sense of timing, when the right moment has arrived for something to turn, to be exposed. He now places Odysseus front-and-center in the hall because he is curious about the source of his guest's grieving and suffering. He has watched him weep whenever Demodocos sings stories of the Trojan War. He first lays out several plausible propositions as to the cause, but he also now wishes to hear the stories that will expose his guest's identity. Implicit here is an acknowledgement of the power of narrative to elicit commanding emotional responses, especially grief and sadness, in the listeners.

Our deepest definitions of who we are connect us and others to the stories we nurture and cultivate in ourselves. We have our historical past, but that is not what we finally relate to when we remember our history. What we tell is a narrative of that past crafted in the present. A personal myth influences our language to craft our story; who our audience is also effects what we highlight of our narrative, because context is never divorced from content. Tim O'Brien confesses that some stories he never told because "what embarrasses me much more, and always will, is the paralysis that took my heart. A moral freeze.... All I could do was cry" (*The Things They Carried* 57). So our stories are not simply accounts of our history; remembering is itself a creative act of imagination which can create a field of powerful emotions that can elevate or destroy.

Meditation:

Recall a story you told about yourself for a particular effect on your audience. Did you leave out parts of it because it was too potent to utter?

III

BOOKS IX-XII

**Reclaiming a Coherent Life:
The Myth of Remembrance**

III

May 3: Book IX

"But your heart turns toward me to ask of my woeful cares,
So that I may grieve still further as I lament.
What then shall I tell you first, what tell last,
Since the heavenly gods bestowed many cares upon me?
Well now, I shall tell you my name first, so that you too
May know it, and then, when I have escaped the pitiless day
I may be your guest friend, though I dwell far off in my halls.
I am Odysseus, son of Laertes, who for my wiles
Am of note among all men, and my fame reaches heaven.
I dwell in sunny Ithaca" (IX. 12-21).

At the request of his host, Odysseus obliges by beginning his story, knowing it will cause him to grieve even more in the telling. But he assents to this new journey, a narrative one, to please Alcinoos. He first ponders what is the best way to order and arrange his narrative—its techne—its proper measure and organization. He proposes his name first, then works out from there to reveal a concealed identity. Telling his story will link him in memory over vast areas of space. His audience knows of him already as well as his heroics at Troy, since Demodocos has sung of him in his epic songs. His thoughts on framing the story for accuracy and effect will then be dramatized in this and the next three books of the epic. His story becomes a crucial pillar in the epic edifice. Telling his story will begin to reassemble a shattered identity from such a long experience of violence.

Naming ourselves to others in one way recreates us into a new context. We reinvent ourselves in our naming, and if our story follows from it, so much richer do we become as we fashion ourselves in language. What we choose to relate and what we keep hidden creates a certain specific self in the minds of our audience. Through our telling, listeners may find resemblances in their story and community begins to emerge between us. Story telling is then community-creating, but it may also alienate us from our audience. A willing acceptance of the other is therefore necessary in conversation. Remembering through conversation may increase self-consolidation (*Searching for Memory* 82) wherein a fuller sense of self is gained in such a gathering, as Daniel Schacter writes.

Meditation:

When did you connect deeply with a stranger through sharing your stories with one another? Did the connection last?

May 4: Book IX

"So nothing grows sweeter than a man's own fatherland
And his parents, even if he dwell in a fertile home
Far off in a foreign land apart from his parents.
But come, let me tell you of the much-troubled return
That Zeus put upon me when I went away from Troy.
The wind bearing me from Ilion brought me near the Cicones,
To Ismaros. There I sacked the city and killed its men.
From the city we took the wives and many possessions
And divided them so none for my sake would lack an equal share" (IX. 34-42).

Through his story, Odysseus furthers his quest for home. He prefaces his narrative proper by stating that being in one's own fatherland is the greatest of sweet feelings. Story telling is a form of homecoming to one's self. He returns to his origins as he relates his history. He then switches to Troy as his beginning narrative. His warring nature is in full throttle as he lands on the isle of the Cicones, "Thracian allies of the Trojans" (*Odyssey*, fn. 1, 115), and kills, pillages and destroys another version of Troy almost as a reflex. He is being witnessed in his telling, which seems a necessary condition for him to truly arrive home. His story is his rehearsal to his return. Destroying is deep in his nature; as he leaves Troy he continues the slaughter that he has learned so well in battle.

The frame of mind of warriors, indeed anyone traumatized by violence, does not shift when they are free of the traumatic field they inhabited. Writers have shown how a war imagination creeps into one's soul and creates further battle grounds, regardless of the physical terrain. War's wounds can infiltrate and dominate the soul, creating "an unpredictable beast in mind and heart," writes Edward Tick (*Warrior's Return* 155). But, as he writes much later, "Witnessing allows suffering to come home. . . . To give meaning to traumatic events of war is a form of homecoming" (233-34). Without this gesture of the imagination to tell one's story, the trauma stays indoors and festers, incapacitates and can lead to thoughts of or actual suicide. Being in the mode of warrior can become itself an addiction, which then keeps one fixed, self-incarcerated, as with any addictive thought pattern and behavior.

Meditation:

Think of a battle you have been fighting in warrior mode for a great part of your life. Have you been able to give it voice and be witnessed?

May 5: Book IX

"Then I gave the order for us to take rapid flight,
But the men, great fools as they were, did not obey;
They had drunk much wine there and slain many sheep
Along the strand, many shamble-footed crumple-horned cattle.
Meanwhile the Cicones went and called other Cicones
Who were their neighbors, at once more numerous and brave,
Who dwelt on the mainland, skilled in fighting with men,
From horses, and, when necessary, on foot.
As thick as leaves and flowers grow in their season,
They came, in early morning. Then an evil fate of Zeus was with us" (IX. 43-52).

Odysseus remembers how his men chose their appetites over restraining and obeying his orders. They are reckless and focused on excessive killing of sheep. Wine brings them to excess; they abandon all restraint. They slaughter more than they need, without boundaries to curb their appetites. Such single-visioned violence incites the wrath of Zeus and the Cicones down on them for their recklessness. They did not pause to consider what the consequences of their actions might arouse; the war of Troy is still very much in their blood as they respond automatically, as they have during years of prolonged battle. Chaos is their medium; right order and measure have been abandoned in their wantonness.

Patterns of violence can take fierce hold of us and deflect reason and caution. Undoing previously learned patterns of self-destruction as well as the destruction of others for material gain are age-old conflicts in the soul. In a culture of war, as Homer's world and ours was and is, vessels of restraint are often side-lined in favor of greed for more material gain and power. Jonathan Shay writes that Homer shows the "first way that combat soldiers lose their homecoming, having left the war zone physically—they may simply remain in combat mode, although not necessarily against the original enemy" (*Odysseus in America* 20). In this condition, homecoming is impossible; one becomes a wanderer in the world without compass or direction. It is to live in chaos and perhaps begin to believe it is normality. Telling and being witnessed in one's telling, can reorder one's history.

Meditation:

Remember a time in which a violent response to a situation proved your undoing and perhaps a reflective reassessment of your thinking/behavior.

May 6: Book IX

"We set up our masts and hoisted the white sails
And took our seats. The wind and the pilots steered them,
And I would have arrived unscathed at my fatherland,
But as I rounded Malea a rushing wave
And a North Wind pushed me off and drove me past Cythera.
Thence for nine days I was borne by destructive winds
On the fish-laden ocean. But the tenth day I set foot
On the land of the Lotus-eaters, who eat a flowery food.
Then we went onto the dry land and drew off water,
And at once my companions took dinner beside the swift ships" (IX. 77-86).

Amazingly, Odysseus relates how he was almost home ten years earlier than his journey finally cost him to reach Ithaca, if only the natural order had not deflected him from his goal. Cythera is an island of Greece which holds the temple of Aphrodite. The winds and wave are as destructive and excessive as he and his men were on the island of the Cicones. Nature seems to have turned her own version of violence on Odysseus and his men. Finally, after ten days, he is led to the shore of the enchanted Lotus-eaters who promise forgetfulness as the consequence of any who eat of the magical plant. Arriving unscathed to his home is not Odysseus' fate; neither is dying on his journey.

Discerning what life forces guide us, attempt to destroy us, or deflect us from our goals, is not only a sign of wisdom but an awareness of what elements of our personal myth are at play in our journey. Life has its own consciousness and pattern or plots for us. We know what it feels like to be in accord with the life energies and what it is like to rub against life's grain. The mythologist Joseph Campbell writes: "I regard the *Odyssey* as a book of initiations, and the first initiation is that of Odysseus himself into a proper relationship to the female power. . ." (*Goddesses* 160). Part of that initiation occurs above, when the natural order resists him, as it may any of us when we refuse to "go with the flow," to be more in alliance with life's forces, both masculine and feminine. Can we ask, when winds and waves blow us off course: Is this the authentic path I need to be on in this chapter of my life? Or must I tack into different winds to be righted?

Meditation:

Remember a time when, blown off course, you came to see that it was a corrective to your pursuing a wrong or premature path. What brought you back on course?

May 7: Book IX

"And the Lotus-eaters did not plot destruction
For our companions, but gave them the lotus to taste of.
Whoever among them ate the honey-sweet fruit of the lotus
Wished no longer to bring word back again or return,
But wanted to remain there with the Lotus-eaters
To devour the lotus and forget about a return.
Back weeping to the ships I led them, by compulsion,
Dragged them and bound them in the hollow ships under the benches,
And I called all my other trusty companions. . .
Lest someone perchance eat the lotus and forget a return" (IX. 92-100; 102).

The lotus is a seductive enemy of memory. To satisfy one's appetites by eating of its fruit is to choose desire over intellect, craving over consciousness. The men are not happy with Odysseus, who resists the charm of the lotus and the desire it engenders in those enchanted by it. They grieve when their leader forces them back on the ship and restrains or constricts them with bonds. Only restraint will allow them to be free of the seductive lotus. In their being limited resides their freedom to return home. Forgetfulness is subtle and carries its own form of violence; Odysseus meets the challenge of this new enemy and retrieves his men. This incident is one of many episodes of binding and loosening in the epic.

To be charmed into forgetting, especially when one of our basic appetites is aroused, is often a seduction we cannot resist. Individuals have lost everything under the persuasive force of sweet blossoms and the permission to forget one's history, goals, achievement, others, and to abandon oneself to the appetite that pushes back our fuller sense of our life, free of cravings. On a collective level, Henry Giroux points out on a national level how a "politics of disimagination" can undermine "our capacity to bear witness to a different critical sense of remembering, agency, ethics and collective resistance" (*The Violence of Organized Forgetting* 26). When appetites dull the senses and create an atmosphere of forgetting, then power and authority moves from the individual to social constructions. Remembering, we grasp, is connected to ethics and agency. To forget or diminish our history is to invite the rages of consumption to replace it.

Meditation:

Think of the world you live in and where you might see forces working to make you disremember and substituting them with cravings and desires.

May 8: Book IX

"They got in at once and took their seats at the oarlocks.
Seated in order, they beat the hoary sea with their oars.
Then we sailed further on, grieving in our hearts,
To the land of the Cyclopes, an overweening
And lawless people, who, trusting in the immortal gods,
Do not sow plants with their hands and do not plow
But everything grows for them unplowed and unsown,. . . .
They have neither assemblies for holding council nor laws,
But they inhabit the crests of the lofty mountains,
In hollow caves, . . ." (IX. 103-09; 112-15).

Each distortion of home Odysseus and his men explore teaches their leader something of home's true nature. The Cyclopes' world is no exception. Perhaps each home reflects the warrior's soul at various stations of readiness to return home. Deep in grief, the men sit and row in right order. The land they arrive at is without law, community, or mutual cooperation. It lacks a sense of measure and mindfulness. The inhabitants exercise the bare minimum in cultivating home or land, preferring to trust that to the gods. Their culture is primitive and closer to nature rather than culture. Their dwellings are of the earth rather than crafted. Little skill influences their lives. No laws restrain them. They are separate and alienated from one another, with only their appetites connecting them.

The Cyclopes are a consumer culture with little room for anything more of a cultural imagination. All else is left by the side of the cave: laws, rituals, forms of civilization, art, music, all of which defined the Phaeacians. Now Odysseus and his men are at the opposite pole from his time on Scheria, which is yet to happen in Odysseus' narrative but has already occurred in his history. Cultures or individuals that focus one eye on consuming lose the depth of field—the texture of life that double vision engenders. Consuming goods for the body can foreclose other forms of nourishment and leave one starving spiritually in the midst of plenty. An imaginal anorexia can seduce the soul; the richness of life can be misplaced or discarded as impediments to appetite's satisfaction. Life becomes barren and without the spiritual and emotional nutrients that can create communities.

Meditation:

When may you have experienced a desire or appetite to the extent that you let all other concerns of life dissolve, perhaps temporarily?

May 9: Book IX

"There we sailed on in. And some god guided us
Through the murky night. There was not light enough to see.
Dark air was deep about the ships, nor did the moon
Show forth from heaven, but it was contained in clouds.
There no one looked upon the island with his eyes,
And we did not behold the great waves rolling up
On the mainland, before we beached our well-timbered ships.. . .
We fell asleep there and awaited the godly dawn.
And when the early-born, rosy-fingered dawn appeared,
We wondered at the island and traveled all around it" (IX. 142-48; 151-53).

Darkness, Odysseus relates, suffuses this part of their journey. The men and ships enter a dark night of the soul, where all is wrapped in obscurity and the feminine light of the moon—lunar illumination--is blocked by the suffocating clouds. The men sense but cannot see either land or sea. They are as well, Odysseus believes, guided by an unknown god through the dark air. Vision's limits are enhanced, as is the one-eyed Cyclopes' vision flat and limited. When they beach their ships they have no clue as to the terms of the land they have reached, or its inhabitants; they are fully "in the dark." Such blindness forces them to trust the divinity who has charted their course for them, but remains unseen. The island, as they explore it, evokes a sense of wonder in them, so foreign is it to their lives.

Night, obscurity, little distinction and no sense of one's direction or here, their landing, are all phases of any of our life's journey. We feel our way forward, pray not to be shipwrecked by rough seas hurling us against hidden rocks, and find comfort when finally there is solid land to beach our dazed and exhausted ship on. The dark night of the soul, a universal condition that no one escapes, puts us in jeopardy and risks our further pilgrimage. When we relate this experience to others, we of course know the outcome, but when we are in it, only our faith in something other than our abilities will serve. To accept invisible divine presences in our journey cultivates its own form of strength. Joseph Campbell suggests that the Cyclops' one eye "represents the bull's eye, the narrow gate through which one has to pass on the way to initiation" (*Goddesses* 162). It is a familiar gate to us.

Meditation:

When in your life did any clear direction dissolve and any control over your future become muted? What did you then rely on as guide or compass?

May 10: Book IX

"There we saw a cave on the verge, close to the sea
High up, overhung with laurel. Many animals
Usually slept there, sheep and goats; a courtyard
Was built high around it out of deep-bedded stones
And tall pines and oak trees with lofty foliage.
There a monstrous man usually slept, who alone
And aloof tended the animals. He did not consort
With the others, but stayed apart and had a lawless mind.
And indeed he was formed as a monstrous wonder" (182-90).

Odysseus describes a minimalist surroundings and a lone inhabitant who keeps to himself. Large, overbearing, exaggerated, if not excessive in size is this monstrous Cyclops, who subsists living in a cave and caring for his animals, his food source. Odysseus and his men have yet to see him at this moment in time, but they have seen him in Odysseus' narrative time. Lawless in mind is the Cyclops, isolated in a setting high up, resting on the margin or the edge, between sea and land. Thick foliage partly conceals his home, which denies social interaction with any other life than his cattle as chattel. He will be identified as the son of Poseidon, god of the waters and brother to Zeus and Hades. Odysseus calls him a "monstrous wonder," as he has never seen the likeness of him before.

We read of figures like Polyphemos above who prefers isolation to community, lawlessness to lawfulness, and mindlessness to mindfulness. He is self-sustained, inclined toward solitude, overbearing and concentrated on making sure there is enough to satisfy his appetites. We can relate to this mythic figure in ourselves who closes in on himself, remains aloof and lives off the grid of civilization. He is a natural force, excessive and rapacious in his appetite wherein there is never enough. He seems to be a mirror of Odysseus at this juncture on the journey, for their traits match up neatly in their distortions of culture's norms and yet necessary in the reformation of the warrior. As Odysseus tells his story, he gains glimpses of his nature through narratives recollected and reflected upon. Living by appetite and instinct, without regard for the communal good, is to live within the suitors' imagination, without boundaries and only one eye for appetites.

Meditation:

Reflect on your own experiences where satisfying your impulses and cravings isolated you from yourself and from a wider community

May 11: Book IX

"I filled a great skin with it and brought it, and also I put
Provisions in a bag. At once my bold spirit
Sensed that the man would approach, clad in his great strength,
The wild man who had clear in his mind neither justice nor laws. . . .
We entered the cave and gazed at each separate thing.
Baskets were weighed down with cheeses, and the folds were thronged
With lambs and kids. All were divided in groups,
And confined; here the first born, there the middlers,
The dew-fleeced apart too. All the pails flowed with whey,. . ." (IX. 212-15; 218-22).

Odysseus' poetic and narrative eye sees the particularities of Polyphemos' world, all encased. He brings with him a strong wine, gifted from earlier grateful friends. He and his twelve men look at the arrangement, an order separating out animals and food, each with its own distinct space and measure. Everything is in service of satisfying appetites, so order has one purpose, an eye to the stomach only. Nothing beyond this one feature serves the Cyclops' world. Order, degree, measure—all have one end: the body's needs in order to continue life on the most basic level. Beyond that seems of little importance. The liquid whey is used to make cheeses and butter to vary Polyphemos' diet. His depth of field goes no deeper than consuming, which is one dimensional, lacking the depth of culture.

We cannot live by bread or goats or kids and whey alone. Some larger measure of life is necessary to exist beyond biology. If our lives are given over to arranging our world to satisfy the body only, we may starve to death if we don't nourish the soul, the imagination and a larger purpose rather than isolated gratification without gratitude. If everything in our existence is separated out from everything else, then what purpose beyond extending our life is served? Consuming is a thin form of sharing ourselves if deeper desires are not addressed. Polyphemos may be that force or impulse in us to close in on ourselves in a mindless way and foreclose on the larger community we inhabit. Odysseus' storytelling puts him in touch with this excess in himself as he outwits the giant.

Meditation:

By what standard, value or idea do you order your everyday life? What are you forced to leave out and what would you like to begin to include?

May 12: Book IX

"Then at first my companions besought me with speeches
To go back again, when we had picked some cheeses and then
When he had hastily driven the kids and lambs out of the pens
On board the swift ship, to set sail upon the salt water.
But I did not listen—that would have been far better—
So I might see the man and he give me the gifts of a guest.
But when he appeared, he was not to be joyful to my companions. . . .
            He carried
A stout burden of dry wood to use for this supper.
Throwing it down inside the cave, he made a din;
And we drew back in fear into a nook of the cave.
But into the broad cavern he drove his fat flocks, . . ." (XI. 224-30; 233-37).

Odysseus becomes more reflective of his own reckless behavior when he confesses that he resisted the restraint his men encouraged him to follow: "that would have been far better" (l. 228). Instead, his own desires outweigh the safety of his crew. He turns into one appetite, like the giant mirror of himself conveys, so he can receive more gifts to consume, assuming the giant knows the codes of hospitality; but his assumption is blinded by the facts he enters now. He begins to realize how naïve his thinking is when Polyphemous enters the cave with a bundle of wood and throws it to the floor. As Odysseus recollects each part of his history, he finds a place or a home for it in order to piece together a coherent story that is self-confirming as well as painful for him. Restorying himself promotes mindfulness and order, which slowly restores the terms of his personal myth.

Our appetite's, often roused by willful desires, can arrest us in our thinking, our clarity and our sense of balance. We may naively assume that codes of behavior we have lived by are values shared universally. This naivete is a fractured form of perceiving that connects us to shaping a reality that may not in fact exist. Our disordered sense of how the world is may finally threaten our existence. Appetites, when excessive, can narrow vision. Our myth evokes seeing less, not more. Appetites can condition us to see the world as something only to consume.

Meditation:

When has your own willfulness threatened your existence, your position, or your purpose in life? What forces or influences helped you realign yourself in a relation with the world that is functional and enriching?

May 13: Book IX

"'Strangers, who are you? Whence have you sailed the watery ways?
For some sort of gain, or do you wander at hazard
The way pirates do who wander over the sea
Risking their lives, bearing evil to foreigners?'
So he said, and our own hearts were shattered within us,
In terror at his deep voice and the monster himself.
Yet even so I answered him with a speech and addressed him thus:
'We are Achaians coming from Troy, driven off course
By all kinds of winds over the great gulf of the sea;
Wanting to go homeward, we came by other passages, . . .'" (IX. 252-61).

Communicating with the giant Polyphemos, whose name means "Wordy," writes Eva Brann (*Homeric Moments* 189), terrifies Odysseus and his men. The Cyclops sees them as threats, as invaders who have landed perhaps to pillage the island. He offers no hospitality but turns the code of guest-host inside out. He begins by demanding who they are rather than guests to be hosted, as with the Phaeacians, before asking for their identities. The Cyclopes are inversions and perversions of hospitality's code. Odysseus tries to oblige this reversal by telling him the truth; a fiction would have worked better. But if Polyphemos is a giant version of Odysseus' own robbing, pillaging and violent nature, then he has yet to learn to speak to this part of himself. Instead he highlights his victory over Troy, and later "the men of Agamemnon. . . The glory of whom is now the most under heaven" (ll. 263-64), which he assumes the world knows about.

At times when confronting new situations, and before we know with more clarity the terms of our engagement with them, we might do well to modify the amount of information we display, perhaps even bend the truth of our identity and intentions initially and be a little less "wordy." Until we know what we are dealing with, it might be wiser to speak with some stealth, not showing our cards too quickly. Odysseus is naïve above, a consequence of war's effect on him not to read the signals of danger as thoroughly as he might. When we journey over our life's circumstances, we are on a different journey, one of knowing the self more deeply. At times, fictionalizing the facts can buy us time to assess an uncertain life event.

Meditation:

When have you let out more information that, in retrospect, you know was a mistake that you later regretted?

May 14: Book IX

"So I said, and he answered me at once, in his pitiless spirit:
'You are a fool, stranger, or have come from afar,
To bid me to be afraid or to shrink from the gods.
Cyclopes have no regard for aegis-bearing Zeus,
Or the blessed gods since we are mightier by far.
Nor to shrink from the hatred of Zeus would I spare
You or your companions, unless the spirit moved me.
But tell me where you have come and put your well-made ships,
Whether on the mainland or nearby, so I may know'" (IX. 272-80).

Now that he begins to sense the intentions of Polyphemos, Odysseus returns guile for guile in a battle of words and wits. He has the craftiness of words but not the *bie*, the force or strength to defeat the monster. He hears that the Cyclopes have no piety toward the gods, so they have erected their appetites as their deities. All is in their worship; their hubris is that they surpass the gods in strength and might. Excess is the virtue employed by this horrific horde such that Odysseus has a large mirror in which to see his own excess, if not his inflation. Restraint is not a part of the monster's behavior; he will next turn violent and devouring. As Charles Segal writes, "heroism. . . has little meaning. It certainly makes little impression on the Cyclops" ("Kleos and Its Ironies" 210).

When we confront another set of values antithetical to our own, how do we react? To push to convince the other of our righteousness? To back away, seeing persuasion as futile? May this be an occasion to camouflage our own beliefs? We are really tested in our views and convictions when opposition steps on to our path. We must choose what is the greater value to make present and what outcome would be of real value, perhaps for both. When we face opposition in thought or behavior contrary to what we believe, can we remember that this other person is feeling the same way as we when they confront our thoughts and beliefs that contradict their own? At what may feel like an impasse, what might we do to either find a compromise or to allow the differences simply to be? Daniel Mendelsohn refers to the Greek term *arkhe kakon* to suggest a bad beginning, an event that will lead to disaster (*An Odyssey* 8). Such is what Odysseus puts in place here.

Meditation:

How do you handle opposition and confrontation, especially when you feel physically or emotionally threatened? What guides do you call on?

May 15: Book IX

"Helplessness held our hearts.
And when the Cyclops had filled up his great belly
By eating human flesh and then drinking unmixed milk,
He lay down in the cave, stretched full length through the sheep.
And in my great-hearted spirit I made a plan myself
To go closer to him, draw the sharp sword from my thigh
And wound him in the chest where the midriff holds the liver,
Striking with my hand. But another spirit restrained me;
For there we too would have perished in sheer destruction,. . . " (IX. 295-303).

Who is this monstrous figure who lives outside the boundaries of civilization in his mindlessness? He may be what the warrior looks like when journeying from war, pillage, booty, then back to civilization. He must renegotiate this part of himself to arrive home and to remember his goal and not his desire for revenge. Exercising his "*thumos,* his fighting spirit," suggests Johnathan Shay (*Odysseus in America* 46), prompts one response. A spirit of restraint governs his other response. Athene's attribute is one of being able to "combine reason with Necessity," suggests James Hillman ("On the Necessity" 28) so to restrain the impulsive appetite in Odysseus. His goal is to craft a way out of this dilemma; *thumos* would not serve him in the long run. When he considers both his men and himself, he is pulled back by an internal spirit restraining his appetite for vengeance.

It is never easy to rub against the grain of immediate gratification when our inner prompting is to react immediately and mindlessly. Holding back, counting to ten, breathing deeply may be the most productive response, especially to violence or any form of invasion that would leave one at a disadvantage. Retraining a habitual response requires a warrior's attitude and strength; they are never easy to interrupt. Something important is to be learned by not following the same patterns that often increase our pain and woes rather than relieving them. As for storying our lives, we are not different from Odysseus; I have written that he tells us not just what happened to him, but on a deeper level what events that happened to him mean (*The Wounded Body* 39).

Meditation:

Recall a time when you successfully thwarted an old response pattern. What were the consequences?

May 16: Book IX

"And when the early-born, rosy-fingered dawn appeared,
He kindled a fire and milked his glorious flocks,
All in due order, and set each young one to his mother.
And when he had hurried at tending to all his tasks,
He again snatched two men together and made them his meal. . . .
With a great whistling, the Cyclops turned his fat flock
To the mountain. I was left deeply devising evil,
If I might somehow avenge me and Athene give me glory.
And this seemed to me in my heart to be the best plan.
In the fold a great club of the Cyclops was lying,
A green one of olive wood." (IX. 307-11; 315-20).

Fully absorbed in his morning chores, Polyphemos sows order, arrangement and a certain measure in his actions as he arranges his food sources. But these virtues are in the service of one end: to satisfy his appetites. He then turns on the men Odysseus leads and devours two of them, then rolls the stone from his cave and drives the flocks to the mountains to graze. The men, like the flocks, are left as captive to the Cyclops' appetites. In time he will consume many men, promising Odysseus to leave him for last, as a generous gesture of the host, in a distorted version of hospitality. Now Odysseus smolders for vengeance, prays to Athene, in seeking glory *(kleos)* and renown. He carries his own appetites forward and is forced into a distorted version of the proper guest in a world of distorted values.

Held hostage by another's power or by an idea, an impulse, appetite or addiction, both demeans and debilitates us. We seek release from such strains against the time it often takes to be unknotted from such caves of banishment. Enslavement can assume a variety of formats, from self-incarceration because of habits of thoughts and behavior, to economic imprisonment, spiritual goals and patterns of suffering. Restraining all drives for quick fixes may be the first step to healing. Turning to our faith and our image of God for help and solace may also encourage liberation from self-absorption. So too can reflecting on our condition rather than reacting to it in haste can open a space for a solution we had not considered to emerge in the cave of our captivity.

Meditation:

To what or whom do you surrender in times of feeling entrapped, perhaps in the cave of your own excessive thoughts and yearnings?

May 17: Book IX

"I took it at once and brought it to a glow in the blazing fire;
Then I hid it well, placing it under the dung
Which was strewn through the cave in great abundant heaps.
Then I ordered the others to cast lots for a choice
Of the one who would dare to raise the pole along with me
And bore it in his eye when sweet sleep had come upon him. . . .
'Here Cyclops, drink wine, now you have eaten human flesh,
So you may see what sort of wine this is that our ship contained.
I brought it for libation to you that you might pity me
And send me home. Your rage may be borne no longer'" (IX. 328-33; 347-50).

After devising his plan to wound the giant and escape with his men, Odysseus sets out to craft it into action as the man of many turns and devices. From the huge olive pole Odysseus "cuts off a piece the size of a cubit" (l. 325) and has his men plane it. Now he heats it in the large fire, then hides it under the animal waste strewn in abundance across the filthy floor. Chance chooses the man who will risk more in afflicting the Cyclops' eye, blinding him. First deeds, now words. First concealing, then revealing. Odysseus persuades the enormous appetite before through distorting the laws of hospitality as guest; the wine is a gift he has brought to please his grotesque host. The guest-host relationship is turned upside down, parodying itself, reminding us of those scenes of the suitors who through their bellies abuse the guest-host relation.

Deceit, guile, *metis,* cleverness, concealment all have a place in life's journey, especially when it points out to us that not all people are playing by the same rules. Force or might alone is often not sufficient for survival. Something else is needed when one's life is at stake: imagination and physical resistance are potent allies and, if need be, a weapon that may insure survival. Plot and craft may enrich one's pool of possibilities. Cleverness can be a virtue, its execution a source of delight in story and in lived situations. Knowing when to remain hidden, and when to emerge or even burst into the open is a sign of wisdom. Finally, Odysseus shows us that one can in a difficult situation, use the shit that we are surrounded by as part of the solution. An excremental imagination may be what allows us to survive.

Meditation

When has a contrivance or clever solution helped you in a difficult or frustrating situation? Was the solution remembered from the past or created in the moment?

May 18: Book IX

"Thrice I brought it and gave it, thrice he thoughtlessly drank.
And when the wine had overcome the mind of the Cyclops,
At that point I addressed him with soothing words:
'Cyclops, do you ask me my famous name? Well, I
Will tell you. Then give me the gift you promised.
Noman is my name. Noman do they call me,
My mother and my father and all my companions.
So I said, and he answered at once in his pitiless spirit:
'Noman I shall eat last among his companions
And the others first. This will be my guest gift to you'" (IX. 361-70).

The guest-host relation is further exaggerated and distorted when Odysseus bends this civilizing relation to his will and outer conditions. Offering the Cyclops one cup of this strong inebriate is proper for a guest; three cups is excessive, but it is what is called for in this scene of distorted measure. Odysseus' "soothing words," companions to the sweet strong wine, have their intended effects. Odysseus also continues the deception by renaming himself, a revealing that is simultaneously a concealing, as are now all his words. Noman, nobody, no name are appellations that deceive, words that fictionalize him further and protect him from excess. Inebriated, the Cyclops' gestures comically in exaggeration that this nobody will be his final meal, a gift in the exchange, after all the men have been devoured. In matters of excess, language itself becomes twisted and gnarled.

Playing along, seeming to be courteous and part of the flow, yielding to superior forces, are all ruses to disarm the powerful through crafted words that conceal true motives; thus brute force is restrained, arrested, made more malleable, even impotent, temporarily. Having a clear intention and goal are essential in a well-crafted plot: craft in words and craft in behavior must be in accord if the hidden plot is to be realized. Craft can lead to restraint over forces that spill from its boundaries. Words can conceal and they can congeal one's purposes without the audience of them having any mindfulness of true intentions. Further, telling our story recreates ourselves in a fictional memory, part mythos, part logos. We create ourselves anew *now* by recollecting the self we were *then*.

Meditation:

Recall when you perfectly executed a well-constructed plot. What was your intention(s) in doing so? What did you fictionalize for effect?

May 19: Book IX

> "And some god breathed great courage into them.
> They lifted the olive pole that was sharp at its tip
> And thrust it in his eye; I myself, leaning on it from above,
> Twirled it around as a man would drill the wood of a ship
> With an auger, and others would keep spinning with a strap beneath,
> Holding it at either end, and the auger keeps on going.
> So we held the fire-sharpened pole in his eye
> And twirled it. The blood flowed around it, hot as it was.
> The fire singed his eyebrows and eyelids all around
> From the burning eye" (IX. 381-90).

Odysseus describes a horrific scene in great detail to render the violence vivid and felt in the gut of the Phaeacians and in ours. The wandering warrior wants to tell a good, engaging and mesmerizing story. He uses a simile from a ship's construction or repair to enhance the horror. We remember that Odysseus is recollecting this gruesome scene, one of his own devices; his memory is fashioning this past event into a coherent shared form to be ingested by his Phaeacian audience, who must be spell-bound by its fantastic brutality. As a people they know nothing about war or strife in the world. Odysseus is both the inventor of violence to disarm Polyphemos as well as the craftsman of the story to render it with great effect and to engender in his audience a sense of wonder. He is the consummate craftsman: a builder, a shaper, a story-teller; it may be the first time he has shaped this event from the past into a formed experience to be shared.

What, we may ask, is the benefit of such a recollection in our own past, when we give shape and form to a horrific experience? What does it serve? Giving language to past events that may have pushed us far beyond our boundaries of familiarity and cast us into violent behavior, may need this moment of recollection to reconcile a segment of our traumatic past. Edward Tick working with veterans, relates how "witnessing allows suffering to come home" (*Warrior's Return* 233) Giving meaning is a form of homecoming in itself (234). Telling creates identity.

Meditation:

Recall when simply relating openly and vividly our past, especially a painful past event to others, gave some relief from its haunting presence.

May 20: Book IX

"'Polyphemos, how is it you are hurt so much as to shout so
Through the ambrosial night and to make us sleepless?
No mortal drives your flocks against your will, does he?
And no one is murdering you by craft or by force?'. . . .
And they answered him and addressed him with winged words:
'If no one is compelling you when you are alone,
There is no way to escape a sickness from great Zeus.
Come now and pray to our father Lord Poseidon.'
So they said and went away; and my own heart laughed
At how my name had deceived him, and my faultless device" (IX. 403-06; 409-14).

Duped first by Odysseus' false naming of himself, and then by having his eye burned out of his head, Polyphemos calls on the other Cyclopes to save him from "Noman." Odysseus' name means somebody and nobody at once. So the Cyclops claims to be suffering from someone and no one. The paradox is too much for the other Cyclopes so they advise Polyphemos to stop howling in pain and to pray to their father, Poseidon for solace. What he complains to them about is both true and untrue at the same moment; he is victim of Odysseus' *metis,* or craftiness and Odysseus is quick to boast to his audience of how clever he is. He would seem to suffer his own form of excess and arrogance in this moment; he has successfully used words to both reveal and conceal himself and his actions.

Ancient Greeks believed in the magic power of the name, of naming and of calling on the name of a god (*The Therapy of the Word in Classical Antiquity,* fn. 24, 50). Names can enchant, provoke, deceive, identify and charm, as Lain Entralgo furthers this power of naming. Our names and our words can deceive to create an illusion of a reality. Interpretation and meaning-making are part of the craft of words as well as their latent force. Confusion, not clarity, can easily be the effects of our words, which we may or may not discover in time. Crafted words may also consciously deceive others to bring about a desired reality that may have a tenuous relation with the facts. Words and their power remains one of the *Odyssey's* major themes, both in storytelling and in oath-taking.

Meditation:

When have you found it necessary to create an illusion through words? What were its consequences?

May 21: Book IX

"I held on relentlessly with an enduring heart.
So then, lamenting, we awaited the godly dawn.
And when the early-born, rosy-fingered dawn appeared,
At that moment he drove the male flocks to pasture,
And the females were bleating unmilked around the pens.
Their udders were swollen. And then the master, afflicted
By bad pains, felt over the backs of the sheep
As they stood erect. And the fool did not perceive
How the men were bound under the breasts of the thick-fleeced sheep" (IX. 435-43).

Once again, Odysseus practices his craft and cunning in tricking Polyphemos to roll the large stone from the mouth of the cave to let his flocks out but keep Odysseus and his men confined. Their leader conceals each man between the sheep and positions himself under the belly of the ram, the last to leave the cave. He tells us earlier that to secure himself against the animal's belly "my hand twisted in his marvelous wool/I held on relentlessly with an enduring heart" (ll. 434-35). Afflicted and now blind, the Cyclops feels each animal for a man riding it, but fails to check the gap between each pair, where Odysseus' men reside. Odysseus plays off of the limited perception of his enemy while exposing his own inflation. The origins of this story of one who comes on a monster "guarding a group of animals, and manages to escape by clinging to the animals—emerged more than twenty thousand years ago during the Paleolithic period," writes Ferris Jabr ("The Story of Storytelling" 38). Odysseus' own myth is crafted in this scene.

Being tricky, wily, and clever are all part of our advantage as individuals. There exists a delight in trickery and craftiness, of being a craftsman of our narratives in revealing such qualities as equally important; our myth resides in the folds of the plot we construct. A personal myth, in Dan P. McAdams' words, is a "special kind of story that each of us naturally constructs to bring together the different parts of ourselves and our lives into a purposeful and convincing whole" (*The Stories We Live By* 12). We construct our lives' coherence through narratives that we choose, organize and express to ourselves and others. Our stories create a reality, even if fictional in parts, that can lead its listeners to their own narratives.

Meditation:

Have you crafted a story to create a particular effect in your audience?

May 22: Book IX

"And when I was as far off as a man's shouts would carry,
I addressed the Cyclops myself with taunting speeches:
'Cyclops, you were not destined to eat in your hollow cave,
For your powerful might, the companions of a strengthless man'. . . .
When we had crossed twice as much water and were far away,
Then I would have shouted to the Cyclops, but my companions around me
From all sides tried to restrain me with soothing speeches:
'You wretch, why did you want to provoke the wild man,
Who even now, when he threw his missile into the ocean,
Has brought the ship back to land? And we really thought we would die there'" (IX. 473-76; 491-96).

Arrogance, coupled with excess, overcome Odysseus' appetite for fame in his ridiculing the now-wounded Cyclops. Polyphemos is his double as both engage in thoughtless, excessive behavior that turns against them both. Lack of restraint is what Odysseus confesses to in the narrative, which is also an admittance of his weakness, now reflected upon through the narrative. Rash and out of control, not unlike Polyphemos' weaknesses writ large, he endangers all his men and the ships because of his self-centered impulse for fame; he succumbs totally to his appetite for revenge and *kleos*. His men constrain him, but only briefly, for Odysseus' appetite is as big as his rivals in this moment. His boasting returns the ships back to the island. He spurns "soothing speeches" from his men; his appetite is beyond persuasive language and the restraining qualities of Athene. He is Polyphemos.

Recklessness is always possible in all our thoughts, emotions and behaviors. Thought, reason, moderation, restraint, keeping one's focus on one's intentions—all are signs of maturing into our own imperfections and our own authentic identity. When Athene's force and presence abandon us, and when the trauma of war or other violent conflicts fester in us, we may lose restraint and bring about further violence, feeding the flames of our injuries and need for retribution. The *Odyssey* is a prolonged poetic meditation on the conflict in us between restraint and recklessness. Interpreting both working in us is a lifetime project. Like one's personal myth, our life is a series of patterns we reinforce and revise when needed.

Meditation:

Recall when recklessness took over your life and what you were able to call upon to bring yourself back into a more moderate disposition.

May 23: Book IX

"So they said, but they did not sway my great-hearted spirit.
But in my angry spirit I answered him back:
'Cyclops, if someone among mortal men should inquire
Of you about the unseemly blindness in your eye,
Say that Odysseus, sacker of cities, blinded it;
The son of Laertes, whose home is in Ithaca.'
So I said. He moaned and answered me with a tale:
'Well, then, the decrees uttered of old have come upon me. . . .
And now, a man small and worthless and feeble
Has blinded my eye when he overcame me with wine.
Come here now, Odysseus, so I may present you with gifts, . . .'" (IX. 500-07; 515-17).

Through his unchecked anger and boasting, as well as his monstrous pride, Odysseus becomes a perfect mirror of the Cyclops he battles, matching him appetite for appetite. Excess, absence of restraint, fully self-absorbed, and with an eager appetite for fame from such a primitive presence he fights with, he leaves all wisdom of concealing who he is and all but gives Polyphemos his street address and zip code. He has offered the Cyclops knowledge that, had it remained concealed, would have deflected the wrath of Poseidon on him and his men. Now the Cyclops knows Odysseus as the figure in the prophecy that preceded this meeting. But the cost is Odysseus' jeopardizing him and his men's successful voyage home at the same time it prepares Odysseus partially to confront the suitors, who are themselves images of the Cyclops' appetites.

Prudence is a word woefully out of use today. Making all transparent, confessing everything, exposing all corners of one's life, is now a national malady promoted by all forms of media. Lost is the virtue of privacy, of not letting everything seep out of us. Keeping certain items of one's life to oneself is a virtue. Not gushing indiscriminately on to another is practiced less often. Not bragging, leaving certain facts, even secrets concealed, can often serve us much more effectively than continually revealing all to gain greater attention.

Meditation:

When have you let certain information leak out of you to make a certain impression, but in hindsight you realized soon after might have been best kept to yourself?

May 24: Book IX

"But my well-grieved companions chose the ram especially
For me alone, when the flocks were divided. On the strand
We slew it and burned the thighs to black-clouded Zeus,
The son of Cronos, who rules all. But he received not the rites;
Instead he kept on plotting how all the well-timbered ships
And the companions faithful to me might be destroyed.
So then the whole day till the setting of the sun
We sat dining on endless meat and sweet wine. . . .
Then we sailed further on, grieving in our hearts,
Glad to escape death, having lost our dear companions" (IX. 550-57; 565-66).

Odysseus and his warrior shipmates have returned to shore after boasting to the Cyclops from the sea. His men have been grieving, waiting to be led by their commander, who now divides Polyphemos' cattle so each receives an equal share. The men agree to give the ram, who Odysseus used to escape the cave, to him. They slay the ram and feast on him as they offer the thighs to Zeus in sacrifice. But the god rejects their offering now, as he will do so again on another island, that of Helios, god of the sun. Both Zeus and his brother Poseidon plot the destruction of everything that Odysseus is carrying to Ithaca, including all the ships. Zeus' intention is to have Odysseus return home with no spoils from the war or acquired in its aftermath. Whittling away his men and possessions has begun.

To have a divinity turn against one is a serious matter. We may feel it as "nothing seems to go right" or "I feel cursed by bad luck" that express some deep sense of having angered or wounded whatever force in the world has turned on us. "I can't seem to catch a break" also witnesses whatever we try to achieve as a failure. It can lead us to depression and despair. Maybe that is its intention: to lead us to a place of surrender because our goals are not right for us. Yielding may be offering us an alternative. Perhaps we are battling our own mythic journey by pulling us from our true path on to one we are not destined to follow. McAdams suggests that "when we comprehend our actions over time, we see what we do in terms of a story. We see obstacles confronted, and intentions realized and frustrated over time" (*The Stories We Live By* 30).

Meditation:

Think of a time where yielding rather than pushing against resistance opened something up for you, showing you another option you had not considered.

May 25: Book X

"Then we came to the island of Aeolia, where dwelt
Aeolos, Hippotas' son, who is dear to the immortal gods,
On a floating island. . . .
A whole month he befriended me and asked in detail
About Ilion, the Argives' ships, and the Achaians' return,
And I told him everything in due order.
But when I inquired about the way and asked him
To send us, he did not refuse, and he made a conveyance.
He gave me the skin of a nine-year-old ox he had flayed
And in it he had bound the courses of the blustering winds.
For the son of Cronos had made him steward of the winds, . . ." (X. 1-3; 14-21).

Odysseus continues to reconstruct himself through his narrative. Each habitation he and his men sail to offers another example of home and its distortion or a peculiar idealization. The island of Aeoloia actually floats. Ruling it is Aeolus, lord of the winds; his world is one of motion, not stillness. He befriends Odysseus and his men and shows them generous hospitality, replete with gift-giving in the form of a sack of winds, which, if used in moderation, will take him and his men home. Restraint is key to the proper use of this marvelous gift. It is up to Odysseus' wise and consistent leadership and his men following his commands concerning this prized gift that will ensure their arrival to the fatherland. Order and measure are the ways home.

Gift-giving is part of the guest-host ritual. What a treasure to receive what is needed to complete one's journey! Such generosity can be honored by using the gift wisely. Any assurance in our lives when we find ourselves blown off course is to be respected and used proportionately. Aided by others in difficult times, we may find ourselves a recipient of a gift that helps us on our journey. Joseph Campbell writes that "the boon is simply a symbol of life energy stepped down to the requirements of a certain specific case" (*Hero* 189). Prudence in its use may be the highest mark of gratitude, which may or may not be shared with the gift-giver. A gift seems by its nature to be something given without regard for attaching any strings to it. Gift-giving is another civilized way of cementing community.

Meditation:

Have you received a gift or given a gift that aided you or another on one's life's path? What was it and how did you use or perhaps abuse it?

May 26: Book X

"Then he set a breeze of the West Wind blowing for me
That would carry the ship and the men onward. He was not
Destined to complete it. We were lost by our own foolishness.
Nine days we sailed alike by night and by day;
On the tenth the soil of our fatherland already appeared,
And we were close enough to see men tending the fire.
Then sweet sleep came upon me in my weariness,
For I always saw to the ship's sheets, and did not give it
To another companion, so we might reach the fatherland quicker.
But my companions addressed one another with speeches
And said that I was bringing gold and silver home
As gifts from Aeolos, the great-hearted son of Hippotas" (X. 25-36).

Odysseus' urge to sleep, to be overcome by fatigue, could not have descended on him at a worse time when he is on the cusp of achieving his goal. In retrospect, when he sails in imagination back to this event now told, he sees its foolishness. He checks out, leaving the warriors to their own devices of excess and suspicion. With their leader gone, the one who kept them in check and on course, the men's appetites and fantasies of being cheated take command. Their appetites are aroused in proportion to Odysseus' growing desire to sleep. It is a moment of self-defeating indulgence. Their leader conspires against himself by slipping into unconsciousness and choosing not to share his knowledge of the bag's content with his men; his miscalculation stretches his journey nine more years, as W.B. Stanford reveals (*The Ulysses Theme* 23-24).

Any of our lives, seemingly ordered, arranged and reasonable, is in constant tension with appetites, selfish desires, concerns of getting one's share in life—all of which can dismast even the sturdiest of ships. When leadership, even just of one's own appetites, through destructive behavior, exhaustion or indifference, relaxes for a moment, the baser elements of our lives squeeze to the surface, demanding satisfaction. Norman Fischer writes that "when the fatigue of inner spiritual conflict grows deep enough, we fall asleep" (*Sailing Home* 115). We say for instance, "I let my guard down for just a moment."

Meditation:

When have your own appetites, even indiscretions in thought or action, tyrannized your sense of order, right thinking and behavior? How did you reclaim them?

May 27: Book X

"'Now Aeolos has given him these things as a favor
In friendship. Come, let us see quickly what they are,
How much there is of gold and silver in the skin.'
So they said, and evil advice won my companions over.
They undid the skin, and the winds all rushed out.
At once a storm seized them and bore them onto the ocean,
Far away from our fatherland, weeping. And I,
As I awoke, wondered in my own blameless heart
Whether I should drop from the ship and perish in the ocean
Or endure silently and stay among the living still" (X. 43-52).

Absent their leader, the force or presence that keeps their appetites in check, the men grow curious, motivated by desire and envy, to see what their commander may be withholding from them. Their fantasies of what is in the skin bag incite foolish thoughts and behavior as they throw mindfulness overboard. Like their appetites, the winds are beneficial when unloosed slowly, in moderation. But in excess they can destroy, dismantle and dissolve order into chaos. Almost home, they lose sight both of their goal and their purpose for momentary pleasure. Odysseus in turn calls his own role blameless for falling asleep; it is a weak excuse because his own foolishness instigated his crews' recklessness. His failure to endure sets the occasion for destruction. His despondency in the last two lines brings him to contemplate "what amounted to suicide" (*The Ulysses Theme* 23).

The *Odyssey* is interested in exploring the qualities of a wise leader and warrior. When any of us is in a position of leadership, we cannot put our own needs first; some larger purpose must guide us. Our wishes and impulses must be muted under the banner of a greater good. The consequences for putting one's own necessities first is that the helm is abandoned, either in an individual life or in a nation's future. What we are responsible for strays off course, inviting loss of control and harm. An authentic leader cannot put one's guard down. Recovering from war or strife of any kind, can leave one exhausted. "War is a beast," writes Edward Tick, and it "dwells in the human heart and soul. Under proper conditions it possesses us until it or we are spent" (*Warrior's Return* 58).

Meditation:

In any form of leadership position or command, even one's own life, what were you forced to overcome or override for a greater good for yourself and others?

May 28: Book X

"The ships were borne in a bad storm of wind
Back to the island Aeolia, and my companions groaned. . . .
I took a herald and a companion along with me
To the famous halls of Aeolos. And I found him
Having a meal along with his wife and his children.
When we came to the hall we sat beside the columns
On the threshold. They wondered in their hearts, and asked
Right out: 'How have you come, Odysseus? What evil god has attacked you?
We did send you off kindly, so that you might reach
Fatherland and home and whatever is dear to you. . . .
Go quickly from the island, most shameful of living men'" (X. 54-55; 59-66; 72).

The consequences of Odysseus falling asleep and his crew behaving with no boundaries or trust in their leader have been disastrous. When they return to seek further hospitality, in excess of the code defining guest and host, he insults the very core of civilized protocol. He takes no responsibility but pleads with King Aeolos to once again supply them, as would a gracious host in ordinary circumstances, but this is a distortion of the guest's code. The king will have none of it; excessive behavior by Odysseus and his men have polluted the gift of hospitality. Aeolos now fears Odysseus, who he believes "is despised by the blessed gods" (l. 74). He banishes them all and they leave "groaning from his halls" (l . 76).

Glenn Arbery writes that "for Odysseus, returning home is precisely what defines him" (("The *Iliad* and the *Odyssey*" 31).Taking advantage of hospitality by misusing the largesse of others is a violation of restraint, appetite and the guest-host relationship, which is a sacred bond between those in need and those who have the wherewithal to satisfy them. Twisting a code of civilized life into a form of greedy acquisition as a consequence of poor choices weakens the fabric of civilization itself. One becomes another form of a cyclopean way of life, lacking all piety and respect for the code that sustains life and generosity. One of the virtues of the guest-host relationship is that it puts a level of moderation on the needs of both in the form of unwritten, but assumed oaths.

Meditation:

Have you been violated by someone who took advantage of your generosity and/or abused a gift or help you offered? Even more, have you been inhospitable to yourself?

May 29: Book X

"Six days did we sail alike by night and by day.
And on the seventh we came to Lamos' sheer citadel,
Lestrygonian Telepylos, where a shepherd driving in the flock
May call to a shepherd, and the one driving out answers. . . .
When they entered the glorious hall, they found his wife
As big as the crest of a mountain, and they loathed her.
Right away she called renowned Antiphates from assembly,
Her husband, who planned a woeful destruction for the men. . . .
From the cliffs they threw boulders the size of a man's load.
And at once an evil din rose up among the ships
Of men being destroyed and ships being crushed together" (X. 80-83; 112-15; 121-23).

Strife and suffering continue to invade the lives of Odysseus and his men. Having missed an opportunity to arrive home, they are fated to suffer more and wander farther because of mindless appetites. They are blown to the island of "savage giants" ruled by King Lamos (Albert Cook, footnote 2, 131). More civilized than the Cyclopes, they are none-the-less savage and devouring, like war itself, absent the glory of heroes. This distortion of home is closer to the avenging realm of suitors Odysseus will confront at home, so in one sense the Lestrygonians are his home in temperament and evil devising. Odysseus continues to put his story together, a way of reordering his own personal myth, which has been shattered by war. His journey home is at first filled with distortions, grotesque giants and savage presences. These images of his myth signal the first step in reintegrating who and what he is. Remembering these grotesque images is a crucial step towards healing from combat as the Phaeacians offer him an entranced audience.

How is any of us equipped to encounter savagery and survive it? Millions of people today confront, flee from and pray to survive with their families, the wild savagery unleashed on them. Their stories relate levels of loss and suffering that seem impossible to endure as they are driven from their homes and country. How might we reflect on these devouring forces in human life that can leave us feeling helpless and hopeless? How might we help them shape their stories to heal?

Meditation:

Recall telling others of a horrendous event in your life that left you traumatized. Did languaging the experience begin healing for you?

May 30: Book X

"To my joy my own ship escaped from the overhanging rocks
Onto the ocean. But the others were lost there all together.
From there we sailed further on, grieving in our hearts,
Glad to escape death, having lost our dear companions.
We came to the island of Aiaia. There did dwell
Fair-braided Circe, dread god with a singing voice,
The blood sister of destructive-minded Aietes.
They were both descended from the sun who gives light to mortals. . . .
There we put in silently to land on the shore with the ship
Into a sheltered harbor, and some god guided us" (X. 131-38; 140-41).

Odysseus has suffered a continuous dismantling of men and ships at most dwellings he has encountered; now only his ship and warriors are left when they land on Circe's island. Their grief does not abate even amidst the joy Odysseus senses for having survived the slaughter by the Lestrygonians. David Wood writes that "coming together as they do, these emotions of grief, sorrow, shame, guilt, and loss endure as a powerful moral injury" (*What Have We Done?* 135) Now they encounter another feminine goddess who can aid them given the right circumstances: a right ordering of the guest-host relationship. Odysseus continues to praise the divine realm, and most likely Athene's presence, which has guided them to this next challenge and station. Their fate, he has accepted, is in the hands of powers well beyond him and his prowess; some plan is unfurling with each encounter as he struggles to unite the shattered parts of himself back into a coherent story.

On our own journey we land on various islands, then remember and relate them in story, which can begin to reveal a pattern, a core myth, one which defines us most uniquely (*The Stories We Live By* 20) as Dan McAdams writes. Our suffering is not meaningless but at times dreadful forms of opportunities for knowing ourselves, and becoming more conscious. We begin to recognize some of the central patterns of our plot, our myth, which contributes to our seeing more deeply the meaning, value and uniqueness of our lives. Our suffering encourages our awakening; our task is to reflect on the narrative that best expresses it.

Meditation:

Can you describe one pattern in your life that may have surfaced through your experiences of suffering and grieving?

May 31: Book X

"In the glen they found the hall of Circe, constructed
Out of polished stone in a place with a view all around.
About her were wolves of the mountains and also lions
That she had charmed herself when she gave them evil drugs. . . .
So did the wolves with powerful claws and the lions
Fawn about them. They were afraid when they saw the dread creatures.
So they stood in the forecourt of the fair-braided goddess
And they heard Circe singing in a lovely voice within
As she went to and fro at a great immortal web such as are
The works of goddesses, fine woven, pleasing, and bright" (X. 210-13; 218-23).

Circe's elegant home is another version of Odysseus' in Ithaca. Living alone, Circe lives close to the natural order, yet her home is of polished stone, aesthetically attractive. She, like Penelope, Arete and Calypso, weave on a loom a work of art. Her domicile is filled with wild beasts who have been drugged by her potions and have lost their wildness. She is an enchantress who affects the nature of things, transforming them. Circe is also an artist of many strategies whose vision "all around" reminds us of Penelope's name and meaning—one who sees all around. Joseph Campbell calls her "the temptress, the seductress; she is the one who leads the hero beyond bounds" (*Goddesses* 166). Odysseus' men appear dumbstruck by both her and her animals, who terrify them. Her weaving is a rich metaphor for the way she can entice and weave her powers to arrest one's nature.

Such a rich texture has Circe's world: artifice, nature, beasts, aesthetics are all present as she sings and weaves. She could be very disarming, yet the wild creatures she enjoys as house pets keep the crew alert and feeling threatened. How to interpret such a rich mixture of the natural and artificial worlds? She seduces by her singing and lulls those who enter into enchantment and restraint or constriction. As an archetype she is capable of intense seduction; we have all heard her song at one time or another when we have been seduced by the song of life that conceals a transforming potion, or entangles us in a webbing hard to escape, so powerful and seductive are its threads. Yet she is also a guide, so one should not dismiss her.

Meditation:

Recall when you were enchanted and threatened by a new situation or person that you had no ready response for. What webbing encircled you and/or what song disarmed you? Was the end result helpful for your own journey?

June 1: Book X

> "And she stirred into the food
> Woeful days that make one forget his fatherland wholly.
> But when she had given it and they had drunk, she at once
> Struck them with her wand and shut them up into sties.
> They had the heads of swine and the voice and the hair
> And the body, but the mind was sturdy as before. . . .
> Eurylochos came back at once to the swift black ship
> To tell the news of his companions and their harsh fate.
> He was not able to speak, though he wanted to, . . ." (X. 235-40; 244-46).

Like a fairy tale, Circe drugs her new house guests immediately to send them into forgetfulness. When they are rendered helpless, she transforms them into swine, yet allows them to retain their human minds. Human speech is replaced by the sounds of pigs. The crew member assigned to lead part of his shipmates, Eurylochos, rushes back to the ship to inform Odysseus of their companions' fate. His grief is so keen that, like the swine-men, he loses language in his grieving. He is overwhelmed as he seeks out Odysseus to report their condition. The captive men's plight is in sharp contrast to the suitors in Ithaca: they maintain their bodily form but their minds have become excessive in pursuing appetites.

As readers we study each of Odysseus' and his men's encounters as they wander toward home. Their adventures put them in touch with many varieties of homes and domiciles, each of which shape their imaginations anew and may even serve them when they arrive home. These various homecomings educate their minds to ponder so many different iterations of danger or abuse their homes may be enduring. But Odysseus will be the only survivor. C.G. Jung comments in *The Red Book*: "What would Odysseus have been without his wandering?" (*The Red Book, Reader's Edition,* footnote 176, 182). These varieties of home shape and form him in new ways from chaos to cosmos. We can also ask what each of us would have been without our own wanderings, false homecomings, seductions, threats, detours, most of which we were not prepared for. What have events we anticipated and integrated added to the core person we are today because these events encouraged or coerced us into reformatting the myth we have been living?

Meditation:

Think of one or two incidents in your life that you sense were most formative and/or transformative in your development. Could they have been prepared for?

June 2: Book X

"And when I was about to go through the sacred glen
To come to the great house of Circe of the many drugs,
Hermes of the golden wand came across my path
As I was going to the house, resembling a young man
With his first beard, at the most pleasing time of youth.. . . .
'Where are you going, alone through the hills, hapless man,
Ignorant of the place? These companions of yours are confined
In Circe's house as swine, and keep to their dense lairs.
Are you going to free them? I do not think
You will return yourself, but will stay where the others are'" (X. 275-79; 281-85).

The gods intervene on behalf of Odysseus throughout the epic; this time Hermes, the god of language, interpretation, messenger from Olympos to mortals, and guide of souls to the underworld, steps in to aid the epic hero. The youthful-appearing god, who will instruct Calypso to release him from seven years of captivity, intervenes to save him and his men from Circe's powers. We recall that Odysseus' narrative to the Phaeacians is a retrospective, so what we learned earlier of his time with Calypso as well as his freedom from her, has yet to happen in his narrative but has already happened in historical time. He tells his story in hindsight with the knowledge gained from his adventures up to landing on Scheria. Only with the help of this god can Odysseus hope to liberate his men from Circe's desires, both transforming them bodily and returning to them their memories.

We tell our stories in hindsight and in so doing include the knowledge we learned going forward in "narrative time" as a form of "historical time." We tell our stories in hindsight to gain foresight in the forward thrust of our personal plot. With such a temporal perspective we in truth tell our stories both forward and backward in and through time present. So we engage the temporal dimensions of past-present and past-future. Our life wisdom accrues from this triple journeying through all three of these narrative/historical time zones. Paul Eakin suggests that "the self I am remembering the self I was, collaborate in the making of a fictional self. . . . I cannot separate out knowledge of myself from the practice of language" (*How Our Lives Become Stories* x).

Meditation:

Describe one discovery you have made in telling a part of your life story. Has it continued to bear out a core element of your myth?

June 3: Book X

"'Well, I will release you from evil and rescue you.
Here, take this excellent drug to the halls of Circe
And enter; so it may ward off from your head the evil day.
I shall tell you all of Circe's pernicious wiles.
She will make you a mixture and drop drugs into the food.
But she will not be able to charm you so. The excellent drug
I shall give you will not permit it. I will tell you the details.
At the moment when Circe hits you with her very long wand,
Draw your sharp sword at once from along your thigh
And rush upon her as if intending to kill her.
She will be afraid of you and ask you to go to bed'" (X. 286-96).

Hermes is the instructor as well as the messenger. He offers a prophecy of the future as well as strategies for creating antibodies to Circe's potions. She changes consciousness through their use. Moly is the root that will deflect Circe's potent elixirs and aid Odysseus' travels home. Hermes' strategy is to restore order to chaos. He is also testing Odysseus' will to follow instructions, to yield to the divine other, and to restrain his own wily nature. His name, *Hermaion,* Antoine Feivre informs us, means "'fallen fruit' or 'windfall'" (*The Eternal Hermes* 14). He knows what future will unfold if the god's words are followed precisely. Odysseus is free to accept or reject his instructions as part of his training to arrive home intact, if alone. He is a windfall to Odysseus when he needs it the most.

No one, it seems, ever reaches beyond gaining from the instructions of others. One is most vulnerable when one thinks s/he has all the answers. The inability to learn through another's tutoring is a flaw that may turn a person into one's own worst adversary. Yielding to the teachings of another, mortal or immortal, is a sign of wisdom and prudence. Restraining one's habitual pattern of thought and behavior in order to yield to another authority can make the difference between survival and shipwreck. Being able to listen to another point of view, to weigh its merits and then act on what seems most conducive to one's well-being is a learned skill. Said another way, this aid may be the arrival of grace.

Meditation:

When did you instruct another or help them over a crisis? When did you receive instruction or direction that helped you avoid some larger challenge because you listened?

June 4: Book X

"'But order her to swear a great oath by the blessed gods
That she plot no other bad trouble against your person,
Lest when you are naked she make you unmanly and a coward.'
When he had said this, the god, the slayer of Argos, gave me the drug
He had plucked out of the earth, and showed me its nature.
It was black at the root, but its flower was like milk. . . .
She gave a great shout, ran up under and took my knees;
And lamenting to me, she uttered winged words: . . .
'Surely you are the Odysseus of many turns, who,
The gold-wanded slayer of Argos always told me,
Would come on his way out of Troy in a swift black ship" (X. 299-304; 323-24; 330-32).

In a repetition of Odysseus leaving Calypso's island after he has persuaded her to swear an oath not to harm him as he prepares to depart, here Hermes instructs the warrior to extract an oath from Circe that she will not harm him if he stays. His sexuality and his manhood are at stake in this oath. He now has the requisite antibody to her charms and magic. Calypso and Circe are linked here in their desire for Odysseus, and with Circe, who has been expecting him, to furnish a glimpse into Penelope's own delight when she finally realizes the beggar who has entered the household is her husband. As Froma Zeitlin reveals, ". . . every female figure in the poem, including Kalypso, Kirke, Arete and even Nausikaa, contributes some element to the complex and composite portrait of Penelope" ("Figuring Fidelity in Homer's *Odyssey*" 140). The "bad trouble" that Hermes mentions again references Odysseus' name.

We cannot journey through life unassisted and survive, much less flourish. Through grace, chance, fate, guides may appear, often when most needed. We too appear as a guide, mentor, helper, supporter, to others; it is part of each of our destinies to assist others distressed, helpless, confused or needing emotional support, physical care, or simply to listen to their plight. We may be akin to the moly Odysseus receives. Its physical contrast is striking: black at the root with a milk white flower, signifying the richness of its hold in the earth and its bloom.

Meditation:

Recall when your presence in the life of another aided that person in avoiding or muting whatever threatened to turn them into something less than they were.

June 5: Book X

"Then I spoke out to her and uttered winged words:
'Circe, fulfill for me the promise you made,
To send me home; the spirit is eager in me already
And in my other companions, who consume my precious heart
In complaining around me whenever you are absent'. . . .
'Do not stay any longer in my home unwillingly.
Yet you must first achieve another journey and come
To the halls of Hades and dread Persephone,
So you may consult the soul of Theban Tiresias.
The blind prophet in whom there is a steadfast mind'. . . .
So she said, and my own heart was shattered within me" (X. 482-85; 489-93; 496).

After a full year hibernating and incubating with Circe and his men, Odysseus feels put upon to continue his homecoming. Because he assumes there is a direct flight from her island to Ithaca, he is crushed when she outlines another journey he must fulfill before reaching Penelope. This underworld journey is a pilgrimage with his men he cannot avoid. To visit the dead is integral to being among the living; in the underworld, however, is a mentor he must consult who will instruct him about the future, one that will take him home and beyond. He must also visit the shades from his past on this journey to the Phaeacians. In the process of storytelling he picks up and pieces together the shards of his life scattered by war. His heart (*thumos*) aches twice in the above passage as he reassembles his devastated myth.

We cannot know, finally, the full trajectory of our life journey. There will always be present side trips, returns to previous locales, even journeys that are so out-of-keeping with what we expected, so that being open to and accepting what we can neither control nor avoid is our best preparation. To question or to resist is perhaps to rupture our destiny by clinging to control. If we insist on this condition towards all that comes our way, then we may feel our heart splinter repeatedly as we suffer through all that is beyond us. His "narrative framework" (*Stories We Live By* 23) is as important a journey as the lived events of his past and future, writes Dan McAdams.

Meditation:

Relate an unnerving or disruptive voyage that threw you off your familiar path in order to reveal something needed to fulfill your journey. Pay attention to the language you use and what you choose to leave out. Both carry your myth.

June 6: Book XI

"Arriving there, we beached the ship and took out the flocks.
Then we ourselves went along the stream of Oceanus
Until we arrived at the place that Circe had said. . . .
I myself drew my sharp sword from along my thigh,
Dug a pit the size of a cubit on all sides,
And poured a libation about it for all the dead,
First of honey mixture, and then of sweet wine,
And the third one of water; I sprinkled white barley on it.
I besought the feeble heads of the dead for many things, . . ." (XI. 20-22; 24-29).

In this journey within a journey, framed by the narrative voyage he is on presently, resides great complexity. To arrive home, Odysseus and his men must descend to the land of Hades and meet the population of the dead. Odysseus follows Circe's instructions carefully and faithfully in order to arouse the shades of the dead to approach him. Ritual actions are essential to create the proper field so the dead will gather and speak. He honors the dead in this ritual in part by sharing with them the nourishment of the living—a mixture of honey and sweet wine and water—and swears to offer sacrifice to them and to Tiresias when he returns home. At this moment he uses his sword as a shovel to construct a pit for the dead, to resurrect lost lives even as many of his warriors have joined their ranks.

Rituals are important in life circumstances both to memorialize the past in the present and to conjoin what is absent into presence. Rituals themselves are embodied storied actions that aid recollection to enrich the meanings of the present. They sacralize space and impose an order on life's events by adding a sacred quality to what is of value and worthy of recollection. Rituals also bring to conscious awareness what has been forgotten or pushed into the unconscious. Value is bestowed on what is ritualized into a present memory; they bestow value to communal involvement by transforming both time and space into a new narrative. To learn of an individual's or a nation's personal or cultural myth, note what events or situations they ritualize, for these rituals embody a value or values that allow coherence in an individual or cultural life. Note too what is ignored.

Meditation:

In your life currently, what event, person or idea might you create a ritual around so to give it greater value in remembrance?

June 7: Book XI

"Then I took the sheep and cut their throats into the pit.
And the black-clouded blood poured out. And out of Erebos
The souls gathered of the corpses of those who had died,
Brides and bachelors and old men who had suffered much,
And tender maidens whose hearts were fresh in sorrow,
And many who had been wounded by bronze-tipped spears,
Men slain in battle wearing gore-spattered armor,
Many of whom hovered round the pit on every side
With a tremendous shout. And sallow fear seized me" (XI. 35-43).

Within the epic genre it most often happens that the hero must descend into the depths to encounter the dead; they are part of the journey towards wholeness and completeness. Only when Odysseus satisfies the ritual of conjuring the dead by adding blood to the pit's contents do the shades step forward and make themselves heard "with a tremendous shout" (l. 43). Those present have suffered in war, have lost loved ones in battle and grieve for them in Hades. The intensity of suffering in this engagement is fierce and sorrowful. They appear too in the bloody armor they fought and perished wearing. Here the further horrors of war are spread out for Odysseus and his men to witness and grieve over. Jane Ellen Harrison writes that for the ancients, often the animal sacrificed in purification rituals shows "a placation to ghosts or underworld powers" (*Prolegomena* 53). Their experience among the dead underscores war's cost. Odysseus' story gives these souls new life.

Underworld knowing is a special form of becoming aware or awakening more fully to the strange terror of war's relentless, destructive appetite. A journey to the underworld highlights life's experiences seen through the prism of death. Funerals, wakes, celebrations of the Day of the Dead are essential rituals of remembrance because through them we are each reminded of our destiny, both invisible and mysterious surrounding its occasion. Mingling with the dead underscores our own inevitable membership in their tribe. As to storying such experiences, Dan McAdams suggests that "the unfolding drama of life is revealed more by the telling than by the actual events told" (*The Stories We Live By* 28). Remembering and relating such events adds to their meaning and power.

Meditation:

What images do you carry of your own death? What images of the dead still live vibrantly in you?

June 8: Book XI

"Then there came the soul of my mother who had died,
Anticleia, daughter of great-hearted Autolycos,
Whom I had left alive when I went to sacred Ilion.
I wept when I saw her and pitied her in my spirit,
But though I grieved heavily, I did not let her
Get near the blood first till I could learn from Tiresias.
Then the soul of Theban Tiresias came up,
Holding a gold scepter; he knew me and spoke to me:
'Zeus-born son of Laertes, Odysseus of many devices,
Why, hapless man, have you left the light of the sun
And come here to see the dead and a joyless place?'" (XI. 84-94).

In such an experience of the dead, especially with his mother, Odysseus must bracket his grief in order to learn from the blind prophet how he will arrive home and what he will confront there. It pushes Odysseus to his emotional limits. Life struggles with death, origins with the present-future. The underworld has its own manner and matter of knowing. Tiresias arrives to ask him, as he names the warrior, why he has entered Persephone's realm—the feminine-ruled Hades. Odysseus needs the knowledge of the dead in order to continue his life.

Homer's world reveals to us the very thin line separating us from the dead. We are always poised to enter it, whether we desire to or not. James Hillman observes that "entering the underworld" refers to a transition from the material to the psychical point of view. Three dimensions become two as the perspective of nature, flesh, and matter fall away, leaving an existence of immaterial, mirrorlike images, *eidola*. We are in the land of soul" (*The Dream and the Underworld* 51).

The Italian poet Dante creates his entire epic poem, the *Commedia* within the arena of the state of souls after death. They are essential to the fabric of our lives, in part because they remind us that one day each of us will join their ranks, and for another, they have access to dimensions we the living do not. Thomas Lacqueur affirms that both names as well as the dead have "been a primal touchstone of humanity, a practice that defines the border between nature and culture" (*The Work of the Dead* 367).

Meditation:

Offer an illustration of your relationship with the dead. What does your connection to the dead add to the quality of your life?

June 9: Book XI

"'But draw back from the pit and hold back your sharp sword
So I may drink the blood and speak to you unerringly . . . .
You seek a honey-sweet return, noble Odysseus;
A god will make it disastrous for you. I do not think
You will elude the earth-shaker; against you he has laid up a grudge,
In his heart, enraged that you blinded his beloved son.
You may get there yet, even so, though you will suffer ills;
If you are willing to check your spirit and your companions, . . .'" (XI. 95-96; 100-05).

Sage advice from the blind seer is the very knowledge and perspective Odysseus needs to hear for a successful *nostos*. Tiresias points out to him his greatest adversary, a divinity who seeks revenge for his son Polyphemos' wounding. Odysseus cannot arrive home without the turmoil stirred up by the god who will make him suffer. Odysseus has brought this on himself with his recklessness with the Cyclops, followed by falling asleep as he nears his homeland. Poseidon's arena is the shape-shifting, often violent waters of the ocean. Tiresias cautions an attitude of restraint, moderation and measured leadership that includes guiding his men into more moderate waters; only then will they achieve a joyful homecoming. Further excesses will destroy them.

We each must identify those pockets in our life that are adversarial, destructive, malignant and vengeful. It is a part of life we must contend with rather than try to conquer or deflect. We carry something of Poseidon's wrath within us; through some measures he must be befriended and integrated. To be unconscious of our adversary is self-destructive. Often we need the mentoring of Tiresias, our inner voice of wisdom unique to us, to point out the direction that our conflicts and obstacles will emerge from. Integrating both of these powers is essential to our growth. "The primal might of Poseidon," Walter Otto writes, "is suggested by the sons whom myth ascribes to him: they are gigantic, unrestrained manifestations of strength such as . . . Polyphemos, and many others" (*The Homeric Gods* 27). They are figures of strength without mindfulness, so dangerous in their unrestrained power and unpredictable like the ocean.

Meditation:

What occasion identified for you an adversary to contend with? What shift in attitude or behavior allowed you to coexist with that force in you?

June 10: Book XI

"I waited there steadily until my mother
Came up and drank the black-clouded blood. She knew me
At once, and, lamenting, she uttered winged words:
'My child, how have you come down under the murky dusk
While yet alive? This is dangerous for the living to see.
In between us there are great rivers and dread streams,
Oceanos first, that it is not possible to cross
On foot; one must possess a well-made ship. . . .
Have you just got this far in wandering from Troy
A long time with ship and companions? Have you not yet come
To Ithaca and seen the wife within your halls?'" (XI. 152-59; 160-62).

The underworld is a place of new knowledge and old knowledge reclaimed. For the dead to speak, there is a ritual for them to perform before they can voice their intentions. Finding his mother among the dead is a surprise for Odysseus who did not know she had died. She cautions him about the terms of her world. Her speech reveals that she does not know what has happened to her son since leaving the battlefield of Troy; she also questions if he has even arrived home from war. Her knowledge is incomplete. It is a poignant and dramatic moment for each of them as the dead and the living reach out to one another with great affection and concern. We glimpse through this scene some of the beliefs surrounding the world of the dead. For Odysseus it is a moment of return to his origins.

How far from the dead are we? The passage suggests that conversation and communion between us and those who have died is more intimate than we might think. Perhaps the dead, our ancestors, complete our living, offer it further meaning and show us the final home we are all destined to inhabit. Hades, the Underworld is understood as a vessel of history. The dead may be more active in the lives of the living than we have considered. Robert Pogue Harrison believes that " to utter, to repeat the words of the dead is to invite their spiritual presence back into our souls" (*The Dominion of the Dead* 75). Odysseus telling his story of the dead to the Phaeacians brings the underworld to life again, as having its own existence.

Meditation:

Who in the world of the departed do you communicate with? What have you learned from that departed person or persons?

June 11: Book XI

"'Too long that woman in her enduring spirit waits
Within your halls. And the miserable nights
And the days always waste away for her as she sheds tears.
No one else yet holds your fine honor, but Telemachos
Possesses the acres securely, and he dines
On well-shared feasts, whereof it befits a judge to partake. . . .
Nor did sickness come on me, such as especially
With grim wasting away takes the spirit from the limbs.
But longing for you and your counsels, noble Odysseus,
And your kindliness, reft my honey-sweet spirit away'" (XI. 181-86; 200-03).

The underworld knowledge Odysseus receives from his mother is painful but necessary for him to hear. Anticleia tells him of the grieving status of his wife wasting away waiting for his return, and of his son, who seems to be faring better in his travels to seek out his father. He learns too of the conditions that brought on his mother's death—grief for her missing son. His lengthy homecoming killed her. Her memories of him as well as his loss proved too much for her. This underworld knowledge crushes him with grief and with what we can imagine is guilt for taking so long to return from war. In his storytelling, the warrior ritualizes his grief; he brings past suffering to public awareness and in so doing objectivizes the grief over loss that, left unsaid, could destroy him (*Dominion* 57-58).

Such prescient knowledge all of us know, through intuition, a sudden insight, a deep reflection, a word or observation from another, we grasp that something has eluded us. Our level of understanding deepens as a result. We need not travel someplace to gain a Hades-Persephone knowledge. In my own experience pilgrimaging through monasteries and retreat centers for three and a half months, my father, who died one year before, appeared and traveled with me for almost the entire trip. We had conversations about his being a father consumed by his addiction to alcohol and my own patterns of behavior that stemmed from that. I spent a significant part of my journey in the underworld being taught by him (*A Pilgrimage Beyond Belief* 131, 132, 137, 153, 158, 284-87). Only when I wrote this memoir where the dead instructed me did I make peace with my past.

Meditation:

Recall your coming to an awareness of a life situation that was given you from an underworld person's perspective.

June 12: Book XI

"So she spoke. And pondering in my mind, I wished
To take hold of the soul of my mother who had died.
Three times I tried and my spirit bade me to grasp her.
And three times like a shadow or a dream she flew
Out of my hands. Sharp grief grew ever greater in my heart. . . .
So we exchanged words with one another. Women
Came up, and noble Persephone sent them forth,
All of whom were the wives and daughters of excellent men.
They gathered in clusters around the black blood.
And I thought about how I might question each one. . . ." (XI. 204-08; 225-29).

Homer shows us the intimate relation that can occur between the living and the dead. This and other passages reveal how important they are for the living. Working with an upper world understanding of the human body, Odysseus tries to embrace his mother, but the shade is an airy nothing, an *imago* of the soul of the person who appears but is insubstantial. His grief grows in realizing she cannot be embraced. More women gather, guided by Persephone, presumably including the wives and daughters of many warriors killed in battle. Odysseus relates the story of many of them in subsequent pages. His connection to history, to the dead and to the qualities of excellence reveals to him the invaluable service of the dead to the living.

When we consider the enormous population of the dead, we realize there are so many more in the region beyond life than those alive. We gain a much broader and deeper imaginative perspective by acknowledging all those who have taken the journey guaranteed to each of us. They are all our kin, our ancestors, as one day we will become an ancestor to so many we have preceded. Thomas Lacqueur's masterful study of the dead acknowledges "the work they do collectively, about how and why the dead make civilization." We are a species, he goes on, "that not only lives with its dead but also is acutely aware, if not always consciously, of their continued foundational importance" (*The Work of the Dead* 81-82). We seem to need to be connected to the dead, through remembrance, rituals, holidays and celebrations, in which they are resurrected in memory to add to our life's meaning.

Meditation:

Have you been mentored by a shade from the dead? What insight have your contacts or remembrances of specific members of the dead bequeathed to you?

June 13: Book XI

"I cannot tell or mention all of the women
I saw in numbers there, wives and daughters of heroes.
Ambrosial night would wane first. Now it is time
For me to sleep, whether I go to my companions on the swift ship
Or stay here. The convoy will be your concern, and the gods."
So he said. And they all became silent in stillness.
They were held in rapture through the shadowy halls.
Then white-armed Arete began to speak among them:
"Phaeacians, how does this man appear to you to be,
In form and size, and in his mind well-balanced within?
He is my guest, and yet each has a share in the honor" (XI. 328-38).

In the midst of his narrative, as has happened before in the process of his journeys, Odysseus grows weary and wishes to sleep. He then turns over his homecoming to the Phaeacians, as he did with his crew members after leaving Aeolia. He pushes for a pause, a gap in the narrative. His audience is completely enchanted by his story because they sit in silence when he pauses; they hold him in thrall as a persuasive bard. Queen Arete steps in graciously to praise her guest and offer further hospitality by acknowledging his balanced mind; each of her subjects shares in the honor the guest is given as a gift. Is he increasing the appetite of his audience to hear more by pausing? He is wily, a man of many turns; these options are possible, as a serialized story in a magazine or newspaper may be a way to increase audience anticipation for the next installment.

The word "rapture," translated here, is a telling term for the effect Odysseus' narrative has on his audience. They are rapt, arrested, even trapped in wonder; their immediate response is silence, not applause. The verb in Greek is "*thelgo* (charm, enchant) and the noun *thelkterion* . . . are not infrequent in the Homeric epic" (*Therapy of the Word* 61) writes Lain Entralgo. When our story is truly told and well-formed, we share persuasively with others our deepest identity and our most important values. It thus contains our personal myth, a vessel for containing our most important concerns, wishes, and aspirations; it is also "a patterned manner of imagining, a style of being present to the world" (*Riting Myth, Mythic Writing* 10).

Meditation:

When has telling your story publicly created a community with another or others?

June 14: Book XI

"'There is grace in your words, and your thoughts are noble.
As a singer would, you have skillfully told the tale
Of all the Argives' sad troubles and of your own. . . .'
"There is a time for many tales and also a time for sleep.
But if you are still longing to listen, I would not myself
Refuse you in this, to tell other more piteous things,
The cares of my companions who perished afterward, . . .
The soul came of Agamemnon, son of Atreus,
Grieving; and others gathered about who had died
And had met their fate with him in the house of Aigisthos" (XI. 367-69; 379-82; 387-89).

Alcinoos praises the skills of Odysseus as bard and poet in recounting a story that has enraptured all who listen. He underscores that there is a time for storytelling and a time for sleep and that it is not yet time for the latter. There is a protocol in life that is part of a civilized people. He lets it be known that his audience would love for him to continue, in spite of his fatigue. What is tested once more is the endurance of Odysseus, his ability to sustain his narrative as a gift to his hosts. He agrees to continue, putting off his desire for sleep. But he may also be further seducing his audience with tales of wonder to seal his journey home. By pausing in his narrative journey, he guarantees his physical voyage home. Now he moves closer to the Trojan War when Agamemnon, leader of the Argives, approaches, grieving less for the horrors of war than for his ill-fated homecoming. He will suffer immediate death at the hands of Aigisthos and Clytemnestra.

To endure, to persevere, to put one's own desires behind those of others is a sign of a mature, thoughtful and disciplined person. Add to it that this is done by one who is still traumatized by war's effects and the loss it brought about, and one sees another side of the heroic temper. The nature of the heroic is at times simply in continuing when our frailty insists we stop. Being able to restrain one's own needs in service to others is admirable and at times unconditional. Achieving such a state can have rewards impossible to see beforehand. With Odysseus, perhaps being asked to continue his narrative also encourages further healing in the telling.

Meditation:

When were you forced or persuaded to push yourself beyond your normal capacities in words or actions? What were the consequences of your persevering?

June 15: Book XI

"He recognized me at once when he had drunk the black blood.
He wailed piercingly and shed a swelling tear,
Stretching his hands toward me in striving to reach me. . . .
'So never be mild yourself, henceforth, even to your wife.
Reveal to her no entire story that you know well,
But tell a part of it and let the rest be concealed.
But your own death, Odysseus, will not at all be from your wife.
Highly Trustworthy and of good care in her mind
Is Icarios' daughter, the prudent Penelope. . . .
Hold your ship on course secretly, not openly,
To your fatherland. There is no longer any trust in women'" (XI. 390-92; 441-46; 455-56).

Agamemnon's violent death at the hands of his wife Clytemnestra and her lover Aigisthos, a suitor in his household, is the cause of so much suffering in the Greek leader. His lesson: conceal as well as reveal; find a balance so as not to tell your entire story, lest it be used against you later. Restraint is what shapes this mode of behavior. Agamemnon speaks less of Penelope than he does the suitors, or anyone for that matter, that Odysseus does not know or trust. Be more circumspect, Agamemnon warns; be less open and protect yourself with *metis*, craftiness and cunning, not force or might. Agamemnon's bitterness is thick and coats his entire attitude toward women generally, with Penelope singled out as the exception. Odysseus takes his warning to heart; it will serve him when he arrives home.

There is wisdom in not going through life spilling the beans in situations that may use your information as a weapon in the future. Better to be prudent, restraining and retaining what you know. On the other hand, Agamemnon's grief-stricken story underscores what Robert Pogue Harrison suggests: "Grief can destroy one if not ritualized in a public lament. Then it becomes public and symbolic" (*Dominion* 18). A mutual healing may then occur in the above passage. Now one's story takes on another dimension; a healing into insight that can be wisdom for others. Our stories organize the events in our past into coherent experiences.

Meditation:

Recall a time when you told your story of pain or suffering to others. Did it help you accept, integrate or understand more fully the terms of that suffering?

June 16: Book XI

"The soul of Achilles, son of Peleus, came up;
The soul of Patroclos and of excellent Antilochos,
And of Ajax who was the finest in body and form
Of all the Danaans, after the excellent son of Peleus. . . .
 'Achilles,
No man in the past or hereafter is more blessed than you.
When you were alive before, the Argives honored you
Equal to the gods. Now you greatly rule over the dead,
Being here as you are. So do not grieve now you are dead,
Achilles'" . . . (XI. 467-70; 483-87).

The underworld, land of Hades, returns Odysseus to his fallen comrades, among them the bravest and finest in combat. He sees his friend Achilles, having had the best of both worlds: *kleos,* or glory in battle at Troy and now ruler over the enormous population of souls in Hades. This realm has been called "the safe depository of tales, the treasure house of myth" (*Homeric Moments* 203) by Eva Brann. Odysseus encourages his dead friend not to grieve, for he has achieved greatness. But something is missing in his calculation, as he sees the dead from the imagination of the living and not the mind of the dead. His knowledge is narrow and incomplete, which may be why the wise Circe sent him to this realm initially. Like his son Telemachos, he has much to learn before returning home. Hades is a domain of seasoning into a relation to the dead and added wisdom about life.

Our human tendency is to frequently see not the reality of someone's situation or condition for itself, but our fantasy of it, filtered as it is through our own personal myth. We see what appears to be happiness and status experienced by others, without knowledge of the deeper back story that could readily change our perspective. The underworld is a viewpoint and we do not need to physically travel there to enter its mysterious space. Our angle of vision is our via or way of understanding everything. When another's situation looks to us as idyllic, we might want to give it another glance, shift our eyes a bit. One additional piece of information could shift our entire manner of perceiving. Hades is, imaginally, an attitude, a perspective and an occasion for deepening what we know.

Meditation:

Recall when your perspective of another's good fortune was altered when you learned something new about their story that shifted your understanding.

June 17: Book XI

"'Noble Odysseus, do not commend death to me.
I would rather serve on the land of another man
Who had no portion and not a great livelihood
Than to rule over all the shades of those who are dead.
Come now and tell me the story of my noble son,
Did he follow to battle and become a chief or not?
Tell me about blameless Peleus, if you have heard anything;
Does he have honor still with the many Myrmidons,
Or do they show him no honor through Hellas and Phthia
Because old age constrains him in his hands and feet?'" (XI. 488-97).

Achilles offers Odysseus a dramatically different vision of his plight in Hades. He would be happier as a servant or slave working the land, guiding the plow behind oxen, than to rule over the massive population of the dead. Life, he suggests, no matter the lowliness of its station, is far preferable than death. Life in any form is what Achilles would trade his status in Hades for: to be in the land of the living, no matter how low the position. Life itself is what he would treasure. Ruling over the dead rather than serving in life is not the warrior's wish. Odysseus gives the impression that he "knows" the world of the dead. He does not; as Norman Fischer suggests, "We simply don't know what death is, and that that's what it is: the unknowable, the incomprehensible, the beyond-all-reach. This is why it is so terrifying" (*Sailing Home* 130). In Achilles' case, he does not know the present condition of his son, so he asks for a story to inform him.

We easily fabricate not only our own reality but that of others. We see what we often project on to the station of another. The hidden reality may never surface, but when it does we are often surprised, even dumb-founded by what attitude, emotion, or sense of their own condition has been in play in their lives. We continually live in a point of view and that angle is the context through which we process and understand ourselves and others. We can easily wish to trade places with another because we see only what is revealed in outer appearances. Jane Wagner asks: "What is reality anyway? Nothing more than a collective hunch. . . " (qtd. in *The World is Made of Stories* 15).

Meditation:

When might you have been surprised by what others created or manufactured about your life circumstances?

June 18: Book XI

"But first numberless bands of the dead came on
With a tremendous shout, and sallow fear seized me
Lest noble Persephone send the Gorgon head
Of the dread monster from the hall of Hades against me.
At once I went on the ship and called my companions
To board it themselves and to untie the stern cables.
They boarded it at once and sat down at the oarlocks,
And a wave of the stream bore it to the river Oceanos;
First there was rowing and after that a fair breeze" (XI. 632-40).

Odysseus' fear increases as the number of the dead multiplies around him and incites his fear of Persephone turning on him by sending the head of the Gorgon; his exit is then rapid, driven by fear of the dead, especially in such numbers. They all yearn to be heard, to connect once more with the world of the living. With his men he flees to the ships to sail out of the realm where he has met so many from his earlier life. They are his memory in so many ways, including his own birth and his hand in their death. The dead seem to have awakened him to dimensions of his life that were buried with them; they are his memory as well as the history of war's enormous destruction. Homer's description of Hades is terrifying and unifying at once.

Each of us must decide if we have had our own underworld experience, which may include being pulled out of our routine world and into the land of a deepening awareness of life, with its fears, mysteries and helplessness. What is dead is not past or ended; the dead are waiting for us to be present to them in life or finally, in death. Thomas Laqueur reminds us that only in the underworld does Odysseus have told to him his fate but he goes beyond that: "Indeed, the dead might be said to see the future of nations. . ." (*The Work of the Dead* 66). It seems that the dead complete the life of the living in essential ways. Days of the Dead might be best understood as necessary for every day of the living. We house the dead in ourselves; they shape our memories and what is most valuable to us on a daily basis. Without the dead we would not live as full or complete a life as they make possible.

Meditation:

Describe what you believe sent you into an underworld region that gave you a way of knowing that was most meaningful to your life.

June 19: Book XII

"When his dead body had been burned, and the gear of his body,
We heaped up a mound, dragged a grave marker up on it,
And set up his well-shaped oar on top of the mound.
We talked out the details, nor did we escape the notice
Of Circe as we came from Hades, but very swiftly. . . .
The divine goddess took her stand in our midst and spoke:
'Rash you are, who have gone alive into the hall of Hades,
Dying twice, when other men die a single time:
Well, come, eat of the provisions and drink wine
All day long in this place, and as soon as dawn appears
You shall set sail. I shall show you the way . . .'" (XII. 13-17; 20-25).

When Odysseus and his men reenter the land of the living, they ritually attend to the body of the dead Elpenor who, drunk and asleep on the roof of Circe's home, woke up and, forgetting where he was, walked off the edge. In the underworld his shade laments his death and the absence of his burial. The warriors burn his body and gear on the ritual pyre to honor him. The space between the living and the dead is non-existent. Robert Pogue Harrison illustrates, "What we find in Homer and throughout the ancient Euro-Mediterranean world is an elaborate ritualization and formalization of mourning behaviors" (*Dominion* 56) developed in part to modify extreme grieving that could threaten the lives of those mourning. Circe underscores the collapse of the distance between the living and the dead by asserting that all those who visit the land of the dead suffer their first death. Now she is ready to aid them sufficiently so they may continue home.

A journey to the underworld can take many forms, but it is a staple in epic literature that the hero, often accompanied by others, travels to this realm as a necessity for his/her success. In our own lives, news about a loved one or news we receive from a doctor can send us tail spinning down into this realm. One may feel something die inside and realize that from this moment forward, life will be lived differently. Aging itself can promote an underworld experience where one's soul must renegotiate one's life, reset one's priorities and suffer into a new mode of seeing, a deeper consciousness of one's purpose, and a grasp of new limits.

Meditation:

How did you recover or rejoin life after an experience that pulled you into the underworld? Or are you currently inhabiting that realm?

June 20: Book XII

"A driving wind full in the sails, a fine companion,
Did the fair-braided Circe, dread god with a singing voice,
Send on for us from behind the dark blue-prowed ship.
At once when we had tended to the gear through the ship piece by piece
we took our seats. The wind and a pilot steered her.
Then, grieving in my heart, I spoke to my companions:
'My friends, not one person or two alone need to know
The prophecies that the divine Circe told me.
But I will tell them, so you may know whether we
Shall die or might avoid death and escape fate'" (XII. 148-57).

We witness the slow metamorphosis of Odysseus from warrior to mentor, even as he was transformed into a poet in Books 9-12. Now he shares what Circe has predicted so that his comrades become part of that future. He has gained the gift of insight into the future through narrative, his conduit for relaying the words from the gods to mortals. In the telling, a different relationship with his men and with the future begins to emerge, making the time with Circe pivotal to the entire epic enterprise. The seductions to stifle homecoming are plentiful and must be negotiated one at a time with a constant focus on the goal. Odysseus carries this divine knowledge in the vessel of narrative as he emerges from the ashes of Troy. Bruno Snell underlines the truth that "In Homer every new turn of events is engineered by the gods" (*The Discovery of the Mind* 29).

Our identity individually and collectively is tied up fundamentally with a "narrative identity that perdures and coheres over a lifetime" (*On Stories* 4); it is a way of gathering, of clustering events that are scattered into a unified memory, writes Richard Kearney. It includes being mindful of one's present, past and anticipated future that signals a rich development in the soul of a person; when it integrates the parts of a leader, it takes on greater importance. One's vision opens out as a leader and can now benefit all who depend on him/her. A common story is infused into the collective to further define its communal myth.

Meditation:

When have you been gifted with foreknowledge that has aided you and others in your life? That knowledge might spring from a dream, a comment to you, or something you have read or even overheard, that gains import over time.

June 21: Book XII

"'She ordered us first to avoid the voice of the marvelous
Sirens, and also their meadow full of flowers.
Me alone she ordered to hear their voice; but bind me
In hard bounds so that I may stay firm in my place. . . .
The Sirens—as it drew near, they struck up their clear-toned song:
'Come near, much praised Odysseus, the Achaians' great glory;
Bring your ship in, so you may listen to our voice.
No one ever yet sped past this place in a black ship
Before he listened to the honey-toned voice from our mouths,
And then he went off delighted and knowing more things. . . .
We know all that comes to be on the much-nourishing earth.'
So they said, sending their lovely voice out" (XII. 158-61; 183-88; 191-92).

The Sirens combine honey-sweet words with lies and delusions to flatter their audience into submission; their persuasive language is used to snag the persons who fall for their deceitful promises with a false story and an impossible set of attractions. They offer the gift of more knowledge so one will be seduced to know more. To draw near to these seductive imposters is to be snared by false oaths that new knowledge is a gift for the ego. Their hook, dangled in front of Odysseus, is more knowledge of the war that consumed a decade of their lives as well as their struggle to reach home. All the men, still grieving over their losses in war, are ripe for seduction. The Sirens' honey-sweet words are fatal.

To be promised more knowledge returns us to the original garden of Eden where the serpent promises Adam and Eve the knowledge possessed by God alone so they may approximate Him in power. Knowing more, when moderated, is a healthy desire; but the Sirens in life claim much more than that. They speak in seductive tones with a counterfeit narrative in promising what they will never deliver. They may be the original con artists. Words can seduce, incarcerate and condemn one. Once we surrender to their empty assertions and our own vanity, we are fixed in a grip that wrests from us our freedom. Promises of rich prophecies are all around us on a daily basis. Sirens' voices are ubiquitous and pornographic in that they offer us a fantasy they are unable to deliver.

Meditation:

What form has a seduction taken in your life? Were you able to escape its seductive voice, its empty promises and its sticky sweetness in part or whole?

June 22: Book XII

"So I said and they obeyed my words right away.
I said no more of Scylla, the unavoidable danger,
Lest somehow in their fear over me my companions
Should cease from the rowing and crowd themselves within.
And then I forgot the hard injunction of Circe
When she ordered me in no way to arm myself.
I put on my famous armor, took two long spears
In my hands, and went up on the deck of the ship
At the prow, for from that place I expected Scylla
First to be sighted, who bore me woe for my companions" (XII. 222-31).

Just before his encounter with the twin destructive forces of Scylla and Charybdis, Odysseus, tied to the mast, and with his men all having stuffed wax into their ears, listened to the sweet seductive call of the sirens without being seduced by them. But now, forgetting once more threatens the safety of the crew and their arrival home. Forgetting is a form of mindlessness; Odysseus forgets the explicit instructions of Circe. Instead, he reverts back to the habits of the warrior. While he tries to calm his men by not bringing up the monstrous Scylla, his armor and spears create both unrest and terror in his crew. He stands at the prow, ready again for battle that is unnecessary. Forgetting the "hard injunction" is to fall out of consciousness; it is also to dishonor the goddess, the source of feminine wisdom and to resort to the more masculine contrivings of a wounded and traumatized warrior.

Old habits of dealing with similar situations require another kind of warrior in us to awaken—one of mindful attention and a shifted intention so we don't regress into unconscious habits of response. We know they often no longer work. But resisting them while not bludgeoning ourselves for the slippage into antiquated habits of dealing with crises may take years to undo. Meanwhile, we struggle to wake up in our lives so to be more conscious of the manner in which we negotiate crises. Habits are expressions of the myths we feed daily. Those same habits, while giving us a sense of security, may be also the source of our self-incarceration.

Meditation:

Recount an especially enduring habit of response you know does not work anymore but that you continue to turn to. Can you think of another, more self-affirming response that you could begin to develop instead?

June 23: Book XII

"There was Scylla, and on the other side godly Charybdis
Sucked back terribly the salt water of the sea.
Whenever she disgorged, like a basin in a large fire,
She seethed, all stirred up. And from overhead, foam
Fell down on the both sides of the peaks of the crags,
And when she swallowed down the salt water of the sea
She appeared all stirred up within, and the rock roared
Terribly about, and the earth appeared underneath
In dark blue sand. Sallow fear seized the men.
We looked toward her in fear of our destruction" (XII. 235-44).

Odysseus continues to spin his narrative like a net to ensnare the Phaeacians in wonder. Circe has told him what to expect and how to respond to the dangers he is now encircled by. Here he brings the monstrous sucking Charybdis to life in her violent drawing in of the sea, followed by her vomiting it forth. He is trapped between two unavoidable dangers. To witness the violence and indiscriminate taking in of everything that the sea contains terrifies the crew. They witness this natural force of destruction at such close range that their lives feel more fragile and impermanent. She is a life principle that threatens all of their *nostoi*. Excess, excitement, swallowing and disgorging—all of these are principles of war and exaggerations that war invites and promotes. Scylla reaches into the ship and pulls six of his men out to devour. She is a force of annihilation that renews violence.

We are not unfamiliar with a form of Charybdis that can without warning enter our lives to suck everything valuable from our grasp that we treasure and may have worked years for and on. It could appear in the form of a physical phenomenon as well as in the guise of an emotional or psychological capsizing that leaves us naked and breathless on a calm shore after being swept into the turmoil of life's at-times unforgiving seas. In recounting the *Odyssey,* Joseph Campbell offers that "while these myths speak of the anxieties and the problems of the moment, what are dealt with are always the same powers that now have to be integrated" (*Goddesses* 178). Experiencing Charybdis in our lives might require a complete reassessment of what we value after she has spent herself.

Meditation:

When has the reality of Charybdis sucked from your life what you treasure, including those you love?

June 24: Book XII

"Then, while I was still on the ocean in the black ship,
I heard a lowing of cattle coming to the fold
And a bleating of sheep. Then there fell on my heart the speech
Of the blind prophet Theban Tiresias,
And of Aiaian Circe, who enjoined me many times
To avoid the isle of the Sun, who delights mortal men. . . .
'So let us drive the black ship on past that island.'
So I said, and their own hearts were shattered within them.
Eurylochos answered me at once with a hateful speech:" (XII. 264-69; 276-78).

After losing many more men in the vortex of Charybdis' turbulence, Odysseus and those remaining continue toward home, grieving once more over the loss of their dear companions. They come now to the land of Hyperion, the island of the sun. Odysseus remembers, even as they approach its shore, the words of both his mentors, Tiresias and Circe, who embody the masculine and feminine voices of the soul; both warned him to avoid this landfall on their return. He tries too late to remember their warnings by encouraging the crew to press on, fatigued though they are. Exhausted, they try to muster the strength to forge ahead, even while one among them, Eurylochos, resists Odysseus' authority and knowledge in favor of landing on the island to rest the men rather than to endure on their journey. Excess does battle with restraint. He barters one form of excess for another in a fashion similar to the suitors.

So often in our experiences we are confronted by "one who resists." This person may be well-meaning but is often ignorant of a larger frame of reference that we may possess. Their vision is close and immediate, not long and panoramic; it can be in the moment easier not to persevere, but to let down our guard and even our authority. Leadership at this moment is a challenge, but it should not capitulate to a more popular or favorable tack. Having knowledge of potential danger through foreknowledge or instruction should not be escorted to the sidelines by someone who may know less but shout more. Being bullied, we can easily lose our compass bearings and succumb to emotions rather than a reasoned response in line with our authority.

Meditation:

When has your authority been challenged by the contrary position of another who was clearly not in a position to know the fuller story?

June 25: Book XII

"'You are tough, Odysseus, with your superior strength; your
limbs do not get tired, but they are made all of iron for you
Who will not let your companions, worn out with fatigue
And sleepiness, set foot on land. . . .
But you bid us to wander as we are through the sudden night,
carried away from the island upon the murky ocean. . . .'
So Eurylochos said, and my other companions agreed.
Then I knew that some god had devised evils
And I spoke out to him, uttering winged words": (XII. 279-82; 284-85; 294-96).

Odysseus' authority is challenged once again by Eurylochos, who earlier challenged him on Circe's island. He is Odysseus' antagonist, one who resists and questions the wisdom of his leader's decisions. The questions are: do I resist or do I rest? Do I avoid harm or court it, even create it? Do I follow instructions or improvise? Sleep can be the cause in any voyage, but pushing beyond one's capacities may jeopardize even more. Outvoted, Odysseus must decide as their leader which option will serve the enterprise and avoid mutiny. He blames it on a god, but it is more likely that Eurylochos' challenge is man-made. Odysseus is put in a position where two alternative and possibly equally deadly dangers confront him.

Whenever we are placed in a position to choose a course of action for others, our values surface to guide us as we negotiate between two goods, two evils, or one of each. Sometimes it is not so clear which is which. Short term relief over long term gain may be our outcome. Hindsight won't help in the moment but it can offer us knowledge in remembrance, which seems to be the point of Books IX-XII. There exists no absolute rule to follow unless one is a dictator. Weighing the benefits and dangers of a decision is to use *metis,* craft, leadership skills, savvy and intuition. Who one is as a person emerges in such moments to seek a compromise. The passage above also underscores Odysseus' name, meaning "trouble," either delivered or received. Having an antagonist in life will bring up trouble and test one's skills in negotiating the turbulence of dissent. Each of the stories Odysseus relates move him closer to home and to mastering restraint or caution.

Meditation:

What values did you rely on in making an important life decision for yourself and perhaps for others as well? In retrospect, how did they serve you?

June 26: Book XII

"'Come, then, all of you, and swear me a mighty oath.
If we find some herd of cattle or a great flock
Of sheep, that no one in evil recklessness
Will slaughter any cow or sheep. But be secure
And eat the provisions that immortal Circe gave.'
So I said, and they at once swore an oath as I bid them. . . .
So long as they possessed grain and red wine
They held off from the cattle in their desire for life.
But when all the provisions had been used up from the ship,
They went out on the hunt, roving from necessity. . . .
        Hunger wore down their bellies" (XII. 298-303; 327-29; 332).

Odysseus turns to oath-taking as a way to solve his dilemma. An oath is a way to buy time and to relax tensions between opposing viewpoints. Oath-taking goes on throughout the epic; it ends in Book XXIV with a divinely-inspired oath. It calms reckless behavior. Entralgo believes that the Greek word, horkos (oath) "has a curative and purificatory power" (*The Therapy of the Word* 60, fn. 39). It requires both parties to relinquish something of value if the oath is to hold. Here the men promise not to hunt or eat of the cattle so long as their own provisions last. The oath forges a peace, temporarily. But appetites, excess, an imbalance in necessities, can easily disarm an oath. Appetite begins to overtake the promise not to hunt the animals populating the island. The oath begins to weaken as hunger strengthens. Appetites will most often supersede agreements of restraint.

Oaths often rest behind civilized life. They allow a healthy tension to exist between opposing values and points of view, even different mythologies striving for dominion. Something of value for each party is present in oath-taking; otherwise, it is easily violated or set aside because no values sustain it. We say: "keep your word." Oaths are word instruments that reveal the power and persuasive force of language. Oath-taking implicates the integrity and honor of the two sides to create an agreement so a truce can come into being. Violating the oath by one side dissolves the responsibility of the other; the oath then collapses.

Meditation:

What oath did you find necessary to create for yourself and others? Has it been sustained or has it collapsed or been modified over time?

June 27: Book XII

"Then I went away, up into the island so that I might pray
To the gods, for one to show me the way to return. . . .
And I prayed to all of the gods who possess Olympos.
But they poured sweet sleep over my eyelids. . . .
And when I had got down to the ship and the sea,
I rebuked them one after another on the spot. Nor could we
Find any remedy. The cattle were already dead.
Then at once the gods showed forth portents to the men;
The skins were creeping, meat lowed upon the spits,
Both roast and raw, and there came up the voice as of cattle. . . .
Then the son of Cronos halted a dark blue cloud
Over the hollow ship, and the ocean darkened beneath it. . . . (XII: 333-34;
337-38; 390-06; 405-06).

Having exhausted the provisions provided by Circe's generosity as a good host, the men throw off the restraints of the oath to follow their appetites. Odysseus is put to sleep by the gods and so loses his command to their hunger. They slay and roast the sacred cattle of Helios. Odysseus has gone to pray to the gods for a solution; when he returns, he rebukes his men. Their attempts to offer sacrifices to appease the gods are rejected. The skins on the spit creep and the meat, still alive, lows in protest and reprimand. Poseidon sends vicious winds to destroy Odysseus and his remaining crew for such a serious violation of their trusted words. The ship will soon shatter in the gale force winds that shriek in protest as well. Again their reaching home is jeopardized by both sleep and the body's mortal limits.

Oaths, pacts, truces, vows, contracts, agreements are all sacred bonds between two or more individuals or groups. They are held together by mutual trust and honor; their medium is usually words crafted together and agreed upon. When one is violated and trust is wounded, there is nothing left to hold the oath in place; it is dismembered. Little can be cultivated or protected, much less furthered. Usually, some appetite overrides the terms of the oath, making its language impotent. Something falls asleep in sustaining the oath that then soon weakens its resolve and efficacy. Like myth itself, an oath requires one remain mindful of it.

Meditation:

List one or two oaths, be they explicit or assumed, that you live by daily or that you discovered had been violated. What were the consequences?

June 28: Book XII

"Then I bound both the keel and the mast together.
Seated on them, I was carried by the destructive winds....
All night long I was carried, and with the rising sun
I came to the crag of Scylla and to dreadful Charybdis.
And she had sucked back the salty water of the sea....
I held there steadily, till she should disgorge back
The mast and keel again. I longed for them, but they came late....
Seated upon them, I rowed on with my hands.
The father of men and gods no longer let Scylla
See me, or I would not have escaped sheer destruction" (XII. 423-24; 429-31; 437-38; 444-46).

For the first time since his journey began many years ago, Odysseus is bereft of any companions whose recklessness as well as his own sacrificed all. Alone, he is returned by the gods to Scylla and Charybdis where once more he must endure their devastation. His own level of endurance and tolerance for suffering is pushed to its limits as he waits for the keel and mast raft to be disgorged by Charybdis. After looping back, this time alone, to where he and his men had suffered through their dismembering, Odysseus sails in solitude, stripped to the barest elements of a ship—keel and mast—as he wanders towards Calypso's island, the only survivor among his men of victory over Troy. Zeus aids and abets his escape.

What are the dismembering forces of Scylla and Charybdis only each of us can answer for ourselves. What is the world we are at times threatened to be drowned or devoured by, and what threatens to "chew us out" or to "suck us dry" and even to spit us out in life? We carry these energies within us and confront both internally and externally. Their destructive energy often requires a guide or protector because our vulnerable nature makes us easy prey to their powers. Norman Fischer writes that "none of us will escape the necessity of sailing through a narrow passage with disaster lurking port and starboard" (*Sailing Home* 146-47). All of Odysseus' adventures have multiple analogies with our own journey.

Meditation:

Identify either Scylla or Charybdis in your own history or in your present circumstances. They may appear as a deep loss in your life, an illness, an accident that debilitates or in one's own self-harming behavior.

June 29: Book XII

"Nine days I was borne thence, and on the tenth night
The gods brought me near the island of Ogygia, where lives
Fair-braided Calypso, dread god with a singing voice.
She befriended me and cared for me. Why tell this story?
Already I have told it in your house yesterday
To you and your goodly wife. It is hateful to me
To tell over again a story that has been clearly told" (XII. 448-53).

Odysseus journeys to the end of his narrative that fills four of the twenty-four books of the epic. He comes full circle, having related all that happened prior to his seven years with Calypso and then being thrown to shore on Scheria and the Phaeacian audience; they have listened with rapt attention and wonder. All the events of his past since the war have now been given a narrative form and coherence. But he ends his tale abruptly and with impatience through a rhetorical question. He has told it once and now again and wishes to be free of it. His impatience to be transported home is insistent. He has endured the wishes of the king to tell his story; now he wants his freedom. Repeating it seems futile.

Narrating our history may reveal not just the formation of our historical identity but also our narrative or storied self. Recounting our past is never a copy of what we have lived; there are instead gaps, fissures, modulations, embellishments that comprise pieces of our personal myth, which guides the way we recollect and speak our past. Tim O'Brien writes of his experiences in combat in Viet Nam: "story truth is truer sometimes than happening truth" (*The Things They Carried* 179). We have been listening to Odysseus mythologize his past into a more complete or deeper sense of himself by relating his ordeals to a willing and receptive audience. Louise DeSalvo tells us that "writing is a way of assimilating events along with the emotional charge that accompanies them. A catharsis is experienced here" (*Writing as a Way of Healing* 22). I believe the same is true of speaking when we gather ourselves into a coherent story and are healed in the process. The acts of remembering and speaking are creative moments in our life and may be counted among the most important we engage. When we can deliver our story to an eager and receptive audience, healing is enhanced.

Meditation:

When you relate your story to another or others, what happens to your relationship to it and to those you speak it to? What shifts in the act of telling?

IV

BOOKS XIII-XVI

Home to the Unfamiliar:
Crafting Concealing and Revealing

IV

BOOKS XIII–XVI

Hero in the Underworld, and Homecoming and Revealing

June 30: Book XIII

So he said, and they all become hushed in silence.
They were held in rapture through the shadowy halls.
Then Alcinoos gave him an answer and spoke to him:
"Odysseus, since you have come to my bronze-based home
With its high roof, I think you will not be driven off course
In your return back, though you have suffered much. . . .
Clothes are laid up for the stranger in a polished chest,
And highly wrought gold and all sorts of other gifts
That the members of the Phaeacian council brought here" (XIII. 1-6; 10-12).

It is an amazing moment in the narrative that Homer describes as he assumes once more the epic's authorship. Odysseus' audience is held in wonder, transfixed in their imaginations by what they have just heard, perhaps in an instant of "aesthetic arrest" by his at-times fabulous and entertaining story. In these four books he has migrated from competent but lost warrior to accomplished poet. He has married force to craft. Alcinoos breaks the stunned silence by congratulating the bard on his narrative and by outlining the gifts Odysseus is to receive for his performance to take home with him. It will be a direct voyage with no wandering interludes or wondering if he will ever arrive safely. Stripped to bare-bone essentials when he landed on Scheria, he will leave with abundance from his generous hosts; within him the guest-host relationship has been reconstituted. Some deep form of healing has also been part of his narrative odyssey, which has helped to stitch him back together after the traumas of war and return.

To establish some form of the measured and mutual respect of the guest-host relationship moves both culture and civilization forward in mutual agreement. It is a form of what the Greeks called "sophrosyne," or sweet agreement. More than a pact or an oath, it is based on mutual trust and understanding. Each participates actively in his social arrangement. Both benefit, and the community in which this ritual is enacted is also a receptive beneficiary. Story telling has the power to forge such a bond into something lasting and joyful. Louise Cowan suggests that the *Odyssey* as comic epic has been one of the great shaping narratives of Western civilization ("Epic as Cosmopoiesis" 24).

Meditation:

Where in your life does the guest-host relationship appear and thrive? What experience have you had in which this bond was violated or disrupted?

July 1: Book XIII

So was Odysseus glad when the sun's light went down.
At once he addressed the Phaeacians, who are fond of rowing.
And to Alcinoos especially did he make known his speech:
"Lordly Alcinoos, exalted among all your people,
Pour a libation and send me home unharmed. Farewell to you!
What my own heart was wanting has now been brought to pass,
An escort and friendly gifts; and may the heavenly gods
Make them blessed for me! On my return may I find
My wife at home blameless, with my friends safe and sound" (XIII. 35-43).

With jubilation in his voice, Odysseus is more festive as he feels for the first time that home is a real possibility. His desire to reach it is muted only enough for him to pour gratitude on to his host. His heart is now close to being satisfied. In his imagination he is already home. He hopes too that when he arrives, all will be as he had left it twenty years earlier. But he has been told better than to expect such a condition. His language and demeanor is full of blessedness and joy as he praises and calls on the gods to sanctify his journey. His grief is for a time assuaged because now his future is full of hope for reunion with his fatherland and his family. After dwelling/telling of the past, he now pivots to what lies ahead.

We can each recall being away from our familiar world for a time and feeling the exhilaration of an impending homecoming. While the adventures one had are not forgotten, the meaning of home is so powerful that it can put into lower case all other memories. Home is one of the most powerful archetypal images we carry from birth to death. As it draws closer, our emotional life may rev up in anticipation. Our origins are so entangled in images of home we carry within that at some point nothing else matters. If we have been in potent conflicts or combat while gone, telling our history in story form is essential to reclaim our identity before arriving home. Telling the story, as Tim O'Brien observes from combat, is a way "to invent myself" (179) anew. Coming home may demand a new form of oneself to fit into it. It is often the most difficult journey for war veterans.

Meditation:

Recall a time of homecoming or of receiving someone who has been gone, perhaps in war, in prison, or another challenging time in their life, and your emotional response to yourself and others.

July 2: Book XIII

At once his noble escorts took those things and placed them
Inside the hollow ship, all of the food and drink.
They spread out a blanket and linen cloth for Odysseus
On the deck of the hollow ship, so he might sleep without waking,
Upon the stern. He himself boarded too and lay down. . . .
For him there fell down upon his eyelids a balmy sleep,
Unwaking, most sweet, nearest in semblance to death. . . .
But at this time he slept without a tremor, forgetting what he had suffered.
When the brightest star rose up that most of all
Comes on to announce the light of early-born dawn,
At that time did the seafaring ship reach the island   (XIII. 71-75; 79-80; 92-95).

Surrounded by luxuriant gifts, Odysseus falls asleep wrapped in a linen cloth, perhaps like one dead, at the ship's stern. The Phaeacians are careful not to disturb his sleep. It is like a balm of peace after so many years of turmoil and violence. He sleeps the deep sleep of the dead and forgetfulness, liberated for a time from the horrors of his losses and battles. It is a transitional death as he migrates from twenty years out in the world back to home. His is a psychological and emotional voyage as much as it is physical. The ship cuts through the waters at a magical speed and after its night sea journey sails into the harbor of Ithaca. When the early dawn is spotted, Odysseus' new life at home is about to begin. He has been prepared by several voices to return home wide awake and transformed.

Being able to step out of a period of crisis or even of never-ending work that allows no respite is a joy in its simple pleasure. For some forms of fatigue, a week's vacation is too inadequate. Odysseus' rest is more akin to a warrior finally returning from battle. Rest is renewal and rejuvenation. Trauma has been so much a part of his life, that without Athene's guidance he would never have made it home. Also, as Edward Tick points out, homecoming too for the warrior can be a source of trauma, even after the veteran has told his story (*Warrior's Return* 122-23), as it will be for Odysseus. Reentry contains its own fierce form of heat and suffering.

Meditation:

If you or a loved one was away from home for an extended time, how were you or they received? What was the most remarkable part to adjust to? Was there a chasm that had opened between the former life and the one now?

July 3: Book XIII

At the head of the harbor is an olive with long leaves,
And close to that is a pleasant and shadowy cavern
Sacred to the nymphs who are called Naiades.
And in it there are mixing bowls and two-handled jars
Of stone. And the bees store up their honey in them.
There are very long stone looms in it, where the nymphs
Weave sea purple mantles, a wonder to behold,
And ever-flowing waters are there. It has two doors,
One toward the North Wind, accessible to men,
And the other one divine is toward the South Wind. . . (XIII. 102-111).

This is our first view of Ithaca, the long-desired place of Odysseus' origin. It is like Calypso's island and like Arete and Alcinoos' palace. Weaving holds it all together. Here the natural and cultural worlds mingle in harmony. The bees use the cultural artifacts to store their honey. Nymphs weave in the cave; they create beautiful mantles, not unlike Penelope who has been weaving a shroud for her father-in-law Laertes to forestall the suitors. Water flows fresh and natural through this idyllic scene that Odysseus has yet to awaken to on the Phaeacian ship. The olive tree is Athene's symbol; its fruits sustain the Greek people. The cavern has two doors, one to be used by mortals, the other by immortals, so it is a meeting place of the divine and human dimensions of being. Confluence and congruence reign within the cavern, a primal form of home.

Our own homecoming may be just as sweet in surroundings as this scene depicts. When we return from an arduous absence, we may find ourselves in a state of wonder over what was once familiar but has over time and our experiences taken on a very different cast. We are welcomed home, paradoxically, by both what is strange and new and what is familiar and comforting. So many objects we love, that reflect the home we have created, step forth to welcome us: our favorite room, chair, view, people who love us, and artifacts gathered over a lifetime. Home may then feel like paradise. People shape our lives, but so do things that have a history and a precious quality to them. Appreciation may be our first response; gratitude our second.

Meditation:

Describe what you gravitate toward when you arrive home from a short venture or an extended time away from all you love. What calls you to it first?

July 4: Book XIII

First they raised Odysseus out of the hollow ship,
The linen sheet and the glistening blanket and all;
They set him down on the sand overcome with sleep.
They lifted out the goods the noble Phaeacians had given
As he was going home through great-hearted Athene's help,
And then put them in a heap by the base of the olive tree,
Out of the path lest by chance some wayfaring man
Might find and despoil them before Odysseus woke up.
Then they started back homeward. Nor did the earth-shaker
Forget the curses he had made originally
Against godlike Odysseus (XIII. 117-27).

Two worlds open up in this passage: one is a scene of abundance where the barren, stripped Odysseus is now in possession of the Phaeacians' largesse. Their gifts are more than Odysseus would have arrived home from Troy with if he were unscathed, as Poseidon complains to his brother, Zeus. The second world is the wounded enraged Poseidon who has kept his word to his brother not to destroy Odysseus in his homecoming, but who now seeks vengeance on his own people, the Phaeacians, who have secured Odysseus' homecoming on their swift ship. He then pleads with Zeus for vengeance, who responds to him: "Do as you wish, and as is pleasing to your own heart" (l. 145), and then instructs him in his destruction.

Even in a safe homecoming, something may have to be paid for. We cannot separate out abundance from threat, security from danger, or the satisfaction on arriving home with the imperfect, even harmful possibilities of such a destiny and a destination. Life seems always to be polluted with contrary forces and powers, benevolent and malevolent presences frequently at war with one another. We may carry home with us the consequences of behavior on our journey. We return home expecting a level of hospitality we yearn for, but as David Denby writes after reading the *Odyssey*, "hospitality may be vicious, the beginning of annihilation" (*Great Books* 81). We cannot often assume very much in life's circumstances.

Meditation:

When have shadows from your journey or journeys followed you home, demanding to be paid for? Or what debt have you had to incur from the homecoming of another?

July 5: Book XIII

And when earth-shaker Poseidon had heard this speech,
He went on to Scheria where the Phaeacians dwell
And stayed there. The seafaring ship came very near,
Running on nimbly. The earth-shaker came near it,
And he turned it to stone and rooted it beneath,
Pressing it with the flat of his hand. Then he departed. . . .
Then Alcinoos spoke out to them and addressed them:
"Ah well, the prophecies have come upon me, spoken of old
By my father, who used to say Poseidon resented us
Because we are secure escorts for everyone" (XIII. 159-64; 171-74).

There seems to be no boundaries between mortals and immortals in the epic. Poseidon's resentment of the Phaeacians because they have protected Odysseus on his last voyage is unleashed on them, thereby fulfilling an old prophecy and partially satisfying the sea god's wish for revenge. He would have preferred to kill him before he arrived home. We learn from Karl Reinhardt that "Poseidon's wrath is there for the sake of the actions of the gods. It is a given element in the style of great epic and prescribed by the genre of the nostos" ("The Adventures in the *Odyssey*" 86-87). His presence is that of a shadow figure to goodness, of resentment and a desire to destroy what is measured and good, as Athene embodies them. Alcinoos remembers the prophecy as soon as the Phaeacian ship is petrified. The destructive element of life seems indomitable but not necessarily dominant.

No good deed escapes some penalty. Goodness, generosity, helping another should not be assumed to draw like to it. Resentments, envy, getting even, revenge, destructive impulses may respond to good or ill works. There are no guarantees. Odysseus arrives home but the price tag is enormous. Whether or not we act in the world to promote good works, or if we act solely to benefit ourselves cannot predict the presences in life that may attack to destroy our noble intentions and actions. Always there seem to be polar energies in the world; when one aspect of these energies is engaged, it would often seem to invite its contrary. Perhaps prophecies often need to be fulfilled to satisfy the menu of a myth, whose "pattern may be promise and fulfillment," writes Laurence Coupe (*Myth* 100).

Meditation:

When have your good intentions or deeds been met with vengeful and/or destructive responses?

July 6: Book XIII

But godly Odysseus woke up
From sleeping on his fatherland soil and did not recognize it,
For he had been gone a long time. A god shed a mist round him,
Pallas Athene, the daughter of Zeus, so she could make him
Unrecognizable, and tell him the details,
Lest his wife recognize him, and his townsmen and friends,
Before the suitors had paid for all their transgressions.
And so everything appeared of a changed form to its lord;. . .
He sprang up, stood still, and looked on his fatherland soil,
And then he uttered a groan and struck both his thighs
With the flat of his hands. And he made a speech lamenting: (XIII. 187-94; 197-99).

The force of good in the form of Athene when Odysseus wakes from the sleep of the dead camouflages him so he may be protected from adversaries now that he is home. The suitors have rung up a huge tab in violating the household. As he is changed by Athene, so is he unable to recognize being home. He groans with disappointment that the Phaeacians have erred in bringing him somewhere other than his familiar Ithaca. Concealment, deceit, disguise are all part of the chaos of homecoming, it seems. He is and is not himself; the land is and is not his home and his journey, he realizes, is not yet finished. He must return home as a stranger, "still lost" as Jonathan Shay describes him (*Odysseus in America* 246).

It is not unusual that a warrior returning home finds a strange, not a familiar welcoming place. Odysseus expresses enormous disappointment in not recognizing his fatherland. Edward Tick reveals the complexity of nostalgia: it is comprised of *algos*, pain, and *nostos*, to return home. Nostalgia is then the pain of not being able to return home *(Warrior's Return* 228). This emotion is what Odysseus feels when he strikes both his thighs in frustration. War can shift one's perception such that home appears as an extension of the battlefield; the warrior's return brings with it violence, rage and a desire to destroy what is most precious.

Meditation:

Have you returned home after a critical absence and felt it was more a foreign than a familiar welcoming place? Or when you were home and a family member or friend returned from a crisis, what might they not have recognized?

July 7: Book XIII

"Woe is me, to the land of what mortals have I come this time?
Are the men proud and savage and without justice
Or are they friendly to strangers and have a god-fearing mind?
Where am I carrying these many goods? Where do I myself
Wander? Would that they had stayed with the Phaeacians
In that place. But I would have come on another of the exalted kings....
As it is I do not know where to put these things. Nor can I
Leave them here, lest they become a prey to others....
    They did say they would lead me
to sunny Ithaca, and they did not bring it to pass.
May the Zeus of suppliants pay them back, who watches
Over all men and punishes whoever errs" (XII. 200-05; 207-08; 211-14).

Despair, disorientation and disappointment mingle in Odysseus as his feelings of betrayal grow. Many assumptions begin to crowd around him as he decides that he has been tricked by his worthy hosts. His disorientation results in creating a narrative that will make sense of his current predicament and offer some assurance for his wandering. He is at this moment completely helpless and at a loss over what he deems a lack of trust. All is out of place. He has no idea of what he should do with the gifts the Phaeacians have bequeathed him. His next move is a blur; safety is a concern but what to do is uncertain. He ends by cursing his former hosts and calls on Zeus to avenge him. David Wood writes that combat vets arriving home feel "as vulnerable to sorrow, regret, guilt, grief and loss as they were in combat" (*What Have We Done?* 221). Odysseus at home is still wandering.

To continue on this theme, the warrior's disorientation is acute. He is home but may have no clue that he has reached his destination. Jonathan Shay writes that "many veterans experienced that disorienting bewilderment. This wasn't the place they left" (*Odysseus in America* 120), leaving them often with a sense of estrangement because they "'fail to know the land'" (121). The trauma of war and the often painful trek home have uncoupled Odysseus from his origins in the same way it may affect a refugee who has wandered for years in an attempt to find a new home or his/her former one. Moral injury is all-consuming.

Meditation:

Has a trauma in your life disconnected you from your home, which can be psychological or emotional as well as a physical place?

July 8: Book XIII

Then the bright-eyed goddess spoke to him:
"You are simple, stranger, or have come from far away
If you ask what this land is. To no great degree
Is it nameless. Very many men know which it is. . . .
It is a good goat pasture and cow pasture. Woods
Are all over it, and it affords year-round watering places.
And so, stranger, the name Ithaca has reached even to Troy,
Which they say is far off from the Achaian land."
So she said, and godly Odysseus, who had endured much,
rejoiced (XIII. 236-39; 246-50).

Athene walks down the beach towards Odysseus, disguised as a young man holding a javelin; she gives him reason for hope when he asks her where he is. He is desperate to make contact with her and to regain a sense of place and purpose. Initially Athene hides her identity when she responds to him; then she names the familiar place, which brings immediate joy to the wanderer of twenty years. She reminds him of how Ithaca is renowned in the Greek world; even those as far as the battle ground of Troy have heard of it. The power of naming the place makes it familiar; without a name it is no place, as earlier when he named himself "no man," he was without identity, homeless and an alien to himself.

The power and pleasure of knowing what a place is called points to one of the gifts of language. To give a name to a person, place, condition or thing gives one a certain control or familiarity with the thing or person named. It now has an identity, a locale, a history and often, a story or stories that accompany the name. Naming can be its own form of therapy. It locates not just the place but the person who hears the names as well. Name creates a reality that is absent without it. Sheila Murnaghan makes the point that the *Odyssey* "enters its most intense phase in Book 13, with Odysseus' arrival on the shore of Ithaka and Athena's more overt involvement on his behalf ("The Plan of Athena" 69). As the goddess reveals the name of Ithaca, she also plans for Odysseus' concealment from Penelope. As goddess she is both revealer and concealer and has the wisdom to discern them.

Meditation:

How might learning the name of something immediately change your relation to it? How has it done so and what happens when you lose the name of something or someone? Does that diminish it in some way?

July 9: Book XIII

So he said, and the bright-eyed goddess Athene smiled.
She reached her hand to him and likened her body to a woman's,
Lovely and tall and skilled in glorious tasks;
And speaking to him, she uttered winged words:
"Cunning would he be and deceitful, who could overreach you
In various wiles, and even if a god should confront you.
Versatile-minded wretch, insatiate in wiles, you would not
Cease from deceits though you are in your own land,
Or from fraudulent stories that from the ground up are dear to you" (XIII. 287-95).

This moment with Athene is one of the most poignant and tender in the epic. She delights in Odysseus being so much like her in *metis* (craft, craftiness) which includes fictionalizing life and oneself in service to a greater good. The line "versatile-minded wretch," is good humored chiding by Athene. Odysseus' nature seems to be one of incessant and excellent story-telling as a way to conceal the truth of things and situations or perhaps their facts. As a maker of fraudulent or untrue stories, Odysseus is seen as a poet, a crafter of words that can be more potent than forceful actions because they can persuade or shape actions based on the narrative plot. She has a deep perception of Odysseus who loves fraudulent stories, stories that are not true; but if the story is truly told, then it is a success.

The heartbeat of our lives occurs in our narratives; the ones we tell ourselves and those we tell others as well as those we hear from still others. Richard Kearney believes the earliest instinct for storytelling, from the very first of folk myths on, expresses "our most viable form of identity—individual and communal" (*On Stories* 4). Our stories comprise our deepest identities. Shaping experiences into words can draw us closer to a communal belonging; they can also conceal our deeper motives when we use a story as a camouflage, a cover, a deceit for ends that may be generous or self-serving. Not only do we plot our lives daily, but since plot means *muthos,* our personal myth is encased in and shapes the narratives we craft. Plotting a plan or scheme is another way to construct stories and express myth.

Meditation:

Describe one story you tell yourself frequently. Is it still true for you or might you drop that story line for one fresher as well as a truer version of who you are currently?

July 10: Book XIII

"Come, let us say no more of this, as both of us are skilled
In shrewdness, since you are by far the best of mortals
In plans and in stories, and I among all the gods
Am famed for planning and shrewdness, and you did not know
Pallas Athene, daughter of Zeus, who always stands
Beside you and guards you in all sorts of troubles
And made you believed by all of the Phaeacians. . . .
Come, I will show you Ithaca's site, to convince you.
This is the harbor of Phorcys, the old man of the sea;
This at the harbor's head the olive with long leaves,. . ." (XIII. 296-302; 344-46).

Athene deems it important to reveal to her charge how they both excel in shrewdness, cunning and craftiness. Mortal and immortal, they mirror one another. Their mutual natures are a perfect fit between an immortal goddess and a mortal man, whose name means "trouble" or "strife." She also wants him to know two important truths: that she is his constant guardian always, whether she is visible or invisible, and that he is indeed home. Now that he has achieved his homeland, he must be brought into its awareness through particulars. By pointing out familiar landmarks to Odysseus, she convinces him of this right place. Place and person are of a piece. He has taken a first step towards reintegrating into his *oikos*.

Where we are from is an essential piece in our most fundamental identity, so much so that a person may naturally ask you where your home is before they ask what your name is. Locating ourselves in place shifts our perspective from wandering to wondering. Ed Casey distinguishes between being *dis*oriented and *un*oriented. "To be *un*oriented is not to know where I am—not yet. This does not mean that I am lost; it just means that I cannot specify my whereabouts. . ." (*The World at a Glance* 91). Even when we arrive home, we cannot know with any certainty what the terms of our homecoming and home actually are. We enter fully into what is partly familiar, partly strange and ambiguous. A narrative congeals them. David Loy writes that "place stories are essential to non-modern cultures. The more homeless stories of modernity weakened such accounts with the fiction of ownership and property—today our most basic story about place" (*The World is Made of Stories* 9).

Meditation:

What must happen for you to make a new place a home?

July 11: Book XIII

Pallas Athene, the daughter of aegis-bearing Zeus,
Put them in well and placed a stone at the entrance.
They both sat down at the base of the holy olive tree
And talked about destruction for the presumptuous suitors. . . .
"Take thought about how you may lay hands on the shameless suitors
Who for three years have held sway over your hall,
Wooing your godlike wife and giving her bridal gifts.
But she always grieves in her heart for your return.
She gives them all hope and makes promises to each man,
Sending out messages, but her mind plans other things" (XIII. 370-73; 376-81).

Athene aids Odysseus in finding a place for his guest-gifts given to him by his Phaeacian friends. They rest by the tree that gives so much to the Greek people, the olive tree of Athene, who now fills Odysseus in on the status of his household and the suitors' continual violations. They have kidnapped his dwelling and courted his wife, accompanied by the assumption that her husband will not return. Penelope in turn, not unlike her husband and the goddess, assents to their desires verbally by both weaving a funeral shroud for Laertes so to lead them on with hope. She knows in her heart he is making his way home. In his mythic reading of the couple, Joseph Campbell suggests that "Odysseus is the sun, she is the moon—they are associated with a calendric mystery, symbolizing the relationship of solar and lunar consciousness, male and female consciousness" (*Goddesses* 176).

Alone at times when we feel overwhelmed by our situation, we may be blessed with comfort from forces beyond us. We may pray to them for guidance and support and seek advice and consolation in our crises. The benefits in being open to aid and support can be as enormous as they are unexpected. Praying for guidance and a way past our difficulties can open us to opportunities that would not present themselves any other way. The ability to yield, to submit, to turn over control of our current situation is an act of wisdom that can aid us in surviving and even flourishing in the midst of friction and futility. Being open to what transcends our mortal limits is a spiritual act that rests on being aware of our limitations.

Meditation:

When have you been comforted and aided by life's mysterious forces? Was it something you wished for or desired, or did it arrive without invitation to aid you in a time of need?

July 12: Book XIII

"Come, I shall make you unrecognizable to all mortals.
I shall shrivel the lovely flesh on your supple limbs,
Destroy the blond hair from you head and cloak you about
In rags a man seeing you wear would loathe you for.
And I shall mar your eyes that were beautiful beforehand,
So that you may appear ill-favored to all the suitors,
And to your wife and your child that you left in the halls.
But first of all, go on up yourself to the swineherd
Who is guardian of your swine, kindly disposed to you also,
And a friend to your son and the constant Penelope" (XIII. 397-406).

Athene reveals her brilliance here in transforming Odysseus into his opposite, into an inverse fiction of himself: a ragged aged beggar whom no one will suspect is a threat to them, least of all the suitors. By concealing Odysseus' identity she will allow to be revealed how the suitors may be conquered and dismantled, less by force then by *metis*. Like stories themselves, what lies invisible in the narrative—its core identity—Odysseus' core appearance is cloaked. Frederick Turner writes that "*The Iliad* and *The Odyssey* are not quite so explicit in their acknowledgement of their fictionality, . . . (*Epic* 280), but here is one crucial play on the reality of fiction that encompasses the larger fiction of the epic plot that stitches the *Odyssey* into a coherent whole. It also points out the faithful honesty and trust of the swineherd Eumaeus who has served Odysseus and his family from the beginning. He embodies the archetype of the faithful servant.

We know how the appearance of something or someone can cloak or mask a more authentic or even false reality beneath. Sometimes only the slightest signals that peak out of the disguise may give us an inkling of a deeper reality just below the surface. So a disguise creates a counterfeit where two realities converge, one visible, the other invisible. Wisdom perhaps rests in part in being able to discern such a dual reality. Developing this mode of perceiving may prove to be one of our greatest skills. "Things are not always as they seem" is a useful angle of vision to maintain, without it becoming an obsession. What story or stories we believe in or give most credulity to is the reality we submit to most readily.

Meditation:

When have you seen through a disguise to a deeper truth? Are there valid situations wherein self-disguise is the best strategy?

July 13: Book XIII

"Stay there, remain beside and ask him everything,
So that I may go to Sparta that is lovely in women
And summon Telemachos, your dear son, Odysseus,
Who went to Menelaos in Lacedemon of the broad dancing-place
To learn tidings about you, if you were still alive" . . . .
When she had said this, Athene touched him with a wand.
She shriveled the lovely flesh on his supple limbs,
Destroyed the blond hair on his head, and put the skin
Of an aged old man around all his limbs. . . .
She threw other clothing about him, a foul rag and a tunic,
Dirty and full of holes, begrimed with foul smoke, . . . (XIII. 411-15; 429-32; 434-35).

The plot of the epic now circles back to retrieve the early books about Telemachos and his quest to find his father and/or the stories that describe him. Athene informs Odysseus of her plot to unite the three of them and to create a new Odysseus, a fiction, by transforming him into a harmless and pathetic beggar. In this new fiction he will present a new public presence that will allow him simultaneously to be himself and another. Now he is prepared to become a public persona once more, crafted into a new person so he can gauge the faithful from the hostile and deceiving forces before him. In fact, as W.B. Stanford has written of the figure of Odysseus, "most significant of all for the possibility of altered adaptations of his myth, one of his chief qualities, as Homer portrayed him, was adaptability" (*The Ulysses Theme* 7). Such an ability, aided by a goddess, to conform, transform and reform reveals how this form of the epic hero survives.

Craft, deceit, shaping a persona that hides an authentic self is not unusual for any of us. What we conceal from others is also a part of our personal myth. We see, understand and judge so much in our lives by how they appear; we must trust how things, people, and events present themselves in their particulars. If we are proven wrong in our assessment, we adapt. When needed, we craft ourselves into a form to meet the demands and exigencies of what is before us. We thus fashion a paradox in that we are present and absent at the same moment. That too is a form of self-crafting, so to make our invisibility provoke visibles that may threaten.

Meditation:

In certain situations, do you feel a need to disguise your true nature to survive?

July 14: Book XIV

He shouted at the dogs and scattered them this way and that
With showers of stones. And he addressed his master:
"Old man, in a little while the dogs would suddenly
Have torn you to pieces, and you would have heaped reproach on me.
To me also have the gods given the other pains and griefs. . . .
But follow me, old man, let us go to the hut, so for yourself
When you are satisfied in your heart with food and wine,
You may tell where you come from and how many cares you
have endured"
When he had said this, the godly swineherd led him into the hut (XIV. 35-39; 45-48).

Disguised in a decrepit fiction, Odysseus enters the space of his faithful swineherd Eumaeos where his dogs rush to attack him. Eumaeos rescues his fabricated master, and tells him that the gods have given him his own suffering: the loss of his master and the devouring compulsions of the suitors. Setting all that aside, the swineherd exercises the code of hospitality that is his habit with strangers. He invites Odysseus into his humble hut, close to where the water and land meet. He looks forward to hearing the fragile guest's stories and the pains life has brought him to suffer. Between the two men a community forms of mutual care and respect. Odysseus moves one more stage toward his household, beginning with one of his oldest and most faithful servants.

Strangers may become friends quickly through their material wounds inflicted on them by the world. All that is required is something as mundane as a shared meal. When a warrior like Odysseus returns home, feeling welcomed by even the humblest servant is enough to begin reintegrating him into the security of a hut and a simple meal. That Eumaeus does not know the stranger's true identity underscores the authentic acts of hospitality to one who has nothing. He shares as host what his guest obviously requires. Their mutual stories nourish one another. William Hazlitt believes that "man is a make-believe animal—he is never so truly himself as when he is acting a part" (qtd. in *The World is Made of Stories* 34). Both reveal the myth that we live within and that lives through us.

Meditation:

Think of when you were shown hospitality that helped to restore you from a challenging situation or when you showed another hospitality in acts of kindness.

July 15: Book XIV

"Eat, now stranger, the food that is furnished to servants,
Plain pork. But the suitors eat the fatling swine
And in their minds do not think of divine surveillance or pity,
For the blessed gods are not fond of cruel deeds;
No, they reward justice and the righteous deeds of men. . . .
But these men know—they have heard some voice of a god—
Of that man's woeful death, and so they do not wish to pay court
Justly, or to return to their own goods, but at their ease
They presumptuously devour his goods, and there is
No restraint" (XIV. 80-84; 88-92).

The swineherd now fills the stranger with plain pork and knowledge of the intolerable conditions of his master's household. He is clear about their abuse of hospitality to strangers or any piety towards the gods, so unrestrained are their appetites. Eumaeos also voices divine principles about what divinities scorn and what they favor. Divine and human are contrasted by the wise old man who has devoted his life to serving this one family's household. He continues to do so even as the suitors habitually violate the customs of hospitality through their unrestrained excess and arrogance. Lack of moderation has led to sustained and excessive violation of the household. Greed has triumphed over graciousness, civility and largesse. Here Odysseus experiences for the first time at home that like-mindedness with another, *homophrosyne*, which will be fully realized and shared soon with Penelope, writes Louise Cowan ("The *Odyssey* and the Efficacy of Imagination" 66).

Greed is the absence of restraint, moderation and due measure, often at the expense of others with less. Greed consumes the one who lives without boundaries or limits and insults both mortals and divinities. Even the gods have their own boundaries to honor. Cowardice seems related to greed, as does arrogance. Given time, greed will turn on those in its grip, but not before the excessive damage is done to those who pay for this imbalance. The cowardice of the suitors is revealed when they hear that Odysseus is dead, which gives them free reign on his household. Lack of piety, of acknowledgement of the gods, feeds the fires of greed wherein it continues to accelerate and intensify without fear of reprisal.

Meditation:

What qualities have you noticed accompany greed? Can it ever be satiated?

July 16: Book XIV

"Yet anyway, wanderers who need entertainment
Tell lies, and they are not willing to speak the truth.
Whoever in wandering reaches the land of Ithaca
Comes to my mistress and utters deceptive stories.
She receives him, befriends him, and asks for the details,
And as she laments, the tears fall from her eyelids,
As is right for a woman when her husband has perished abroad.
And you too, old man, would quickly fashion a story
If someone gave you a mantle and a tunic and clothes.
By now the dogs and swift birds have probably
Torn the skin from his bones and the soul has left him, . . ." (XIV. 124-34).

Eumaeos continues the conversation with the fictional beggar on the nature of stories themselves. They have the capacity to conceal when they seem to reveal, to deceive when they seem to speak the truth, to create a reality when their motive is to gain power over the listener. Penelope is the desired target for these false narratives about her husband. Each one makes up a different Odysseus, perhaps suggesting that this figure is the image of stories themselves as well as the center piece of this epic. She weeps for his loss but in her heart may remain a disbeliever of these unproven tales. She holds in her heart a conviction that he will return. The swineherd tells Odysseus he too would tell a false tale if he were rewarded with clean clothing to make him more believable. Helen Foley writes that "In short, Penelope is not fully herself without her husband" ("Penelope as Moral Agent" 96) and perhaps the same could be said of her husband.

We cannot know for certain whether the stories we are told as truth are in fact so. Fictions can serve as truth, even on a deeper level than the realm of factual occurrences. They can also serve self-interested ends that run counter to truth. Trust is the fragile thread that binds truth to narrative. Stories may blend some proportion of enough truth to make them credible, yet enough falsity to seduce the listener or reader. Motive is all. Homer may give us pause when he reflects on his own creation.. What do we believe and what do we question in stories we read or hear? he asks us as audience.

Meditation:

What is your marker for believing or rejecting the truth claims of a story presented to you?

July 17: Book XIV

"But longing takes hold of me for Odysseus who is gone away.
I am in awe to speak his name, stranger, though he is not here.
For he loved me exceedingly and cared for me in his heart.
But I call him 'honored sir' even when he is far away."
Godly Odysseus, who had endured much, spoke to him then:
"My friend, since you wholly deny it, you do not still think
That man will come, and your heart is ever unbelieving;
I shall say it, not just that way, but with an oath:
Odysseus shall return. Let me have reward for good news
Right away when that man arrives at his own halls;
Clothe me in a mantle and a tunic, lovely clothes" (XIV. 144-53).

The play and power of stories as creations of *metis*—craft—but also what can plot deceits through seducing a listener and so dismay him/her continues between Eumaeos and the disguised Odysseus, who is wrapped in a ragged fiction. Does Eumaeos suspect that this stranger is now who he claims and wishes to speak lovingly of Odysseus to reveal the stranger's identity? Possibly. The swineherd's repeated idea uttered above of Odysseus having died, makes this scene all the more poignant. Then Odysseus swears an oath that he shall return. He speaks of himself in the third person as an absent-presence. So he appears split from his narrative in crafting another identity, but such deceit is needed for a higher end.

We each may disguise and conceal ourselves for a host of reasons. Concealing something of ourselves is a form of disguise, yet the fictions we tell may be their own way of revealing what is true. A story like Homer's epic may in its "as-if" expression, carry more truth about the human condition than can any research process or sociological data. The truth of who we are may best be revealed in well-crafted narratives that have become classics in the literary tradition. On one level, the *Odyssey* reveals the trauma of a warrior returning home without faith or trust in the place he left to risk his life. When that trust and welcoming is absent, warriors "are spiritually traumatized" and their "belief systems shattered," believes Edward Tick (*Warrior's Return* 129).

Meditation:

What do you learn about being human through fiction you have enjoyed reading? What is the nature of their reality through narrative that is analogous to your story?

July 18: Book XIV

Odysseus of many wiles addressed him in answer:
"All right, I shall tell you this quite truthfully. . . .
I declare I am of the race of those who live in broad Crete,
The son of a wealthy man. And many other sons
Were both born and nourished in his hall, legitimate,
From his wife. A bought mother bore me, a concubine.
But Castor, son of Hylax, of whose race I declare I am,
Honored me as he did the sons rightfully born. . . .
I took a wife among men who had a large portion,
Because of my excellence, since I was not a good-for-nothing
Or a coward in battle. And now it has all left me" (XIV. 191-92; 199-204; 211-13).

Living in a fiction wrapped in beggar's cloth is Odysseus' implement in successfully returning home. Athene's craftiness and wisdom rests behind this disguised way of entering his household. He fabricates to survive. He crafts another self to further conceal his true identity and from which he can witness the truth. He is not ready yet to reveal himself to his swineherd; it is not yet *Kairos*, or the opportune time. The decade of war, coupled with his decade's long struggle to return home, has left him suspicious, fragile, and frustrated with his homecoming. Running like skeins of truth in his narrative above are small pieces of his true identity which he will unravel slowly in order to reunite with his family.

Stories can be effective shields, even a full suit of armor, to fend off others and keep one's self sealed in a cocoon of one's own devising. Some may become so ensnared in their crafted narrative that they lose touch with their core story. Some may lose a sense of themselves through trauma, so it is safer to craft a counterfeit in place of one's authentic self. However, David Loy argues that "One meaning of freedom is the opportunity to act out the story I identify with. Another freedom is the ability to change stories and my role within them. I move from scripted character to co-author of my own life (*The World is Made of Stories* 33). Poetry itself is a form of fantasy, a fabrication that is revelatory about some crucial elements of being human, wrestling with challenges, and suffering wounds in the process. We then can relate to such narratives as analogies of our own plot.

Meditation:

When have you found it necessary to script your own chronicle that you knew was not who you believed yourself to be?

July 19: Book XIV

And you addressed him in answer, swineherd Eumaeos:
"Ah, wretched stranger, you have stirred my heart very much
As you tell the details of how you suffered and wandered.
But this I think is not in order, nor will you convince me
When you speak about Odysseus. Why does a man like you need
To lie fruitlessly? Well do I myself also know
Of my master's return, that he has been very much hated
By all the gods, as they did not subdue him among the Trojans
Or in the arms of his friends, after he had wound up the war" (XIV. 360-68).

The only time in the epic the narrative refers to a character in the second person with some consistency is with Eumaeos. It may be a show of intimacy or favoritism, a congratulatory gesture because the swineherd sees through Odysseus' story as a foil, but he does not know the identity of the one relating the fictional narrative. The swineherd seems to have a sharp intuitive knowledge of what is true and in what order a story is to be told; by his standards of truth, Odysseus' narrative does not measure up. He chastises his master by challenging his veracity. He has been moved deeply, nonetheless, by the narrative and is upset by the effects a false story has on him. The power of narrative is once more the centerpiece of this section of the plot, a plot about a plot and soon, a plotting against the suitors. Not that a story is true or false, but that it is well-told seems to be Eumaeos' concern.

We cannot know for certain when a story is a vehicle for delivering false news or true statements; the emotions cannot not know the difference. It always depends on the authority we give the teller and the circumstances in which the story is delivered. Eva Brann writes that "Odysseus is a versatile and controlled liar. His lying tales are collages of fact; they have verisimilitude because they are a neat mosaic of probabilities, facts that surely happened to someone, some time, probably to him" (*Homeric Moments* 247). People may tell a story to conceal what "really happened." Some tell true stories that are disbelieved, like the mythical Cassandra prophesying the future to incredulous ears. One can tell a story with the express intent of manipulating others, so powerful is its energy.

Meditation:

When you knew a story you heard was untrue, what was your response? Did you call the teller or writer out on it?

July 20: Book XIV

"Do not blandish me or charm me at all with lies,
As I shall not respect and befriend you for that, but in fear
Of Zeus, the god of strangers, and pity for your person."
Odysseus of many wiles addressed him in answer:
"Surely you have an unbelieving spirit in your breast,
When I do not bring a man like you around by oath, or persuade you.
But come, let us make an agreement. Let the gods
Who hold Olympos be henceforth witnesses for both.
If your master does return to this very home,
You will dress me in clothes a mantle and a tunic, and send me
On a trip to Dulichion, where I would like in my heart to be" (XIV. 387-97).

Odysseus takes a different tack now with Eumaeos; he knows he needs him for a successful reentry into his home. Jean Houston refers to Eumaios as "the last true guardian in Ithaca even though he exercises authority over only part of the estate" (*The Hero and the Goddess* 308). The swineherd's impatience grows into high frustration. To calm him, Odysseus suggests an oath be struck between them. He offers that they both agree by the gods on an arrangement that they witness. If Odysseus does return in the fiction he is promoting in being present already, then the swineherd will give the stranger much finer clothes to wear. It is an unfair oath because it has already been accomplished; but it is also a fair oath because it buys Odysseus time to plan his strategy to retrieve his home by crafty means.

Once again, an oath is called forth to interrupt growing tension and possible violence. The oath disarms this accelerating animosity. Some agreement between opposing forces by means of language agreed upon is a major step forward in civilized life to quell potential violence. Each must relinquish something of value to the oath itself. Both parties must sense the other side is also sacrificing something of value for the oath to gain a proper tension in establishing peace. The oath itself is a storied way of creating a compromise, one that opens rather than forecloses possibilities; without it, options vanish and violence or silence or resentment settles in to forge dissatisfaction on both sides of the conflict. Oath-taking is a rich and civilized form of story-making.

Meditation:

Recall a situation when you came to an agreement in order to modulate a possible violent escalation or when the agreement defused factionalism.

July 21: Book XIV

"But now is the time for dinner. May my companions soon
Be here inside, so we may make a tasty dinner in the hut."
In this way they addressed such words to one another.
Then did the swine approach, and the men who were swineherds. . . .
Then the godly swineherd called to his companions:
"Bring the best swine, so I may slaughter it for the stranger
From far away. And we too may enjoy it, who have long
Had sorrow as we labored for the swine with shining tusks,
And other men do devour our hard work scot free."
When he had said this, he split wood with the pitiless bronze,
And they led in a very fat pig five years of age (XIV. 407-10; 413-19).

Now that the terms of the oath or agreement have been settled, both sides can enjoy hospitality and the feast it encourages. The oath has released the tension between them. Camaraderie replaces conflict. A feast shared brings out the best in guest and host. We turn to the domestic chores of creating a feast. The robust pig slaughtered is a bridge between Odysseus and his swineherd and helpers. Jonathan Shay suggests that perhaps Eumaeos "has already guessed who this wizened beggar is because he not only orders the fattest boar killed for their supper, but also presents Odysseus with the choicest cut from the loin" (*Odysseus in America* 126). Or perhaps it is the swineherd following the protocols of the guest-host relationship. Or both. It is certainly a welcome respite from the suitors devouring the household in violation of just such protocol and a cornerstone of Greek civility. Homer's devotion to detail includes here the age of the meal to be devoured.

Few pleasures surpass that of a feast in which *communitas* is established through the body's appetites and the pleasures of eating and conversing. Food consumed in the glow of conversation and shared experiences and common pleasures reinforces civilized life as well as sustains physical well-being. It is also a healing moment for Odysseus now among faithful individuals who have served his family in his absence. We can imagine his own soul being nourished in this temenos space between the violence of Poseidon's seas and the devouring and murderous attitude of the suitors, a small Tahiti between two venues of violence.

Meditation:

What do you most enjoy about a feast with friends and new acquaintances? What else is fed than just the body?

July 22: Book XIV

Odysseus spoke to them, testing the swineherd out,
If he would take off his mantle and give it to him, or urge
Another of his companions to, since he cared much for him.
"Listen now, Eumaeos, and all you other companions,
I have a boast, and will tell a story, for crazing wine
Bids it, that sets even a man of many thoughts on
To sing and to laugh gently, and it drives him to dance,
And he brings out a story that would be better untold. . . .
But I, when I went, left my mantle with my companions
Foolishly, since I thought I would not freeze in any case" (XIV. 459-66; 480-81).

Odysseus would appear to feign being inebriated so to loosen the restraints of the guest and enjoy excess in storytelling. He wishes to test the generosity of his host by crafting a story of being with Odysseus in battle and losing his mantle that protected him from the elements. He prefaces the story by saying he should not tell it but decides to. He reveals what might best be concealed. The focus again is on narrative's capacity to conceal and reveal simultaneously, to flesh out the truth through a lie or a distortion of it. It is part of Odysseus' own personal myth to do so. We saw above that for the good story he told, Odysseus received a sumptuous meal; Andrew Dalby points out that in the Homeric world, "most performances [for that is what Odysseus enacted] were likely rewarded. . . with food and a place near the fire" (*Rediscovering Homer* 171) rather than with money. Odysseus' success as bard who tells entertaining stories continues to evolve. He pushes Eumaeos once more to show his generosity as a proper host.

Motive is often difficult to detect accurately. Stories told may have an ulterior design, a concealed motive, a hidden itinerary. It may be designed to elicit a particular response from its audience or to shift the hearer's opinions or beliefs in something the story carries within it. We may even tell ourselves certain stories not once but repeatedly to convince ourselves to believe something or deny certain painful truths. Some may become fixated in their own story telling and carry that narrative to their graves without ever questioning its veracity or usefulness.

Meditation:

What story do you tell yourself frequently that you believe helps you navigate each day? Is there any part of that story that is actually no longer serving you, but you have not yet considered letting it go?

July 23: Book XIV

Then you addressed him in answer, swineherd Eumaeos:
"Old man, the story is excellent that you have told.
And no profitless word did you speak improperly.
So you shall not want for clothes or for anything else,
Of the things that befit a long suffering suppliant one meets—
For now. But at dawn you shall bundle your own rags on,
As there are not many mantles and changes of tunic
To put on here, just a single one for each mortal man.
But when the beloved son of Odysseus comes
He himself will give you clothes, a mantle and tunic,..." (XIV. 507-16).

Once again, Odysseus sings for his supper, as he did on Scheria. Eumaeos praises him for his craft as a story teller. Like a literary critic, he tells the stranger he has told a story truly and well, although we are in a position to realize it is a fabrication with no word out of line. His story tells of leaving his mantle and thus having nothing to cover him at Troy. Eumaeos relates that Telemachos, Odysseus' son, will amply dress the tattered old man in garments far richer and newer than the rags he now wears. Odysseus is once more testing the depth of Eumaeos' fidelity to him and how he will reward the stranger for a story well-told. Homer may also be testing the limits and the skills of his own story-making talents, whose poetic prowess conveys the deep psychology of a warrior-bard.

Stories delight, entertain and often carry a second or third meaning in their structures. Stories can persuade, exhibit craft and skill as well as camouflage the truth. They may consciously conceal, or select out elements to discard and others fabricated to create a particular effect in the audience. Our narratives may reveal our identity, motives and values. Their natures are always protean. They also carry a *mimetic* function, meaning, in Aristotle's use of the term *mimesis,* that stories can, Richard Kearney writes, render "a creative redescription of the world such that their hidden patterns and hitherto unexplored meanings can emerge" (*On Stories* 12). So a story can seem very simple and entertaining on the outside, yet carry a deep mythos of meaning on the inside. Our narrative self is imbedded in the style and manner of expressing our fiction, not as lies but as our truth.

Meditation:

What might have led you to tell a good and engaging story with the intention of concealing yourself or something you preferred to remain hidden?

July 24: Book XIV

When he had said this, he rose up and made a bed for him
Near the fire. And on it he threw skins of sheep and goats.
There Odysseus lay down. He threw on him a mantle
Great and thick, which lay beside him as a change
To put on when any terrible storm arose.
So Odysseus slept. And beside him those young men
Were sleeping. But to lie there was not pleasing
To the swineherd, to be sleeping apart from the swine.
He went out to go and get ready. Odysseus was pleased
That the man took care of his livelihood when he was away (XIV. 518-27).

While just earlier Eumaeos informed Odysseus that extra mantles are very rare, he promises that when Telemachos arrives he will furnish more of them to the stranger. He strives to make his disguised mentor (which some have suggested the swineherd intuits who he is), comfortable and secure. Eumaeos, however, is more content and accustomed to sleep with the animals he cares for, so he gathers his things to join them. Odysseus is pleased to witness the fidelity of his servant towards his valued goods. Each of these incidences bring the warrior a step closer to home. Being home includes being able to trust anyone and everyone. Eumaeos wins over his master's trust by acting hospitably without knowing, perhaps, his guest's identity. The poet consistently addresses Eumaeos in the second person, seemingly to establish a more personal relationship with this character. A greater intimacy is established between the poet of the poem and the character who loves stories and can smell a counterfeit one when he hears it.

We cannot fully know someone and our relation to them without it including how they may behave without knowing they are being watched. We each cultivate a social self we exercise in public and a more private self we engage when alone or with family and friends. Here Homer shows Eumaeos acting in private as an authentic servant differently than he behaves in public. Some live by two different and even opposing sets of values when alone and when in society. They may both be true. Eumaeos, however, is the archetype of the faithful servant in all situations; he exhibits a generosity of spirit with strangers and with who is familiar.

Meditation:

Describe one quality or behavior that separates you in your private life from how you behave publicly. What is the motivation for this separation?

July 25: Book XV

She found Telemachos and the noble son of Nestor
Lying in the forecourt of glorious Menelaos.
The son of Nestor was overcome with soft sleep,
But sweet sleep did not hold Telemachos. In his heart
Concern for his father kept him awake through the ambrosial night.
Bright-eyed Athene stood close to him and addressed him:
"Telemachos, it is no longer good to wander far from home,
And leave behind in your home the possessions and the men,
Presumptuous as they are, lest they divide and devour
All your possessions and you have gone on a fruitless journey" (XV. 4-13).

The plot shifts in space but not in time to pick up Telemachos' own journey as he searches for his father's story at the palace of Helen and Menelaos. Athene enters to continue her plan to reunite father and son, and then both of them with Penelope, while avoiding detection by the suitors. As she encouraged him initially to sail from Ithaca in search of his father, now she persuades him to return home; her ploy is to awaken in him an urgency to return before the suitors have devoured all possessions and forced his mother to marry one of them. Helene Foley speculates on this exchange between Athene and Telemachos that the young man "should look to his possessions because Penelope may decide to marry and take Telemachos' goods with her" ("Penelope as Moral Agent" 98).

The interior voice we sometimes hear encouraging us to take action or to rethink a plan or way of life we have engaged is here understood as divine intervention. Many of us pray for guidance on a daily basis; our belief is that presences and invisible powers beyond us, whose presence is a "higher power," as it is sometimes called, are at work in the world. Giving ourselves over to such oracles or guiding presences can be a way of life. It admits we cannot often know the outcome of our actions, much less control all of them, so we petition help from energies that can bring us some sense of agency and comfort in our decisions. One might think of prayer in this same way, as a ritual-making presence of energies or beings that assist us with their wisdom that is well beyond our own. "To complete the hero quest," writes Joseph Campbell, "the hero must bring the boon,. . . the culled wisdom back into the community for its benefit" (*Hero* 167).

Meditation:

What forces outside yourself or within you do you call on for guidance?

July 26: Book XV

"I will say something else to you; store it in your mind.
The best of the suitors lie ready in ambush against you
In the strait between Ithaca and the rugged Same,
Wanting to kill you before you reach your fatherland. . . .
But first of all go on up yourself to the swineherd
Who is guardian of your swine, and kindly disposed to you also.
Rest the night there. And send him on inside the city
To give the message to the prudent Penelope
That you are safe for her and have arrived from Pylos."
And when she had said this, she went off to tall Olympos (XV. 27-30; 38-43).

Athene's care for the entire family of Odysseus is consistent from the epic's early lines to the end of Book XXIV. She is the grand plotter of mortals' lives with her wisdom and attentive care, her prescience and good will. As a divine goddess she once again imparts good judgment to Telemachos and moves him closer to a reunion with his father. She reveals that even when we believe we independently make life choices and implement them, that other forces may also be actively guiding us. Telemachos proves a worthy student and recipient of her directions. He has been schooled to yield to her instructions because he knows she is a worthy mentor. That she instructs him to end his voyage at Eumaeos' hut that inhabits the space between the solidity of land and the uncertainty of the sea, is a fitting place to be reunited with a father he has known only through narratives. Now he returns with the person of his father existing in his memorial imagination.

Who or what voices and influences we yield to in life define our personal myth, which includes those mentors we have learned to trust and believe in. In times of feeling lost, frustrated, uncertain or defeated, we have to turn to presences that can help us reground ourselves amidst periods that challenge who we are. Athenian presences in our lives are less crutches than they are teachers, ancestors, or wisdom figures that we turn to when we recognize our own frail powers of discernment. Such can take the form of internal authorities or others we believe will show up when we extend an invitation. Having mentors over a lifetime is a gift, even a form of grace, because they fill in for us where we are still developing.

Meditation:

Has prayer, in whatever form or way you choose to petition, helped you in your interior life or from outside?

July 27: Book XV

"Send me off right away to my dear fatherland,
For already my heart is longing to return home."
Then Menelaos, good at the war cry, answered him:
"Telemachos, I shall not hold you back here a long time,
Wanting to return as you do. I would resent another
Who, receiving a guest, acted excessively friendly
Or excessively hostile. All things are better when in measure. . . .
It is glory, splendor, and refreshment all together
For men, after dining, to go far on the unbounded earth" (XV. 65-71; 78-79).

While a gracious guest, Telemachos knows he must follow the muse of wisdom, Athene, as she instructs him to complete the circle of his journey by returning to Ithaca. Menelaos, the gracious host, understands from his warrior days that moderation and proper measure comprise a virtuous way of life. Excess in any form is a deterrent to a life of moderation, proportion and balance—all virtues of a civilized social arrangement. Learning to live a life of due measure is a form of wisdom and piety. To venture out into life itself is to invite these three qualities of glory, splendor and refreshment that may have faded from a life of routine and familiarity that can numb the soul. He yields to Telemachos' request to leave.

Measure and proportion are qualities the world teaches us when we risk the call to adventure. Joy and splendor often accompany one adventuring, risking and growing. Being transformed, not simply in-formed, by one's experiences is a crucial and necessary aspect of life generally; such moments revive and enliven us. Menelaos' wisdom imparts to the young adventurer what Athene had hoped he would learn once outside the suffocating excess of the suitors. The mythologist Joseph Campbell reminds us that "it has always been on myths that the moral orders of societies have been founded" (*Myths To Live By* 11), so we pay attention to what values, ideals, prejudices, and aspirations we and the culture we live in promote; therein lies its mythic substrate. Myths are foundational and fundamental to the life of an individual or a people; Telemachos above is being initiated further into their value as his own maturing self continues to unfurl. His education has as its central focus his imagination as a way of knowing the world. Athene is imagination's voice and presence in the soul of each of us.

Meditation:

What key or core values do you take with you when you venture into the world?

July 28: Book XV

"Farewell, young men. And to Nestor, shepherd of the people,
Give greetings. To me he was always mild as a father
While we sons of the Achaians waged war in Troy". . . .
A bird flew to the right of him, as he was speaking,
An eagle bearing a huge, bright goose in his claws,
A tame one from the courtyard. The men and the women
Followed them shrieking. He came up close to them
And rushed off to the right before the horses. When they saw it,
They rejoiced, and the spirit was warmed in all their minds (XV. 151-53; 160-65)

Menelaos sends Telemachos and Nestor's son, Peisistratos, off with a warm greeting to the wise Achaian, Nestor. At this precise moment an eagle passes over carrying a large goose from the courtyard. This event, a portent, delights the crowd gathered to wish the young men a safe journey. Their interpretation is that such an event is a good omen, and implicates Telemachos as he heads home. The gods can appear in various guises and enact a reality that gives mortals a glimpse into the future. An omen is another form of speech, a revelation of another order, one of divinity, speaking or commenting or passing judgment on the works of mortals by means of the natural order. Little space exists between the natural, human and divine worlds; together they create a living organic cosmos.

Depending on one's belief system, one may choose to accept that life has many layers and expresses itself in more than one register, the literal level. Behind the literal may be other forms of knowledge given through the natural order that mirrors the divine realm and deeper dimensions of the human order. Accepting this multiplicity of meanings can offer a richness and complexity to our lives that is bountiful, nuanced and fruitful for understanding our role on this stage of being/becoming. An omen is like an oath: both tell a narrative in another register, link worlds that are still distinguishable one from another, and impart knowledge that does not address reason so much as the mythic imagination. Donald Cowan speaks in this regard of Athene's crucial importance, "as inspiration for the active and vital imagination, and as help and guide to heroes. . ." ("The Stages of Learning" 75).

Meditation:

When have you received a sign of what is to come or what is currently, but defied interpretation?

July 29: Book XV

Helen of the long gown began speaking before he could:
"Listen to me, and I shall prophesy the way the immortals
Have put it in my heart, and how I think it will end.
Just as the bird seized the goose reared in our home
When he came from the mountain where his descent and his birth are,
So Odysseus who has suffered many ills and wandered much
Will return homeward and do vengeance. Or else already
He is at home and breeds evil for all the suitors."
Then sound-minded Telemachos answered her:
"May Zeus, Hera's thundering husband, make it so" (XV. 171-80).

Nestor's son, Pesisistratos, has just asked the gift-giving Menelaos to interpret what all have just witnessed. The leaders take a moment to ponder what nature has just revealed, and through her, the gods. But before he can speak, Helen enters to offer her own reading. She speaks almost automatically and with an air of assurance and conviction. Her belief is that the referent of the eagle carrying the goose in its talons is analogous to Odysseus returning to confront and rid his household of the overstuffed geese, the suitors, who have grown fat on Odysseus' fare. Her analogy is convincing and hopeful, as Telemachos expresses immediately after her prophecy. Helen speaks with such certitude because she believes her vision has been prompted by the gods who have shared their knowledge with her.

Writing on magic and prophecy in the ancient Greek world, Richard Onians notes that "Magic, power, is in the words: the force of magic does not reside in the things; it resides within man and can escape only through his voice" (*The Origins of European Thought* 68). Speech is the center of gravity for both information and for prophecy as well as for magic. Interpretation is also a form of magic. How we see is as mythic as what we see and what we remain blind to; it is expressed in language, in the power of words to create realities now and forthcoming. What we believe is the source of our knowing is also mythic and can shift over time as we understand more. Our myth mirrors and serves as metaphor for our understanding.

Meditation:

Offer an aspect of your way of interpreting events. What do you assume? What do you imagine to be true from what you witness or experience directly?

July 30: Book XV

Greatly disturbed, you spoke to him, swineherd Eumaeos:
"Alas, stranger, what is this thought that has come about
In your mind? You must surely long to die on the spot
If you wish to enter the company of the suitors,
Whose presumption and might reaches iron heaven. . . .
But stay, no one is troubled at your being here,
Not I or any other of the companions who are with me.
But when the beloved son of Odysseus comes,
He will clothe you in garments, a mantle and a tunic,
And he will send you wherever your heart and spirit bid" (XV. 325-29; 335-39).

We want to remember that this entire time with Eumaeos is under the cloak of an elaborate fiction, perpetuated by Odysseus, who is like an actor in a drama and whose identity requires further concealment. It is like a casting interview for Odysseus to see how convincing he can be in his role of beggar. The swineherd cannot believe this decrepit man before him desires to penetrate the surly and excessively hostile world of the suitors, but he bases his observations on the man's appearance, not his concealed reality. He pleads with him to await the arrival of Telemachos and his generosity. When Eumaeos says "no one is troubled," he recalls "Noman" who troubled Polyphemos and may be hinting that he suspects the identity of the stranger.

Homer's story asks us to think deeply about our own identity and whether it is singular or plural. We may have multiple faces we turn to the world. Our identity may not be so fixed and certain as we or others believe. What is at play in the passage above and in our own lives is the power of the imagination to create realities that exist only in the creative act, not in the phenomenal world. Imagination allows us to manipulate who we are and to craft the identity of others according to our own desires and intentions. We say of someone we know whose actions are "not like him. He could never do X." "We do better," Paul Eakin writes, "to speak of 'registers of self and self-experience,' for there are many stories of self to tell, and more than one self to tell them" (*How Our Lives Become Stories* xi).

Meditation:

When might you have felt that your self-identity was up for grabs? What was your response to such a feeling?

July 31: Book XV

"The wind and the water carried and brought them near Ithaca,
Where Laertes bought me with his resources.
In that way did I see this country with my own eyes."
Then Zeus-born Odysseus aroused him with a speech:
"Eumaeos, you have stirred the heart very much in my breast
As you tell the details of the pain you suffered in your heart.
But Zeus has provided good for you along with evil
When, having suffered much, you reached the home of a man
Who was mild, and who furnished you with food and drink
Kindly. And you live a good life.. . ."
And so they told such stories to one another (XV. 482-91; 493).

Eumaeos opens up to Odysseus with his own history that carries his listener deeper into the swineherd's identity. Disguised but authentic in his feelings for his faithful servant, Odysseus is moved in his heart by Eumaeos' suffering. Their stories share their respective grief with one another to create a strong bond in that universal human experience of affliction, pain and sorrow. Odysseus reminds him of the justice of Zeus; offering good with evil is a measured distribution of these inevitable human attributes. Their mutual narratives solidify a bond between master and servant that cannot be equaled. Like oaths, stories can bond us in empathy to the sufferings of others when we relate it to our own distresses.

When we share our story with another, we open ourselves to a sweet vulnerability that can't be willed. Our life's plot is our myth enacted, then remembered in the present, so there exist images of self-then and self-now as well as two stories, one lived and the other its expression in narrative form. Telling our stories elicits in others a similar desire because we hear echoes of our past in the fabric of another's tale and its potent emotions. Both fabrications infer a weaving of one soul with another through distinct narratives. John Scheid and Jasper Svenbros' *The Craft of Zeus: Myths of Weaving and Fabric* reveals that "Homer is familiar with the metaphor of verbal weaving" (114), though he did not use it to describe his own poetry. But it is certainly a rich figure of speech to characterize the way telling our stories to one another weaves us together in profound, often permanent ways.

Meditation:

What conditions have to be in place in order for you to share your deepest story of yourself with others?

August 1: Book XV

Theoclymenos called him aside from their companions,
Took his hand, and spoke right out directly to him:
"Telemachos, not without a god did that bird fly to the right.
I knew when I saw it head on it was a bird of omen.
There is no other descent more royal than yours
In the land of Ithaca. You are the strongest always."
Then sound-minded Telemachos answered him:
"Would that this speech, stranger, might be fulfilled.
And then you would soon know friendship and many gifts
From me, so that someone who met you would call you blessed" (XV. 529-38).

Telemachos' soon-to-be friend and a seer, Theoclymenos, pulls him aside and interprets the meaning of a hawk with a dove in its claws who just flew to their right. The implication is that Telemachos is descended from a strong lineage and that he will prevail at home. His observations boost the Ithacan's confidence; he befriends this young man whose prophecy is a gift to him. He provides Telemachos bounty in his quest and then calls to his good friend, Peiraeos, to take Theoclymenos in and show him abundant hospitality. We see here a miniature version of Odysseus' stories to the Phaeacians who reward him with grand largesse for his knowledge and his story-telling excellence. Telemachos, ever the learner, heeds the words of this prophet and is both lightened in his heart and enlightened by his interpretation.

Individuals enter our lives like fate or perhaps "by chance" to offer us wise counsel, a new direction or to fulfill some gap in our existence at a given moment. They are gifts from divinity, from life itself or other sources beyond our understanding. Through them we glimpse a comprehension we have not considered before. It could be a recommendation to contact someone, a book to read, a film to see or a new adventure to consider. The options are infinite. When we depart from that person we are often uplifted, have a new insight, even given a new path to pursue. They show us how interdependent we all are, and, as messengers, we may understand them as voicing something from a divine source.

Meditation:

When have you been a gift to a stranger because of something you brought to them that they needed? When has this happened to you as recipient of some insight or understanding that you would have not been able to locate on your own?

August 2: Book XVI

"Eumaeos, surely some companion is coming here
Or some other acquaintance, since the dogs do not bark
But fawn around him. And I hear the low noise of his feet."
The speech was not yet fully said when his dear son
Was standing in the doorway. The swineherd started, dumbstruck.
From his hands the bowls fell that he was tending to
As he mixed the sparkling wine. He went over to his master
And kissed him on the head and on the both lovely eyes
And both of his hands. A swelling tear fell from him,
As a father receives lovingly the dear son he sees
Coming in the tenth year from a faraway land,... (XVI. 8-18).

Like a son is Telemachos to Eumaeos. The actual father, Odysseus initially offers no response to his son, who is not named yet by the swineherd. He may simply not recognize him after twenty years when he left him as an infant. Or he may, in sustaining his concealment, not risk a response just yet. The love of the swineherd for the young man who has appeared so suddenly, seemingly out of nowhere like a god, is both startling and welcoming. We can only imagine Odysseus' own shock at this new presence. The man who is not Telemachos' father reacts as Odysseus, the true father would if he revealed himself. The true father shows no emotion at this initial encounter. Eumaeos does not know the identity of Odysseus while Odysseus at this moment cannot respond to his son.

The war has taken Odysseus so long from his family that he cannot recognize his own son and knows almost nothing about him. The world's warriors share this common thread: they may return home and not recognize their immediate kin, so estranged are they from that earlier reality. Their return home must occur in increments in order to be successful. Too much home at once can devastate the warrior whose world has been violent, uncertain, wounding and often dismembering. Coming home is not one action but a complex weave of many. David Wood observes that "The clash of needs can be emotionally painful, and rebuilding relationships an added challenge" (*What Have We Done?* 223).

Meditation:

Have your experienced a situation in which returning home felt like entering a strange, foreign territory? What helped or hindered your adjustment?

August 3: Book XVI

Then he himself went in and crossed the stone threshold.
His father Odysseus yielded him a seat as he entered.
But Telemachos, for his part, checked him and spoke out:
"Sit down, stranger. We will find a seat somewhere else
In our hut. Here is a man who will furnish one"....
But when they had taken their fill of food and drink,
Telemachos spoke out to the godly swineherd:
"Father, where did this stranger come from? How did sailors
Bring him to Ithaca? What men did they claim to be?
For I do not think he could have arrived here at all on foot" (XVI. 41-45; 55-59).

After engaging familiar rituals of hospitality, Telemachos does not address the stranger's origins or why he is there, but he questions Eumaeos when he refers to the stranger in the third person. He wishes to know why he is there but chooses not to ask the old beggar directly. His knowledge of the stranger will come indirectly, even second hand; Odysseus remains silent, concealed, not wishing to give any hint to either Eumaeos or his son, whose exercise of hospitality is impeccable and who Odysseus learns much about the qualities that define him. Father and son are placed in a position of being complete strangers to one another, even as Eumaeos may or may not know of Odysseus' true identity. As a story, it is a delightful series of tensions between the three that Homer's brilliance creates and sustains.

The warrior's return may be accompanied by silence, uncertainty, a certain resistance to tell his story or even to exhibit fully who he is, since he may have been changed radically by war and would possibly create an emotional deluge if he spilled his story on to family and friends. The warrior may also return appearing as a stranger who makes him only partly recognizable. It may feel like entering the home of foreign people, so devastating can war's alteration of the person be. The rules of hospitality may be the best curative to such a painful and fragile reentry into a life that feels distant, as war feels so incomprehensible to those who have not experienced it firsthand.

Meditation:

When has your loved one or a close friend felt or appeared as a stranger to you such that you found yourself saying, " I don't even know who you are"?

August 4: Book XVI

"Yet, indeed, since this stranger has come to your house,
I shall clothe him in a mantle and tunic, lovely garments.
I shall give him a two-edged sword and sandals for his feet,
And I shall send him wherever his heart and spirit bid.
But if you wish to, care for him and keep him in your hut. . . .
I for my part should not allow him to come there
Among the suitors, for they have too much reckless presumption,
Lest they mock him, and that be a dread grief to me" (XVI. 78-82; 85-87).

Telemachos, still unaware that the stranger is the goal of all his searching and grieving, nonetheless confers on him the respect and dignity of a royal guest. He reveals to his concealed father the ethos of his character. His mother has raised him to be hospitable to even the lowest and poorest of mortals. He also offers information on the suitors as a dangerous throng of thugs who will most likely abuse Odysseus because they operate out of "reckless presumption." If they violate this beggar and the code of hospitality, Telemachos will suffer grief as well "since they are far stronger." He does not yet recognize just how true his own words are. The other value that breathes here between father and son is that of *homophrosyne,* or like-mindedness that Marilyn Stewart writes, "comes to life in the action of the *Odyssey*" ("Imagination and Mapping in the *Odyssey*" 88). Watching his son's behavior, Odysseus must be well-pleased to witness his generous character.

It is so easy to mock, degrade and trivialize the poor, the marginal and powerless because they pose no threat politically or otherwise. They can be left along the roadside as refugees and as refuse, dangerous characters, suspicious immigrants demonized by leaders and citizens alike. Judged solely by their appearance and by stereotypes of them can put them in their place at the bottom; there they become easy victims of their own unimportance. For an individual to offer one of them assistance shows a soul's largesse and pulls that person from the stubborn quicksand of a stereotype into a space of their own.

Meditation:

Have you reached out to someone in need to ease their suffering or to help them on their journey? Have you been aided by someone at a time when no one seemed to even notice your existence?

August 5: Book XVI

Then godly Odysseus, who had suffered much, answered him:
"My friend, since surely it is proper for me to reply,
My own heart is torn to pieces when I hear
About the reckless deeds you say the suitors contrive
In your halls, against the will of a man as good as yourself. . . .
I would rather be killed in my own halls and die
Than perpetually to look upon these sorry deeds:
Strangers being maltreated, and men disgracefully
Dragging the servant women through the lovely halls, . . ." (XVI. 90-94; 106-09).

Even in disguise, Odysseus speaks as himself obliquely so as not to reveal too much of his identity. So even concealed in appearance, he reveals his true feelings of being distressed at knowing the conditions of his own household. He now realizes the terrible suffering his son and wife have endured while he remains hidden in his disguise. He speaks out of the frame of the "other" while remaining himself in order to have revealed what he needs to know within his concealment. He also tells Eumaeos and Telemachos his plans and desires. His outrage and woundedness seep through his words in his lament over the complete dissolution of the guest-host community he has just witnessed and experienced in its finest expression in Scheria and now here in his fatherland. His language bonds him to his son.

Violence against one's household, and by extension one's homeland, can be a dismembering experience to endure. To be forced from one's home and land to become a refugee is to inflict terrible loss on a family. When the appetites of the powerful are unleashed on a community that has no resources to protect itself, then those afflicted may be exiled from all values they hold close as defining presences. One's identity is questioned when violent force is leveled against an individual or even nations. David Loy reminds us that "Our identities are constructed from what we detest as well as what we love" (*The World is Made of Stories* 64). To be attacked in one's home where these identities are forged and cultivated is to threaten the very nature of one's sense of self.

Meditation:

What opportunity have you seen and acted on to alleviate suffering of the homeless or violence in the home?

August 6: Book XVI

"For thus did the son of Cronos make ours a single line.
Arkesios sired Laertes, a single son,
And his father sired Odysseus alone; Odysseus sired me
Alone, and left me in the halls, and got from me no joy.
So now there are countless enemies in the house,
All the noblemen who rule over the islands,
Dulichion and Same and wooded Zacynthos,
And all those who are masters in craggy Ithaca,
Are paying court to my mother and wearing down my home, . . .
        Soon they will tear me to pieces myself" (XVI. 117-25; 128).

A mature Telemachos steps forward in this passage to give the disguised stranger a progress report on the state of his household. He also offers a genealogy stretching back several generations to illustrate how he has a clear sense of his own history on a broader scale. Sandra Easter writes eloquently of these figures in our past: "our ancestors have both a physical and psychic reality. Their bones and flesh lie in the ground on which we walk every day. . . (*Jung and the Ancestors* 1). They define us from their graves. Telemachos shows us in pointing to his ancestors how far he has grown from the whining young man who left in search of his father, guided by Athene's wisdom and counsel. His father witnesses this through the veil of his fiction. He brings his father up to date on his mother's critical condition as well as the general dissolution of the home. He also acknowledges that he himself is in immediate danger. Father and son bond over their shared histories.

To place one's self within a family heritage where one traces his/her roots back in time is to see one's life within a much larger vessel of awareness. It is to see one's self as part of a historical continuum. The long view can both humble and elevate one's status because the view of self in a progression of time is immensely helpful and sobering. History then becomes a living mythic presence in a life more grounded because of a greater awareness of one's origins. In our origins is our originality as well as our destiny. Gaining a historical perspective lifts us out of self-centeredness and places us within the grand fabric of time's treasures. Not knowing one's past leaves one an orphan in the world, rootless and naïve.

Meditation:

What do you know of your own ancestry? What has your own lineage taught you about yourself and those in your family?

August 7: Book XVI

"Go quickly, father, to constant Penelope.
Tell her I am safe and have arrived from Pylos.
I myself shall remain here, but you come back here
When you have told just her. Let no one else of the Achaians
Find out about it, for many devise evils against me."
And you addressed him in answer, swineherd Eumaeos:
"I know, I see; you say this to an understanding man.
But come, tell me this, and speak out truthfully,
Should I go or not by the same path to tell Laertes,
That wretched man, who, while he grieved much for Odysseus,
Used to oversee the fields, . . ." (XVI. 130-40).

Telemachos also reveals his leadership qualities and a measured way of thinking when he instructs Eumaeos to relieve Penelope's fears about her son. He thinks of her over his own needs and fears about his own life. Conceal your message, he tells the swineherd, even as his concealed father stands and witnesses his son emerging before his eyes take charge and plot a reasoned plan. Eumaeos wonders about the grief of Odysseus' father, for whom Penelope has been weaving a funeral shroud in order to stave off the suitors' advances, and whether he should be informed of his grandson's return. All of the information passing between them Odysseus assimilates and uses to evaluate his own strategy to reclaim the *oikos*.

To watch our own children or those of others mature into their unique identity and gifts is a wonder to witness. At a certain age they begin to unfurl their own talents and life trajectory. It is a great mystery how all of this ripens and matures into a unique person. We may see in them our own developing soul years ago and perhaps memories of our own parents' maturation. These fundamental patterns unfolding reveal the original creation of each human being. It becomes especially poignant when we witness them in moments of crisis step into their own authority to reveal their independence through expressing more of the qualities of their personal myth. As parents we can only wonder at this miracle and feel gratitude at the treasure of a child growing into their own identity. They are mirrors of ourselves, whether or not, like Odysseus, we were part of their upbringing.

Meditation:

Recall a moment or two when you grew into an awareness of your own original self, or that you witnessed one of your own children journey into this space.

August 8: Book XVI

"But now from the time you were gone in the ship to Pylos,
They say he no longer eats and drinks the way he did,
Nor looks over the fields, but with groaning and wailing
He sits and laments, and the flesh shrinks round his bones."
Then sound-minded Telemachos answered him:
"That is the more painful. Still, let us leave him, though we are grieved,
For if things were somehow free for mortals to choose,
We should first choose the day of my father's return.
But you, when you have told the news, come back and do not
Wander in the fields after that man" (XVI. 142-51).

Eumaeos looks to Telemachos for advice and direction, both under the watchful eye of their master and father hidden in the shadowy folds of disguise. He listens to his son's growing talents in leadership. Odysseus' instincts are to remain hidden, concealed and inconsequential to allow his son to create strategies for returning home. Eumaeos speaks of Odysseus' father Laertes in his deep grieving and disintegration, exactly what killed his wife. From the swineherd Odysseus learns more of his family's suffering and his father's rapid decline. Laertes is paralyzed by both grief and fear, while Telemachos is full of vitality with a plan to reclaim the home from those who would murder him and kidnap his entire estate. In between father and son is Odysseus, tracking a middle course.

Father, son, and servant gather to reclaim the household. Add one more—the father of the returning warrior. Families have been shattered by so many forms of violence: addictions, emotional rages, infidelities, warring forces bombing homes, killing the young and elderly. What power does one have against such destruction? This outlines the central dilemma when contrary forces invade to disrupt and dismantle the serenity of home, shattering the intact vessel of wholeness. Only craft, a fertile imagination and perhaps concealment are clever enough to reclaim the household. Finally, as Edward Tick writes of the warrior coming home, "resolve must be present not only during conflict but afterward" for it indicates the truth of a people's character (*Warrior's Return* 123).

Meditation:

What forces have tried to shatter your home or relationships and what responses worked to reclaim them?

August 9: Book XVI

He spoke, and roused the swineherd. He took sandals in hand,
Bound them under his feet, and went to the city; nor did
The swineherd Eumaeos escape Athene as he went from the lodge,
But she came up close. She likened her body to a woman's,
Lovely and tall and skilled in excellent tasks.
She stood and appeared to Odysseus at the hut doorway,
Nor did Telemachos see her face to face or perceive her.
For in no way do the gods appear clearly to all men.
But Odysseus and the dogs saw her. They did not bark;
They slunk with a whimpering to the other side of the lodge. (XVI. 154-63).

Telemachos' words are potent and persuasive, perhaps in part the consequence of Athene's influence and mentoring. As Eumaeos departs she appears in the doorway, a threshold place, in the form of a beautiful woman and well-skilled (*metis*). Only Odysseus has eyes to see her, as do the dogs surrounding him; she reveals her human form to the swineherd but conceals it from Telemachos. The gods appear in various shades and nuances to individuals; they are not bound by uniformity; some gods are always vague and most often invisible. Christine Downing reminds us in writing of the Greek Gods that "of course, none of us has access to an unmediated relation to these divinities. We know them primarily as communicated through Greek literature of the classical and Hellenistic world. . ." (*Gods in Our Midst* 22). Here Athene also conceals herself to appear in a non-destructive way.

The experience of a god's presence in our lives, who perhaps appears to us in dream or in the form of a person, is difficult to either prove or dispute. But that we can be visited by the sacred in an experience we have had, even in the form of an apparition, a voice of direction or inspiration or in any number of formats is unquestioned. The sacred as well as the demonic pervade religious and mythic traditions; being open to their possibilities is a form of reverence. "Common to all of them, writes Walter Otto of the Greek pantheon, "is immortality, and they are called the eternal ones who exist forever" (*The Homeric Gods* 127). To be visited by a deity is a moment when eternity slices into our mortal temporal existence.

Meditation:

Recall what you believe was an experience of the numinous or sacred or divine revelation that impacted how you think or behave or shifted an attitude.

August 10: Book XVI

She signaled with her eyebrows. Godly Odysseus perceived it
And went out of the room along the great farmyard wall
And stood in her presence. Athene addressed him:
"Zeus-born son of Laertes, Odysseus of many devices,
Now is the time, say the word to your son, and do not conceal it
So you may both work death and destruction on the suitors,
And come to the renowned city together. Nor shall I
Myself be long from you as I desire to fight."
Athene spoke and touched him with a golden wand (XVI. 164-72).

Such a brilliant poetic device to have Athene silently signal to Odysseus by raising her eyebrows and to have him respond in understanding this subtle gesture. She informs him that the right time, the appropriate time (*kairos*) has arrived for him to shed his concealment as her strategy to protect him. Her intention was to keep him hidden (*kalypsoed*). Now is the right time for Odysseus and his son to meet for the first time, to embrace and then to begin plotting the overthrow of the excessive presences in his household. This is a pivotal moment in the epic when the plan to reclaim the *oikos* occurs on the margins, at the threshold between land and sea. She also reassures him that in the battle with the suitors she will be there to fight with him.

A visitation by the goddess is often accompanied by an expression of wisdom or information crucial to further survival; they are most often spoken but are not limited to words. They can alter significantly the trajectory of one's life or moderate the direction one has been traversing. These sacred instances are called in some traditions conversion experiences; they may be permanent or temporary in their affects, but one must be willing to give oneself over to them. One has the right to refuse or deflect the call, but at great risk of not fulfilling one's destiny. Athene's name itself, as James Hillman cites Karl Kerenyi, "refers to a 'containing receptacle, a kind of vessel, a dish, beaker or pan'" ("On the Necessity of Abnormal Psychology" 26). Here she holds both father and son at the moment when the father will reveal he is now home.

Meditation:

Have you heeded the call from a divine or numinous or mysterious presence that changed your life's direction? It could have appeared in many forms: a presence, a dream, a book, a conversation overheard, to name a few.

August 11: Book XVI

At first she placed a cloak and a well-washed tunic
About his shoulders, increased his body and his youth.
His skin became dark again, and his cheeks filled out,
And the beard around his chin turned into dark blue.
When she had done this, she went back again, and Odysseus
Went into the hut. His dear son marveled at him.
He cast his eyes the other way, alarmed lest it be a god (XVI. 173-79).

We sense the care and affection Athene feels toward Odysseus as she once again returns his body to its original, even heightened stature in the process. Here he is created anew, so much so, that Telemachos thinks he may be in the presence of a god, so craftily does Athene make him shine in his mortality. Odysseus willingly accepts himself back again. It is a preparation to meet his son after two decades so they might conspire to retrieve the home and rescue Penelope from enormous pressure to marry one of the suitors. The moment is pivotal in the long journey home for both of them. Finding one another is one of the essential moments of the father and the son's homecoming.

Living in disguise has its advantages. They can be overt or covert, as when one disguises who one is in demeanor and the personality they put into the world; it can also be overt disguises to hide one's identity. Odysseus engages both forms. Reaching a point where one can present oneself in one's true nature, disposition and appearance in shedding concealment, is both liberating and affirming. Being hidden from family and friends can dismember one's relationships. Restoring oneself and restoring relationships after being absent and a stranger rather than a familiar presence, can renew the soul and reaffirm one's deepest identity. Returning a family to its original unity after years of exile revitalizes every member. Edward Tick writes that "wandering and wounded warriors need a tribe waiting to receive, hear and tend them. If we are that tribe, they will come home and serve the greater good" (*Warrior's Return* 161). The moment above when Odysseus begins his reintegration through his son and swineherd inaugurates this most important part of the journey.

Meditation:

Describe when you were alienated from your family, your friends, and even from yourself and what it felt like to reunite with any of them.

August 12: Book XVI

"You appear other to me, stranger, than a moment before.
You have other garments, and your skin is not as it was.
You must be some one of the gods who possess broad heaven.
Well, be gracious, so we may give pleasing sacrifices
And well-made golden gifts to you. Be sparing toward us."
Then godly Odysseus, who had suffered much, answered him:
"I am not any god. Why liken me to immortals?
But I am your father, for whose sake you are grieving
And suffer many pains, receiving the assaults of men" (XVI. 181-89).

For the first time Odysseus and his son are alone and see one another clearly and lovingly. Telemachos notices all the changes that have occurred to the stranger and can only assume he is divine. His fear is apparent in his plea to spare him and the others at the swineherd's domicile. Odysseus then identifies himself not as an immortal but as the young man's father. The words "suffer" and "suffering" gather around him as he acknowledges his son's own grief at his loss. An instant connection absorbs them both as a lifetime of absence pervades the loving air embracing them both. Each is returning home from a journey. Norman Austin observes that "the son, in order to become spiritually like the father, traces out a reduced, and to some degree symbolic, journey in imitation of the father" (qtd. in Jean Houston, *The Hero and the Goddess* 268). Two forms of the heroic surface in their meeting.

How can we imagine such a reunion when family members find one another after years of not knowing their blood kin or discovering they have such a person in their lives? We witness this increasingly with the use of Facebook and other social search engines wherein people find relatives they have never met or even known existed. Some part of both individuals or groups are completed, or shattered fragments put back into place, or a missing piece of the larger family finds a home. The joy of the reunion is tempered by the years of absence where so much of both lives was not able to be shared. But the grief felt about this loss is often overridden by the joy that attends such a reunion.

Meditation:

Have you been reunited with a relative or a close friend, perhaps from early childhood, after many years or decades of separation? What did this reunion add to your own existence?

August 13: Book XVI

When he had said this, he kissed his son and sent a tear to the ground
Off his cheeks. Before, he had always held them back without blenching.
Telemachos—he did not yet believe him to be his father—
Answered him right away with words and addressed him:
"You surely are not my father Odysseus, but some god
Enchants me, so that I may grieve and lament still more;
For in no way would a mortal man in his own mind
Devise these things, unless a god came by in person
Who might easily if he wished make one young or old" (XVI. 190-98).

Incredulous and guarding his own feelings of vulnerability, Telemachos is wary even after the father's affection seems so genuine. Odysseus allows himself to express the deep grief and joy over his son's presence, one he has been watching for some time prior to revealing himself. His son sees a cruel joke afoot, a divinity trying to trick him to increase his sense of loss by offering a counterfeit of his father. No mortal, he asserts, would or could do such a thing unless guided by a divinity. Here both father and son speak the truth, given Athene's role in concealing, then revealing Odysseus. All of this is Athene's doing, expressions of her *metis* and her strength. As Sheila Murnaghan writes of Athene, "As she stimulates the extension of mutually supportive relationships between aristocratic males from father to son, she activates the very process of heredity on which the aristocratic and patriarchal culture of the poem is based" ("The Plan of Athena" 66). The scene above is a key example of Murnaghan's insight.

What life circumstances have each of us experienced when we found ourselves saying, "I can't believe it" or "This can't be happening" or "Unbelievable!" because what we are experiencing has stepped outside our limits of probability? In that moment we may become aware of other forces, presences, or active agents affecting our lives by increasing our capacity to know and to acknowledge the vaster dimensions of our being. In these moments we may feel the numinous gather around us like a mist to push us into another reality.

Meditation:

When has your life suddenly opened to embrace or include the numinous, the inexplicable, the paradoxical, any of which may have deepened your awareness?

August 14: Book XVI

"Telemachos, it is not seemly when your father is within
To wonder exceedingly and to be amazed.
No other Odysseus, indeed, shall ever come to you here.
I am the very man; suffering evils, wandering much,
I have come in the twentieth year to my fatherland.
And now this is the work of the forager Athene,
Who has made of me what she wishes, for she can do that,
Sometimes in the semblance of a beggar and sometimes
That of a young man who has lovely clothes on his skin" (XVI. 202-10).

Telemachos' incredulous response to his father is met with a mild rebuke. Odysseus wants his son to see he is a mortal, not a divinity, and to accept him on those terms. Odysseus' anguish is apparent: after twenty years of warring and wandering, he is at last in the vicinity of home; yet Telemachos is skeptical that the man in front of him is his father. Odysseus explains that the gods have the power "to glorify a mortal man or to disguise him" (l. 212). Athene has altered her beloved Odysseus in various acts of *metis* in order that he survive and make his way home to fulfill his destiny. He has yielded to her wisdom and now has reclaimed part of his family and property. He is also reclaiming his family's history, which includes severe suffering to rival his own.

Few escape the range of being that includes the poverty of a beggar and the wealth of a leader. Life is often more uneven than we would prefer. At times, we are thrown against the rocks and at others against the soft cushions of good fortune. All of our plots are comprised of such extremes. Call it the doings of divinity or the impulses of our higher self; our plot must absorb them all. In this way our character is forged anew. A sign of wisdom may be the ability to discern what we have control over and what we must yield to as the presence of another reality that also wants a say in our plotline. Our own embodiment can be an "aperture or the corridor into invisible presences that can be imagined only through the flesh" (*The Wounded Body* 17), as I have written in another context.

Meditation:

To what do you attribute your own shifts and machinations of your life's fortunes? Are they exclusively your doing, or do you believe that another presence is also at work in your unfolding destiny?

August 15: Book XVI

When he had said this he sat down. Telemachos
Embraced his noble father and moaned, shedding tears.
In both of them there arose a longing for lamentation.
They wailed piercingly and more incessantly than birds,
Sea eagles or falcons with hooked claws whose children
Farmers have snatched off before they were fully fledged.
So they lamented and shed tears from under their eyelids,
And the light of the sun would have gone down on their moaning
If Telemachos had not at once spoken out to his father:
"In what kind of ship, dear father, did sailors
Bring you to Ithaca? Who did they claim to be?" (XVI. 213-23).

Fully revealed to one another now, father and son emotionally fall into one another's embrace without reservation and painfully, but not without joy at their reunion. They hold one another and go beyond language in their lamentation for all the years they were apart; now in being reunited the simile is a rich one: they are compared to birds whose young have been stolen by farmers from them before they were developed; their parents now grieve for their loss. Laments for years lost mingle with joy at seeing who and what one another is. The two emotions may never be reconciled, so vast is the time war and wandering have split the family.

News reports often find a rich story in revealing how family members, apart for decades, or not knowing the existence of the other, are reunited or united for the first time. These connections are both joyful and sad, fulfilling and discouraging. No one who has the experience in one's own life or who witnesses this moment in the lives of others can remain unaffected. Separation is a grief-laden moment; that same grief returns when family members are reunited. In some faiths, people believe that at the death of a loved one, they believe it is temporary, for they will be reunited in an after world. Telemachos expresses what many feel after years of being separated from family. Norman Fischer writes, "he finds it difficult to accept that Odysseus stands before him now, a perfect match for his fantasy" (*Sailing Home* 179). Disbelief and non-acceptance are not uncommon responses in family members or loved ones because the risk is great that they may be deceived by an imposter.

Meditation:

What has been your experience of separation and then reunion with loved ones?

August 16: Book XVI

"Now I have come here at Athene's instigations,
So we may plan about slaughter for our enemies.
Come now, speak out, and number the suitors for me,
So I may know how many men they are, and what sort.
Then as I deliberate in my own blameless heart
I may consider whether we can oppose them ourselves,
Alone without others or shall seek for others."
Then sound-minded Telemachos spoke to him in answer:
"Father, I have always heard of your great renown
For being a skillful fighter with your hands and prudent in counsel.
But you speak of something enormous. Awe holds me" (XVI. 233-43).

Odysseus is clear to his son that he is guided by the goddess of war and wisdom; he needs her counsel because the household has been usurped by young men with enormous appetites who disrespect all codes of hospitality. Odysseus seeks the number of men he is to challenge and Telemachos shortly lists them: one hundred eighteen and from an impressive number of tribes. His crafty mind is set in motion to see if the number is low enough for them to overthrow the suitors, or if he is to enlist more men to aid them. Craft *(metis)* weds with force *(bia)* in reclaiming the household. Odysseus may refer to his heart as "blameless" because he had to be a warrior at Troy rather than at home to protect his property. I think his claim can be argued because he defeated himself on more than one occasion and extended his time away from home because of it.

When in our lives we are confronted by adversaries and we have no clear game plan to compromise or overthrow the source of conflict, to whom do we turn? We can solicit outside companions to aid us; we can discern a crafty way to engage the source of the conflict; we can surrender; or we can see if an oath, in which each side sacrifices something of value in order to gain a lost balance or equanimity, is possible. The goal is to restore both integrity and wholeness to our lives by dismantling or reducing the challenge. Some sane measure of opposing energies is needed to restore equilibrium before violence is a default position.

Meditation:

Recall a situation in which suitors' appetites invaded your life and household. Here a suitor could be in the form of a disease that ravaged or devoured so much of what you treasure or a betrayal by someone or your own reckless appetites and needs.

August 17: Book XVI

"Take thought for someone well disposed to defend us."
Then godly Odysseus, who had suffered much, addressed him:
"I shall tell you, then, mark it well and listen to me,
And consider whether Athene with Father Zeus
Will protect us, or I shall think up some other defender."
Then sound-minded Telemachos answered him:
"These are excellent defenders of whom you speak,
Both seated high upon the clouds, and the two of them
Rule over all others, both men and the immortal gods" (XVI. 257-65).

It is rare that much time passes when Odysseus is not referencing divinities in his plans and his actions. The gods are laced throughout his soul and body. Rarely are they very far from his consciousness. The stories of the gods and goddesses Homer both appropriates and invents, for they are, as Carl Kerenyi writes, "the products of humanity at a more general and impersonal level" and serve us as "examples of the more general human lessons that mythology teaches us" (*The Gods of the Greeks* 11-12). With his human flaws he nonetheless turns always to divine guidance through Athene's constant mentoring. He sees here that his son is of the same mind and heart as his father. Furthermore, if they are not willing to assist Odysseus, he will call on other deities to reinforce his campaign to re-civilize his home.

A mark of our human condition from its origins has been to create/discover deities either within or outside us. We recognize that another dimension of reality, to which we are suppliants, is a comfort and a real source of strength and solace when strife and suffering impinge on our lives. Submitting or yielding our will to the conditions of a god or guide or guru can help us survive what might kill us if we tried to handle it on our own. At one point our poet of the *Odyssey* claims that "Okeanos [is] the origin of the gods" and "the origin of everything" (*The Gods of the Greeks* 15). Like us, the gods have an origin, a beginning narrative that extends from prehistory into the present; their wisdom is worth pursuing. Such a belief can offer us comfort when we accept that something beyond us also has a hand in our lives; we are only partly the impetus to our destiny.

Meditation:

To whom do you turn when life becomes overwhelming and out of control, when you feel that you have little voice in its management?

August 18: Book XVI

"Well now, you go on home at the appearance of dawn
And mingle in with the presumptuous suitors,
And the swineherd will bring me later to the town
In the semblance of a beggar, miserable and old.
And if they dishonor me in the house, let the heart
In your own breast endure it that I suffer evilly.
Even if they drag me by the feet through the house out the doors
Or throw at me with darts, look on and restrain yourself.
No, just order them to cease their foolishness,
Speaking to them with soothing words" (XVI. 270-79).

Odysseus outline his strategy for taking the suitors off guard by letting them believe they are in full command of the household and he, a pitiful beggar. He calls on his son to endure the disrespect he will surely confront. His father's instructions are clear: persevere through their abuse, admonish them gently with non-threatening words so to give the impression they have nothing to fear from the beggar or him. Restraint is the operative virtue he calls on his son as a warrior to practice. Endurance and restraint are the initial weapons to deploy against the consumers of his home. Craft will be their initial assault strategy to disarm those who for years have violated the laws of civilized life.

Force may work at times to correct an impulse. But craft reveals an intelligence and a keen imagination that can disarm and defeat a less astute adversary, especially one grown unconscious from excessively serving appetites as their god. A subtler approach, more indirect and thus more effective, is disguise, fiction, a fabrication of reality to bring the stronger force into a more vulnerable condition. Something in craftiness shows a richer way of imagining a solution or resolution to problems. There exists even a greater delight in resolving a conflict by some contact and contract with another reality that the adversary does not see until too late. Books XV and XVI are crucial sections because in them "Odysseus' life threads begin to be woven back into the fabric of his fatherland and his family as he imagines entering his own home," as I have written on the *Odyssey* (*The Wounded Body* 46).

Meditation:

Have you resolved a conflict by craft rather than force? What was your strategy to defuse or domesticate what could have been a violent or unpleasant situation?

August 19: Book XVI

"I shall tell you another thing, and keep it in mind.
When Athene of many plans puts it in my mind,
I shall nod to you with my head, and then you yourself take note
How many weapons of war are lying in the halls;
Pick them up and put them in a nook of the lofty chamber,
All of them. And appease the suitors deceptively
With soft speeches when they miss them and ask you questions:
'I have put them out of the smoke, since they no longer look like those
That Odysseus once left behind when he went to Troy, . . .'" (XVI. 281-89).

From beggar stranger to father to teacher is Odysseus' trajectory with his son. He now instructs him in the art of deception, fine-tuning the craft of *metis* in order to disarm the suitors with appearance and words that deceive. Odysseus once more becomes a fiction-maker, a master fabricator. The above reads like the dress rehearsal of a performance. He offers Telemachos his character role to perform to keep the suitors ignorant of their future. He will remove their weapons to protect them from the fire's smoke. Raising no suspicion while plotting their destruction is the goal of the performance. Norman Fischer offers that Telemachos here also witnesses how "our youthful, ambivalent, and fearful selves—our Telemachos selves—be united with our wily older selves, because it takes both to oust the suitors" *(Sailing Home* 181). Odysseus cannot go this part of his journey alone, unaided.

Fabrication of reality may be necessary in certain life conditions where the balance of power is so askew that nothing less than a believable fiction will favor an effective advantage. The end goal requires craft mixed with force. Here the fiction is used to reclaim one's home; its leverage is a fictional narration to create a credible world for the other to believe in. It must be cunning and consistent. Without success, one's intentions are paralyzed. The mystery of narratives is that when successfully accepted by a believing audience, then one has created a credible reality that exists only in the imagination, not in the historical field of life. But the psyche cannot and is not interested in the difference, finally, if the story is truly told. Whether it happened historically does not affect its veracity.

Meditation:

Have you been forced to fabricate a fiction for others to accept because of a threat to your existence on any level?

August 20: Book XVI

"Let you and me alone find out the bent of the women,
And we shall further try out certain of the menservants,
To see where one honors us and respects us in his heart,
And who does not heed you and dishonors the man you are."
His illustrious son spoke out to him in answer:
"Father, you shall know my disposition, I think,
And soon, for no slackness of mind holds me at all . . . .
A long time in vain would you go and test each person
By visiting the fields. And they in our halls unharmed
Devour goods insolently; there is no restraint" (XVI. 304-10; 313-15).

Now that Odysseus has revealed himself, he wishes to discern in his own household who has concealed their infidelity, but while he was gone have revealed it. Now it is time for unmasking the men and women who have violated their trust by dishonoring and disrespecting his family and home. Telemachos believes such a task is far too unwieldy; there must be a better way than individual interrogations. The chance that those unfaithful to the household may unite to destroy father and son is always possible. Odysseus will listen to his son's wise counsel and act on it. Craft must hover above force, for they have an abundance of the former and little of the latter. Telemachos highlights again the absence of restraint that brings the appetites into such prominence in his home. Their devotion to excess, coupled with an outrageous mindlessness, will be used against them as Odysseus' greatest weapon.

When do parents begin to recognize and listen to the wisdom of their children? Some never do, or perhaps when they are wise enough to see it and their children in their full authentic light. Deferring to our children, both in their thoughts and in their physical strength when we parents grow more limited, strengthens the bonds between us. There is a grace in yielding in certain matters to our children; they reflect us in their own development, bringing to us both unique assets and weaknesses. We are wise to listen to them so they feel a true sense of being heard *and* seen. They may also reveal how to reimagine what is familiar.

Meditation:

When has your child or children brought you needed assistance either in words or deeds? Did you see your own earlier self in their words and/or actions such that they returned you to qualities of your former development?

August 21: Book XVI

The suitors were grieving and depressed in their hearts;
They went out of the hall along the great wall of the courtyard
And they sat down there out in front of the portals.
Eurymachos, son of Polybos, began speaking to them:
"Friends, a great task is arrogantly achieved
By Telemachos, this voyage. We thought he would not achieve it. . . ."
Antinoos spoke to them, son of Eupeithes:
"Well now, the gods have delivered this man from harm!
Lookouts were sitting day by day on the windy heights,
In quick succession always, and at the setting sun
We never rested a night on land, but on the ocean. . ." (XVI. 342-47; 363-67).

The suitors show their intentions and their hopes in a scene where they feel defeated because outsmarted by the gods. They had thought to successfully ambush and slay Telemachos on his journey home, but he was assisted by Athene and escaped their fate for him. Despondent, they sense their limits begrudgingly; they also show their boundaries in accepting that divinity might be assisting the young man despite their efforts. But they offer no libations or honor to the gods, only a recognition that some or one was helping the young man survive on his return. They mistook their limited thought for Telemachos' inability to navigate past them. Now they are forced to admit that the gods seem to favor him and that they are more limited than they believed.

We can plan, organize and execute our life phases as be we can, but to believe that all the terms of such actions are in our control is foolish. We are often so surprised that our expectations do not bear fruit that we may be forced to witness ambiguity, uncertainty, paradox and other presences we are unable to harness. Life itself, infused with presences that can undo our best plans, should be expected, if not embraced. St. Augustine observes that "you must be emptied of that with which you are full, so you may be filled with that whereof you are empty" (qtd. in *The World is Made of Stories* 73). The ability to yield to what is offers a way to freedom that many do not learn or learn to ignore.

Meditation:

Recall when a carefully wrought plan was dismantled by unexpected intrusions. What were those invading presences that forced you to change course or adopt a different attitude in your life's journey?

August 22: Book XVI

"Sailing in the swift ship we awaited godly dawn,
In ambush for Telemachos that we might capture him
And kill him. And meanwhile some god has brought him home.
But let us here think of a woeful destruction
For Telemachos, and let him not escape us. I think
These deeds will not be accomplished while he is alive.
He himself is skilled in deliberation and thought,
But the people no longer wholly bear favor toward us. . . .
And they will not approve when they hear of the evil deeds.
I fear they will do some evil and drive us out
Of our own land,. . ." (XVI. 368-75; 380-82).

Antinoos (against mind), the leader of the suitors, recaps what they had planned to do and what they anticipate doing. Slaying the son of the king before his rise to his own authority becomes a primary objective for them. They too plan to engage hiddenness as ambush to destroy Telemachos, who has grown in their imaginations to be a real threat to their consuming habits. But some turn is taking place in Ithaca's people; they are growing weary and wary of the suitors' outrageous and sustained behavior. Antinoos knows what he and the others are planning is wrong and that the people may soon turn against them. The shelf life of the suitors' limitless consumption is drawing to a close. It is the right time for both Telemachos and Odysseus to return to their home. Knowing full well that the gods are assisting Telemachos, they nonetheless continue to plot his death.

Behind bullying and usurping the goods and possessions of others lurks a cowardice and fear of being discovered and exposed. Not uncommon is it for those who rise to a position of power to throw off all limits of measure and propriety because no one is strong enough to rein them in. Their own weak sense of what is just must have restrictions on them; otherwise, their appetites will run over the rights of others. Its motive is short term gain and self-interest at the expense of a common benefit. Antinoos' words reveal how destructive forces in the social order are motivated as much by fear of discovery as it is by greed and keeping what should be commonly shared property within the domain of the few.

Meditation:

When have you witnessed a common good trampled by self-interest that benefitted the few, not the many? Were you able to push against such a move?

August 23: Book XVI

But the prudent Penelope had another thought:
To appear to the suitors with their presumptuous pride;
For she had heard death was to be in the halls for her son.
The herald Medon, who found out their plans, had told her.
She went on into the hall along with her serving women.
And when the godly woman arrived before the suitors,
She stood beside the pillar of the stoutly fashioned roof;
Holding the glistening headbands before her cheeks
She rebuked Antinoos and spoke out directly: (XVI. 409-17).

Like any mother who hears of possible harm to one of her children, Penelope courageously steps forward to confront those who plan to murder her only son. Her rage over their insolence would seem to suffocate any fear she might have for her own safety. She steps forward and stands by the supporting pillar of the roof, as she too is a pillar of the household, keeping it intact and strong. Without any hesitation, she addresses Antinoos, the suitors' leader. Her son's life may depend on the effect she has on him and the others who follow his lead. She is accompanied by all those women who have remained faithful to her and the household. She also is certainly grateful to Medon for revealing to her the suitors' murderous plot, even as they tried to keep it concealed.

Courage in the face of death, especially of one's own member, is a deep primal response to danger. When one is confronted by such a crisis, a parent will drop all hesitation and fear to protect one's own. No hesitation, no doubt, no second guessing are prudent actions to confront the threat head-on. One does what is within one's power to hold the family together in the face of forces that can kill. A parent may feel that to continue living when a family member is at risk would have little purpose. As with her husband and their son before her, Penelope steps into her role as hero, as defender and as deflector of trouble. She is driven less by the fact of whether Odysseus lives or not and more that she will not sacrifice her son to the impious presences in her home. While Gregory Nagy writes that "Penelope defines the heroic identity of Odysseus" (*The Best of the Achaeans* 38), she is also defining her own heroic stature in what follows.

Meditation:

To what ends would you go, or have you gone to protect a family member? To protect yourself or a friend from harm?

August 24: Book XVI

"Antinoos, for all your pride and evil devices, they say
You are the best of your peers in the land of Ithaca
For advice and speeches. But you are not really so.
You madman, why do you devise murder and death
For Telemachos, and do not heed the suppliants
Who have Zeus for a witness? It is not holy to plot ills for one another.
Do you not know that your father came here in flight
And in fear of the people? . . .
They wished to destroy him and to tear out his own heart,
And to devour his great and satisfying livelihood.
But Odysseus held them back and restrained them, though they
    wanted that." (XVI. 418-25; 428-30).

Penelope fights nobly against the source of the one plotting her son's death by rebuking Antinoos. She reveals to him what he has concealed about himself, that he is the best of the Achaians in appearance only; below his counterfeit demeanor he is impious, treacherous and hypocritical. She then shifts to history to bring forth the context in which his own father came to the region and was seen as a threat to the citizens, who wished to destroy him. Only because Odysseus restrained them with his own pleas was the man spared. Now it is time for Antinoos to remember her husband's act by sparing Telemachos. Again, restraint proves more efficacious than engaging in physical conflict, which she would lose.

Exposing someone in power can jeopardize one's own life. But without a warrior spirit speaking the truth to one's adversary's character, words may carry no persuasive force. Like Penelope, who has no physical power but does have craft and cunning, her words must be her strongest ally in deflecting the murderous desires of an enemy who may be beyond shame. One relies on her power of persuasion wherein her language rises to the level of restraining another's destructive impulses. Helen Foley shows how Penelope's moral stance "forms part of the *Odyssey*'s emphasis on ethical norms such as justice and on the quieter values that promote social cohesion" ("Penelope as Moral Agent" 105).

Meditation:

Have you found yourself in a situation where your only weapon or defense was your words? Did they prove effective in heading off or deflecting the violence of another or others?

August 25: Book XVI

But she went on into the shining upper chamber
And wept there for Odysseus, her dear husband, until
Bright-eyed Athene cast sweet sleep on her eyelids.
At evening the godly swineherd came to Odysseus
And his son. They were preparing dinner attentively,
Sacrificing a year-old swine. And Athene
Stood close beside Odysseus, son of Laertes,
Struck him with a wand, and made him an old man again.
She clothed his skin in wretched garments, lest the swineherd
Look straight at him and know him and go announce it
To constant Penelope. . . (XVI. 449-59).

Two women bookend Odysseus and his son. Penelope weeps for him while Athene transforms him. The goddess attends to all those in the family, comforting Penelope with sweet sleep as well as hiding Odysseus in an aging body; she then assists Telemachos by showing her affection for him. Athene's wand gives the scene a fairy tale or folkloric atmosphere as she prepares them to retrieve the household. Craft, guile, deception, disguise demand a constant oscillation of reconciling and revealing, opening up and closing down. Athene's wisdom knows the right timing and the right response, both signs of her deep wisdom. Eumaeos' hut is the model of order, courage and arrangement.

Any period in our lives can be like the one described above, a transitional period, where we can find ourselves for a time between two worlds—one not yet achieved, the other perhaps only dimly grasped. It is a mythic place, often called liminal, where two different worlds need a bridge to help one cross from one to another. The father, Odysseus, is prepared carefully by the goddess to achieve a hidden end by hidden means. Such pauses allow us to re-collect ourselves, offer patience in planning and let conditions arise so that timing is careful and prudent. Lena Ross writes that "Transition, then, would appear to have an implied function: to carry one over to a different state of being" ("Transitional Phenomena in Clinical Practice" 90).

Meditation:

When has a transitional state or condition in your life surfaced, where you found yourself temporarily moving between two worlds? What was it that moved you from one to another?

August 26: Book XVI

"Just now over the city where the hill of Hermes is,
I was going along when I saw a swift ship coming on
Into our harbor. There were upon her many men.
It was loaded down with shields and with two-edged spears. . . ."
So he said, and Telemachos smiled in his sacred strength.
He looked with his eyes at his father and avoided the swineherd.
And when they had ceased from their toil and made dinner,
They dined, nor did their hearts want for a well-shared meal.
But when they had taken their fill of food and drink
They remembered rest, and they took the gift of sleep (471-74; 476-81).

Telemachos' maturation is evident when Homer refers to his "sacred strength." He has a wisdom about him that was absent in the early scenes of him in his home before initiating his quest. The three of them are busy recreating in their imaginations a well-ordered household; there surfaces as well a rhythm and measure in their tasks, ending with sleep to prepare them for executing their plan against the suitors. The swineherd reports seeing a ship coming into the harbor dressed for war. Telemachos and his father share a recognition, for this is the ship that had been out waiting to ambush Telemachos as he returned. Now they will enjoy the gift of sleep; it replenishes and renews. It rejuvenates and restores strength and resolve. One feels in reading that a threshold is about to be crossed to bring the warrior and his son more fully home.

We find ourselves often anticipating a moment when one's carefully thought-out plans draw near to being achieved. We cannot know the outcome but we know that now is the time, the right time (*Kairos*), to execute it. Not acting at the right time can suffocate its execution. After a certain time, thinking and planning must migrate into action. Much risk is in play. One cannot know the adversary or the force of the challenges ahead. But one can know that the time has arrived to move on one's intentions. It is often a moment requiring great courage. In some individuals this moment may be viewed as one of grace's presence to guide one to a hoped-for end. That grace cannot be sought, but as a gift it can be received with humility and gratitude.

Meditation:

Recall a situation when you knew that you must take action after pondering your options and perhaps seeking advice from others.

V

BOOKS XVII-XX

Reclaiming One's Self: Cleansing the Household

August 27: Book XVII

"Uncle, I am going to the city, so that my mother
May see me; I do not believe that she will cease
From hateful wailing and tearful lamentation
Until she sees me in person. I give you this order:
Lead this wretched stranger to the city, so that there
He may beg a dinner. Whoever wishes may give him
A loaf and a cup. . . .
And if the stranger gets very angry, it will be the more painful
For himself. Yes, indeed, I like to speak the truth."
Odysseus of many wiles addressed him in answer:
"My friend, I do not wish to be held back myself" (XVII. 6-12; 14-17).

Telemachos' journey puts into action their plot to reclaim the household from violation and excessive consumption. Eumaeos remains unaware that the ragged wretch is his master so he will not reveal Odysseus' identity. He must remain concealed so their scheme to win back the household will be successful. Telemachos treats the stranger with a nonchalance that furthers Eumaeos' belief that this beggar may receive tokens from the suitors but is of no real consequence. And if he urges the suitors to become angry, he will suffer for his own lack of restraint. Then Telemachos proclaims that he likes to speak the truth, even as his father in disguise announces that he does not wish any longer to be restrained. Both assertions are true, one spoken in openness, the other within the foliage of disguise.

Deception can be a virtue when the unadorned truth can be a fierce weapon against one. Disguise and craft, craftiness, are then a delight to witness. Part of its entertainment rests in its replacing one reality with another and holding the tension between them so that the hidden, true realism, is rendered harmless until the propitious moment. Writing of war, Tim O'Brian observes: "I want you to know why story truth is truer sometimes than happening truth" (*The Things They Carried* 179). Within a certain disposition, what one conveys to be the truth of identity or situation is negotiable and depends on what ends it seeks to serve. How one crafts appearances in words or wardrobe is then taken for what is true. The truth of the story is more crucial than the truth of the event that it speaks about. The difference matters.

Meditation:

When were you deceived or forced to deceive another? Thinking back on it, what was each or both in service of?

August 28: Book XVII

Then he went in himself and crossed the stone threshold.
The nurse Eurycleia was by far the first to see him.
She strewed fleeces upon the cleverly wrought armchairs,
And then she broke out in tears and came straight to him.
The other serving women of hardy-minded Odysseus gathered,
And they kissed him affectionately on his head and shoulders.
The prudent Penelope went on out of the chamber,
Resembling Artemis or golden Aphrodite.
Weeping, she threw her arms around her beloved son;
She kissed him on the head and on both lovely eyes (XVII. 30-41).

Telemachos' return home is welcomed with an outpouring of love for him; no one thought they would see him again. The mother who bore him, the woman who helped raise him and the women who served him all gather to celebrate his homecoming. By craft through Athene's aid he has walked across the threshold, placed his spear against a pillar of the home and surrendered to their affection and joy. This threshold also signals a new life and role for the young leader. As the pivotal figure, Telemachos has just been resurrected with his father and now with his mother. Through his efforts and the divine goddess he will aid in reuniting his parents soon, after they reveal themselves to one another. There is as well a fatedness in the action of reunion; all of the wanderings and woundings are slowly finding a home, which itself must now be cleansed.

Homecoming can be a blessed event. Something absent in the household that gives it purpose and a form is reestablished. The spirit of the place is renewed; that mysterious quality of presence once more reveals itself. The goddess Hestia, divine presence of hospitality and hearth-warming reenters, even in the face of adversity. I have written in another essay that "As the guest-host relationship is so central to the action of Homer's *Odyssey* when the wandering hero struggles to regain the hearth in his home with the assistance of his son and wife, Penelope, so does Hestia offer a rich and welcoming ground for ideas and images to be entertained" ("Hestia: Goddess of the Heart(h)" 99). Along with Athene's craft, Hestia's hospitality is a major force in the epic. Focusing is one of her strongest attributes.

Meditation:

Describe your response to someone precious to you who has returned home after being away for a time. What did their return add to the quality of your life?

August 29: Book XVII

She washed herself and put pure garments upon her skin,
Vowed to all the gods she would sacrifice full hecatombs
If somehow Zeus might bring about deeds of retribution.
Telemachos then went on through the hall
Holding a spear, and two swift dogs accompanied him.
Moreover, Athene shed a marvelous grace about him.
All the people wondered about him as he came on.
The bold suitors gathered together around him,
Speaking fine words but plotting evils in their minds.
And then he avoided the entire group of them (XVII. 58-67).

In her own way Penelope prepares herself for Odysseus' arrival as a beggar, though she does not know it. Telemachos also prepares: he carries a spear and with Athene's power, he has a sense of grace mantling him that is so potent that it brings wonder to all the people who witness his arrival. The beautiful poetic touch is that he is described with two swift dogs who are by his side. The suitors also reveal a hypocritical face by speaking well of him but in their concealed minds continue to plot his death. Knowing this instinctively, Telemachos gives them a wide berth. He is portrayed as the new warrior and serves as a preamble for the arrival of his father, who will continue the fiction of his identity.

The discomfort of being in a position where others seek our overthrow or bad fortune is intense and can debilitate us. We seek acceptance and a life free of suffering. but life circumstances can throw us into a vulnerable position. What do we do? Who or what do we call on when we are certainly without much power or means of defense? What craftiness or cleverness do we access to resolve a tense and unpleasant situation? In addition, how do you understand the aura or mana that surrounds a person to make them seem out of the ordinary in appearance and stature, where a sense of grace surrounds them and compels others to draw near that person? It is a magnificent moment when divinity gives a brilliance to a mortal that brings them closer to the divine that may inhabit each of us but is not seen except when they wish to intervene to aid or thwart circumstances.

Meditation:

How have you responded when threatened? What resources, perhaps that you did not know you possessed, came to your aid?

August 30: Book XVII

"Telemachos, when I have gone up into the upper chamber
I shall lie down in my bed, which is made full of groans for me,
Ever sullied with my tears since the time Odysseus
Went to Troy with the sons of Atreus. . . ."
"All right, then, mother, I shall speak the truth to you.
We went to Pylos and to Nestor, shepherd of the people.
The man received me and kindly befriended me
In his lofty home, as a father would his own son
Come afresh after a time from somewhere else. . . .
But of hardy-hearted Odysseus, alive or dead
He said he had never heard anything from anyone on earth" (XVII. 101-04; 108-12; 114-15).

Exasperated by the situation and getting little information from her son, Penelope answers she will return to her bedroom, full of grief and tear-stained, as it has been since Odysseus originally left for battle. Her sadness prompts her son to reveal at least some of the story of his travels in quest of his father. He recounts all that he was told, both from Nestor and later, Menelaos. He omits the part where he was reunited recently with his father and their mutually-crafted plot to overthrow the suitors. What remains concealed is where the power of surprise incubates. What is not said is finally more potent than what is expressed. This passage also returns us to the beginning of the epic as one of many places where the well-crafted plot folds back and remembers itself in the making.

Deception has a renowned place in our lives as well as in our life story when it serves purposes of survival and sustains what is of value, or protects the feelings of another. We story the world we move through all the time, shaping it with intentions as we go, as Telemachos demonstrates above. Dan McAdams suggests, "Storytelling appears to be a fundamental way of expressing ourselves in our world to others" (*The Stories We Live By* 27). We see as well that expressing the blatant truth can create destructive consequences, especially when one discloses it at the wrong time or in the most inauspicious moment. Great harm can ensue when the story we tell is expressed within an uncertain or precarious context.

Meditation:

When have you withheld the whole truth of an event in order to preserve a situation or to protect yourself and another, or both?

August 31: Book XVII

There Melanthios, son of Dolios, came upon them
While he was leading goats that were best among all the herds,
As dinner for the suitors. And two herdsmen followed along.
When he saw them he upbraided them and spoke directly,
A striking, disgraceful speech. He stirred Odysseus' heart.
"Now a man wholly foul leads a man who is foul;
So the god always brings a like to his own like.
Miserable swineherd, where are you leading this wild pig,
This tiresome beggar, desecrator of feasts,
Who stands by many door posts and rubs his shoulders on them,
Begging for morsels, but not for basins or swords?" (XVII. 212-22).

Melanthios, a resident lackey, brings the best of Odysseus' goats for the suitors' consumption. He pauses to berate and demean the swineherd and the disguised Odysseus. A miserable, arrogant fellow, he relishes attacking the two ragged-looking men, with no clue who is concealed. Yet he still brings trouble on himself in the form of a bully who has no sense of hospitality, so he treats them both with disdain. He judges Odysseus by his appearance and spins a tale about his behavior as one who seeks food but has no wish to wash or fight. He judges from an arrogant and condescending point of view, as befits the suitor's attitude. Melanthios' ignorance allows him to speak the truth: that the god always matches mortals according to likeness. He does not grasp just yet the reality of his pronouncement.

None of us can completely avoid bullies, tyrants or individuals who abuse their power against those who cannot defend themselves; their victims are those who cannot retaliate, most often because they have no power. Their goal is to intimidate to perhaps improve their own feelings about themselves. Melanthios is an image of the brutal soul who tries to gain self-worth through intimidation. His own poverty is revealed in violent words and threats. Many have suggested that behind the overt verbal and/or physical abuse of the bully lies a coward suffocating in fear that one hides with contrary gestures.

Meditation:

When you have been confronted by the cruel spirit of a bully, what was your strategy of dealing with the assault? Have you changed your tactics over the years because you found a better strategy to deal with this character type?

September 1: Book XVII

So he said, and in his foolishness rushed with a kick
On his flank. But he did not drive the man off the path;
Odysseus stood steadfast. And he deliberated
Whether to rush on the other with the staff and take his life
Or to lift him by the middle and dash his head to earth.
But he braced himself and checked his mind. The swineherd
Looked at the other and scolded him; he raised his hands and
Prayed aloud;. . . .
"May the man himself come, and may some god bring him.
Then he would scatter all these vainglories far and wide
That you bring now in your insolence. . ." (XVII. 233-39; 243-45).

Melanthios, not satisfied with words, and easily provoked, turns to physical violence in kicking Odysseus. The violence brings Odysseus to react in kind in his mind, but realizes whatever draws attention to himself diminishes his success in reclaiming the household. With great effort he restrains his appetite for revenge. Restraint, concealment and craftiness are his strongest weapons at this juncture, not force and might. What he as a warrior knows is that there is a place for each strategy, depending on the circumstances and not on one's appetite to seek vengeance. Eumaios comes to his master's aid, unknowingly, by calling to the gods to return Odysseus home. We as audience experience a certain delight in the swineherd's words, for we know that he is standing next to the one who pleads for his arrival. An act of restraint on a larger level will reconcile forces in the epic.

Remaining concealed or hiding one's intentions gives one a power that can far exceed blatant overt force. What is called for, as Marilyn Stewart writes, "is patience and heroic endurance. It demands waiting and listening and taking in as much as possible" ("Mapping in the *Odyssey*" 89). There is authority in covert action. Patience, holding back, keeping one's hand hidden confers a mindful advantage over brute force, especially when those much more powerful know they are. Often their guard is then relaxed. They believe their might will win in any circumstance. Mindfulness over muscle can ultimately conquer forces far more compelling and destructive than one's own.

Meditation:

When did you decide to yield, to hold back, because you took the long view rather than the immediate short view in a threatening situation you found yourself in?

September 2: Book XVII

Then godly Odysseus, who had suffered much, answered him:
"I know, I see. You say this to an understanding man.
Go forward now, and I shall remain here behind,
For I am not unacquainted with tosses or with blows.
My heart is enduring, since I have suffered many ills
On the waves and in war. Let this one be added to them.
There is no way of concealing an eager stomach,
The accursed thing that gives many evils to men,
On whose account also well-rigged ships set out
Over the barren ocean, carrying evils for enemies" (XVII. 280-89).

Odysseus responds to Eumaios' two plans of having either him or Odysseus enter the house first. He gets the strategy of the swineherd's two possible options. The warrior then reflects on what war and wandering have taught him. Being abused by others is only another form of being in battle and having to endure hardships at the hands of hostile presences. Odysseus is most interested in reclaiming a cosmos that has been shattered in his absence. His desire is to reshape the order of his household, and more broadly, of his people. Louise Cowan has written that "epics give form to the myth of a people and places that myth within a larger, moral universe" ("Epic as Cosmopoiesis" 17). Seen in this light, Odysseus must restrain himself here and further on if he ever hopes to reclaim what his people need: their abiding and sustaining myth.

Odysseus' reflections ask us to consider the source of evil and suffering, as well as their intimate relation in history, from a broader perspective. Self-interest, the hunger for more wealth, the reckless acquisition of property, land, possessions--all serve mortal cravings, not noble impulses. In the *The Bhagavad Gita*, the god Krishna instructs the warrior Arjuna that "Greed is but desire swollen to grotesque form. The wise one knows that desire is the eternal, insatiable archenemy, . . ." (36). Strip them away and one exposes the monstrous form of greed and power, both insatiable hungers for more. Without a broader epic vision of human life that is more inclusive, one migrates, knowingly or not, to serving the self in an endless repetition of satisfying hungers that defy satisfaction.

Meditation:

Where does the desire for more infect your own life and those around you? What have been the consequences of pursuing such stubborn desires?

September 3: Book XVII

And so such things did they say to one another,
And the dog held his head and his ears up where he lay,
Argos, stout-hearted Odysseus', that he himself
Had once reared and did not enjoy, but he went off beforehand
To holy Ilion. . . .
But now he was lying unwanted while his master was gone,
In much dung from mules and oxen, which was heaped
In abundance before the gates, till Odysseus' servants
Should bring it when they had a great plot to fertilize.
There the dog Argos lay, full of the vermin of dogs; (XVII. 290-94; 296-300).

A small but profound scene in the epic when Odysseus meets his faithful dog, who in his neglect and filthiness is an emblem of the condition of the household polluted by the suitors. Neglecting Odysseus' beloved pet indicates the neglect of the hearth; the dung that Argos is mired in is a painful metaphor for how the home has gone to waste. But in the current situation, he has been cast aside, along with the excrement of animals. Steeped in vermin and absent spirit, Argos is exhausted, unwanted and ignored by all around him. As a remnant of a life that has been lost in the household, he is treated with the same indifference as is the waste of other animals. He has no reason or purpose to live, except to wait faithfully for the return of his master under the harshest of conditions.

Our pets are powerful reflections of ourselves. They care for us, humanize us, and bring out some of our best qualities. We care for them as we would any family member. When they are abused through neglect, beatings, or by withholding affection, or any other form of mistreatment, it tells us something about their caretakers. The animal nature in any of us is given expression in how we care for our pets. In his reflections on the dog, James Hillman writes: "What essential intelligence is embodied in that hairy coat, behind those soft eyes and black muzzle of that angel we call a dog?" (*Animal Presences* 151). So there is a spiritual quality about animals, especially those we domesticate and love. They are also psychic realities that influence our own thoughts, behaviors and attitudes toward the natural world.

Meditation:

What role has an animal pet contributed to your quality of life, and you to its?

September 4: Book XVII

And then, when he perceived that Odysseus was nearby,
He fawned over him with his tail and dropped both his ears.
But then he was no longer able to go closer
To his master. The man looked away and wiped off a tear. . . .
"Great wonder is it, Eumaeos, that this dog lies here in the dung;
He is handsome in body, but I do not clearly know
Whether along with this look he used also to be swift to run
Or was simply the sort of table dog that belongs to men. . . ."
But the fortune of black death took Argos away
Once he had seen Odysseus in the twentieth year (XVII. 301-04; 306-09; 326-27).

We remember how Telemachos, on returning home, was accompanied by a spear and two swift dogs. Here Argos attempts in his weakened condition to rekindle his relations with his master by fawning over him. Odysseus, fearful of someone seeing his pet's affection for him and revealing his identity, must refuse Argos' gestures of affection. No one sees Odysseus' grief not just over his former companion's affection, but that he cannot comfort Argos in his short time before dying. Argos, however, seems content now to having seen his master one last time, after waiting twenty years for his return. His pet is the sterling emblem of fidelity, of enduring in suffering for his beloved master; in this he rises above all the suitors in his fidelity and in bearing his unfortunate neglect. One might wonder why Telemachos did not care for him.

Perhaps fidelity and unconditional love are two of the most prominent attributes our pets bestow on us. They are absolutely forgiving and accept us on almost any terms without qualifications. As such they add immeasurably to the quality of the household. James Hillman reminds us that "the dog's association with the underworld and death occurs widely in folklore, in stories of revenants, hauntings and uncanny intuitions, and in the myths of many cultures" (*Animal Presences* 158). It is not unusual, then, for our pets to sound an alarm of danger or otherwise warn us of possible disaster or threat. Our pets can then be bellwethers for what is to come. In this sense, the incident of Argos' passing suggests the end of a condition, perhaps of the household as it has become and with death as the forerunner of its revitalization.

Meditation:

Relate your favorite story of a pet that stirs affection in you.

September 5: Book XVII

Odysseus entered the halls close behind him
In the semblance of a beggar, miserable and old,
Walking with a staff. Sorry garments clothed his skin.
He sat at the ashwood threshold made of the portals
Leaning on a cypress post that a workman once
Had skillfully planed and drawn straight to the line. . . .
"Bring this and give it to the stranger and tell him
To go around to all the suitors and beg in turn
For shame is not a good thing for a needy man" (XVII. 336-41;345-47).

After twenty long-suffering years Odysseus arrives home, a stranger to all he knows. Not a victorious warrior but a tattered beggar is his status. He and his beloved Argos share a similar appearance and fate in being cast aside, rejected as inconsequential. But Odysseus does not wish to imitate King Agamemnon's homecoming that ended in his murder by his wife Clytemnestra and her lover, Aigisthos on the evening of his arrival. Disguised as someone harmless in appearance, Odysseus chooses to sit at the threshold between two worlds: that world he has spent two decades negotiating and the interior world that is a smaller version of what threatened him often in war and his journey home. He occupies a transitional place where the home is well-constructed, perhaps by his own skills at carpentry. Meanwhile, Telemachos instructs Eumaeos to show proper hospitality to the stranger by giving him an abundant supply of bread and meats to enjoy as a gesture of abundant hospitality.

Preparations for war often include setting up a concealed surprise for the enemy. Disguise, deception and surprise are traits Odysseus honed in battle at Troy and in journeying home. Now he is the image of the Trojan horse, meant to appear as a gift to the Trojans but concealing death within it. Advantage is its goal and patience its main avenue in. Restraint is its rightful disposition. When craft is chosen over a show of force, the edge such a design affords one may be the difference between victory or slaughter. One can feel the tension in this uneasy marriage between concealment and revelation. Crossing the threshold from one to the other is an art form that, with Athene's cosmetics, Odysseus has achieved.

Meditation:

Recall a situation in which you knew the right time to reveal something would assess its success or failure.

September 6: Book XVII

The suitors made a din through the halls. And Athene
Stood close by Odysseus, son of Laertes,
And urged him on to gather loaves from the suitors,
So he might know who were righteous and who lawless;
And yet she did not intend any to escape from misfortune.
He went along begging of each man, from left to right,
Stretching his hand everyway as though he had long been a beggar.
They pitied and they gave and they marveled at him
And asked one another who he was and whence he came (XVII. 360-69).

The suitors are a raucous bunch, noisy and self-absorbed. Into this din Athene instructs Odysseus on how to separate them into two groups—righteous and lawless, though it seems that neither group will escape her justice. His indicator will be their generosity in giving or in holding back from the filthy beggar. Odysseus stars in his role very convincingly, taking on the gestures and demeanor of a beggar. Yet there must be something else in his deportment, for even as they offer him sustenance, they marvel at him as well. They grow curious about this intrusion into their midst and want to know his origins. They do not suspect him of being other than he appears, which will prove their destruction. Athene's strategy is brilliant: she knows that thrusting him into their midst will be more successful than having him linger on the margins of their feasting.

Athene may be the most polysemous of all the divinities. In the above situation she reveals that "One of her later epithets was Pronoia, *providential,* foresight, for her structure of consciousness can espy predictabilities, prepare for them, and thus normalize the unexpected" James Hillman writes ("On the Necessity of Abnormal Psychology" 26-27). This last part, to "normalize the unexpected" is her creation, with Odysseus a willing and obedient student. He plays his role well and while rousing the curiosity of the suitors, gives them no reason to suspect that who they have convinced themselves will never return stands in their circle. Her ploy is to have each suitor identify himself as generous or lawless, upholding or violating the code of hospitality.

Meditation:

When have individuals been so disarmed that they revealed to you elements of their nature you were unaware of but may have suspected?

September 7: Book XVII

So he said, and Antinoos upbraided the swineherd with a speech:
"Notorious swineherd, why did you lead this man
To the city? Are there not enough vagrants for us,
Insatiable beggars, defilers of the banquet?
Do you treat it lightly that those who are gathered here
Devour your master's living; that you called this man here too?
And you addressed him in answer, swineherd Eumaeos:
"Antinoos, though you are noble, you have said what is not good. . . .
But always you are harsh beyond the other suitors
To the servants of Odysseus, and especially to me" (XVII. 374-81; 388-89).

The tension begins to be more palpable as Antinoos steps forth to berate the swineherd for bringing another hungry mouth to feed. Enough vagrants already populate Odysseus' table, which would include the suitors themselves. Excess seems to be the atmosphere Odysseus has returned to confront. Ironically, Antinoos accuses Eumaeos of excess in swelling the population of beggars. The old swineherd's response reveals a history of abuse; Antinoos is a tyrant over the servants of the household and particularly over Eumeaos himself, the one who cares for the animals that the suitors have been consuming for years. Antinoos has distinguished himself through his excessive, unchecked bullying. What he accuses Eumaeos of is precisely what he himself has become.

It is not unusual that bullies speak in moralisms from a disposition of self-righteousness. Perhaps it is their way of camouflaging their true intentions. They will always find fault with those beneath them who have no real power or way to defend themselves or to retaliate. The bully tyrannizes over situations they may have no business intruding into. Their life is often one of excess with little restraint. Their treatment of others demeans their target to raise their own fragile sense of self above their victims. In the above passage we witness the opposition of the restraint of Odysseus in disguise and the excessive overt behavior of the bully. Eumaeos is the voice that bridges the two with his words to Antinoos. That Antinoos would accuse a few beggars of defiling the household when he and his entourage have been abusing Odysseus' home for years is beyond hypocrisy.

Meditation:

When have you found yourself under the tyranny of a bully? Did you have any strategies to counter their power over you?

September 8: Book XVII

Then sound-minded Telemachos answered him:
"Silence, and please do not answer this man so much with words.
Antinoos has the habit of always giving evil provocation
With harsh speeches, and he urges others also to do it."
So he said, and he uttered winged words to Antinoos.
"Antinoos, you care for me nicely as a father for his son
When you order me to drive the stranger from the halls
With a word of constraint. Let a god not bring this to pass.
Take and give to him; I begrudge it not. In fact, I command it" (XVII. 393-401).

The first showdown between Telemachos and the leader of the suitors begins here. Strife will build in subsequent confrontations. Odysseus' son berates Antinoos for his selfishness in not giving to the beggar generously, as is the custom that hospitality calls for. He calls out Antinoos' bullying way with others to intimidate them into submission. He is cutting in his comparison of their relationship of a father to his son who orders his son to drive out the stranger who is their guest. He then rises above Antinoos by taking on his role as leader of the household and insists the beggar be given sustenance by Antinoos, whose nature does not allow him any largesse towards others. Gregory Nagy writes of the word *xenos* (stranger-guest): "Anyone who would consider even a mere beggar as his or her xenos displays the maximum of generosity. . ." (*The Best of the Achaians* 232). Telemachos embodies such largesse and his father is there in disguise to witness his son's developing authority.

After a time of trying to compromise to keep the peace, one may reach a threshold. To cross it is to invite trouble on an intensified scale. When violations of a belief become intolerable, then one must take action, first through words, then with physical force if necessary. Words set the table for what is to follow. Deeds then must punctuate one's words when justice is at stake. Arguing further at this juncture will only encourage greater excess that in time may destroy everything of value. One must exercise moral courage to face a force that is beyond being persuaded and Athene, goddess of persuasion, knows this. She guides father and son to physical action because words are reaching a point of exhaustion.

Meditation:

Have you been forced to take action against injustice when repeatedly provoked?

September 9: Book XVII

All the others gave and filled his wallet with bread and meat.
And soon Odysseus was again ready to go back again
To the threshold and get a taste from the Achaians free.
He stood by Antinoos and addressed a word to him:
"Give, my friend, you do not seem to me to be the worst
Of the Achaians, but the best, since you look like a king,
And so you ought to give bread more liberally
Than the others. I shall speak your fame through the boundless earth.
For I myself was once blessed, and I inhabited
A rich house among men, and gave to a tramp like this. . ." (XVII. 411-20).

Odysseus' craft with language is highlighted when he addresses Antinoos directly. The other suitors have made gestures of generosity, though always with Odysseus' goods. He calls Antinoos friend, which he takes as an insult. When Odysseus refers to the leader (the king) not as the worst of the Achaians but perhaps the best, he has planted the seed in Antinoos that he may indeed be the worst among all gathered at the feast. So as the best he should be most generous, thereby placing Antinoos in an awkward position; if he does not give liberally to the beggar he will not be seen as the best of the Achaians. Gregory Nagy reveals something of the phrase worth noting. In the *Iliad,* there were three warriors claiming to be the best: Agamemnon, Diomedes and Ajax in the contest held for this honorific, "aristeia Akhaion" in Greek (*The Best of the Achaeans* 30). We know that Agamemnon is murdered without warning when he returns home. Odysseus may be sealing Antinooos' death knell here by calling him the best of the Achaians; he will be murdered first by Odysseus in his own home.

Words, like physical disguise, can express the truth through a fiction. In fact, a disguise can allow us to speak in ways that its absence would prohibit. So we can, like Odysseus, have it both ways—to use the fiction to speak the truth, as Homer also engages through his epic fiction. Stories can be understood as a disguise that allows the truth to unfurl. At this moment Odysseus would seem to embody the essence of poetry and poetic utterances. The truth is present, but for a limited and reliable audience. Poetry reveals what prose may fail to express.

Meditation:

Have you been able to speak the truth about something or someone through or by means of a fiction? When has poetry revealed a truth that changed your thinking?

September 10: Book XVII

Then Antinoos answered him and addressed him:
"What god has brought this trouble, this annoyance at the banquet?
Stand as you are in the middle, apart from my table,
Lest you soon arrive at a bitter Egypt and Cyprus,
Because you are some bold and shameless beggar.
You stand beside all in turn, and they give to you
Wantonly, since they have no restraint or remorse
At giving of others' goods freely, since each has much."
Odysseus of many wiles withdrew and addressed him:
"Well now, your mind is not a match for your appearance.
You would not give salt from your house to your own suppliant, . . ." (XVII. 445-55).

Antinoos first wonders what deity has visited this trouble on them in the form of a beggar. Unwittingly, the suitor uses the word that conveys the meaning of Odysseus' name: trouble or strife. He orders the beggar to stand clear of him before he winds up in a condition similar to Odysseus' fictional travels related earlier. Antinoos is angry with his fellow suitors who show no restraint in giving goods to the beggar, forgetting for a moment his and others' own wanton consumption of what is not theirs; they have enjoyed such bounty in Odysseus' absence. We remember Odysseus' distinction made to the son of King Alcinoos, that there are two kinds of men: one looks good but speaks poorly, while the other is less comely in appearance but speaks eloquently. Antinoos is the former version.

Disguise reveals the truth more clearly than when one is fully revealed. Fiction is a mask that brings the truth forward. Fiction is a form of play. Costumes, masquerades and humor place one in a position to know more clearly. The fiction of the epic is a form of deep revelation. By means of poetic fabrication one reveals himself with far greater clarity than a documentary. In addition, as Richard Kearney observes, "storytelling may be said to *humanise* time by transforming it from an impersonal passing of fragmented moments into a pattern, a plot, a *mythos* (*On Stories* 4). Story's fabrication fictionalizes the truth as poetic revelation.

Meditation:

Describe one pattern you discern in the fabric of your narrative.

September 11: Book XVII

"Listen to me, suitors of the illustrious queen,
So that I may say what the heart in my breast bids me to.
There is no pain in a man's mind or any grief
When he battles over possessions of his own
And is wounded for the sake of the oxen or shiny sheep.
But Antinoos hit me on account of my woeful belly,
A cursed thing that gives many evils to men.
But if perchance gods and Furies exist for beggars,
May the end of death find Antinoos sooner then marriage" (XVII. 468-76).

At this juncture in his quest to retrieve his home, Odysseus' best weapon is words. He distinguishes between a man who fights to defend his own possessions and is wounded thereby. Such is understandable; but when one is injured because of his appetite, which often leads men to commit evils for the sake of satisfying it, that is unjust because appetites are out of one's control. Appetites can be accursed when they rule a life instead of reason and due measure as well as piety towards the gods. He calls on both gods and Furies to enact justice over those who are victims of others' wrath because of their appetites. Odysseus claims Antinoos threw a footstool at him because he was hungry and simply sought what would appease his appetite. For that unjust act, Antinoos may indeed die before all the others. His disguise cloaks his words and allows him to speak the truth without being discovered.

From a position of deception one can speak the truth and not have it tracked back to its true source. The fiction of one's appearance offers a place of refuge for the facts displayed through that portal. So not just the content of a narrative is important but so too is the context by which it is conveyed. When the source is disguised, it offers a richer opportunity to reveal the truth of what is present now as well as a prophecy of what is to come. Concealing is a rich and complex origin for revealing what is or is soon to be—true. The famous Spanish painter Pablo Picasso once claimed that all art is a lie that expresses the truth. Odysseus at this moment may be best understood as a lie, an artistic one, that allows the truth to be entertained without deadly reprisal.

Meditation:

When did a fiction reveal a necessary truth to you? What truth were you able to reveal from a place of its fictional "hiddenness"?

September 12: Book XVII

So he said and they all grew presumptuously angry
And this is what one of those overbearing young men would say:
"Antinoos, you did not do well to hit a hapless wanderer.
You are cursed, if perchance he is some heavenly god.
Yes, the gods in the semblance of alien strangers
Do appear in all forms and go about among cities
Looking upon the excess and the good order of men."
So said the suitors and he did not attend to their speech.
Telemachos was nursing a great grief in his heart
For the struck man, but he cast no tear on the ground... (XVII. 481-90).

It is a moment of clarity for the young suitors, presumptuous though they are. One of them reminds Antinoos that this stranger may be a god in disguise mingling among them to see if they exercise piety or recklessness. Divinity notes where excess reigns and where good order exists among mortals in their social arrangements. Perhaps more restraint on Antinoos' part, he suggests, would be prudent in their current climate. Yet Antinoos in his arrogance and excess will not or cannot have the suitors' warning to constrain his language toward the new beggar in their midst; he is incapable of hospitality. At the same time, Telemachos struggles to hold back his emotional pain at seeing his father both physically and emotionally abused in his own home. He dare not let the suitors see him responding with compassion and suffering for the stranger.

Each of us makes up our own minds concerning the presence of deities, the transcendent, the sacred, the ineffable or whatever god image we live by in our lives. We may understand the divine as an extension of ourselves or without, or in all things, including others. Regardless, our relation to the transcendent reflects some essential qualities of both our collective as well as personal mythology. It is core to our being because it is our belief about god, gods or their absence, or about the various forms they may assume. What we believe about divinity further reflects the power of the myth we live by. Poetic knowledge itself, as Jacques Maritain suggests, "is the intrinsic moment of contemplation from which creation emanates" (*The Range of Reason* 18). It is a rich connection to the divine.

Meditation:

What belief in god, the sacred or holiness in life shapes your attitude towards others and aids you in understanding the nature of your own narrative?

September 13: Book XVII

"They carry on their revel and drink the sparkling wine
Wantonly. Many things are wasted. And there is no man
Of the kind Odysseus was, to ward off harm from the house.
But if Odysseus were to come and reach his fatherland,
With his son he would at once avenge the men's violence."
So she said, and Telemachos sneezed loud. About the house
It resounded terribly. And Penelope laughed.
At once to Eumaeos she uttered winged words:
"Come to me, and summon the stranger so, face to face.
Did you not see that my son sneezed at all the words?
So death will come not unfulfilled for the suitors, . . ." (XVII. 536-46).

One of the most ordinary events in the entire epic occurs here: sneezing. Sneezing has been associated with the god Hermes, a figure central to the epic at key moments. He is the messenger from gods to men and this sneeze may be his handiwork, as Penelope, after laughing at her son's outburst, perceptively notes that something has been given a sign through the sneeze: the death of the suitors. Penelope begins to assume the starring role as she steps into the midst of the plot from here to epic's end. She also compares her husband to "no man," a name Odysseus' addresses to the Cyclops, and we relish the pun. It was another moment of fashioning a disguise, a fiction, so to escape the devouring force of Polyphemos. Odysseus is again disguised to battle the excesses of the Cyclopes in his home.

Laughter happens infrequently in Homer's epic. Sneezing only once. The outburst from Telemachos is akin to the outburst of Odysseus shortly when he throws off his disguise and unleashes his fury on the suitors. At moments in life we feel a prediction in our words, perhaps only later, in hindsight. Following an intuition or an instinct, we may say or act in a way that is unclear even to us as we draw life into motion through a hope, a wish or a desire. Penelope, having enjoyed a good laugh, attends to the stranger. Similarly, we may sense in the progression of events, to invite something we wish to face directly. Onians remarks that "the sneeze in ancient Greece was regarded as prophetic, an indication that what one was thinking of just then would be fulfilled" (*Origins* 104).

Meditation:

When have you trusted an instinct or impulse and acted on it because it felt like the right time and circumstances to do so?

September 14: Book XVII

Then godly Odysseus, who had suffered much, spoke to him:
"Eumaeos, straight off, I would tell all truthfully
To the prudent Penelope, daughter of Icarios.
For I know well about that man; we have got the same woe.
But I fear the throng of the difficult suitors
Whose insolence and force reach iron heaven. . . .
So now go bid Penelope to remain in the halls,
Though she is eager, till the setting of the sun.
Then let her ask me about the day of her husband's return,
Seating me closer to the fire" (XVII. 560-65; 569-72).

The complexity of the situation unfolding continues to thicken. Odysseus plays himself not playing himself. To Eumaeos he speaks as a beggar; he will continue this role when he speaks to Penelope by telling her he and her husband suffer the same fate. Odysseus is two people at this juncture: one concealed, one slowly revealed. With Penelope the two identities will unite, for what he says of Odysseus is what he says of himself. But as himself and as beggar he fears the volatile and unpredictable suitors and knows if his disguise is discovered all in the household will be lost. He asks that she come at sunset to hear his story, that of one character with two plots and/or as two characters with one plot. He claims that he wants to be near to the fire "for the clothes I have/ are woeful" (ll. 572-73). But perhaps he wants her to see his face close up as they share their stories.

Is it not possible, indeed preferable, to be multi-plotted, to harbor more than one person within? We have an innate unity but it does not mean we cannot enjoy a diversity within such a unity. We can "prepare a face to meet the faces that you meet" in the words of T.S. Eliot ("The Love Song of J. Alfred Prufrock" 4) It does not mean we dissemble; it means we may be more of an assemblage of persons with a solid core that constellates them. Perhaps our authentic self resides in between these facets of faces and the stories we tell others about ourselves or tell ourselves about ourselves, what I have been calling one's personal myth. Perhaps it is truer to say that each of us is a congress of personages, all of whom carry something true about who we are.

Meditation:

How many roles are you regularly asked to play or are forced to play to survive, to keep your world intact, and to hang on to your sense of self?

September 15: Book XVII

Then the prudent Penelope addressed him:
"The stranger is not senseless; he thinks the way it may be.
For never, in this way, surely, did any among mortal men
So devise reckless deeds in their insolence."
So the woman spoke, and the godly swineherd went off
To the conclave of suitors, where he had told her everything. . . .
He went after the swine, and left the enclosures and the hall
Full of banqueters. They were enjoying themselves with dancing
And with song, for the evening of the day was already coming (XVII. 585-90; 604-06).

Dusk falls on the household as the suitors repeat their well-worn pattern of partying well into the night. Penelope's attention is drawn to the stranger's request delivered by both of their faithful servants. She discerns immediately the truth of the stranger's words of caution and considers his reading of the suitors as accurate. Perhaps right here she begins to see the beggar in a new light, even a familiar illumination, and wishes to trust him. Once more, however, she prepares for the invaders into her house as she has done countless evenings before. But perhaps there is hope that has arrived in the form of the stranger in rags who has nothing to lose in the person of his disguise and everything to lose in his authentic identity. Perhaps as well the last image of evening suggests darkness on many levels.

One has to wonder when caught in life's predicaments what force, presence, chance or interruption might break open a calcified life and free those trapped in it? Some devising from outside, some gesture of generosity, some heroic presence must intervene in the lives of those who cannot uncouple from some oppression or condition of being taken advantage of. One can call it providence, fortune, a fresh breeze, a rebalancing energy—anything to allow those oppressed to breathe freely again. Sometimes the cure is in stories themselves, of which Gary Snyder writes: "The world is made of stories. Good stories are hard to come by, and a good story you can honestly call your own is an incredible gift" (qtd. in *The World is Made of Stories* 103). Stories in this sense can be salvific presences for our stuck plot.

Meditation:

At a time of oppression in your life, what entered to free you? Did it come from within you or an outside aid or guide to assist you?

September 16: Book XVIII

So Antinoos spoke, and his speech was pleasing to them.
Odysseus of many wiles spoke to them with a plan in his mind:
"My friends, there is no way for an old man worn out with grief
To fight against a younger. Still, my criminal belly
Urges me on, that I be overcome with blows.
But come, all of you, and swear a mighty oath,
That no one favoring Iros will recklessly
Strike me with heavy hand and overpower me for him."
So he said, and all of them swore as he had asked (XVIII. 50-58).

Antinoos has just set the terms for Odysseus to fight another beggar, Iros. He has also encouraged a fight between them; the winner will be favored by being allowed to dine with the suitors, becoming temporarily one of them. Odysseus agrees to the fight because he is guided by his belly to do so. In this way he implicitly admonishes the suitors for following their own "criminal" bellies to excess. He calls for restraint by having them swear an oath that none of them will interfere and favor Iros' winning. It marks the beginning of violence to subdue all the suitors as well as puts in place a container—oath-taking—to counter their excess. The fight with Iros is a micro-version of the larger blood bath that is soon to follow. The oath the suitors take here will, on a larger scale, end the epic.

Compromise in the form of an oath allows both parties to win and lose at once. Each loses or sacrifices something of value; each wins something of moderation and balance. Oaths, as the *Odyssey* has highlighted often, balance two sides through the tension an oath has the capacity to hold in place. Within the oath excess evaporates or is sacrificed by placing limits on it. The oath works only if both parties hold to the intentions of its words. It is an Athenian move when the oath is a vessel of compromise because the oath marries *metis* to *bie,* force or might with craft. Sheila Murnaghan reminds us that Athene "is a fitting emblem for a poem that at once acknowledges the power of women and equates the successful conclusion of its story with the enlistment of female characters in the male-centered project of the hero's Return" ("The Plan of Athena" 63). Oaths may then unite the energies of masculine and feminine forces in sustained tension.

Meditation:

When has an oath as a form of compromise brought peace into your life? The oath might be with yourself to cease self-harming.

September 17: Book XVII

They led him out to the middle; both men held out their hands.
And then the godly Odysseus, who had endured much, considered
Whether to strike him so his soul would leave him as he fell
Or to strike him softly and to stretch him out on the ground;. . . .
Then they both drew themselves up. On the right shoulder
Iros hit him. But the other struck his neck under the ear and crushed
The bone inside. At once gory blood came out of his mouth.
He fell bellowing in the dust. He knocked his teeth together,
As he kicked the ground with his feet. Then the noble suitors
Held their hands up and died with laughter (XVIII. 89-92; 95-100).

Even in battle, Odysseus shows restraint because his prowess over Iros is excessive. Mind rules the matter of his battle. The suitors will suspect him of being more than his appearance reveals. By showing excessive force against his rival, Odysseus will bring excessive might of the suitors down on him, his family and those who remained faithful to him. He moderates his response; it is not yet time to unleash greater fury. He finds a balance so as not to drive the soul out of Iros. Once again, he is linked with "the middle," which occurs often in the poem. He is the man of the middle way. Ancient Greece, according to Onians, believed that "the soul and seed of life were in the head" (*Origins* 113), which Odysseus grasps when he strikes Iros in the neck but does not strike his head directly.

Some life situations may require us not to reveal completely our attributes, strengths, achievements, capacities and intentions. We hold back, speak only so much, conceal our full nature because something bigger is at stake that we must achieve or protect. Letting all our feelings be revealed may give a moment's satisfaction but harm us in the long run. Our own excess can undo us and our plans to accomplish something we deem crucial to our lives. Restraint for a higher end, we learn to bide our time until the right time—*kairos*—presents itself. Moments of restraint and moments of more explicit action in themselves form an elaborate weave where the one restraining holds a tension with what desire urges one to perform or think. The weave itself seems to be the most poignant image in human life, for there is very little that is not woven into a grander design.

Meditation:

Recall a situation when holding back proved to be a better plan than revealing all your cards at once.

September 18: Book XVIII

And this is what one of the overbearing young men would say:
"Stranger, may Zeus and the other immortal gods
Grant you what you wish and is most dear to your heart,
Since you have stopped this insatiable man from wandering
In the district. And soon we will bring him to the mainland,
To King Echetos, destroyer of all mortal men."
So he said, and godly Odysseus rejoiced at the omen he heard.
Antinoos put a large stomach before him
Full of fat and blood. And Amphinomos
Lifted two loaves out of the basket and gave them to him (XVII. 112-21).

The suitors, used to being amused, are extremely pleased with the entertainment afforded by the two beggars fighting and Odysseus' handling of Iros. Odysseus has dragged his foe, deeply wounded, out of the house. They laud this newcomer to his own home with no suspicion of his disguise. Unknowing, the young suitor hopes the stranger will be granted all he wishes. As the audience in the know, we hear the irony in this and other comments about the beggar to whom they now show generosity; Antinoos offers him a large stomach full of fat and blood from one of the animals, an apt image for the suitors themselves. Another offers him an abundance of bread as reward for his entertainment. The belly is what keeps the suitors from any more than a superficial level of mindfulness.

Not showing one's hand by underperforming is a compromise; to settle a score and to remain disguised shows craft and a moderation of force. Restraint can be a virtue on a number of levels. One of them allows action without drawing suspicion. One's response is moderation and mindfulness. Excess is closer to mindlessness. The heroic can be as much about holding back as it can be in pushing forward. Timing seems to be the wise guide here, another attribute of Athene. Craftiness is a form of mindfulness that serves one when one's situation is populated by mindlessness. Remaining possessed and patient are weapons that hold off being discovered when forces around a person are too big to overthrow. *Kairos* rather than *Chronos* is the gift of noticing when the time is both right and ripe. The *Odyssey* offers us a handbook on how to behave under the most adverse and challenging circumstances, not just to survive but to serve a higher end.

Meditation:

Restraint: how has it served you in one important life situation?

September 19: Book XVII

The bright-eyed goddess Athene put it in the mind
Of Icarios' daughter, the prudent Penelope,
To appear to the suitors so she might the most expand
The hearts of the suitors, and might get more honor
From her husband and her son than she had before.
She laughed inanely and spoke quite directly out:
"Eurynome, my spirit longs, as it did not before,
To appear to the suitors, though they are detestable;
And I shall say something to my son, that it would be better
Not always to associate with the presumptuous suitors,
Who speak nicely but are thinking of evil for the future" (XVIII. 159-69).

The gods continually favor the mindful and avoid the mindless. Athene encourages the thought in Penelope to appear and arouse the suitors more than they have been so she can increase her honor for her family. Athene increases her longing to be heard and seen, though Penelope knows how duplicitous they are. She sees through their courtesy towards her; they carry in their hearts malice and a crude cunning to destroy the household if Penelope's efforts are thwarted. She will soon have occasion to see into the newly-arrived and now favored beggar's costume as well. All these recognitions she confides in her trusted housekeeper.

The value of a trusted confidante is immeasurable. One can share one's most guarded secrets with them, or test a notion or a plan to get a second opinion. A confidante is a person one can speak most candidly to without fear of reprisal or betrayal. At their best, a confidante will not mince words or conceal the truth from one who trusts them. At times their candor may be their greatest asset. Wisdom in this regard is knowing who to trust and with what confidences. When one is under siege, having this ability is Athene-inspired to guard one against adversaries. Athene, James Hillman observes, "is necessity moved from other world to this world, from blindness to bright-eyes. . . to the practical intellect's foresighted protective measures in regard to necessity. . . ("On the Necessity of Abnormal Psychology" 27).

Meditation:

Have you served another as a confidante or had the gift of one to advise you in times of stress and turmoil? What value did you find in either of these two positions?

September 20: Book XVIII

But the bright-eyed goddess Athene had another thought.
She shed sweet sleep over the daughter of Icarios.
And she sank back in sleep, and all her joints relaxed
There in her armchair, while the divine goddess gave her
Ambrosial gifts, so the Achaians might wonder at her.
First she purified her lovely face with ambrosial beauty. . . .
And then she made her taller and fuller to look upon
And made her to be whiter than sawn ivory.
When she had done that, the divine goddess went off,
And the white-armed servants came out of the hall,
Coming up with their voices. Sweet sleep let go of her (XVIII. 188-93; 196-200).

Athene continues to attend to Penelope to sculpt her attractiveness still further to increase the ardor of the suitors and thereby distract them from the beggar who they have taken in. A beautiful woman already, Penelope's loveliness is heightened still further by the touch of the goddess. In her beauty Penelope exerts a power different from her husband but no less effective in the grand unfolding plot. As she sleeps, Athene transforms her, as she had done before in tutoring Telemachos and Odysseus. She is a goddess of transformed perceptions; her gift is to craft alluring figures to make them more god-like and irresistible in strength and beauty. Now Penelope is prepared to excite wonder in the suitors.

The multi-million dollar cosmetic industry and fitness programs have as their intention to alter a person's appearance to make one more attractive, alluring and powerful in their presence, as Athene has done repeatedly. Cosmetics comes from the word *kosmos* in which through craft and skill one is transferred to a cosmic order, having to do with proper order and arrangement. Power emanates from a person's level of attractiveness. In some cases we call them "stars," or having "star power," so intimate is their association with the cosmic order. In such a transformation, one's presence is felt more keenly. *Aisthesis,* the root of aesthetics, has to do with showing forth or making more present in ways that pleases the viewer. One is often disarmed by such beauty, as was the case with Helen of Troy that brought the god Paris to desire her beyond all others.

Meditation:

Describe an attractive star, or someone you know, who emanates a divine beauty. What is it that attracts you to this person?

September 21: Book XVII

"Would that chaste Artemis might bring soft-death upon me
At once now, so that I should no longer waste my life away
Mourning in my heart and longing for my dear husband,
Who had excellence of all kinds, since he was foremost of the Achaians!..."
And when the godly woman had come to the suitors,
She stood by the pillar of the stoutly fashioned roof,
Holding the glistening headbands before her cheeks.
A devoted servant maid stood near her on either side.
The men's knees were loosened on the spot and their hearts
Were charmed with desire,
And they all voiced the prayer of lying beside her in bed (XVII. 203-06; 209-14).

Penelope remains front and center in the epic. She voices her own frustration to her women servants and seeks an end to her endurance and patience in holding back the suitors while waiting for her husband's return. Yet she rises and goes down to where the suitors are gathered, all hoping for a chance to gaze on her divinely-crafted beauty. Her loveliness holds them in thrall; their knees slacken and their hearts palpitate in a new vital rhythm at sight of her. They feel the Eros kindle in them and their thoughts move quickly to fantasies of caressing her in bed. Such a distraction will serve Odysseus when he reveals his full nature and stature.

Eros, beauty, desire, satisfaction are all potent human-divine forces and pressures in life. To be aroused by beauty can be both pleasurable and painful. It can lead to an animal lust to mate, or a deep desire to worship and protect, or a pure pleasure and joy of life in celebration of itself. Eros, beauty and desire can also be used to seduce, to control and to conquer others. These attributes each have their own *metis*; Penelope is the fullest embodiment of these qualities that are as potent as any her husband exhibits in the plot. Such seduction is part of Aphrodite's presence, when one is pulled by an aphrodisiac into a condition where beauty and allure easily lead to seduction. Her son was Eros, god of love and erotic impulses. Such distractions can disarm and weaken those who are in their grip.

Meditation:

When have you felt an overwhelming desire for another? What in this fantasy feels most seductive in your animal nature?

September 22: Book XVIII

Then Antinoos, the son of Eupeithos, addressed her:
"Daughter of Icarios, prudent Penelope,
Let whoever of the Achaians wishes bring gifts here,
And you receive them. For it is not good to refuse a gift.
And we shall not go to our fields or anywhere else
Until you have married the noblest of the Achaians."
So Antinoos said, and his speech was pleasing to them.
Each one sent for a herald to bring his gifts.
For Antinoos one brought a great, beautiful tunic,
Embroidered. And twelve brooches were on it in all,
Made of gold, fitted with well-fastening clasps (XVIII. 285-95).

By forcing gift-giving and receiving, Antinoos has told Penelope that time is up. She must now choose. All are weary and impatient and, of course now that Odysseus has arrived home in disguise, the suitors push Penelope to choose one of them for her new husband. Odysseus' cleverness is like the cleverness he revealed in Troy with his idea of the hollow Trojan horse in the belly of which the Greeks hid until the Trojans dragged it inside the wall of their city. Odysseus hides once again, this time within the folds of his filthy clothing and disguise executed by Athene; as a new beggar in their midst, Odysseus has been accepted and is now set on the margins of their attention. Time now constricts after twenty years; it is constricting around Penelope's freedom. Stalling is over; the pressure builds for her to commit to one of them. Enticements to goad her on include a parade of riches as gifts befitting her stature and value, but they are more like bribes than objects of generosity.

Gifts can be given generously as well as used as goads, bribes, persuasions where they cease being gifts at all but more like pressure points because they seek something in return. They are not freely offered; there are strings attached. To equate gifts with freedom is that they are freely given and received. But more can be at stake here. Gifts often have visible or invisible price tags connected to them and if we are wise, we watch for those loose ends dangling from the packaging of the gift. It may be wrapped in graft.

Meditation:

Describe a gift or favor you received that, over time, you realized, may have been freely given but with strings or other necessities attached to it.

September 23: Book XVIII

But fair-cheeked Melantho upbraided him shamefully;
Dolios fathered her, and Penelope cared for her,
And reared her as her own child, and gave her toys to her liking;
Yet even with that, she did not keep Penelope's grief in mind; . . .
"Wretched stranger, you are a man knocked out of his mind,
As you do not wish to go and sleep in the bronzesmith's house, . . .
    Wine possesses your mind, or your mind is always
The way it is now, so that you utter vanity.
Are you beside yourself for beating the tramp Iros?
Take heed lest a better man than Iros stand up against
you. . ." (XVIII. 322-25; 328-29; 332-35).

Melantho's rebuke follows Odysseus' directive for all of Penelope's faithful servant women to come to her assistance and he will keep the torches burning as they do her work in weaving. Those present laugh at the beggar's bold talk, acting as if he were master of the household. Melantho rebukes his audacity, accusing him of having a deranged mind. She steps out of her own boundaries in her insults, violating the code of hospitality and ignoring Penelope's suffering in her newly-constricted situation with the suitors. Melantho assumes Odysseus has grown arrogant after defeating Iros in their fight and now feels he has a position within the household. She tells him to be careful lest someone greater beat him. These rebukes come from a woman who Penelope cared for and helped to raise. Her arrogance draws a surprising response from Odysseus.

Being insulted rather than cared for in the home of another can be devastating. Being insulted by another in your own home can unsettle and enrage the host. For Odysseus, both are true. He is hidden in his own home, therefore open to abuse. Again, disguise is a powerful condition because it invites others to speak unmediated, freely, openly and truthfully. In disguise one can witness others completely exposed in words and actions. It is a cunning social arrangement to get at the truth through the appearance of a fiction. In this way it is like poetry itself. Melantho speaks blindly because she cannot entertain the possibility that this beggar is someone in disguise. Her imagination is incapable of seeing options.

Meditation:

Have you been insulted in your own home or as a guest in the home of another? What were the consequences based on how you handled this violation?

September 24: Book XVIII

Odysseus of many wiles glowered at her and spoke:
"Soon I shall tell Telemachos what you say, bitch,
When he comes here, so he may cut you up limb from limb."
When he had said this he terrified the women with his words.
They went through the hall, and the limbs of each one went slack
In alarm. For they thought that he had spoken the truth.
And he himself stood by the flaming braziers keeping the light up
And looked at all the men. The heart in his breast planned
Other matters, and those were not to be unachieved (XVIII. 338-45).

Beginning slowly, Odysseus' disguise begins to reveal gaps where the man behind the fiction emerges. His anger over Melantho's arrogance is naked and raw even as the source remains concealed. His appearance remains a ruse but his words are without restraint and authentic. He stands by the fire as the caretaker of illumination and the heat of the torches. Their energy is his energy. His thoughts of vengeance in exacting justice, the narrator tells us, will come to pass. Who he fully is begins to blaze outward. The servant women have a felt sense of the accuracy of his words and not the ravings of a drunk beggar; this awareness terrifies them for they sense what is to come and their complicity in what has happened.

No one does not hide their true self with a mask or disguise of some kind. In certain situations the energy may be so powerful that it bursts forth from behind the mask. We get a glimpse of ourselves that may startle and surprise; we see ourselves perhaps as others have known us, but as we have not. Great discipline is needed to keep our naked self concealed. It is hard work and one may wonder at times if the effort is worth the payoff. Once others see us in our more authentic expression, there is no turning back. As to warriors like Odysseus returning from combat and who continue to suffer the traumas of war at home, there is also a "moral trauma" which Jonathan Shay calls "betrayal of what's right" (*Achilles in Vietnam* xiii). Odysseus must restrain from a premature exposure.

Meditation:

When have you allowed a part of your hidden self to be revealed? What were the circumstances that made you feel comfortable enough or courageous enough to make such a crucial move?

September 25: Book XVIII

Eurymachos, son of Polybus, began speaking to them,
Abusing Odysseus, and he caused laughter in his companions.
"Listen to me, suitors of the illustrious queen,
So I may tell you what the heart in my breast bids me to. . . .
Stranger, would you like to labor, if I should take you on
At the very field's very verge—the pay will be enough for you—
Gathering stones for the walls and planting tall trees?. . .
But since you have learned foul deeds, you do not wish
To approach work, but want to beg through the district
So that you may have food for your insatiable belly" (XVIII. 350-53; 358-60; 363-65).

The name of Odysseus means to cause or receive trouble or strife. Now as his disguise tatters he becomes truer to his name. Eurymachos takes on himself abusing Odysseus. Behind the abuse is Athene, who spurs on more afflictions in order to strengthen his restraint and to bring his force, his energy, up to another level. By the flames he is more fired up by the added abuse from one or another member of the household. The belly is again referenced to underscore how appetites' yearnings can break restraint down and lead to violence and death. Such is the scene unfolding now. When Eurymachos refers to the "field's very verge," he unknowingly makes a connection to that other field that Homer uses in Book V as a metaphor when Athene covers Odysseus' eyes when he is exhausted after landing on Scheria. It carries the spark of Odysseus' fire and life force.

When we lose restraint or allow situations of attack or belittling to get the better of us, the belly often takes central command. Now we react out of appetite—to get even, to exact revenge, to answer kind with kind—and lose all sense of freedom. Belly behavior cancels mindfulness. We begin to behave blindly to show who we are on a different level. Restraint evaporates. Moderation breaks down. Raw energy then may be released and our careful plans are interrupted, perhaps permanently.

Meditation:

Has an increased emotion suddenly erupted in you to consume all mindfulness and commandeer your life, if even for an instant? Were you able to muster restraint to counteract this impulse?

September 26: Book XVIII

And Telemachos spoke to them in his sacred might:
"You fools, you are enraged and no longer hide in your hearts
Your eating and drinking. One of the gods stirs you up.
But since you have dined well, go on home and lie down,
Whenever the spirit bids. I shall not pursue anyone."
So he said, and they all bit their lips with their teeth
And wondered at Telemachos, that he spoke boldly. . . .
But when they had poured libation and drunk all they wished
They went off, each one to his own home to sleep (XVIII. 406-12; 428-29).

Telemachos continues to assume his own authority by telling the suitors who and what they are. His image of their revealing themselves, no longer hiding their intentions or natures, reflects on Odysseus himself, who is ready to emerge from his disguise and assume his role as leader and steward of his home. Telemachos orders them out of the house; his sacred might in his words frightens the suitors, who hold him now in wonder. They feel a fear generated by his courageous words and sense his divinity and leadership shining forth. Their sense of wonder, even awe, is aroused by his forthrightness. When they have lingered long enough to satiate their appetites, they return to their homes, perhaps for the last time. He reassures them that he will take no further action when they leave if indeed they go directly to their own dwellings.

Watching someone we know, or ourselves for that matter, gain voice and authority is something to wonder at. It can signal a shift from a private to a public life. It is a moment when one gains his/her own authority and steps into one's own integrity and is present to it. Here Telemachos steps into his authority to wrestle abnormal behavior back into a normative one. Cedric Whitman believes that "the function of a norm is to regularize" (*Homer and the Heroic Tradition* 252); part of Telemachos' function is to bring the abnormal back into line with the tradition of hospitality as he simultaneously prepares for the more fierce norm-restorer, his father. Part of the heroic tradition in Homer is to rebalance what has been skewed or torqued out of its original purpose and form. His treatment of the "abnormal" suitors' behavior pulls Telemachos into that tradition.

Meditation:

Recall when you or someone you witnessed, or when you yourself, crossed such a threshold into their own power and autonomy.

September 27: Book XIX

"Telemachos, we must put the weapons of war inside,
All of them, and beguile the suitors deceptively
With soft speeches, when they miss them and ask you questions:
'I put them out of the smoke since they no longer look like those
That Odysseus once left behind when he went to Troy.
But they are befouled, so much has the smoke of the fire got to them. . . .'"
So he said. And Telemachos obeyed his dear father.
He called the nurse, Eurycleia and spoke to her:
"Good mother, come hold the women back in the halls,
So that we may put away the weapons of my father up into the chamber,. . ."
(XIX. 4-9; 14-17).

Odysseus slowly begins to unfurl his plan to disarm and conquer the suitors, as he did in Troy and as he repeated in his wanderings home. Just as in Troy, he shows his talents as an artificer to draw up a strategy of deception: to put forth one reality while unfolding a concealed second one. Beguiling the suitors with the idea of removing all weapons to preserve them from the smoke in the hall seems on the surface a plausible reason to remove them. He also suggests that when they drink to excess, they may draw swords in conflict because "iron of itself draws a man on" (l. 13). Telemachos, while having the ability to command, knows also how to obey at the same time. *Metis* surfaces in place of *bie* to cultivate this segment of his plan. By removing the weapons Odysseus increases his *bie* through *metis*.

When out-forced, then craft and clever disguise can disarm through language. The appearance of a situation can be crafted by the words chosen to describe or explain it. The words may correspond to the phenomenon or they can create a reality very different and often at odds with its true nature. The experience then is shaped through the words chosen rather than the action itself. So powerful is persuasion that it can override the truth of a situation. The ability to discern truth from falsehood actually determines what reality one will finally believe. A key quality to make oneself believable is relatedness, which Donnell Stern calls "the nexus from which experience emerges" (*Partners in Thought* 4). So, the "soft speeches" intended for the suitors is to create a sense of relatedness and trust.

Meditation:

When have you used words to deflect yourself or others from the truth as you understood it?

September 28: Book XIX

And the prudent Penelope went out of her chamber
In the semblance of Artemis or golden Aphrodite.
They put a chair by the fire for her where she used to sit,
A chair whorled with ivory and silver that Ikmalios
The craftsman had once fashioned; to it he had attached
A footstool under the feet; and over it a large fleece was thrown.
Then the prudent Penelope sat down on it.
White-armed serving women came out of the hall
And were taking away a great amount of bread, and the tables,
And the cups from which the insolent men had drunk (XIX. 53-62).

This scene that combines both domestic beauty in contrast to the insolence of those who devour without boundaries is a potent one. Penelope is transformed in her loveliness. The craftsman's chair is described as an artful object to be admired as well as used; the aesthetic is most often present in Homer's world to wonder at. Perhaps the suitors glance her way and see the beautiful chair she sits in. Perhaps their appetites blind them to such beauty, so consumed are they by their own addiction to consumption. Penelope's presence nonetheless adds luster to the scene and even ennobles it. None of this of course is lost on Odysseus, who has been made to suffer more through Athene's directives. Meanwhile, as if no one is noticing, the servant women begin to clear the hall of feasting, including the tables where insolence has sat for so long.

Mortals are blessed at certain moments in appearing like a divinity to be admired and to elicit wonder in others. These moments reveal such a thin space between divinity and mortality. These worlds may blend more frequently than we realize. We cannot rule out the passage above as part of Penelope's own weaving of a plot through her beautiful presence that arrests. Nancy Felson-Rubin asks: "What if Penelope, weaver of plots (as her name, from *pene*, "woof" or "web," suggests), calculated her move to fit simultaneously into several possible plots?" ("Penelope: Character from Plot" 167). Her beauty is such a powerful presence that it distracts and disarms the suitors. Beauty is a form of plot-creating. When we experience the beautiful we grow to appreciate life in its greater splendor.

Meditation:

Have you witnessed when beauty, allure and attractiveness was itself the central quality of a plot to convince, persuade or deceive?

September 29: Book XIX

Melantho upbraided Odysseus again a second time;
"Stranger, will you still bother us here even now through the night,
Prowling through the house; and will you be ogling the women?" . . .
She rebuked her servant and spoke out to her directly:
"Bold woman, fearless bitch, you indeed do not escape my
notice
When you do this enormous deed, that you shall wipe off on your head.
And you know this full well, as you heard me say it myself,
That I intended to ask the stranger in my halls
About my husband, since my griefs come thick and fast" (XIX. 65-67; 90-95).

Melantho is the emblem of the haughty servant women who have chosen to align with the suitors against Odysseus and his family. Her arrogance in berating a stranger guest violates all protocols of hospitality. Her insults to the stranger, whose disguise masks her master, Penelope is quick to rebuke, in part because as she feels time evaporating, she desires to question him about her husband. Melantho's insults will not make the stranger very amenable to her questions after he has been once again abused. One can feel the tightening and constricting of the plot as its energy coagulates more intensely in this scene, and time draws closer to Odysseus' revelation. Penelope's language mirrors the level of anger and frustration she feels at this violation that thwarts her own plans to interrogate the stranger. Melantho seems intent on thwarting Penelope's plan of interrogation.

Protocols, conventions of behavior, rules of etiquette, care for others—all are forms that hold civilized life intact. It socially bonds those familiar with civil elements deserving respect and hospitality. One cannot know when one might need similar assistance, or when a god might appear in disguise as a mortal. Violating these codes can reveal how close below the skin resides chaos and violence. Such generous behaviors conserve the integrity of those who receive them and those who bestow them on others. The arrangement protects the human order from descending into the realm of appetites and addictions to satisfy oneself at the cost of others' respect and needs. Chaos may then be that condition aroused when self-interest and base appetites capsize moderation and balance.

Meditation:

When have you witnessed the violation of protocol or good conduct toward yourself or others?

September 30: Book XIX

Then godly Odysseus, who had endured much, sat down there.
And the prudent Penelope began speaking between them:
"Stranger, I myself shall ask you this question first:
What men are you from? Where are your city and parents?"
Odysseus of many wiles addressed her in answer:
"My good woman, no one among mortals on the boundless earth
Would find fault with you. Your renown reaches broad heaven,
As though of some blameless king who in a god-fearing way
Holds sway over numerous and valiant men, . . ."
And so ask me anything else now in your house,
But do not inquire of my race and my fatherland,
So that you may not fill my heart up further with pains . . ." (102-10; 115-17).

The conversation is the first one between Odysseus and Penelope, even though from her perspective it is the first one between her and the stranger that has found his way into their midst. One can imagine the fierce restraint the warrior home from Troy must exact as he sits so closely to his wife. As she seeks his origins to encourage him to speak, Odysseus praises her reputation and asks that she not probe his heritage because his pain in being away from it is too acute to respond to her. He is speaking of his current situation of not "being at home" in his true identity. So two narratives are playing out at this moment. Perhaps sensing that Penelope might be suspecting his identity, Odysseus works to deflect her.

Each of us has our own manner or style of expressing ourselves. It is not easily disguised. How we speak mirrors the structure and patterns of our consciousness. Those who know us are difficult to fool if we are in disguise. We tell our stories in certain patterned ways and reveal our identity even when we struggle to conceal it. A discerning ear may catch nuances and shades of our actual identity regardless of our counterfeit appearance. Physically changing how we appear is a much easier task than disguising speech patterns from familiars. "We have a story generating function to make [our myth] coherent, writes Laurence Coupe (*Myth* 6). The way we tell our stories reflects our mythic style.

Meditation:

Have you found it necessary at times to effectively hide your real feelings or thoughts on a matter from others for reasons that you believed essential?

October 1: Book XIX

"But longing for Odysseus, I pine away in my heart.
They are eager for marriage and I weave deceits.
First some god inspired my mind with the thought of a robe;
I should set up a great loom in the halls and weave on it
A large and delicate fabric. I told them at once:
'Young men, my suitors, since godly Odysseus is dead,
Wait, though you are eager for this marriage of mine, till I finish
This robe, so that the yarn may not waste in vain,
This burial sheet of hero Laertes for the time
When the ruinous fate of long sorrowful death seizes him,
Lest one of the Achaian women in the district blame me
If he who had won so much lie without covering.'" (XIX. 136-45).

Penelope confesses to the stranger her strategy for postponing marrying any of the suitors. She begins by professing her continued love for and fidelity to the man sitting across from her in concealment. She then reveals how a god sent her an idea to weave a funeral shroud during the day for her father-in-law and to unweave at night what she created that day. She succeeded in the ruse for three years; finally exposed by unfaithful maidservants,"uncaring bitches/they came and caught me, and all shouted at me together" (ll. 154-55). She was then forced to complete it so that now her marriage to one of the young suitors appears inevitable.

John Scheid and Jesper Svenbro suggest that "poetic composition is a metaphorical weaving, the result of which is a "richly patterned" fabric" (*The Craft of Zeus* 120). So in the passage above, two weavers converse: the weaving poet Odysseus and the shroud-crafting Penelope. They are both inspired by the divine talents of Athene whose intent is to reunite the household. They are also both poets in the act of making or shaping a reality through story, disguise, ruse, and deceit which are all forms of fictionalizing to attend to and shape a reality that will reunite the forces that comprise the intact household. In the process both are revealing and concealing in a delicate rhythm that is reminiscent of their life together before Troy and a long separation.

Meditation:

Offer your own version of weaving a pattern in words, fabric, pottery or painting in order to represent a reality that you wish to share with others.

October 2: Book XIX

"But tell me of your descent, wherever you are from,
For you are not from the oak of ancient tale or from rock."
Odysseus of many wiles addressed her in answer:
"Respected wife of Odysseus, son of Laertes,
Will you never leave off inquiring of my descent?
Well, I shall speak out to you, and you will give me to more woes
Than those I am held in. For this is the rule, when a man
Has been away from his fatherland as long as I now have,
Wandering to many cities of mortals, suffering pains.
Yet even so I shall tell you what you ask and inquire about:" (XIX. 162-71).

Penelope is insistent on knowing the stranger's origins while Odysseus becomes frustrated with her persistence. Both are strong demanding characters whose patterns of behavior with one another are so familiar to both. Odysseus is concealed and she wants him revealed. He knows and she does not. She wishes to pierce the veil of his nature, for perhaps she suspects already his true identity. When he tells her he will yield to her desire to know, he begins to craft his story that follows. She draws from his history that is in many ways analogous to her husband's; he speaks in a code she understands. On one level they are retrieving their old relationship under the noses of the suitors who are not attuned to such subtleties. As with the Phaeacians, Odysseus is reluctant to tell his story.

Coded language can be very effective when one wishes to reveal what has been concealed while keeping it hidden from those who have not enough history to know code words and habits of speaking together, which is now in full display but camouflaged simultaneously. Both of them are schooled in craft. Crafted words can reveal while concealing. It is an art form resting on a social arrangement and personal history. Glenn Arbery observes that "disguise and restraint have become the clear pattern of the truth that Odysseus is building, with great care, out of his painful circumstances" ("Odysseus' Nostos: Concealment and Revelation" 118). As he builds, so does Penelope weave; her weaving represents a pulling together all of the essential parts of the *oikos* that have been frayed and made threadbare. She fabricates while he dissembles. Our fabrications of ourselves can be seen as a way to restrain certain thoughts or actions in others.

Meditation:

Have you spoken in code to another in order to hide something of value?

October 3: Book XIX

"A great North Wind held them back and did not allow them
To ride at anchor near land; some harsh god raised it up.
The thirteenth day the wind fell, and they put to sea."
He spoke many falsehoods and made them seem like the truth.
Tears flowed from her as she listened and her flesh melted.
Just as snow melts down upon the peaks of the mountains
Which the East Wind melts when the West Wind pours it
down, . . .
So her lovely cheeks melted as she poured down her tears,
Weeping for her husband who was sitting by. Odysseus
Felt pity in his heart for his wife as she lamented,
But his eyes stood fast, as though they were horn or iron. . . (XIX. 200-06; 208-11).

Creating a fiction of himself so to deflect Penelope's curiosity about his identity becomes a necessity; she does not know that who she weeps for is next to her in disguise. Fiction becomes the great deflection. On this reality Donald Spence asks: "Is the story we hear the same as the story being told? If yes, then it is an account of 'the way things are'" (*Narrative Truth and Historical Truth* 27). Odysseus successfully takes lies and clothes them in the garments of a true story, one that Penelope ostensibly believes in and responds to. The lines above are the final ones of a longer, more elaborate ruse that he crafts. He even names himself as "Aithon" as "my well-known name" (l.183). Odysseus speaks of himself in the third person, someone he met in his travels. He then watches in deep sadness as his wife he longs for suffers further wounds about her husband's fate.

So many necessities may cause one to claim a false story as true; a counterfeit narrative is passed off as authentic. There are times when deception feeds a higher good, when the truth can be extremely harmful, even deadly, if exposed at the wrong time, or ever. Sacrificing the truth through a bogus narrative may eventually pay off, but keeping a fiction in place may be a necessity, especially when the power balance is skewed in the adversary's favor. For a time the fiction travels in the world "as-if" it is fact.

Meditation:

Describe a story you have been told or read that you simply could not believe. What was it about the narrative that denied your ability to accept it as true?

October 4: Book XIX

"And now, stranger, I think I shall test you out,
If truly in that place with his godlike companions
You entertained my husband in your halls, as you say.
Tell me what sort of clothes he had on over his skin,
What sort of man he was, and what companions went with him."
Odysseus of many wiles addressed her in answer:
"My good woman, it is hard to say, for a man who has been so long
Parted, since already it is the twentieth year
From the time he went thence and left my fatherland.
But I shall tell you the way my heart pictures it for me:" (XIX. 215-24).

Penelope is a devotee of the particular. Her interrogation begins with testing the stranger as to the personal clothing her husband wore when he met him. She also wants to know his observations on Odysseus' character traits as well as those who companioned him. In the process she is learning the stranger's manner of speaking, how he thinks and responds to her. Odysseus slowly answers some important details, like the twenty years he has been gone. These conversations reveal to her not just the stranger's veracity but his deeper personal traits. In Book XIX, "Penelope gradually arrives at the point where she is willing to make a (at least in her own view) socially responsible decision to move toward remarriage" as Helene Foley argues ("Penelope as Moral Agent" 101), so this stranger may be, she believes, her last chance to escape that fate.

Yes, we can camouflage our physical appearance, but the way we think and speak is more difficult to cover, especially from those who know us intimately. We each have certain patterns in our speech as well as body gestures that are subtle yet detectable by others who recognize them. We can then both conceal and reveal ourselves to intimates where others who are strangers will not detect anything other than what they hear and see since they have no history of the person to pull from. So while Penelope and Odysseus may be heard by others, they will be hidden in plain view in their recognitions. We can and sometimes do speak of ourselves in the third person.

Meditation:

Have you been surprised by your own ability to dissemble, to hide yourself as you reveal yourself at the same moment? On the contrary, can you discern when someone you know intimately is not telling the truth?

October 5: Book XIX

"But cease from lamentation and hearken to my speech.
I shall tell you unerringly and shall not conceal
That I have already heard about the return of Odysseus;
He is nearby in the rich land of the Thesprotians,
Alive. And he is bringing many excellent treasures,
Begging them through the land. But his trusty companions
And his hollow ship he lost on the wine-faced ocean. . . .
He swore to me personally, pouring libation in his house,
That a ship had been drawn down and companions were ready
Who would conduct him to his beloved fatherland" (268-74; 288-90).

As the interrogation/conversation deepens, Penelope breaks down under the crush of memories that fuel her grieving. Odysseus slowly reveals himself in the veracity of his story, which continues to grow closer to his historical truth that mingles with his narrative truth. He seeks as story teller to find analogies with his current disguised character in order to speak his reality through the veil of fiction. He couches his historical self within the fiction that is a safe container from which to disclose the very immediate future and to give Penelope hope she sorely needs at this critical moment. So, paradoxically he is on his way in the narrative and already present in his fiction. Brilliant. Odysseus would seem to embody a salient feature of poetry and of narrative-making, itself.

The lovers of story will delight in this unfolding drama that Penelope sets in motion, much like Athene's role throughout the epic who originates action. At this moment they are sisters in craftiness as Penelope helps to reveal something we all participate in daily: the mingling of the fictional and historical beings we are. We tell ourselves stories every day to create a reality coherent in its fictional/factual elements that comprise who we are. Our personal myth is a blend of these two worlds that keep our lives interesting, with purpose as a conglomerate of fantasy and fiction. Myth-making is the imaginal blending of the two. Myths are as much our attitudes, our way of interpreting events and situations, our judgment calls, as they are about our storied selves.

Meditation:

What fiction do you tell yourself daily as a means or method of continuing to live a meaningful life? If you were to lose sight of the fiction, what do you think would happen to your life trajectory?

October 6: Book XIX

"Dear stranger, never yet has a man so sound in mind
Of strangers from far away come more welcome to my house,
Because you so thoughtfully speak of all that is sound.
I have an old woman whose mind is packed with thoughts,
Who nourished that hapless man well and brought him up,
Taking him in her own hands when his mother first bore him.
She shall wash your feet, though indeed her strength is slight.
Come and stand up now, prudent Eurycleia;
Wash a man the same age as your master. Perhaps Odysseus
By this time is just like him in his hands and feet,
For quickly in misfortune do mortals become old" (XIX. 350-60).

Penelope knows. On a growing level of awareness she suspects this stranger as an image of her husband. She continues to craft a way to further her hunch. By offering further hospitality to the beggar through Eurycleia's washing him, she knows her handmaiden will recognize the scar left by a boar wound in his youth. If it is not there, then no harm done and she will know with certainty that the ragged-looking man is not her husband. She suspects him because she recognizes the habit of his sound-mindedness. She recognizes his thought patterns as they resonate closely with hers. Some may read her lines as coming from one who sees in the appearance of a stranger the resemblance of one long lost and in a moment of nostalgic grief wants to pamper him. Yet it is also clear in another part of the conversation with Odysseus that "the recent maturing of her son is the decisive reason for her giving up on her husband's return," as Uvo Holscher writes ("Penelope and the Suitors" 138).

Our deepest identity may reside in our patterns of thought and speech/writing. We know another through those patterns that are fueled by the personal myth of the person. Intimacy increases from entertaining these patterns of thought and behavior as we share ourselves through them as well. We "know" another through our awareness of their habits of being incarnated even in a disguised body. We can often "hear through" their disguise to the essential person hiding within. We may also believe a fuzzy reality when we are desperate.

Meditation:

Have you found particular thought, speech and gestural patterns in your children or those you know that seem to carry elements of your own basic nature?

October 7: Book XIX

" . . . . And now understand the speech that I speak:
Many long-suffering strangers have reached this place:
I think I have never yet seen one who resembles him
As you resemble Odysseus, in voice, body, and feet."
Odysseus of many wiles addressed her in answer:
"Old woman, that is what all men say who have seen us both
With their eyes, that we are very similar to one another,
As indeed, you yourself have discerned and said."
So he spoke, and the old woman took a glistening basin
That she used for washing feet; she poured in much water,
The cold; then she transferred in the hot. (XIX. 378-88).

Deception is a craft, even an art form and Odysseus has perfected it in his life journey; it is his nature to craft and be crafted by circumstances. Here he sits with the woman who raised him; she knows his persona perhaps even better than does Penelope. She sees, through his disguise, a twin of her master. From head to toe she knows him, and knows his feet from perhaps countless times of washing him as he grew up. Odysseus knows this and so deflects her scrutiny by proclaiming everyone sees in the two of them a remarkable resemblance. She then prepares the bowl for the ritual of washing. The cold and hot waters suggest two natures in the guest she is now serving when she mingles the two temperatures.

Over time deceptions wear out, become threadbare, or unravel so that imperfections appear in its façade. Some can sustain the deception over time. Others lose the energy to continue the disguise. Our true identity begins to seep out through the small gaps of our disguise. The truth of who we are wants to be witnessed and acknowledged; our disguise as scaffolding begins to fall apart to reveal our authentic nature. For warriors returning from the trauma of battle, they may return in disguise, unrecognizable to family and friends. The self that others knew is disguised, their real self often still on the battlefield. So too with wounds, that like Odysseus' are hidden, below the surface, but needing attention and honor. Edward Tick writes that one may feel a "social invisibility" of their true self (*Warrior's Return* 143).

Meditation:

Think of someone, yourself included, who returned from a transformative period in their life and who returned "a different person" from the one who left.

October 8: Book XIX

>   Odysseus
> was sitting by the hearth, and suddenly turned toward the
> darkness.
> For at once he was apprehensive in heart lest when she touched him
> She notice his scar and the facts become apparent.
> She went near and was washing her master, and right away knew
> The scar which once a boar dealt him with its shining tusk
> When he had come to Parnassos to see Autolycos and his sons,
> His mother's noble father who excelled among men
> In trickery and oath making. The god Hermes himself
> Endowed him, for he burned the thighs of lambs and kids
> Pleasing to the gods, who zealously attended the man (XIX. 388-98).

As concealed, so revealed. In this flash back, one of the first in literature, Odysseus' true identity has been slowly rising to the surface with each contact with the feminine presences of Penelope, Eurycleia and the masculine presences of the suitors as well as Telemachos and Eumaeos. Now his early history as a boy who is wounded by a boar tusk creeps to the surface, along with his fear that the scar inflicted by the animal will reveal immediately to the servant woman his full identity. She knows his history and the story of the wound. He tries to shift from the light into the shadows even as his past steals out of the shadows into the light. From his grandfather he has inherited all the attributes of a trickster.

On our bodies are residues of our history in the form of scars, tattoos, birthmarks, nicks and cuts that left a trace: a broken tooth, a finger that healed crookedly, a twisted toe and a host of other identifying markers the body holds in memory. To those who share our past, those marks identify us immediately. Even as our bodies age, they do not relinquish who we are by the marks that life grooved in us. Our flesh carries the residues in the form of stories that inscribe us. In our own stories, as I have written elsewhere, "the wound becomes the distortion through which we revision its phenomenology as a lived experience. Wounding is one way the body shows its hyperbole. . . (*The Wounded Body* 11).

Our wounds are as much psychic markers as embodied emblems.

Meditation:

Identify a mark on your body, natural or artificial, and relate the story of its branding you and perhaps dramatically shaping your identity.

October 9: Book XIX

"Autolycos, now find yourself a name you may give
To the dear son of your child; he has been much prayed for."
Then Autolycos answered her and addressed her:
"My son-in-law and daughter, give him the name I say.
I myself come here as one who has been enraged at many,
At men and at women, throughout the much-nourishing earth,
And let him be named Man of Wrath: Odysseus. For my part,
When he reaches his prime, and comes to the great house
Of his mother, to Parnassos where I have my possessions,
I shall give him some from them and send him back in joy" (XIX. 403-12).

We have been transported seamlessly into the past, to the origin of the hero and his naming, all by means of Eurycleia's discovery of Odysseus' scar. She takes the infant and places him on his grandfather's knees and asks the older man to name him. He responds to a name that he himself would find as appropriate as his own name because he has spent so much of his life enraged. So he names him Odysseus, man of wrath, also translated as one who gives and receives trouble. He also promises that when the infant comes of age, that he travel to Autolycos' home in Parnassos to receive bountiful gifts from him that Odysseus will enjoy as well as learn further of the guest-host relation in hospitality.

Naming, being named or being called forth by a particular name can imprint one with an identity emanating from the name's meaning. Names define us, mark us, like a scar, from birth. Some change their names later in life, feeling they were incorrectly named; others grow into their names, seeing a wisdom in whoever named them originally. Nicknames sometimes split the difference, calling forth a moment in one's life that invites an informal name to override the birth name. Naming can mark us for life, like a wound, a scar or a powerful trait. Sometimes we alter our names in adult life or pick up a nickname at a moment in our journey, like a tour in the military or a special circumstance when a nickname sticks as more fitting of our nature. So our names deeply imbed us in a particular identity.

Meditation:

Reflect on the circumstances that surrounded your own naming. What is its history and the conditions that brought you to bear this name? Have you considered or have you changed your name?

October 10: Book XIX

And when the early-born, rosy-fingered dawn appeared,
They went on the hunt, both the dogs and themselves,
The sons of Autolycos. With them godly Odysseus
Went along. They approached the sheer mountain covered with
woods
Of Parnassos, and soon they reached the windy ravines. . . .
                              With them godly Odysseus
Moved close to the dogs, brandishing a long-shadowed spear.
And there in the thick copse was lying a great boar
The blowing winds' watery force did not blow through to it,
Nor did the Sun strike it with the beams of his rays,
Nor did the rain get all the way through, so thick
It was, and a plentiful deposit of leaves was there (428-32; 437-43).

The plot has shifted to the past and to a very young Odysseus on a boar hunt with his cousins; there they encounter the animal hidden in one of the ravines, within a thicket so tightly overgrown that rain and wind cannot penetrate it. The boar is secure within this sturdy natural home. As we read it closely, we see that the description is identical to the one that ended Book V, where Odysseus, naked, exhausted and alone, not unlike an animal, crawls between two olive coverings, one wild and one tame, and sharing a single root. There, as with the boar, he is protected from the elements and makes himself a bed of dry leaves and Athene sheds sweet sleep on him. He then emerges reborn.

Some incident or incidents from our childhood or young adult days may have defined us. Their memories linger and continue to haunt and even shape our current life. We sense some plot line from the connection of one or more early incidents to our current condition. We feel the form of some coherence, perhaps, some home ground that defines us as unique and as part of a larger community. It is a mythic consciousness or mythic awareness that takes us out of ourselves while at the same time allowing us a more intimate sense of who we are. A myth, I have written elsewhere, "is a patterned manner of imagining, a style of being present in the world" (*Riting Myth, Mythic Writing: Plotting Your Personal Story* 10).

Meditation:

Recall a vivid incident in your past that you sense defined you and may continue to in your life today.

October 11: Book XIX

The boar got the start and struck him
Above the knee, and gashed his flesh deep with a tusk,
Charging at him slantwise, but did not get to the man's bone.
Odysseus wounded him, hitting him on the right shoulder.
And the point of his shining spear went straight on through him. . . .
Autolycos and the sons of Autolycos healed him
Well, and they provided him with glorious gifts,
And sent him in joy speedily to his dear fatherland,
To Ithaca. . . .
The old woman took the scar in the palms of her hands and knew it
As she touched it; she let the foot drop that she held,
And his shin fell into the basin and the bronze clattered (XIX. 449-53; 459-62; 467-69).

In this rich pivotal moment between past and future, Odysseus is wounded and fulfills the name he was given as an infant. He is a fearless warrior at this young age when he hunts the boar in hiding. Out of the wound emanate gifts and a fuller sense of his identity. He is then healed and receives gifts from his relatives when he is ready to sail home, just as the Phaeacians sent him home with gifts after twenty years of his wandering. Then a quick shift in time to the present when Eurycleia recognizes the scar and knows his identity immediately; she knows the narrative imbedded in the scar. She knows the identity of the beggar through his healed wound and is about to rejoice. She also at this moment "unmasked his vulnerability and humanity" as Christine Mitchell Havelock observes ("Intimate Act of Footwashing" 196).

We are, as with Odysseus, wounded into our deeper identity. James Hillman suggests that "the wound that is necessary to initiation ceremonies ends the state of innocence as it opens in a new way at another place. . . . it is as if the soul can find no path out of innocence other than physical hurt" ("Puer Wounds and Ulysses' Scar" 229). When we are wounded from the past and see ourselves through our afflictions, we may recognize that in them reside our fictions, our values, and what we stand for. Others know us by our wounds, by where we have suffered.

Meditation:

Describe a wound you have carried and the identity that suppurates through it. It can be a physical or psychological marking.

October 12: Book XIX

But the other could not sight her face to face or perceive her,
For Athene had turned her mind. Odysseus groped for her
With his hands, and took her by the throat with his right hand,
And with the other he drew her closer to himself and spoke:
"Good mother, why do you wish to destroy me? You brought
Me up at your breast yourself. Now, having suffered many pains,
I have come in the twentieth year to my fatherland.
Since you recognized me, and a god put it in your heart,
Be quiet, lest someone else in the halls find out" (XIX. 478-86).

Odysseus knows that he could be forced to kill someone he loves if that person jeopardizes the element of surprise in his homecoming. Eurycleia is one of those he loves but would silence quickly in order to reclaim his home and family. We can feel the tension in his voice as it becomes possible all will be revealed in an instant. Now he is close to putting his plan into play but such an unforeseen event like his maidservant recognizing his scar and blurting out this fact could undo all he has crafted until now. Athene reveals her own powers over the mind by shifting Penelope's attention so she does not see the look that Eurycleia sends her way to acknowledge the man who she has just washed is Odysseus. Athene is the goddess of mind, mindfulness and when necessary, controlling the mind's attention.

Surprise is a strong weapon against stronger forces. Being concealed is another. Sometimes we survive because of our surprises; it is crafted and may be its own force against those who would undo us. Surprise carries an intimacy about it that may allow one to survive. Holding back surprise action is another form of restraint; it is a strategy of the wise to protect and preserve themselves. We at times touch the Odyssean part of ourselves in cultivating the unexpected but then holding it in check until the right time unfolds before us. One's physical prowess is far less important than the strength of one's mind in crafting the avenue of surprise in order to protect something or someone of value.

Meditation:

Have you been surprised by the sudden revelation of another? Have you held back some surprise information or action that gave you an advantage over another or others?

October 13: Book XIX

And then the prudent Eurycleia addressed him:
"My child, what sort of speech has got past the bar of your
teeth?
You know how much my strength is steadfast and unyielding.
I shall hold out like iron or some rigid stone.
I shall tell you another thing, and keep it well in mind.
If a god does subdue the noble suitors underneath you,
Then I shall tell you about the women in the halls,
Those that dishonor you and those that are innocent" (XIX. 491-98).

Eurycleia asserts herself, her fidelity and her honor before her master. Has Odysseus in his stress over being recognized not given her proper due? He may also suspect everyone, even those who have proven their fidelity to him in the past. She speaks with a certainty about her own strength and her honor as a faithful servant of the household. She adds one more layer: to expose those servant women who crossed over into the camp of the ungrateful and greedy and to name all those who remained faithful to the family. Odysseus in turn will tell her in a moment that her discernment will not be necessary because by observing he will see which have betrayed his *oikos*. Erich Auerbach, writing of the most famous scar in history, points out that "the Homeric poems conceal nothing, they contain no teaching and no secret second meaning" ("Odysseus' Scar" 13). Even in a poem where so much is concealed, for us it is revealed.

Trust, honesty, loyalty are noble qualities in the soul of each of us. It makes betrayal, deceit and absence of fidelity toward the good and noble painful to accept. Manipulating others for self-gain through feigned loyalty must be recognized quickly so its corrosive contagion does not spread and gain power. The very survival of the household rests on a recognition of trust in all its members. Restoration of the home, of order, of moderation and of a virtuous mean is a challenge when one desires to protect it. Marilyn Stewart writes that "the *Odyssey* traces a journey of the human mind in touch with its desire for interaction with other minds, a like-mindedness that is the source of all human harmony" ("Imagination and Mapping in the *Odyssey*" 86).

Meditation:

When your own household has been threatened or attacked, what was your strategy to restore its wholeness?

October 14: Book XIX

"So my heart is aroused, divided this way and that,
Whether I should wait with my son and steadfastly guard
All my property, the maids and the high-roofed house,
Respecting the bed of my husband and the talk of the people
Or by this time should follow the best of the Achaians
Who woos me in the halls and offers endless bridal gifts. . . .
But come, listen to this dream and interpret it for me:
Twenty geese are eating the wheat in my house,
Out of the water, and I am warmed to look on them.
Then a great crooked-beaked eagle came off a mountain,
Broke all their necks and killed them. They were heaped
Together through the halls, and soared to the divine air" (XIX. 524-29; 535-40).

Penelope speaks her heart to the stranger who she has drawn close to the fire. Odysseus hides his scar in the rags he wears. His wife offers a couple of alternatives on what her future might be. Do I continue waiting, she wonders, or do I give myself over to one of the suitors? She watches his own reactions to her choices. Then she tacks in a different direction by asking him to interpret her dream. Might they be speaking to one another through the dream? Perhaps. She knows her husband's mind and how he would work the dream in his cleverness. He will be careful not to fall for her request and so reveal himself.

Indirection can be a forceful rhetorical tool. To move this way and that through images can be a sophisticated way of communicating with others. It is the way of art, of craftiness and subtlety. Penelope and Odysseus know one another's minds and play on their respective talents. For some, communication happens without speech, so freely at home are they with one another. We can also pick up on the character of another without speech but by proximity. We give off our personhood through our bodily presence. As Penelope keeps the stranger close by her, she begins to respond to his identity and wants to test that with various challenges she places in his path. She is weaving her suspicions into her contests. Nancy Felson-Rubin informs us that "her name, from *pene,* "woof" or "web" ("Penelope's Perspective" 167) fits her calculating plans.

Meditation:

Are you so close to another that you communicate with one another without words?

October 15: Book XIX

"My good woman, there is no way to interpret this dream
By twisting it off another way, since Odysseus himself
Has shown how he will achieve it. Destruction is plain for the suitors,
All of them; and not one shall ward off destiny and death."
And then the prudent Penelope spoke to him:
"Stranger, hard to handle and confused in their stories do dreams
Come, and not all in them is brought to pass for men.
For double are the portals of flickering dreams.
One set is made of horn, the other of ivory" (XIX. 555-63).

Odysseus knows his wife and her strategies, so he slips past her invitation to interpret her dream; too much exposure before its time. She in turn wants to hear how his mind works so she can identify him as her husband, her last opportunity before succumbing to the suitors' demands. She is less interested in the content of the stranger's speech than she is in his mind's way of interpreting events and dreams. She will relate in a moment that dreams come through two doors, one bearing falsehood, the other bearing truth. Dreams themselves offer various ways of knowing. She seeks this stranger's help in making some distinctions about how to interpret her latest dream; he in turn offers that the suitors will feel the pain of death, just as the geese do at the hands of the eagle. The dream is her domain.

Our sleeping/dreaming life also offers ways of knowing but they too require discernments, choices, interpretations and a sense of their truth. Perhaps to fully come home one must at least acknowledge the oneiric qualities of the household. To be at home with our dream life and images promises a greater involvement of ourselves in homecoming. We can sense with Penelope that she continues to deepen and strengthen the weave around the stranger, drawing him further into her emotional and psychological life. As Jonathan Shay makes clear, "Penelope takes the beggar into an even deeper level of her private confidence" (*Odysseus in America* 134). We sense that she may believe that if she exposes herself to him more fully, he will or may admit his true identity.

Meditation:

Do you carry with you a powerful dream you return to often to test or discover its validity for you? Has your sense of the dream's meaning shifted over time?

October 16: Book XIX

"And as for those who come through the sawn ivory,
They deceive, carrying words that will not be fulfilled;
But those that pass on outside through the polished horn
Do fulfill the truth whenever any mortal sees them.
But I do not think my awesome dream has come
From those gates. That would truly be welcome to me and to
my son. . . .
This dawn of evil name shall come that will make me leave
The home of Odysseus, for now I will set up a contest
Of axes, which the man used to stand up in a row
In his halls, as trestles, all twelve of them.
He would stand at a great distance and shoot an arrow through.
And now I will set up this contest for the suitors": (XIX. 564-69; 571-76).

Penelope teaches us about the veracity of dreams. If the dream comes through the polished horn, it will not come to pass. But if the dream migrates through the horn of ivory, it will be fulfilled. She at this point commands the narrative; her plan is to set up the old contest of the twelve axe handles, all in a row; she will give herself to who can penetrate all twelve with a single arrow, knowing full well that her husband was able to achieve such accuracy in the past. Some part of her knows this may be the final test to prove or disprove the stranger's identity. Since she probably suspects the man is her husband, she knows how to assemble proof. If he is not, she will leave his house for a suitor's.

Coming home is not without its own challenges. To think otherwise is naïve. Rules, customs, mores all govern the household and should be adopted in any homecoming. The home's own imagination completely absorbs the traveler. One must first become a guest in one's own home, then move to the position of host. Both roles are called for. Penelope is the presence of that shift from guest to host. Jonathan Shay notes, "Odysseus is not yet in a safe, civilian setting. His life is as much on the line as it was on the plains of Troy" (*Odysseus in America* 138), so he must stay in combat mode and not relinquish his identity for a moment.

Meditation:

When have you been a guest in your own home, be it where you grew up or one you founded? What circumstances put you in this role and not in that of host?

October 17: Book XIX

"The one who most nimbly strings the bow in his hands
And shoots an arrow through all twelve of the axes,
Him will I follow, leaving this very lovely
Home of my marriage, full of the goods of life,
Which I think I will ever remember, even in dreams . . . ."
"Respected wife of Odysseus, son of Laertes,
Do not delay this contest any longer in the house.
Odysseus of many wiles shall come to you in this place
Long before these men who handle the well-made bow
Have stretched the bowstring and shot an arrow through the
 iron" (XIX. 577-81; 583-87).

Penelope continues to command the narrative by recalling the famous axe contest. She reveals her frustration and resolve to end her place in the household if necessary, but she is also teasing the stranger out of hiding. Emily Wilson writes in the Introduction to her translation: "The process by which she comes to acknowledge the stranger as the difficult, secretive, aggressive husband is extraordinarily long-drawn-out , and the exact moment at which she recognizes him remains a mystery—like so much about Penelope" (*Homer: The Odyssey* 63). Odysseus in turn tells her: set up the contest now and Odysseus will appear to confront the challenge with such speed that no suitor will have time to even try to string the bow. The two characters who dance around one another continue to draw closer with each advance of the plot. Their conversation is at once concealing and revealing.

Certain rituals reveal who we are over others. As the warrior returns home, he participates in a game, a contest, that simulates battle but is far less deadly. However, not in this case. Warriors returning home, Edward Tick has observed, carry with them in their emotional duffle bag the haunting by a soul wound (*Warrior's Return* 242). That wound continues to fester and may erupt repeatedly if not mitigated in part by "the spiritual warrior archetype" (248). In such a hosting, the returning warrior may more fully reenter his own household. Rituals can disguise deeper intentions and places by looking like something it is not. Rituals unite.

Meditation:

When has a ritual hidden another reality? When has it allowed another reality to become present and prominent?

October 18: Book XIX

"Stranger, if you should like to sit by me in the halls
And delight me, sleep would never be shed on my eyelids.
But it is not possible for men to be without sleep
Forever. The immortals have set down a limit
For everything among mortals on the grain-giving earth.
Well, I shall go up myself into the upper chamber
And lie down in my bed, which is made full of groans for me,
Ever sullied with my tears since the time Odysseus
Went off to see evil Ilion, the unspeakable. . . ."
She entered the upper chamber with her serving women
And then wept for Odysseus, her dear husband, until
Bright-eyed Athene cast a sweet sleep upon her eyelids (589-97; 602-04).

Penelope's familiar air with the stranger, which has become his name, perhaps a synonym for "no man," is a way of seducing him to reveal himself. Odysseus keeps his desire locked up within by heroic restraint. Penelope gives him a sense of her philosophy: the gods impose limits on all things mortal. Violating those limits invites hardship and suffering. She also once again fills him in on the history that has accrued since his departure two decades earlier. She enters her room to weep for Odysseus, but there is no question that her suspicions as well as her desires have been aroused by this ragged beggar's presence. Then Athene aids Penelope, as she has Odysseus, by promoting sleep.

To be so constrained when returning home after a long absence is a horrible form of limitation. Home should be where you reveal yourself fully and act freely. Anything less is to be a stranger in one's home. True, Odysseus is home but he is not "at home." The suitors may take many forms; they are in their violation of limits, invaders of the home as dwelling. They must be both eliminated and integrated into the household for Odysseus to come fully home, where he is able to dwell, not visit, be forced to the periphery, or abused. Home is as much an emotional and psychological attitude as it is a physical place. "Being at home in the place world," writes Edward Casey, is the third stage in "being oriented" and finding one's right place in the world (*The World* 114).

Meditation:

When have you been home but not *at* home? When have you been in the home of another but never felt at home as a guest?

October 19: Book XX

But godly Odysseus went to bed in the portico.
Under him he spread an undressed hide, and above
Many fleeces of the sheep the Achaians had been sacrificing. . . .
Then Odysseus lay awake devising evils in his heart
For the suitors. And the women who up to then
Used to lie with the suitors went out of the hall,
Entertaining one another with laughter and with mirth.
As for him, the heart was aroused in his own breast.
He deliberated much in his mind and in his heart,
Whether to rush among them and bring death on each one
Or else allow them to lie with the bold suitors
A last and final time (XX. 1-3; 5-13).

Now that night has fallen, Odysseus' imagination brings bloody vengeance to mind. He sees those unfaithful to his wife and how their actions violate all those who have faithfully served his family. Part of his impulsive nature wants to rid the household of its pollution in the moment, as he did so often at Troy, while another tells him to respect limits and to restrain even though his heart "growled within him, indignant at their evil deeds (l. 16). He chooses wisely to allow the violators to enjoy one last night together before he unleashes his fury to reclaim his past. His blankets are made of his own sheep that the suitors had sacrificed to satisfy their appetites and their impiety. The epic is on the brink of another Trojan conflict, for now Penelope and Odysseus share sleeping but in separate beds.

To return home from war only to find oneself dressing for yet another battle is a homecoming end-stopped in its joy. But the warrior may have to sacrifice a proper arrival home because of circumstances that keep him or her in a fighting posture. One can only imagine the pain that Odysseus or any warrior returning home seeking asylum from the chaotic violence of war is forced to bear until the right time for the household to be righted. War's appetite seeks to be replaced with an appetite for peace and calm; if that is immediately impossible, then more patience and restraint is necessary to be alert and on-guard until the appropriate time is offered.

Meditation:

What has been your experience in handling warring parties within the walls of your own home? What strategies did you enact to reclaim its peace?

October 20: Book XX

So this way and that did he toss about, pondering
How he might lay his hands upon the shameless suitors,
Being one man against many. Athene came close to him,
Descending from the sky; she likened her body to a woman's.
She stood above his head and addressed a speech to him:
"Why are you awake, ill-fated beyond all mortal men? . . .
Stubborn man, some will trust an inferior person
Who is a mortal and does not know such wisdom as mine.
But I myself am a god, who constantly protects you
In all your trials. I shall speak to you openly" (XX. 28-33; 45-48).

In his own home, trying to calm his own restlessness under his own fleeces, Odysseus remains a stranger in his familiar setting. He is frustrated and feels explosive by his lack of power to conquer the suitors, who travel together like a large pack of hungry animals. Athene recognizes his distress and comes to him from Olympus to counsel him. She seems to berate him for his lack of faith and trust in her wisdom to advise him in his vulnerable condition; she reassures him that she is always close by to protect him and promises him candor in all her insights. Karl Kerenyi writes of Athene that "she is the rescuer from every danger and peril, the advisor for every tight spot, and the highest wisdom. . . . She maintains life and health" (*Athene* 9). Odysseus' task is to submit to her wisdom and to remember how often she has guided and saved him from death.

Not knowing who around us is the wisest or the best guide can be frustrating when we seek out advice or help in planning how to overcome adversaries. Some may refuse to believe in divine intervention. Others may choose poorly and listen to those who lack the knowledge or wisdom to be effective companions in our turmoil. Transiting from the larger world back to home may prove to be an arduous journey. We need the best resources in ourselves to achieve some level of success. It is not unusual, on a broader scale, for warriors returning from combat to be treated harshly and attacked on their return. They are often forced, as Edward Tick writes, "to carry the traumatizing consequences of being dishonored" (*Warrior's Return* 125).

Meditation:

Who do you call on to guide you when the road is extremely rough or obscure?

October 21: Book XX

>   "You shall soon rise up from your ills."
> So she said. And she shed sleep over his eyelids;
> Then the divine goddess herself went back to Olympos.
> While sleep, the looser of the limbs, seized him, loosing
> The troubles of his heart, his wife, who had a sense of devotion,
> Woke up and wept while sitting up in her soft bed.
> And when she was sated in her own heart with weeping,
> The divine woman prayed to Artemis first of all:
> "Artemis, queenly goddess, daughter of Zeus, would that now
> You might strike my chest with an arrow and take my life away. . ." (XX. 53-62).

Here at the last hour when Odysseus returns, Penelope wishes that her life would end at this very moment. She holds secure "with Odysseus in my mind's eye" (l. 81). She could now die with his image in her imagination. As he falls asleep, she wakens; they pass each other in sleep and dream, so rooted are they in one another' soul. As his sorrows are loosened by Athene's charm, Penelope's intensifies. As he rests exhausted and frustrated, she wakes yearning for death. They are inverted images of one another, drawn together by their mutual love. In their differences they create an image of wholeness. She wishes that Artemis—huntress and protectress of animals and warriors—would descend to end her life.

Home is not necessarily an oasis of tranquility amidst the chaos of the world; it may only be a smaller version of it. No guarantees that home will bring tranquility from what Odysseus continues to suffer while in disguise. Yet he has a large challenge ahead in purifying this space whose pollution is systemic. Home can disarm us with its own dysfunctions. In Odysseus' situation, he is back at Troy in his own home so the trauma of war is intensified, not diminished. As readers, we feel the massive tension permeating the household as time itself seems to have been exhausted; there is so little left for anything to change. The dramatic tension is palpable; we can feel in our memories conditions in which time's seemingly inexhaustible presence is suddenly limited. Despair, giving up, exhausting our human resources to survive is a terrible moment suffered alone.

Meditation:

What is your worst or least comfortable experience of coming home or of being at home?

October 22: Book XX

Godly Odysseus heard her voice as she was weeping,
And then he thought it over; she seemed to him in his heart
Already to know him and be standing at his head.
He gathered up the mantle and the fleeces in which he slept
And put them on a chair in the hall; he carried the hide out,
Set it aside, and raised his hands in prayer to Zeus: . . .
So he said in his prayer, and the counselor Zeus heard him,
And he thundered at once from glittering Olympos
High up out of the clouds. Godly Odysseus rejoiced. . . (XX. 92-97; 102-04).

Broken-hearted listening to his wife weep close by, Odysseus wakes, straightens out his sleeping arrangement and prays to the god Zeus to reveal signs of why the god has allowed him to return home only to find the situation he is in: increased and sustained suffering. In addition, both Penelope and her husband have connected in grief and yearning for one another. Their imaginations continue to seek one another out. The thunderous response to his plea gladdens Odysseus' heart and offers him a certainty towards his actions. Edward Casey observes that "Zeus is the ultimate sky-god; like an eagle, he can spot anything that is happening on earth below him" (*The World* 187). It is one of the most poignant moments in the entire poem, where mortals and divinities conspire to the good and the noble by participating in correcting the wrongs done to his household.

Whether we call it prayer or communication with the energies of the cosmos, marking contact with the transcendent or higher powers, it is a road to some comfort in the midst of suffering and longing. To be in contact with higher powers in the cosmos that sustain our resolve can make the difference between despairing and rejoicing. In this connection our idea of home expands and deepens. We are home in a much more authentic and lasting way. Mary Lou Hoyle writes that "the poem has shown home to be of such great importance that the gods themselves retrieve the absent husband. . . . The good home is at the heart of this comic epic. . ." ("From Comedy to Tragedy: The Shift in Perspective" 135). So might we add that the hearth is at the same time their hearts. To say so is to put ourselves in the welcoming space of the goddess Hestia.

Meditation:

May not homecoming include God, the gods or the presence of the transcendent? Is coming home also a movement of the spirit, in addition to body and soul?

October 23: Book XX

The others were sleeping, since they had ground up the wheat.
But one had not yes ceased, the weakest; she was still working.
She stopped the mill and said a word, a sign to her master:
"Father Zeus, you who rule over the gods and men, . . .
Fulfill now, even for my poor self, what I say:
May the suitors this day for the last and final time
Partake of a delightful banquet in the halls of Odysseus,
Those who have undone my knees in heart-hurting toil
To make barley flour. May they dine now for the last time."
So she said, and godly Odysseus rejoiced at the omen and thunder
Of Zeus (XX. 109-12; 115-21).

Even the lowliest servant in Odysseus' home is not without her own feelings toward the wreckage created by the suitors. She is the last to cease her labors, after which she turns to Zeus in prayer. Although seemingly so insignificant a figure, she nonetheless pleads that this night be the last day the suitors have to enjoy their bounty at Odysseus' expense. She admits to being abused in her work to satisfy the appetites of the young men who inhabit the house like a pestilence. She wishes that this day of dining be their final insult on the household. Odysseus nearby, hears her pleas and rejoices a second time in confirmation of his plans as well as the resounding response from Zeus.

When our home is violated, so too are all those who claim it as a sanctuary and a place of respite and renewal. The home is not the physical property. Rather, the home is an attitude of hospitality and largesse, a condition of generosity that extends to all who know it and the family that inhabits it. The home is synonymous with one's identity, dreams, values and properties of the soul that extend themselves into the world. We extend to others a welcoming atmosphere when they appear and are treated as guests. The house is where we live; the home is where we dwell, repose, be. Martin Heidegger reminds us that "To dwell, to be set at peace, means to remain at peace within the free, the preserve, the free sphere that safeguards each thing in its nature" ("Building, Dwelling, Thinking" 149).

Meditation:

How do you understand the adage of "being at home"?

October 24: Book XX

But Melanthios the goatherd came up close to them,
Leading goats that were outstanding in all the flocks
As a meal for the suitors. Two herdsmen followed with him,
And they tied the goats up inside the resounding portico;
And then he himself spoke out to Odysseus with taunts:
"Stranger, will you now still give trouble in the house,
Begging of the men, and you will not go on outdoors?
I think the two of us will not be separated wholly
Till we have tasted fists, since indeed you do not beg
Decently. And there are other banquets of the Achaians, too"
So he said, and Odysseus of many wiles said nothing,
But moved his head in silence, deliberating evils (XX. 173-84).

As he plots the end of the suitors, yet another adversary presents himself, a goat herder and servant of the suitors, to taunt Odysseus the beggar. He accuses Odysseus of not begging according to protocol and threatens him with a fight. Odysseus knows that any direct confrontation with anyone can expose his true identity before the time is right, thus ruining his chances to reclaim his home as well as risking the lives of his family. Odysseus in silence must plot out a strategy on the spot to silence or disarm Melanthios. To increase his gauling, the goatherd brings forward some of the finest of Odysseus' stock. Homer's pun on "trouble," a word used by his adversary, is, we recall, the meaning of Odysseus' name, who is unknowingly referred to by his correct name by the goatherd.

Whether in reclaiming one's home or in any life situation, danger can arrive at our doorstep that may threaten our reputation by our response, or may delay or cancel our future plans. Life seems to insist on moments of adversarial elements intruding to disrupt or effect our desires. Do we react and thereby feed the adversary, or do we more calmly plot a resolution that will leave little detrimental residue? As Odysseus teaches us, at times of sudden strife, silence may be our most potent response, for it does not feed what the adversary is being nourished by. In our silence the opposition has less ground to gain traction by his/her attack.

Meditation:

Describe an adversary you successfully out-maneuvered, disarmed or otherwise deflected? What was your strategy?

October 25: Book XX

Meanwhile the suitors were contriving death and destiny
For Telemachos; still a bird came to him on the left,
A lofty-flying eagle and he held a trembling dove.
Amphinomos spoke out to them and addressed them:
"My friends, this plan shall not concur with our wish,
The murder of Telemachos. Let us take thought for a banquet. . . ."
Telemachos, managing for advantage, sat Odysseus down
Inside the well-built hall next to the stone threshold,
Setting down an insignificant stool and small table.
Beside him he put portions of entrails and poured wine
In a golden cup, and addressed a speech to him: (XX. 241-46; 257-61).

The suitors' intention is to devour Odysseus and his family as well as his household. One among them, Amphinomos, still believes in portents and oracles. He takes the sign of the eagle holding the quivering dove to indicate that they should not yet kill Telemachos. Perhaps a feast is more appropriate and more beneficial to their appetites, he suggests. They quickly agree. As Telemachos hosted Athene disguised as mentor early in the epic, here he protects and hosts his beggar father by setting a small table exclusively for him; he then serves him personally. His son mixes setting an insignificant stool for his father, but pours wine into a golden cup, to reveal the explicit beggar and implicit leader at the same instant.

Something extraordinary appears to all in the form of an eagle clutching a trembling dove. We might watch for signs and tokens perhaps from another realm that break through the curtain that separates us from invisible presences as wisdom guides. Following only our appetites, we of course can pay them no mind. On the other hand, we may read them as signs of how to think and act. The suitors pay little attention to the omen, just as they see nothing suspicious in Telemachos setting the beggar down in a place of honor and treating him like the royalty he is. He follows up with a speech warning the suitors to bring no harm to this guest. Their response is wonder and fear that he speaks so boldly (ll. 262-67). The son is not the father but is the one who prepares the conditions for the father's presence.

Meditation:

Has your life been changed or influenced by an omen or sign that bore its truth out in your future? What was the sign and how was it delivered to you?

October 26: Book XX

And Athene by no means allowed the suitors
To refrain from grievous outrage, so that still more pain
Might enter the heart of Odysseus, son of Laertes.
There was a man among the suitors who had a lawless mind.
Ktesippos was his name and in Same he made his home.
Relying on his own prodigious property,
He wooed the wife of Odysseus who was gone so long. . . .
"Come then, I too shall give him a gift, so that he also
May give a prize to the water pourer or someone else
Of the servants who are in the home of godly Odysseus" (XX. 284-90; 296-98).

Athene continues to pour more suffering on Odysseus. She seems to be the divine embodiment of outrage who gives free reign to the suitors' wrath so Odysseus will feel more pain. She introduces the mean-tempered Ktesippos who will be an instrument of further insults and disrespect in challenging Odysseus' powers of restraint, holding back and remaining concealed, even oblivious, as Calypso's name intones. Ktesippos, in a camouflaged gesture of gift-giving, conceals a malignant motive. He tries to disarm the beggar so to make his "gift" have maximum impact. He feigns hospitality as a guest interested in gift giving in order to appear at least initially as following the code of guest.

When we feel that wall that marks the extent of our capacity to be abused, to be made uncomfortable or to handle physical or emotional pain, something else or someone may enter to test us even further. To be tested beyond what we have accepted as our maximum can push us to give in to it, to tolerate it and to stretch who and what our identity is. Looking back, we may even feel gratitude for the challenge. James Hillman writes of Athene as the goddess who links norms of "images, and ideas with behavioral pathologies. In other words, we are obliged to recognize the *pathologizing of Athene*" ("On the Necessity of Abnormal Psychology" 31). She highlights the norms through excess, pathology, and abnormality, which is what is happening to Odysseus above. Out of this ordeal at home he will reveal himself as stronger and more determined.

Meditation:

Recall a situation when you were pushed to and perhaps beyond what you believe were your limits. Were you surprised by where your boundaries really were?

October 27: Book XX

When he said this he threw an ox's foot from his stout hand,
Picking it up from the basket where it lay. And Odysseus
Dodged it by quickly ducking his head, and smiled in his heart
A very scornful smile. It struck the well-built wall.
Telemachos rebuked Ktesippos in a speech:
"Ktesippos, this was much better for you in your heart
That you did not hit the stranger. He dodged the missile himself.
For I would have struck you through the middle with my sharp spear,
And your father would be arranging a tomb for you, not a wedding,
Right here. So let no one show any unseemly deeds
In my house. For I am now aware and know the facts, . . ." (XX. 298-309).

The arrogant Ktesippos now reveals his actual motives. He takes the foot of an ox and hurls it at Odysseus, as we would imagine he had numerous spears and arrows hurled at him for ten years in Troy and more on journeying home. Even while he avoids being hit, his adversary's deed leaves an impression on him. As Odysseus smiles scornfully, he reveals his feelings of rage to himself. His son, however, steps in to help his father remain concealed. The time is not yet right for Odysseus' revelation, which will be keener with these new outrages leveled against him. Telemachos advances further into his own authority and speaks bluntly to the braggart and to all others, warning them that he will not tolerate any more abuses to the guest. The young man is ready to go to war to protect his family, for he is becoming even more aware of the desperate and dangerous condition at home.

Holding back, remaining quiet, restraining oneself can allow other life forces to step up to assist us. We know how this works. By being patient even when emotions run high to react quickly in violent words or deeds, we can allow life's forces to intervene and other forces to appear. Doing so is an act of faith and self-control. Odysseus learns further restraint in this moment of strife and must feel great pride in watching his son assume the role of authority as a response. We all find times where we must conceal ourselves "just as Odysseus does; it seems absolutely necessary to do so. We develop convincing personae and clever strategies to cover up our wounds," writes Norman Fischer (*Sailing Home* 183).

Meditation:

When has holding back instead of lashing out taught you something about how life can have a moment to intervene and about your own ability to self-constrain?

October 28: Book XX

"But I am ashamed to drive her out of the hall against her will
By a word of constraint. May a god not bring this to pass."
So Telemachos said. But Pallas Athene aroused
Quenchless laughter in the suitors and set their wits astray.
They were already laughing with the jaws of other men,
And they were eating meat spattered with blood. Their eyes
Filled up with tears and their hearts sensed an anguish coming.
Godlike Theoclymenos also spoke out among them:
"Wretched men! What evil is this you suffer? . . .
                            The sun
Has perished out of heaven, and an evil mist has rushed in" (XX. 343-51; 357).

Telemachos' use of the word "constraint" dominates this entire section. Holding back, curbing appetites, conserving energy is the rule as the tension mounts toward the inevitable explosive events to follow. In contrast, Athene casts a spell on the suitors so they laugh their wits away. Their food is spattered with blood and one of them calls them all out on their deranged behavior. The atmosphere is charged with an ominous and deadly foreboding. Even the natural order responds to what is about to be unleashed from restraint: the sun has migrated down from heaven and an "evil mist" fills the void. The portents are frightening in the face of a Dionysian madness; the world is about to be unhinged. Athene's fierceness is now to see the full light of day.

There exist moments when the power of portents signals another reality unfurling. The time before a hurricane or tornado or tropical storm, the air grows still, the sky exhibits a strange color and barometric pressure plummets. Birds cease their songs and a terrifying feeling of impending disaster assumes control and becomes ubiquitous. One knows excessive violence and destruction is on the horizon; it may not yet be named. One feels, however, the force field gathering. Writing on death in the Greek world, Jean Pierre Vernant writes that "the terrifying world of death is a world of confusion, chaos, unintelligibility, where nothing and nobody can exist anymore" ("Death With Two Faces" 61). Only life has value.

Meditation:

Think about when forces, natural or humanly-contrived, have unsettled you by their presence. What was your response to such a momentous event?

October 29: Book XX

> But he did not heed their speeches.
> No, he glanced at his father in silence, ever on watch
> For the time when he might lay hands on the shameless suitors.
> The daughter of Icarios, prudent Penelope,
> Put down a beautiful stool opposite
> In the halls where the men were and listened to the words of each. . . .
> No other more joyless supper might ever come to be
> Than the one the goddess and the mighty man were soon
> To set out. For the others were first to contrive sorry deeds (XX. 384-90; 392-94).

The pattern here is that Odysseus seems to be given harsher punishments and rebukes. The suitors are offered a more lavish meal. The former sharpens his resolve while the latter are lulled into luxury. Athene's brilliance reveals itself in her preparing the suitors to be completely off guard, saturated in appetites and dull of wit; Penelope takes up a ring side seat, for she knows instinctively that something is preparing to burst forth. Andrew Dalby writes that "Very cleverly, the *Iliad* and the *Odyssey* tell us about our relation with the gods in a way that makes sense to us whatever our religion" (*Rediscovering* 199). Odysseus and Athene work together as a pair—mortal with immortal—to level the appetites that have devoured so much of his household. His wrath, spurred on by Athene's further disturbances, is at a fever pitch.

Preparation to launch a counter-offensive against injustice can assume many forms. Like Odysseus, we may practice restraint, but even that must end. Surprise is the most effective weapon against an enemy that seems unconquerable; one creates a world, a fiction, that blinds one to the possibility there could be another plot ready to boil over. Watched pots have the capacity to overflow their boundaries, even in the presence of those who cannot see it coming. The suitors' guard is down. They are incapable of reading the communications that Odysseus and his son are conveying in their presence. They have been given the feeling of security and complete control, even as their minds express confusion.

Meditation:

Have you found it necessary at times to construct an alternative plot in order to deflect harmful or dangerous forces from seeing the reality that is in front of them?

VI

BOOKS XXI–XXIV

From Reunion to Unity: The Weight of Words Over Weapons of War

October 30: Book XXI

Now the bright-eyed goddess Athene put it into the mind
Of Icarios' daughter, the prudent Penelope,
To set the bow before the suitors and the gray iron
In Odysseus' halls as a contest and a start for slaughter.
She stepped up on the high stairway of her quarters
And in her stout hand took hold of the well-curved key,
A lovely one of bronze. And an ivory handle was on it,
And she went with her serving women into a chamber. . . .
There a springy bow was lying, and also a quiver
For arrows, and in it were many arrows that bring grief;
These gifts a friend had given him who met him in Lacedemon, . . . (XXI. 1-8; 11-13).

Nothing in Homer's world lacks a history. An item's history is what gives it life and animation. In addition, few thoughts are aroused without Athene's abiding presence and influence. Guided by her wisdom, Penelope recalls the bow and the contest. She acts immediately on this idea, for the time is right for the contest. Glimpses of their household come into view: the bronze key to open the container of the bow is a beautiful creation. Her faithful servants follow her. The bow and quiver have been waiting for her; they have lain dormant for two decades. Then, as with every object in this epic, its history and its current status come to light, for all things have stories and through them, meaning. Iphitos gave him the staunch weapon; we learn of the narrative that brought the bow and quiver to Odysseus' home—hospitality.

To balance the malice of the suitors, we are reminded of a more civil world marked by gift giving, friendship, lasting relations, fidelity, beauty and value. The home is a complex and nuanced place in our lives, marked often by spirits of violence, estrangement, tension, love, new life, the coming and going of strangers who become friends, and friends who may become strangers, if not enemies, of one's well-being. All become part of that large archetypal condition we call Home. Home comprises both the hearth and one's heart. It is the space of the daughter of Cronos, Hestia, goddess of hospitality and warmth, both of hearth and heart, as I have written ("Hestia: Goddess of the Heart(h)" 93-102). Her hearth fire is central.

Meditation:

What three qualities best define the quality of your home?

October 31: Book XXI

. . . Iphitos, son of Erytos, a man like the immortals,
Who gave him the bow. And never would godly Odysseus
Take it when he went off on the black ships to war.
 But he left it lying there in the halls as a reminder
Of his dear friend. And he did carry it in his own land. . . .
Right away, she quickly took the thong from the hook,
Inserted the key, and shot back the bolts of the door,
Aiming them straight; and they groaned like a bull
Feeding in a meadow, so loud did the lovely door sound
As it was struck by the key and was quickly opened wide (XXI. 38-42; 46-50).

Homer's detail is delicious to read in its particulars; they are as vivid as a film and constructed with equal care. Penelope has taken over the plot and shows her own powers of ingenuity when guided by the goddess of war and persuasion. Her stealth and restraint match her husband's, who she has once again begun to hope for. The bow, left in memory of his friend's generosity, is now called upon to act. Now it is prepared to war against the suitors. In the above description Penelope too has a straight aim, a determination, an accuracy that equals her warrior husband in disguise. His expertise in shooting the arrows through the axe handles is mirrored here in his wife's determined accuracy. The doors groan like the sound of a bull feeding in the meadows, bridging the human, cultural and natural orders and giving us an image of Odysseus' own ferocity.

Reclaiming the home requires each involved to step into a heroic space to exhibit fully what their capacity allows and demands. Here, unguarded, the feminine powers gather in Penelope who, like her husband and son, serves a larger cause, an epic purpose: the restoration of the *oikos* and by extension the reclamation of the city. Our home's comfort as a place of refuge when we return from our adventures in the world can be lost or degraded in so many ways, as can the larger home of our country. Home is more a psychological and emotional condition than a physical habitation. Its condition infects our own. How we dwell is as much a part of our personal myth as the place we inhabit. Home is a mirror of our own soul's condition and health. But dwelling presupposes a building or a rebuilding of something lost, even a refounding, for a home can be lost.

Meditation:

What may you have done to restore the calm and tranquility of your home?

November 1: Book XXI

She stepped up on the lofty planking. And their chests
Were standing, inside of which fragrant clothing was stored.
From there she stretched herself up and reached the bow
From its peg,
Along with the bow case that surrounded it handsomely.
She sat down right there, putting it on her own knees,
And wept aloud as she took down her husband's bow.
And when she had her fill of tearful lamentation,
She went on into the hall among the noble suitors,
Holding in her hand the springy bow and the quiver
For arrows. In it were many arrows that bring grief (XXI. 51-60).

Homer keeps his focus on the suffering, courageous Penelope who is flooded with memories of her absent husband, but who nonetheless pushes on with preparations for the contest. It is a domestic version of competition that mirrors in miniature the horrific competition of Troy. Penelope's grief almost overwhelms her, but as a warrior in her own right, she suffers through and delivers the bow and grief-creating arrows into the midst of the suitors. Her courage and tenacity are equal to her husband's; without her, the conquest of the suitors would not happen. As Sheila Murnaghan also observes, "keeping Penelope in the dark allows Athena and Odysseus to use her in a particularly daring and masterful way" ("The Plan of Athena" 69) because at this moment Penelope gathers her intentions to marry the suitor who successfully strings the bow and shoots the arrow through the axe handles. Her desire hides Odysseus' identity and his design, for now the suitors believe their time has come for one of them to marry Penelope.

Grief can suffocate; grief can paralyze. Its power in reexperiencing pain from the past, however, can be over-ridden by actions for the future in the present moment. Penelope knows she must first sit and cry in lament; then she must rise and act. Only then can the grief moderate and even invite a glimmer of hope. This she does with the courage of a warrior heading into battle. We see the exquisite complicity of Athena-Odysseus-Penelope forming a conjunction to reclaim the dwelling. Each brings their own level of consciousness, of mind, to bear on a single exploit: the recovery of the household and a new beginning.

Meditation:

When has grieving almost conquered you but you pushed against it with action?

November 2: Book XXI

"I will set up the great bow of godly Odysseus.
The one who most nimbly strings the bow in his hands
And shoots an arrow through all twelve of the axes,
Him will I follow . . . ."
So she said, and she called to Eumaeos, the godly swineherd,
To set up for the suitors the bow and the gray iron.
Eumaeos took them, weeping, and set them out . . . .
Then Antinoos rebuked them and spoke out to them directly:
"Foolish yokels, who consider only the things of the day.
You wretches, why are your dripping tears? . . . .
So he said, but even so the heart in his breast hoped
To string the bowstring and shoot an arrow through the iron (XXI. 74-77; 80-82; 84-86; 96-97).

Penelope gathers the narrative around the history of her husband, his greatness and the contest of the bow. She agrees to submit to the victor, which takes their attention far from the intrusive beggar in their midst and focuses their desires intensely on winning her. Eumaeos, ever the transition figure between the natural order and culture, sets up the axes. Antinoos, poor replica of the heroic ideal, tries to take the lead when he hides his own ambitions to string the bow and win Penelope in marriage. His deception contributes to his death at the hands of Odysseus, a form of absent presence who has had ample time to discern the intentions of the suitors generally and certain ones singled out for harm.

The place of the feminine in the home's governance is crucial to the masculine achievement of restoration. Martin Heidegger offers a fine insight here when he writes that "We attain to dwelling, so it seems, only by means of building. The latter, building, has the former, dwelling, as its goal" ("Building, Dwelling, Thinking" 143). If building is masculine and dwelling is feminine, then both are necessary to fulfill the home's nature. Penelope allows us to glimpse the more intimate and personal qualities of the home. She can lead us into its deeper structures in its order and arrangement. Far from a passive figure, she is an active creator and participant of the plot.

Meditation:

What feminine presence orders and structures your home so that it is more than a building and truly a place in which to dwell?

November 3: Book XXI

He went and stood on the threshold and tested the bow.
Three times he made it quiver, striving to draw it,
And three times he slackened his strength, hoping in his heart
To string the bowstring and shoot an arrow through the iron.
And he would have drawn it the fourth time, bending it with his strength.
But Odysseus nodded and checked him, impelled as he was.
Then Telemachos spoke out to them in his sacred might:
"Well, how weak and cowardly I shall be even in the future,
Or else I am too young and cannot yet rely on my hands
For warding some man off if he gets angry first" (XXI: 124-33).

So like his father, Telemachos steps up to try to string the bow by bending it to his strength and will. He perseveres in multiple attempts to succeed until his father, with only a slight head gesture, signals constraint. Telemachos, a disciplined young warrior, immediately steps back and refrains from a fourth attempt. He covers his ambitious attempts by self-effacing in front of the suitors. He admits to weakness and is no match for the men in front of him. His camouflage works, his *metis* is successful; that contest he does win. Emily Wilson writes that "*metis* suggests cunning plots and deception employed in the service of self-interest. . . . *metis* is a very useful quality for a person who hopes to survive in a dangerous environment" (*The Odyssey* 36).

Knowing the right time for surprising an adversary is as crucial as knowing what behaviors night be appropriate and which might just disarm one's cover or disguise. Entailed in such wisdom is knowing limits, knowing the strength of one's adversary, knowing human nature well enough to sense what might draw suspicion, and knowing how to psychologically disarm one's opposition so that less strength than theirs may prove victorious. One can feel the tension in the scene above, not just in the tension of the bowstring but in carefully keeping the suitors distracted while leading them to the brink of their own destruction. Such a strategy approaches an art form, with Athene/Odysseus as the great artificers.

Meditation:

When have your own limitations actually proven to be a strength rather than a liability? How might you have used what is weak or inadequate in your abilities to your advantage?

November 4: Book XXI

"Here I am, home, myself having suffered many pains;
I have come in the twentieth year to my fatherland.
I realize that you alone of the servants I come to
Are longing for me. I have heard none of the others
Praying for me to reach home again on my return,
And I shall speak the truth to you both as it shall be. . . .
Come now, I shall show you another manifest sign
So you may know me well and trust me in your hearts:
A scar a boar once inflicted on me with his shiny tusk
When I went to Parnassos with the sons of Autolycos" (XXI. 207-12; 217-20).

Having heard and believed the faithful allegiances of Eumaeos and Philoitios, Odysseus reveals to them who he can trust and who to avoid. Others through speech have uttered their allegiances that Odysseus has overheard or seen in action. As a reward or symbol of recognition that solidifies his claim of who he is, Odysseus lifts the rags from his thigh to expose one of the most famous scars in history. He received the original wound as a boy when visiting his grandfather Autolycos. Hunting a boar with his cousins, he is gored before killing the animal who leaped out at him from a copse in the wilderness. He confirms to them that the human body in its markings and scarrings is a symbol of one's identity. He too is coming out of hiding and revealing much of what he has concealed until now.

Partly revealing but mostly continuing concealing has been Odysseus' master plot. His life-long wound is a signature to this claim of who he is. It punctuates his veracity. We are all to some degree known by our wounds, whether physical, psychological or spiritual; they are among the deepest expressions of our identity. Our plot line is marked by our scar lines. It emblazons who we are. Our wounds mark us because they were instrumental in shaping us. For Odysseus, his scar, as I have noted elsewhere, is "an etching, a line of demarcation between two worlds. . . . The white scar of the animal wounding the human order, is a place between two destinies" ("Nature and Narratives" 49). The scar stitches in his leg the worlds of animal and human natures. The scar unites the flesh and the two worlds even as the original wound separated them.

Meditation:

Tell the story of a wound or an affliction you carry that is integral to the formation of your present identity.

November 5: Book XXI

When he had said this he drew his rags away from the great scar.
Both of them, when they had seen and well noted the details,
Wept and threw their arms around the skillful Odysseus,
And they kept kissing him, embracing his head and shoulders.
Odysseus kept kissing their heads and hands the same way. . . .
"Stop wailing and lamenting lest someone come out
Of the hall, see us, and then tell it within too, . . .
When all the others, the whole number of noble suitors,
Will not allow the bow and quiver to be given to me,
Then you, godly Eumaeos, carry the bow through the house,
Place it in my hands, . . ." (XXI. 221-25; 228-30; 232-35).

Full of affection and joy for another's being alive and faithful to one another, as well as being reunited, the three men shower love on one another until Odysseus has the presence of mind to suddenly restrain them for fear of exposure to the suitors. Constraint once again rules their conduct in order to reclaim home. He instructs Eumaeos to bring him the bow when all others have failed even to string it. He knows the suitors will howl that he, a mere beggar, should not have any opportunity to participate in the contest, for fear he would succeed and shame them all. They cannot afford even the remotest chance of his success.

This is the pivotal trial that must occur in order to reclaim the *oikos,* what he worked his life to gather and provide his family with. It is a moment that precedes violence and bloodshed. Its moment weds *metis* with *bie,* craft with force. Only then may we win back what belongs to us, including our home, possessions and our identity that were poured into its creation. We note too that the bow without arrows is a harmless, even impotent weapon; arrows without the thrusting power of the bowstring is also inadequate. Together, bow and arrows can do inestimable damage when they cooperate with one another. They are a rich metaphor for what needs to occur to reestablish the home. One element without its counterpart or partner is harmless, just as Odysseus needs both his wife and son as well as faithful servants to be victorious.

Meditation:

Think of a situation wherein you won back something treasured in your life through craft assisted perhaps by force.

November 6: Book XXI

"Place it in my hands, and then tell the women
To lock up the closely fitted portals of the hall,
And if anyone inside hears in our enclosures
A groaning and beating of men, let her not go forth
Out the door at all, but be there in silence at the task.
And you, godly Philoitios, I order to bolt the gates
Of the courtyard with a bolt, and quickly lash on the cord."
When he had said this he entered the well-situated halls,
Then he went and sat down on the stool from which he had stood,
And the two servants of godly Odysseus also went in (XXI. 235-44).

First is the creation of the plan. Next is its implementation. Both measures are essential for a successful campaign, here one not of leveling a citadel like Troy but of reclaiming a citadel that gives one his identity and origins back after decades without them. While the gates of Troy were opened by means of the Trojan horse, Odysseus' invention, here the reverse is true: the doors are closed in the dining hall so no one escapes the leveling of justice. Odysseus is audacious to plan such a *coup* with only two servants here to initiate it. Each has his assigned role; failure in any one part or strand of this webbing will incite failure of the whole master plan. Then all return to their regular places in the hall so as to deflect any suspicions. Two realities are at work at this juncture, one that conceals and one that reveals.

Developing an imaginative strategy is a delight to witness. How resourceful we can be, how Odyssean in thought, when all adversaries are weighing against us; pushed hard by necessity, we can surpass our normal beliefs about ourselves and transcend what we thought were our limits. At times we must challenge the myth we normally live by because life circumstances thrust us beyond ourselves. Trust in the gods or divine forces and presences is what this epic has repeatedly illustrated. Even when Athene is not physically present in some form, for instance, does not mean her influences are not guiding the heroic in us. Louise Cowan reminds us that "epics raise to the heavens the specific peoples they enshrine" ("Epic as Cosmopoiesis" 4).

Meditation:

Think of when necessity challenged you to think and/or act beyond what you thought was your capacity. What were the consequences of your response?

November 7: Book XXI

When they had poured libation and drunk what their hearts wished,
Odysseus of many wiles spoke to them with a trick in mind:
"Listen to me, suitors of the illustrious queen,
So I may tell you what the heart in my breast bids me to . . . .
Come then, give me the polished bow, so that among you
I may test out my strength and hands, whether the force
Is in me still that once was in my supple limbs,
Or whether wandering and lack of care have ruined me already."
So he said, and they all grew instantly angry,
Fearing that he might put the string on the polished bow (XXI. 273-76; 281-86).

Odysseus prods the suitors before they have each had a turn to string the bow. He requests one meager chance to try, before they have have attempted it themselves. He disarms them by suggesting he probably no longer has the endurance to string a bow because he has neglected his powers and failed to remain strong. His words outrage them, a thin veneer which conceals their insecurity and fear that by some trick he might just succeed in achieving what they have yet to attempt. Their insults begin to fly at Odysseus, still disguised as the most ragged among them. By angering them, Odysseus draws out their fear, the flip side of anger. He is spinning his own web around them through language, whose most persuasive conveyor is Athene.

Disarming others by craftiness is itself a fundamental weapon one might use when outright force is not possible in the moment. Ingratiating oneself by self-deprecation adds and confirms the disarming of others. Distracted by the beggar's claims, they are not in a position to read the signs. We can gain the upper hand in a situation where force belongs to one's adversary, which can blind them to what exists directly in plain view. Surprise is the silent partner in disarming others more powerful and numerous than one's own resources. Eva Brann notes the obvious truth that "Odysseus is a versatile and controlled liar. His lying tales are collages of fact; they have verisimilitude because they are a neat mosaic of probabilities, facts that surely happened to someone. . . (*Homeric Moments* 247).

Meditation:

What situation allowed you to disarm others or another by your words or gestures that contained something of the truth but was distorted by embellishments?

November 8: Book XXI

Antinoos rebuked him and spoke out to him directly:
"Wretched stranger, you have no sense, none in the least.
Are you not content to dine among us exalted men,
Secure, not to be deprived of food at all, and to hear
Our speeches and our discourse? Nor does anyone else,
Whether stranger or beggar listen to our speeches. . . .
And so I declare great trouble for you if you should string
This bow. You would not encounter any gentle use
In our district. We should send you speedily
To King Echetos, the destroyer of all mortal men,
In a black ship" (XXI. 287-92; 305-09).

The outrage and fear of the suitors is followed by an overt threat by their leader, Antinoos, who before coveted the idea of successfully stringing the bow. He first points out that Odysseus is privileged to be fed by them and allowed to listen to this group of "exalted men" as they discourse and offer speeches among themselves. The second observation is that the beggar better not succeed in stringing the bow, for it will be rewarded by death at the hands of another King who destroys mortals sent to him. Antinoos' use of the word "trouble," as we have seen repeatedly, is the meaning of Odysseus' name. The irony of course is that Odysseus has in his heart declared "great trouble" for all the suitors that will soon emerge violently. They would all be shamed by this beggar in their midst who shows more prowess than any of them. E. R. Dodds explores both shame and guilt in archaic Greece in his chapter, "From Shame Culture to Guilt Culture" (28-63).

We can be intimidated and bullied because of many motives, including jealousy, envy, fear, or the inadequacies of others, first by being seduced with favors or brought to fear because of a dangerous future if we succeed in winning over others. Carrot and stick served up together put one in touch with surrender and fear. Envy of our possible success can drive others to suffocate our potential and end-stop further achievements. Succumbing to such demands can be an unfortunate limit on our potential—imagined or actual. Envy is a powerful force when leveled against us, for its ultimate intention is to obliterate us.

Meditation:

Have you ever been coerced to be grateful through external gestures rather than it arising naturally from within?

November 9: Book XXI

Then the prudent Penelope spoke to him:
"Eurymachos, there is no way that good reports may exist
In the district for those who dishonor and devour
A noble man's home. And why make a reproach of this?
The stranger here is very large and of a well-knit frame. . . .
Come now, give him the polished bow, so we may see.
For this do I proclaim, and shall be brought to pass.
If he does string it and Apollo give him the praise
I shall clothe him in a mantle and tunic, lovely clothes. . . .
       I shall give him sandals for his feet
And send him wherever his heart and spirit bid" (XXI. 330-34; 336-39; 341-42).

Penelope continues to play a key seductive role in keeping the attention of the suitors on her as Odysseus, unbeknownst to her still, weaves his plot of slaughtering all of them. She disarms Eurymachos and the others suitors by stating that if the strange beggar is somehow able to string the bow and Apollo praises him, she will not marry him; instead, she will give him abundance in clothing, a javelin "and a two-edged sword" and then send him on his voyage. What a seduction of the suitors. Nancy Felson Rubin offers the keen insight that "Like a skilled chess player, Penelope knows when she proposes the contest that she is choosing a move that will fit into more than one strategy or plot trajectory" ("Penelope's Perspective" 178). By sending off the beggar if he wins the contest, she continues the courtship with the suitors and modifies their fears.

To reclaim a lost life because of war or other violent trauma, one cannot accomplish such a retrieval alone. One needs others' generous and fearless spirits to assist them. One builds one's community back up, one person at a time in the household. A life or period of intense prolongation of trauma does not allow chaos to pivot quickly to cosmos. Time and others are essential, especially when more violence is necessary. Through her disarming words uttered above, she has just bought her husband more time, which also allows her to study him further. The contest between them, that the suitors are oblivious of, is between two patterns: concealment and revelation.

Meditation:

Have you been in a situation where you were aided by others or another or have helped another to reclaim their own life?

November 10: Book XXI

But Telemachos from the other side shouted a threat:
"Uncle, bring the bow out. You will soon not do well to heed all,
Lest, though younger than you, I drive you to the fields
And throw stones at you. I am mightier than you in strength.
Would I were that much mightier in strength and with my hands
Than all of the suitors who are inside the halls.
Then I should soon send one of them grimly on his way
Out of our house since they are devising evils."
So he said, and all of the suitors sweetly laughed
At him, and they relaxed their oppressive anger
Toward Telemachos (XXI. 368-78).

Odysseus' other family member follows closely after his mother to further disarm and distract the suitors. He creates a public display with his words towards the swineherd Eumaeos in mock insults, ordering him to give the stranger the bow. He couches his words in self-denigration by highlighting his weakness in the face of his oppressors. Their response is "sweet laughter," which suggests that they see Telemachos' outburst as good entertainment and finally, harmless. They readily accept that he is no threat to them and that they can moderate their vengeful plans to slay him. Here craft substitutes for might and effectively distracts and disarms the lot of them. Language itself is the great disarmer of angry vengeance. It lulls the suitors into a feeling of safety in their numbers.

Metis, or craft, crafted words, craftiness, building something through craft—all play a part in a non-violent *coup.* Lain Entralgo writes of the power of the word in the *Odyssey:* "the whole epic is in a way an enthusiastic homage to superiority in the use of words and their power to touch men's hearts" ("The Therapeutic Word in the Homeric Epic" 29). It disarms others such that limited *bie* or force, energy, power can follow with consequential effect. All three—Odysseus, Penelope, and Telemachos--contribute in their own way effective forms of *metis* so that *bie,* which is to follow, will be successful. Surprise rustles below *metis* to create and ensure force's maximum effect. The ever-present fourth is Athene.

Meditation:

Have you witnessed and can point to when *metis* and *bie* were used in an effective pairing in your life or in a situation you witnessed?

November 11: Book XXI

The swineherd carried the bow through the house,
Stood beside skillful Odysseus, and put it in his hands.
Then he called forth the nurse Eurycleia and addressed her:
"Prudent Eurycleia, Telemachos orders you
To lock up the closely fitted portals of the hall.
And if anyone inside hears in our enclosures
A groaning and beating of men, let her not go forth
Out the door at all, but be there in silence at the task."
So he said and for her the speech was without a wing.
She locked up the doors of the well-situated halls (XXI. 378-87).

Even the servants play instrumental roles in sealing the house from intruders and securing all those within from escaping. The house becomes a closed vessel in which justice is to be served to all who are within. Heating up the vessel is about to commence. As servants, they are not scrutinized like the family members, so they are freer to participate in the details of preparation; none of the servants is to respond to any sounds coming from the great hall. Let each servant stay with their respective duties. That Telemachos' speech conveyed by Eumaeos is without wings suggests that his words carry a somber *gravitas* because they signal the violent deaths of the suitors.

Now begins the execution phase of Odysseus' plan to reclaim the household while dispensing a violent justice from years of hospitality's abuse. No one enjoys being put upon, threatened, taken advantage of or robbed of their life's labors. Now, homecoming assumes a richer meaning. To come back to the home demands encountering impediments to enjoying all dimensions of the sacred *oikos* free of tyranny or oppression. Homer's epic asks us to consider the place of violence and killing as part of homecoming and reclamation. Edith Hall reflects as well that one can never truly go home until one has used one's mental capacities of knowing. Homecoming is a way of thinking (*The Return of Ulysses: A Cultural History of Homer's Odyssey* 163)

Meditation:

Have you been "put out" of your own home or reached a place where you no longer felt it was a safe domicile to inhabit? Were you driven out or were you able to retrieve its original safety?

November 12: Book XXI

He was already handling the bow,
Turning it in all directions, testing it this way and that,
For fear worms had eaten the horns while the master was away.
And this is what one of them, looking at his neighbor would say:
"This is some fancier and an expert with bows,
And perhaps such as these are lying in his home too,
Or else he wants to make one, he handles it so
This way and that in his hands, the beggar skilled in evils. . . .'
So the suitors said. But Odysseus of many wiles,
At once when he raised the great bow and viewed it on all sides. . . .
So without effort did Odysseus string the great bow.
He took it in his right hand and tested the cord.
It sang sweetly beneath like a swallow in its sound (XXI. 393-400; 404-05; 409-11).

We witness Odysseus caress the bow when exploring all its dimensions to gauge its soundness, like a singer "skilled at the lyre and at singing" (l. 406) will test his instrument. Even the bow must be faithful to retrieving the home. Those observing him see he is an expert at the bow and has a sure hand in holding it, which provokes both envy and fear in the suitors. His turning the bow in all directions is also a description of Odysseus' own ethos, being a man of many turns, wily and circumspect, weaving his way around things and men. Then to the stringing of the bow, an act done with great ease and familiarity. Like the lyre's strings, the bow string sings out sweetly now that it is wedded in tension.

In camouflage, what is an act that prepares for slaughter is seen as a far more innocent one of preparing a bow for a harmless contest, not combat. All are preoccupied with Odysseus' ease in being the only one to whom the bow yields its strength under his guidance. Music, not mayhem, emanates from the bow. It acts like a lyre rather than a deadly weapon. Such is the success when one orchestrates the perceptions of one's adversary. Only the subtle imagination can see that the bow, now strung, and the lyre, played for song, story, poetry, share a unity.

Meditation:

Think back to when you successfully altered the perceptions of another or others in order to gain an advantage or surprise.

November 13: Book XXI

He put it to the bridge, drew the string and the notches,
And shot the arrow right from there, sitting on the stool,
Aiming it straight, and he did not miss one handle tip
Of all the axes. The arrow heavy with bronze
Went straight on out the end. He spoke to Telemachos:
"Telemachos, the stranger seated in the halls
Does not discredit you. I did not miss my aim,
Nor did I toil long to string the bow. . . ."
So he said and signaled with his eyebrows. Telemachos
The dear son of godlike Odysseus, girded on his sharp sword,
Put his own hand round his spear, and stood close to him . . . (XXI. 419-26; 431-34).

From contest to war pivots in this scene when Odysseus first exposes his power as an archer, who combines in perfect balance and harmony *metis* and *bie*. His constraints are all about to fall away when he executes his arrow through all twelve axe handles, a feat that may give the plot a magical feeling of a fairy tale. Odysseus pronounces his victory and tells his son he did not shame him with a poor performance, even as he signals him to dress up immediately in war gear. Meanwhile, the suitors still do not know at this moment that Odysseus has returned home and shown his skills as a warrior and a marksman. They are about to have the story perpetrated on them dissolve before their frightened eyes.

Odysseus carefully step-by-step unfolds and enacts his plan to subdue the suitors. A careful execution of his plan is necessary if the entire effect is to be successful. Only a plan whose logic has been thought through at every turn is poised for success. When so much is at stake, one must evaluate every assumption one holds in order to raise the probability of success. Homer wants us to reflect on the power of deception as a craft to gain a higher end: restoration of what has been dismembered. If it can end here, without violence, then so much the better. But there are cases when the adversary is way beyond rational negotiation, as seems to be the case with the suitors, who have habituated themselves to plundering the household and will not relinquish it without a fight.

Meditation:

Think of an important plan or strategy and its desired effects you mapped out. What made it a success or a failure? Was it, finally, necessary?

November 14: Book XXII

Then Odysseus of many wiles bared himself from his rags
And sprang upon the great threshold, holding the bow
And the quiver full of arrows. . . .
"This inviolable contest has been brought to an end.
And now I shall know another mark that no man has ever hit,
If I happen to hit it, and Apollo grant me glory."
So he said, and aimed a bitter arrow at Antinoos.
The man was about to lift up the lovely libation cup,
A gold double-eared one, and he held it up in his hands. . . .
Odysseus took aim and shot him with an arrow in the throat;
The point of it went straight on through his tender neck (XXII. 1-3; 5-10; 15-16).

Book XXII opens with the carnage that is to last until all the suitors are destroyed. That Odysseus springs to the threshold places him between two worlds: war and peace, concealing and revealing, constraint and violent outburst, wanderer and domestic. When he refers to "no man" has ever hit" (l. 6), we recall that he named himself such when he hid his identity from Polyphemos. Now his words are followed by action slaying another Cyclops, Antinoos. The leader of the suitors dies first, caught completely off-guard in the act of consuming. The disguise Odysseus assumed with the help of his faithful household members is now discarded. Antinoos's receiving "the bitter arrow" in the throat seems apt justice for his speeches that heaped insults on his family and plots to murder his son.

Violence is both uncertain and often a first response in a crisis. Odysseus uses it last and at last. The suitors were stalling for an opportunity to slay the family and coerce Penelope into marriage. Does violence in history have a rightful place? We must use prudence in using it as an appropriate response to enemies when individuals or groups in the world lust after power, control, and the conquest of those much weaker. But as Mary Lou Hoyle asserts, "We read the *Odyssey* not merely for its exciting stories but in order to relearn the difference between war and peace ("The Sword, the Plow and the Song" 88). Neither one is to be taken for granted or in the case of war, leveled recklessly at enemies or adversaries or at those we simply disagree with. Its effects wound both victors and victims.

Meditation:

In your mind, when is violence in slaying others a prudent and necessary response, if ever? Can violence serve a good and beneficial end?

November 15: Book XXII

"Dogs, you thought I would no longer come home in return
From the land of the Trojans; and so you wore my house away
And slept alongside my serving women by force
And underhandedly courted my wife while I was myself alive,
And you did not fear the gods who possess broad heaven,
Or that there would be any vengeance of men in time to come.
Now the bonds of destruction are fastened on you all."
So he said and sallow fear got a grip on all of them,
Each one peered for where he might flee sheer destruction (XXII. 35-43).

Even though there are over one hundred suitors, each one feels vulnerable after hearing Odysseus' accusing words that list violations of the home. Their transgressions extended to property, his servants and his wife; he does not mention their plans to assassinate his son. They also violated his sacrifices as a warrior and a defender of Greek pride and honor; more importantly they disrespected the gods whose presence has been defamed. They forgot their obligations as citizens and threatened the integrity of the polis by their appetites. Now, the bonds of destruction ensnare them. Their cowardly nature has been called into account. His words are as terrifying at this instant as his bloody plan.

Any conscious subterfuge that violates the home or the homeland spreads out to infect all citizens in a soul sickness. As a pollution or an infection, it rips at the fabric of civilized life and the sacred *oikos* that undergirds and supports it. Greed and violation can be justified by a twisted reasoning that can metastasize into a consensus; it may be acceptable until other language enters to reveal publicly its true nature. Glenn Arbery suggests that this is the moment of *aletheia*'s presence, a revealing of truth, a disclosure of a code that is just and right ("Odysseus' Nostos: Concealment and Revelation"116). It embodies a moment of disclosure in which the truth of things is offered; when those who have violated its truth hear it, they are terrified, as the above scene shows. In a review of Edward Tick's *Warrior's Return*, I wrote that "healing rituals occur largely through remembrances. But one must feel safe so their remembrances are held as valuable" ("Review of *Warrior's Return*" p. 5). The suitors' other great transgression is their failure to remember Odysseus' struggle to return home.

Meditation:

Where do you call out injustice today by naming the truth of circumstances?

November 16: Book XXII

Eurymachos alone spoke to him in answer:. . . .
"And here he lies already who was guilty of them all,
Antinoos. He it was who instigated these deeds,
Not so much wanting or desiring the wedding at all. . . .
     that over the well-tilled land of Ithaca
He might himself be king, and might kill your son in ambush.
Now he is slain, as was his due. Spare your people
And we shall give satisfaction in the land hereafter
For all that has been drunk up and eating in the halls,
Each one bringing separately a recompense worth twenty oxen" (XXII. 43; 48-50; 52-57).

Eurymachos' words only inflame the crisis as Odysseus is about to unleash and further reveal his true feelings and actions. The frightened suitor deflects all responsibility by scapegoating the dead Antinoos, hoping that his slaying is enough of a payment to Odysseus. Like the others, Eurymachos's hope is to be spared any responsibility for his part in the violation of the home and by extension, the city. He quickly offers an alternative to compensate Odysseus further with goods devoured by them with the simple act of replacing them in kind. Then, to his rattled mind, all will be equal. Each suitor will bring goods to fill the coffers depleted by their collective appetites. Blaming the ambitions of the dead is a characteristic thought pattern of suitor strategy.

When greed and cowardice are exposed, how quickly those souls claim innocence by deflecting responsibility and furthering their display of cowardice. Greed and cowardice seem to be wedded. Seeking full pardon when exposed is its predictable end. No telling when, if exonerated, these pollutants will seek vengeance in the near future. Eradication and penalties in the immediate moment is the only just way to reduce the chance of further trespasses and continued violence, though the latter is unrealistic. For violence has a way of reproducing itself in response to itself. The cycle is unremitting, which is why violence as a response to itself is often futile because based on a false premise. Perhaps one of the suitors' greatest violations is disremembering the soul's suffering and damage in warfare.

Meditation:

Have you had to exact a swift and immediate penalty on others to reestablish a sense of justice and balance?

November 17: Book XXII

Odysseus of many wiles glared at him and spoke:
"Eurymachos, not if you gave me all the paternal goods
That you possess, and any others you added from somewhere,
Not even then should I yet stay my hands from slaughter
Until the suitors had paid for all their insolence.
And now it lies with you either to fight face to face
Or to flee, whoever would avoid death and destiny.
But I think that no one shall escape sheer destruction."
So he said and their knees and their own hearts went slack
On the spot (XXII. 60-69).

All of the restraint Odysseus practiced, the abuse he endured and the waiting he suffered has now found its language of non-compromise. Justice will be harshly observed. He calls their transgressions expressions of insolence—towards the gods, hearth, home and city. He goads them to fight or flee, knowing all exits have been sealed and weapons removed. The suitors are like Odysseus and his men in the cave of the Cyclops earlier, when Odysseus wrestled with his own appetites for fame and recognition, disregarding his men. Now he is the host who will exact justice on the appetites of his adversaries. He also claims, "no one" shall escape being destroyed, punning on his own fictional name to Polyphemos. His words suck the power out of them, so forceful are they to the ears of the suitors.

Jonathan Shay writes of Odysseus and compares current combat veterans to him. He cites another writer, Amelie Rorty, "who defines the Homeric word *thumos* as 'the energy of spirited honor.' It is closely allied to the English word 'character'" (qtd. in *Odysseus in America* 156). What Eurymachos does not grasp is that the violation of Odysseus' home is not measured by goods and services he and others have abused, but by something less visible: honor itself has been ransomed. Shay writes as well: "I believe that *thumos* is a human universal that evolved out of war in our ancestral evolutionary past and still explodes in killing rage, when violated" (156). *Thumos* in this sense is closely allied with justice. Justice must be measured and proportional, as an effective oath shared by two parties must carry a proportional tension so that both sides feel that gain is worth sacrifice.

Meditation:

Where do you see justice meted out to those rich and powerful violators of virtue and honor itself?

November 18: Book XXII

The two servants put their fine armor on the same way.
They flanked the skillful and subtle-minded Odysseus.
He himself, so long as there were arrows to defend him,
Kept aiming at the suitors in his house one by one
And always hit his mark. They fell one after another. . . .
He himself put the four-layered shield round his shoulders
And placed on his mighty head the well-fashioned helmet
With a horse hair crest; terribly the plume nodded on top of it.
And he took two valiant spears fitted out with bronze (XXII. 114-18; 122-25)

Now that the torrent of arrows have been depleted, Odysseus and his faithful servants don armor and head gear and turn to their javelins to continue slaying over one hundred suitors. The battle that rages in his hall has close analogies with the Trojan battles that finally made their way as well within the walls of Troy's citadel. Homer wants us to remember that long battle through the image of Odysseus' helmet hair-crest when "terribly the plume nodded on top of it." This same motion occurs in the *Iliad* when Hector, leader of the battle in Troy, donned his helmet to fight. His young son burst into tears, terrified when his father's plume nodded before him, revealing in a domestic scene, before Hector is slain by Achilles, the horror of war.

The terrors of war carry the god Ares in its features and energy. Athene too is a warrior of words and fighting prowess. To have divinity supporting one's efforts, the balance of a skewed society offers hope to that party. That killing is often used to satisfy appetites on many levels is an illness that must bring forth more violence as an assumed response. Homer, however, is working towards a vision of settling disputes and differences that does not include war; rather, it highlights the power and efficacy of words. War carries within its folds its own mythology. James Hillman writes that "the spirit of war and the rage of battle are archetypal, forced upon all animal life, all gender, all societies. No gland can contain it. It is irreducible,. . . (*A Terrible Love of War* 86). The forces needed to resist it must be different from the appetites that invite and encourage it. Wars' appetites are legion, universal and all-consuming, approaching the force and power of an addiction.

Meditation:

What boundaries have you created for yourself regarding injustice and violence?

November 19: Book XXII

    Agelos spoke to them, declaring his speech to all:
"My friends, this man shall soon hold back his invincible
 hands.
Mentor has gone from him, uttering empty boasts,
And they are left alone out in front of the gates.
Do not all of you let your long spears fly together.
Come now, you six hurl your javelins first, so that Zeus
May perchance grant that Odysseus be hit and we gain glory. . . ."
So he said, and they all threw their javelins as he bade,
Eagerly. But Athene made them all of no effect.
One of them hit against the pillar of the well-based hall,
Another one hit against the closely fitted door . . . (XXII. 247-53; 255-58).

As the suitors scramble to survive, one of them, Agelos, devises a strategy they are eager to implement. He suggests a way to increase the odds that Odysseus may be killed by one of the javelins. In this plan they believe they will win glory. They are only too ready to be led by anyone, so they follow his instructions. But Athene protects him by deflecting all their efforts to slay Odysseus or his comrades. As protectress Athene "was providentia, foresight, for her structure of consciousness can espy predictabilities, prepare for them and thus normalize the unexpected," writes James Hillman of this goddess ("On the Necessity of Abnormal Psychology" 26-27). She is the presence of mindfulness, of seeing through, thus she can deflect the invasions of adversaries.

Depending on our point of view, or our way of interpreting assistance that may appear seemingly out of nowhere to help us when we are insufficient to help ourselves, we will assign credit to what we believe in. The assistance is often mortal, but behind the figure may be a divine presence or impulse using someone as an instrument of divine aid. There are signals in our lives that perhaps behind the phenomenal world are forces that watch over us. Hubert Dreyfus and Sean Dorrance Kelly suggest that "the Greeks were deeply aware of the ways in which our successes and our failures. . . are never completely under our control" ("Homer's Polytheism" 63).

Meditation:

Recall when you stepped forward to help someone or someone aided you, with no desire for recompense. Did you sense something more was present in this situation?

November 20: Book XXII

"I pray to you Odysseus; respect me and pity me.
There will be grief for yourself hereafter if you slay
A singer like me who sings for gods and for men.
I am self-taught, and a god has planted all kinds
Of lays in my mind. I am fit to sing before you
As before a god. And so do not be eager to cut my throat. . . ."
So he said, and Telemachos in his sacred might heard him.
At once he addressed his father, who was close beside him:
"Hold off, do not wound this guiltless man with the sword.
Let us also spare the herald Medon, who always
Looked after me in our house when I was a child,. . ." (344-49; 354-58).

Odysseus in his rage may still be able to exercise restraint towards the faithful and the innocent as the slaughter accelerates in his hall. He pauses to hear Phemios plead for his life, which Telemachos, overhearing him, supports by cautioning his father not to slaughter the innocent and those of real value, like the singer of tales. He takes the opportunity to plead for Medon as well, who cared for Telemachos when he was a child. Odysseus hears their pleas and passes by them without harming either. "Hold off" is the cry of restraint that has been expressed by Homer throughout the epic to this point. Discernment marks a successful victory.

Justice, vengeance, and violent retribution can so overrun an individual or group to such an extreme that they slay anyone who moves—the innocent included—so no discrimination is offered anyone's cry for mercy. Odysseus reveals how justice may truly be a rhythm between punishment and restraint. What justice, finally, is exacted if the innocent and the guilty are treated alike? No justice is served in such a chaotic rush to restore it, which can create more violations. In fact, as Andrew Dalby writes, "By the end of the poem Odysseus has wiped out two generations of Ithake's young men; that's when we wonder, briefly, whether his return has been the best outcome for the city" ("Reading the *Iliad* and the *Odyssey* Afresh" 201). Perhaps then the slaying of the suitors must be constantly reevaluated according to whose point of view the slaying is assessed by.

Meditation:

Have you been in a position to punish or correct others and were you able to discriminate the guilty from the innocent? Are you able to distinguish these two qualities in yourself?

November 21: Book XXII

Odysseus peered round his house lest some one of the men
Might still be concealed alive, avoiding black fate.
But he saw they had all fallen, in great numbers,
In blood and dust, like fish that the fishermen
Have drawn up on the curved beach out of the hoary sea
In a net that has many meshes; . . .
But the sun in his shining is taking away their life;
So then the suitors were heaped up on one another. . . .
Then she found Odysseus among the bodies of the slain,
Bespattered over with blood and with gore like a lion
Who goes along when he has eaten from an ox of the field. . . (XXII. 381-86; 388-89; 401-03).

The carnage completed, Odysseus scans the pile of corpses for any signs of life but sees none. His blood bath is finished. He himself is covered in blood, like a lion who has just finished feasting on an ox. The animal imagery is extended to the suitors who are heaped up like fish from the nets of fishermen; fish and suitors each long for friendlier and more familiar surroundings. The palace is a site of gore and carnage. Eurycleia, the faithful servant, finds her Odysseus moving slowly among the gore satisfied with his achievement. It will soon be time to scrub the palace clean. His image of a gore-cloaked lion gives the sense that this deed he has just finished is as natural as a lion feasting on its kill. That it is not increases its horror.

After violence of war on whatever level, there is a quiet time of reckoning and of assessing the consequences heaped on the defeated and victors alike. It is not, perhaps, a time for joyful celebration but rather a deeper reflection on what the cost has been to restore order and balance in the household and the city. Violence and violation have led to a reclamation of what is central to civilization: *oikos* and *polis*. Mythologist Joseph Campbell has written, "There is also the cruel fact to be recognized that killing is the precondition of all living whatsoever: life lives on life, eats life, and would otherwise not exist" ("Mythologies of War and Peace" 169).

Meditation:

In any battle you have fought, what was your response and feelings after it ended? Was the outcome worth the price tag?

November 22: Book XXII

Now when she saw the corpses and the unspeakable blood,
She made ready to exult, since she beheld a huge deed.
But Odysseus checked her and held her, eager as she was,
And speaking out to her, he uttered winged words:
"Old woman, rejoice in your heart; hold back and do not exult.
It is not holy to boast over men who have been slain.
The gods' fate has worsted these men, and their cruel deeds,
For they have honored no one of the men upon the earth,
Either evil or noble, whoever encountered them.
And so in their recklessness they met a sorry fate" (XXII. 407-16).

This passage encapsulates the action of Homer's epic. War seems inevitable at times and is nothing to boast about because the violence inherent in war can inflict deep soul wounds. Restraint is what Odysseus calls for to his faithful servant who helped raise him and who suffered the lengthy occupation of the suitors. She wants to cry out in joy at the home's liberation, but Odysseus restrains her, as he did when she discovered the scar on his thigh and wanted to rejoice at his homecoming. The death of adversaries in battle is no cause for celebration; rather, it is perhaps more appropriate for a time of lamentation and loss. Odysseus' own restraint, now that he has realized his warrior mode, shows his own level of exhaustion. Recklessness is the primary adversary of restraint.

War requires moments of restraint, pulling back, modifying and restraining fighting. Reckless warfare leaves those who practice it without boundaries or discipline in many circumstances. Edward Tick points out that "since war wounds were taken for the community and nation, they must be acknowledged, witnessed, honored, and supported there" (*Warrior's Return* 157). Far from doing this, the suitors took advantage of the absent leader of the household by confiscating his home and family. Now Odysseus is forced to carry yet another war wound, this time from carnage in his own home. Tick continues: "Understanding the war wound as something both moral and social that we have unwittingly forced our veterans to carry alone, we can shape actions and responses" to aid them (*Warrior's Return* 158).

Meditation:

What might be an appropriate contribution to the healing of warriors' wounds when they return to a home that is no longer familiar because of their trauma?

November 23: Book XXII

"And when you have set in order the entire house,
Bring the serving women on out of the well-based hall
Between the round room and the excellent fence of the courtyard,
And strike them with the long-edged swords until you have taken
The lives of all away, and they have forgotten the love
They had under the suitors, where they lay with them secretly."
So he said, and the women all came in a body together,
Lamenting dreadfully and shedding a swelling tear. . . .
And then the tables and the beautiful armchairs
They cleaned off, with water and the porous sponges (XXII. 440-46; 452-53).

Odysseus orders Eurycleia to gather all the servants who violated the household by turning on his family and sleeping with the suitors, thereby insulting and demeaning hospitality's code. All of them gather and, weeping, are forced to help Telemachos and others clean up the carnage of over 100 young *aristoi* slain. They wipe down the furniture, lamenting and grieving, knowing their fate will probably equal that of their lovers. They dutifully fulfill their roles as servants, but now under a strict set of constraints. There is cold justice in the way that Odysseus conveys his orders to his aids, sounding very clinical and dispassionate in his directions to strike each with the long sword until they have all perished.

Often justice takes the form of those who have been defeated repairing the damage of the battle. Soldiers become servants, survivors becomes slaves. The ripple effect of war can continue to grow, enlarge and swell its population. War, battle, has its own psychology. The goal is often a balancing of forces, powers or energies to restore a cosmos from the shards of chaos of death and dismemberment that has tattered the fabric of a civilized society. Jean Pierre Vernant offers what has happened and is about to repeat itself: "If death did not appear in epic as the ultimate horror, if it did not assume the mask of Gorgo, so as to embody all that is beyond humanity. . . then there would be no heroic ideal" ("Death with Two Faces" 58).

Meditation:

When has restoration and even amends been the consequences of chaos in your life? Did you experience a death in this process that transformed you?

November 24: Book XXII

"I would not take away with a clean death the lives
Of these women who have heaped reproaches on my head
And upon my mother, and have slept with the suitors."
So he said, and a cable from a dark blue-prowed ship
He threw round a pillar of the great round-room and tied it on,
Tightening it up high, so none could reach the ground with her feet. . . . .
So they held their heads in a row, and about the necks
Of all there were nooses, that they might die most piteously.
They struggled a little with their feet, but not very long (XXII. 462-67; 471-73).

A sadness accompanies this description of the unfaithful servant women being hanged together for violating the sacred space of the household. Their actions were more than selfish pleasure by those who abused Odysseus' *oikos,* a sacrosanct place that contains the gods themselves and was to be honored and respected. Homer wishes us to contemplate the horrific details of retribution. Left to the wave of insults to the household, they would have destroyed his family, belongings and the home itself. The line "they struggled a little with their feet" carries a horror in its detail that punctuates the hard justice enacted.

Glenn Arbery, commenting on this scene, writes, "It is a harsh scene, and it seems pitiless, but Odysseus carries it out as a ritual purgation of the sacred *oikos,* and he allows no immoderate exulting" ("Concealment and Revelation," 118). Everything must sooner or later be paid for. There is no compromise with certain violations when the appetites of many threaten the civil structure of a people. Dishonoring what is sacred must be corrected to retrieve a balance and harmony between the household, the *polis* and the gods. Upon such a trinity the myth of a people is founded and nourished through rituals. Chaos is the consequence of the inequity of these three arenas, leading in time to a dissociation of the realms that should be united in a common cause. Achieving balance can be brutal. The conclusive end of this ordering is what the Greeks called *Alitheia,* truth. Marcel Detienne suggests: "To judge by our historical documentation, it began with Homer" (*The Masters of Truth in Ancient Greece* 26).

Meditation:

Have you experienced an imbalance in aspects of your life, your family or the nation in which violence played a positive role in rebalancing what had become distorted? Does balance in your life equate to a truth in your life?

November 25: Book XXII

They brought Melanthios through the forecourt and the yard,
Cut off his nose and ears with the pitiless bronze,
And tore off his private parts for the dogs to eat raw,
And chopped off his hands and feet in their furious spirit. . . .
And he addressed Eurycleia, his beloved nurse:
"Bring brimstone, old woman, the cure of ills; bring me fire
So that I may purge the hall. You yourself go tell
Penelope to come here with her attendant women
And urge all the serving women in the house to come" (XXII. 474-77; 480-84).

Plotting with great patience and restraint, action measured and planned, then purging the household of the bodies and offal in a catharsis of the war, followed by a gathering of all the faithful is an elaborate ritual. Melanthios' death is horrible, described in terrifying detail. Arrogance and infidelity is dismissed through his death. Then Odysseus turns to his ever-faithful servant, the reasoned Eurycleia, and directs her to bring fire and brimstone to cleanse the household of the enormous carnage through yet another ritual. He calls to his wife, who still *may* not know of his true identity, to join him with all those who supported her.

Normalcy is something to be wished for and to strive for after a period of upheaval and disorder. One cannot lay to rest the upset, the illness, the disordered life until it is replaced, cleansed, purged so that its tangible memory is modulated. The cleansing completes the violence and disorder's deletion as well as the infidelity and greed that channeled it. Psychologically, it resets all those involved so life can begin to assume an atmosphere of balance and harmony within its once disordered parts. But far from being denied and deleted, that earlier condition should be integrated, become part of the private or communal memory as a touchstone for being able to see its rise in the future. This ritual finalizing the warrior's return Edward Tick suggests requires an act of self-forgiveness, re-humanizing and giving full expressions to the emotions by all involved in the reentry pilgrimage (*Warrior's Return* 220)

Meditation:

What may you have been called upon to correct or "right" a disorder to achieve an earlier form of normalcy, or perhaps a new ordering principle extracted from the rubble of the old?

November 26: Book XXII

"First of all now let a fire be made for me in the halls."
So he said, and his dear nurse Eurycleia did not disobey.
Then she brought in fire and brimstone, and Odysseus
Thoroughly purged house and courtyard and hall. . . .
They came out of the hall bearing torches in their hands.
They gathered round Odysseus and greeted him in welcome;
They kissed him and embraced his shoulders and his head
And his hands. And a sweet longing took hold of him
For moaning and wailing; in his mind he recognized them all (XXII. 491-94; 497-501).

It sounds as if Odysseus alone purged the household of suitors and their infidelity and abuse that accompanied them for so many years. It may be part of the healing of his own warrior spirit to install in his soul's homecoming the catharsis it longed for to retrieve his life from chaos into cosmos. Then all gather round him to offer a proper homecoming they were denied until now. They shower him with affection. The "sweet longing" he feels is part of his *nostos*. Only now does he recognize each of them in his mind and heart after the bloodbath he has executed. Again, violence was an essential element at this stage of the people's development. By itself, it will solve nothing, but it does offer a reprieve.

Delayed for so long over circumstances out of his control, vets may come home to themselves after they have physically entered their household and city. War does dislocate veterans from themselves; many spend agonizing years after being home struggling to bring those parts of their moral injuries home with them. They seek to reclaim some degree of wholeness in the form of body prosthetics as well as psychic prostheses. Wholeness can take years to regain or reintegrate. Many vets today commit suicide in alarming numbers each day. I wrote elsewhere of Odysseus, that "body and narrative share a common heritage in the self-creation or construction of the domestic hero; one cannot have a full identity, Homer implies, without an intertwining of both human embodiment and a history fully remembered and reinstalled in one's life" ("Nature and Narrative" 49).

Meditation:

Has an illness, an accident, combat, or a form of abuse taken you many years to finally liberate yourself from? Or do you still suffer the wounds today?

November 27: Book XXIII

"Wake up, Penelope, dear child, so you may see
With your own eyes what you desire all your days.
Odysseus has come and reached home, though arriving late.
He has killed the bold suitors who disturbed his house
And devoured his property and oppressed his son."
And the prudent Penelope spoke to her:
"Dear mother, the gods have made you mad, who have the power
To make a man senseless, even one who is quite sensible;
And also they put the slack-minded on the way of prudence.
They have injured you, you were balanced in mind before.
Why do you mock me who have a heart full of grief, . . ?" (XXIII. 5-15).

A clash of narratives occurs between the excited story of Eurycleia, who knows Odysseus is home and has purged the home of the suitors, and the incredulous response of Penelope who seems to have given up on her husband's return and remains caught in the old narrative.Not just of disbelief, but a wounded Penelope feels outraged at the claim of her servant who must have been infected by the gods to make such a pronouncement. Only some form of insanity, Penelope suggests, would bring Eurycleia to make such a bewildering assertion that her husband is home. She dismisses her story with dispatch.

When we have become convinced of a certain reality or a sure belief, it is very difficult to allow a new narrative to invade and topple that fixed position. Life can mold us into a particular myth so no other options are possible, so invested can we become to a certain conviction about reality. Penelope, like any of us, has become so addicted to a belief she is convinced will always be true that she cannot hear others' alternative stories. Dan McAdams makes a keen observation: "we are all challenged to structure our needs for power and for love, and to fashion a myth within the social and historical context to which we are ethically and interpersonally beholden" ("The Meaning of Stories" 35). Our narratives must conform to the reality we give the most credence to. A sign of wisdom is the ability to reassess our narratives and unload them when they no longer serve our beliefs.

Meditation:

Have you found yourself disbelieving a story's truth because you had become so invested in another that changing one's narrative mind is too frightening?

November 28: Book XXIII

"But come with me so you may both enter into gladness
In your own hearts, since you have suffered many ills.
And now this long desire is already fulfilled;
He has himself come alive to his hearth and found in the halls
Both you and his son. Though the suitors acted to him
Evilly, he has punished them all in his own house."
And then the prudent Penelope spoke to her:
"Dear mother, do not chuckle yet and make a great boast.
For you know how welcome in the halls he would appear to all,
And especially to me and the son we both had.
But this story is not really so, the way that you tell it" (XXIII. 52-62).

Odysseus has sent Eurycleia to Penelope to bring her to him now that danger has passed for the time being. She tells Penelope the story of Odysseus' return and his vengeance on the suitors, a truth Penelope, who has slept through the slaughter, will deny. She continues to believe her husband is lost and the gods have initiated the killings. So she deflects Eurycleia's story, telling her it is false as told. Penelope is not ready to surrender herself to a warrior who may be a false version of her husband. She has invested too much in protecting the *oikos* to let her guard down at the word of another. She prefers to deny than to yield to a delusion.

Our narrative truth is so entangled with our identity that to give up one is to relinquish both. Penelope's identity here reveals how stories define our reality and shape a perspective on life's unfolding. To be deceived after reinvesting so much in a particular narrative's continuation is life-threatening to one's foothold. To risk changing it is courageous and confusing at once. Kevin Bradt writes, "How we know, the modalities and techniques of our knowing, not only affect what we know but actually construct the versions of reality known" ("Rejecting Story: Modern Psychotherapy" 63). Our most dominant narrative is then our most influential force in not just what we know, but how. Epistemology comes face to face with our personal myth. We each realize how hard it is to relinquish a narrative that has offered familiarity even at the cost of veracity. To change our story is to reshape the myth we live by. At this juncture, Penelope is negotiating between two myths.

Meditation:

What has brought you at least once, to shift your narrative to accommodate a new understanding of reality? Did the story hold?

November 29: Book XXIII

When she had gone on in and crossed the threshold of stone,
She sat across from Odysseus, in the gleam of the fire
By the other wall. And he sat against a tall pillar
Looking down, waiting to see if his goodly wife
Would say something to him when she saw him with her eyes.
But she sat a long time in silence, and stupor came over her
heart.
With her gaze sometimes she looked him full in the face,
And sometimes did not know him for the vile clothes he had on his skin
(XXIII. 88-95).

Such a poignant moment for them both. Odysseus and Penelope face one another in silence against the gleam of the fire. Like shadows cast by the fire on the opposite wall, he sits expectant while she reposes in a silent stupor, wondering if she should reveal her feelings or keep them concealed. He looks so shabby in his dress, but beneath them he is the husband she has kept the house intact for. She sees him but cannot believe him. She sees him and doesn't see him for who he is. He remains to her both revealed and concealed. The word "stupor" reveals how confused and bewildered she is over his authentic identity. At once, she both believes and doubts his true identity. He remains quiet, gauging her reactions to him in the form he appears to her.

When someone returns home from combat, a long deployment, being detained, or studying or working far from home, nothing can be as it was, exactly. Changes both external and internal have their own life force field that transforms both family and the one returning home, hoping perhaps, to pick up where they left off. That is most often not to be. One may feel a stranger in his/her own home and be treated as such by both family and friends. Distance in both time and space will often create new ways in which people view one another. Edward Casey writes of the ancient Greeks being visuocentric, a way of gazing because of "its ability to make distinctions" (*The World* 173). It is a way, he continues, "of determining depth" (173) of another. That is what Penelope's gaze may be questing after: the depth of the person she faces. It is her pivotal moment.

Meditation:

Think of a time when you greeted someone, family member, relative or friend, after many years. Were you able to see them deeply?

November 30: Book XXIII

Telemachos rebuked her and spoke out to her directly:
"My mother, cruel mother, you have had a heart that is harsh!
Why do you turn from my father so and do not sit
Beside him and ply him with speeches and question him?
No other woman, indeed, with a resisting heart
Would so stand off from the husband who had suffered many
 ills
And come back for her in the twentieth year to his fatherland.
Always the heart in you is harder than a stone" (96-103).

Exasperated with Penelope's unwillingness simply to accept this ragged warrior as her husband, Telemachos accuses her of cold-heartedness. But she does not know with certainty he is her husband, though her son does. Telemachos wishes his mother would treat Odysseus as he does, given what he knows. He is not able in his lack of restraint to see this man as his mother does; she will not risk easily believing in one who may be attempting to deceive her. She is caught in a tension between concealment and revelation and feels the anguish in being so torn. She requires both more time and more proof to adjust to a reality she had about entirely given up on. Her beliefs shape her gaze Her heart is not hard but cautious and guarded, for she too has suffered much at the hands of the presumptuous men. She struggles in her own heart to let go of deceiving and being deceived, which have become habits of being for her.

At times we find ourselves very cautious and circumspect around another or others we at one time may have trusted. As separation and time pass between people, some struggle to accept this familiar, yet new person in their midst. Addictions, traumas and all forms of violence can change a person almost to the point of being unrecognizable. One may have to forego the old image of a person and courageously accept this reformed individual who has reentered their lives. Change occurs on both ends: in the one who has been gone and the ones who suffered while staying in place. The adjustment can be enormous for both sides of the loss. Finding a new myth that might unite them is part of the struggle not only of individuation but of integration of members with one another.

Meditation:

Have you had to accept someone you know who has suffered major changes in who they are? What do you imagine they have had to adjust to in you?

December 1: Book XXIII

"My child, the heart within my breast is amazed,
And I am not at all able to speak a word or to ask
Or to look him in the face directly. If really
He is Odysseus and he has arrived home, we two
Shall know one another, and more fully. There are signs
For us that the two of us know, hidden from others."
So she said, and godly Odysseus, who had endured much, smiled.
At once he uttered winged words to Telemachos:
"Telemachos, permit your mother to test me out
Within the halls. She shall quickly discern even better" (XXIII. 105-14).

From the large battle at Troy, to the skirmishes and restraints on his journey home, to the battlements of his own dwelling, to this contest of identity with his wife, Odysseus is closer to his goal than ever. Only when the family is fully united can he be said to be "at home." Penelope opens just an inch to share with her irate son that there are so many intimate ways they may know one another if this ragged stranger is truly her husband. Odysseus delights in her observation and asks his son to allow her to quiz him on his claim of being who he is. He adopts this strategy because he knows his wife, even after two decades. They know one another in concealed or hidden ways; now the contest is to reveal one to the other.

We know another intimately through so many gestures and styles and ways of speaking to that person alone. Subtle, nuanced, slight yet powerful, individuals who have lived close to others for years or decades know the other almost intuitively and in unspoken ways. We identify and love others through their habits, gestures, quirks, styles of speaking and ways of responding to a variety of situations that are as unique as their own fingerprints. We also know intimate others through their stories and the way they frame them. Richard Kearney writes that "every human existence is a life in search of a narrative." In part, we want to find the right story for ourselves because, he goes on, we each "strive to discover a pattern to cope with the experience of chaos and confusion" ("Narrative Matters" 129). Penelope is on her own quest to discover her husband's core narrative, and by it she will know him to be true.

Meditation:

How are you best known by intimate others who have been in your life over time? How do you know yourself as you continually change in multiple ways?

December 2: Book XXIII

> Odysseus of many wiles addressed him in answer:
> "Well then, I shall tell you what seems to me to be best,
> First of all, wash yourselves and put tunics on,
> And order the serving women in the halls to take their clothes.
> Then let the godly singer, holding his clear-toned lyre,
> Be the leader for us in a reveling dance,
> So a listener outside would think this was a wedding,
> One who walked on the road, or one of those who dwell
> round about;
> So that a wide report about the slaughter of the suitors
> Shall not first get through the town, before we have gone outside
> To our own well-wooded land" (XXIII. 129-39).

Again, Odysseus the artificer, the craftsman as well as the crafty man, sets up a virtual reality of merriment in the household to camouflage or conceal the aftermath of the bloodshed in the home. His intention is to restrain the information that so many who violated the household have been punished, but that fact must remain for now in the privacy of his household, a held-back revelation in a snug container. As the creator of alternative realities, Odysseus shows the power of his *metis* in order to protect his own Troy from invasion by the townspeople who have lost sons in the slaughter. He is intent on controlling the public narrative. Now what is most crucial to conceal is the story of carnage.

Artifice to encourage restraint and the truth of a situation has guided the epic from the beginning. Forces take a back seat to artifice as a calmer, more civilized way to deal with possible all-out violence. Tact, deflection, ploy are optional ways to moderate or avoid bloodshed. We know that putting out a fire with water and not kerosene holds greater promise for peace and perhaps, reconciliation. Odysseus, the supreme story-creator and teller, fabricates a fictional field that, while not symbolic *per se*, nonetheless shapes the consciousness of all those who hear of it or step into it; the story becomes a container as D. Stephenson Bond suggests, that shapes consciousness ("Play: Where Two Worlds Touch" 111) and so allows the control of reality to remain in the hands of the artist, like Homer.

Meditation:

Think of when you used artifice to disarm a potentially violent or potentially explosive situation. Was dissembling part of your strategy?

December 3: Book XXIII

And the women adorned themselves, and the godly singer took
The hollow lyre and aroused the desire among them
For sweet melody and also for excellent dancing.
The great house about them resounded at the feet
Of men frolicking and women with lovely gowns.
And this is what a man who heard them outside the house
would say:
"Someone indeed must have married the much-wooed queen.
The cruel woman, she did not hold out for her wedded husband
And tend the great house steadfastly till he arrived."
So a man would say: they did not know what had been done (XXIII. 143-52).

The dancing and frolicking deflect anyone outside from knowing what is being camouflaged inside by the wedding gala. It also allows all those who remained faithful to Odysseus' household to celebrate his homecoming and the now inevitable reuniting of husband and wife to further heal their home. It gives those outside an opportunity to create their own narrative of the unseen but powerfully heard and erroneously interpreted—a celebration that often accompanies the genre of comedy. It is imagined by passersby that Penelope has surrendered in marriage to one of the young suitors when it might be truer to say she has remarried her husband and they are now celebrating that (re)union.

Deflection is a work of art. It can create a reality that sounds and appears as one thing to hide another reality that must be concealed from all who would disrupt and perhaps respond violently to what actually occurred. The literary theorist Northrup Frye has written that "literature, like mythology, is largely an art of misleading analogies and mistaken identities. Hence, we often find poets, especially young poets, turning to myth because of the scope it affords them for uninhibited poetic imagery" ("Myth, Fiction, and Displacement" 35). We see the large misleading analogy of the wedding feast reconstructed behind closed doors before the terms and conditions of that restoration are made public. Creating an "as-if" reality behind closed doors is a very old archetypal arrangement that Homer's epic is itself a model of poetic narrative for.

Meditation:

When have you found it necessary to conceive and make a reality behind the scenes, in concealment, to reach an end that overt dealings will not allow?

December 4: Book XXIII

But the housekeeper Eurynome washed great-hearted Odysseus
Inside his own house and anointed him with olive oil.
She put a lovely mantle and a tunic over him.
Then Athene poured much beauty upon his head,
Made him bigger to look at and stouter, and made his hair
Flow in curls upon his head like the hyacinth flower. . . .
So she poured grace upon his head and his shoulders.
He stepped from the bathtub in form like the immortal gods,
And he sat back down on the chair from which he had risen,
Across from his wife, and he addressed a speech to her: (XXIII. 152-58; 162-65).

Odysseus continues his journey home when he is washed by one of the faithful servants. When Eurycleia washed him it was a "wash of identity." Now Eurynome's washing and anointing him is a "wash of homecoming." He discards the concealing raiments that served him so well; now his body needs renewal. It is a washing as well of a threshold crossing in which he discards one myth and assumes the mantel of leader in his household and community as Penelope's husband. As Athene once shriveled his body to disguise him, she now enchants his body to enhance his beauty. He is a sight to behold and wonder at, so full of grace is he now. Like a god does he appear. We witness the qualities of his being shine.

So many stories exist, especially about warriors returning home who their family members frequently hardly recognize or understand. They often remember someone quite different both in gestures, mannerisms and even physical formation. Some need more time soaking in the tub of their family's surroundings to clean off clinging traumas from conflict to reveal themselves in this new life they have perhaps abruptly entered. Walter Otto writes that "the Homeric poems are based upon a clear and unified view of the world. . . and their "religious outlook is clear and contained" ("Religion and Myth in High Antiquity" 15). Odysseus, now cleansed, takes on the appearance of one of the immortals; there is a unifying energy between gods and mortals. This analogy, highlighted repeatedly in the poem, assures us of a vision of unity. For Odysseus to reclaim himself is at once to reclaim this unified world view Otto identifies.

Meditation:

Who in your life was returned to you which required many adjustments on both sides in order to find a balance between who left and who returned?

December 5: Book XXIII

"Strange man, I do not at all exalt myself or slight you,
Nor am I too much amazed. I know well the sort of man you were
When you went off from Ithaca on the long-oared ship.
Come now, Eurycleia, spread for him the thick bed
Outside the well-based bedroom which the man made himself.
Put the thick bed out for him there and throw bedding on,
Blankets and mantles and the glistening coverlets."
So she said, testing her husband. But Odysseus
Grew angry and spoke to his wife, who had a sense of devotion: (XXIII. 174-82).

Penelope keeps her own counsel after Odysseus has made it clear that she has "a heart implacable beyond that of womankind" (l. 167). Exasperated, he has ordered Eurycleia to make him a bed right there in the hall so he may rest. She continues to test him to reveal what she has not been ready to receive unconditionally: his true identity. But she knows his patterns of thought and behavior as well as the true condition of their immovable bed. She knows his myth. She orders Eurycleia to pull it out of the bedroom so he may sleep on it away from her. Penelope knows that beside herself, he alone has knowledge of the bed's permanent fixture and will react quickly and harshly to her order. Her own *metis* pushes him into the light of his full identity, now fully revealed.

One way to expose another's identity is to use information that can only be known by another, but distort it. If the uncovering is a forgery, that individual will not question the information presented because the person does not know the truth. Through craft one disguises the truth by offering an alternative to conceal it. It is a clever dance between revelation and obfuscation. The paradox of narratives is that they can appear to be informing one of the truth of life or the pretense of life; on the surface they will sound the same; one may have to get beneath the story to its motive. Thomas Berry has posed two questions on story's nature. "If the world is made of stories, are its problems a result of being enthralled by—in thrall to—pernicious stories? Is the solution to such problems. . . gaining a better understanding of storying?" (qtd. in *The World is Made of Stories* 19).

Meditation:

When have you been faced to conceal information by creating a false story about yourself or another? Was the outcome what you expected?

December 6: Book XXIII

"My wife, this is a heart-hurting speech you have made.
Who has put my bed elsewhere? That would be hard
Even for one very skilled, unless a god came in person, ...
No mortal man alive, not even one in his vigor,
Could dislodge it easily, since a great token was made
In the well-wrought bed. I worked on it, and nobody else.
The long-leaved bush of a wild olive grew inside the yard
Flourishing in bloom. It was thick as a pillar is.
So I built the bedroom round it till I finished it
With close-fitted stones and roofed it well up above." (XXIII. 183-85; 187-93).

Odysseus reveals the pain he endures at Penelope's hesitation to believe who he is. He also balks at the possibility that the bed he crafted around Athene's tree to anchor it permanently and to pay homage to the goddess has been relocated. He is incensed at the notion that the bed is now unmoored. Only if a god descended into the household and moved the bed could it be done; it is beyond mortals' limits. To counter his feelings, he offers a full and detailed account of how he built it, fine artificer that he is. Both crafty as well as a craftsman, he prides himself on his abilities to use both words and wood to craft realities both beautiful and functional by design. He continues his careful description in succeeding lines.

Some things only certain individuals know and often through the intimacy of a relationship of long-standing. We have moments in life when knowledge is secret, kept under wraps, within one or between two people. It bonds and unites them in a way not available to others. It allows a code of connection that eliminates all ambiguity about one another's history and identity, which includes the manner or style of speaking that history. We may sense here that there is often knowledge that should not be shared with others outside the compact it holds. "Homer is familiar with the metaphor of verbal weaving" write Scheid and Svenbro (*The Craft of Zeus* 114). Through their dance with words, Penelope and Odysseus are also weaving their histories back into alignment with one another through a rich series of fabrications that lead to a dramatic tapestry.

Meditation:

When has knowledge known only to you or you and another, kept a sense of unity around the relationship, where that knowledge is what binds one in fidelity to another?

December 7: Book XXIII

"And I stretched over it an oxhide thong shining with purple.
So I declare this token to you. I do not know at all
Whether the bed is still steadfast, wife, or already
Some man has put it elsewhere, cutting the olive base beneath."
So he said, and her knees and her own heart went slack
As she recognized the steadfast tokens Odysseus had shown to her.
Then she wept, ran straight over, and threw her arms
About the neck of Odysseus, kissed his neck and spoke:
"Do not scowl at me, Odysseus, since in everything else
You have been the wisest of men" (XXIII. 201-10).

As the details pile up for Penelope, who knows only she and her husband share the particulars of his craftsmanship, her wall of defenses begins to shatter and scatter; her husband's true identity shines through in his vivid and accurate description of what he crafted. Her cautious suspicion melts under what he reveals and she constrains herself no longer. His revelations break her out of concealing her emotions; now after twenty years she can reclaim a life she almost gave up on. She asks for his forgiveness and he, knowing she is as steadfast as he, will yield to her pleas. He recognizes the suffering she has endured in keeping the *oikos* intact and is far from interested in chastising her for her heroic efforts.

When we establish a long-lasting intimate history with another, we have knowledge of one another that even other family members are not privy to. Certain habits, rituals, shared temperaments and other traits are known only through history's intimate moments. Such is this instance when now both Penelope and Odysseus are at home, although further action will be required to establish the household. Our lives and relationships are built on a thousand particulars wrapped in the sentiment of *sophrosyne,* a sweet accord between the couple. Edward Casey writes eloquently of place: "We pay a heavy price for capitalizing on our basic animal mobility. The price is the loss of places that can serve as lasting scenes of experience and reflection and memory" (*Getting Back into Place* xiii). Nowhere are we more grounded bodily and memorially than when we are "at home."

Meditation:

Consider some of the intimate details of your life you share with another that keep the relationship intact and thriving. What seems most prominent?

December 8: Book XXIII

"We should enjoy our vigor and reach the threshold of age.
But be not angry at me now for this, and do not resent
That I did not embrace you this way when I saw your first,
For always the spirit in my precious heart went cold
Lest someone among mortals come and deceive me
With speeches. Many men think up evil devices, ...
Now you have convinced my heart, harsh indeed though it be."
So she said. In him rose a still greater desire for wailing.
He wept, holding his pleasing wife, who had a sense of devotion. . . .
So welcome was her husband to her as she looked upon him (XXIII. 212-17; 230-32; 239).

One of the tenderest moments of the epic occurs here as Penelope tries to reconcile with her husband and explain to him of her reluctance to offer herself to anyone for fear of being deceived. When he hears her words and feels her caresses, he breaks down after all this time of disciplining himself with self-control, constraint and hiddenness. All concealing on both their parts are erased quickly as they begin to reassemble and speak their love for one another after twenty years of separation. The power of the word to heal is never more pronounced in the epic than it is here. We can only wonder at Telemachos' reaction as he watches his parents reunite in their deep love for one another. Both the Trojan War and Penelope's war with the suitors at home look to be completed.

Home is that rare arena where one can be completely open and authentic with one another. It should be a place of intimate, serene and loving existence, free of outside invasions and descriptions. In the *oikos* is authenticity, a place of abundance and growth. Any force that violates its boundaries must be removed, sometimes by force and brutal directness. The house is the structure, the home is where one dwells in peace and harmony. Edward Casey writes that "the *Odyssey* is therefore at least as much a narrative of place as it is a narrative of events. It is a narrative of *events in place*" (*Getting Back into Place* 277). Places have their own sense of personages and are living entities that we encounter, often repeatedly. The archetype of home with its reclaimed harmony should be the end of the journey

Meditation:

What are the most important characteristics for you in your home? What draws you back to it each day? How are you affected by not being at home?

December 9: Book XXIII

In no way could she quite let her white arms go from his neck,
And rosy-fingered Dawn would have appeared while they wept
If the bright-eyed goddess Athene had not had another thought.
She held the night long on its course, and then kept
The golden-throned Dawn upon Oceanos, and did not allow her
To yoke her swift-footed horses that bear light to men,
Lampos and Phaethon, who are the colts that bring the dawn. . . .
"But come, let us go to bed, my wife, so that now
We may lie down and take pleasure beneath sweet sleep."
And then the prudent Penelope addressed him:
"The bed shall be for you indeed whenever you wish
in your heart. . ." (XXIII. 240-46; 254-57).

Some enchantment like a fairy tale descends on the narrative in this moment; Athene practices her magic to hold back the dawn so this sweet connection between the two can be prolonged and relished. The mythic, natural and cultural worlds all cooperate in the service of love itself after so many years of separation. Ares is replaced by Aphrodite, with Athene its orchestrating presence. From pain to pleasure is highlighted. The bed and its pleasurable comforts replace the battles that have occupied Odysseus for so long. James Hillman writes that "Mars and Venus are always in the bed of the image, even when the tale says they fly off and away from each other. They remain an inseparable archetypal conjunction. Where Mars is Venus will be" ("War is Sublime" 109).

"Make love, not war" seems to want to split Mars from Venus, Ares from Aphrodite. From Hillman's insight, they are always in bed together. Odysseus as Ares is now in his own bed with his Penelope-Aphrodite. If the suitors are a symbol for a malignancy that can infect a household, then *sophrosyne*, or sweet accord, is its antibody. Now as the home is restored, so will the entire citadel follow, but not without more warring that ends in peace. For to have the household and the city violated is to invite further chaos. Cosmos begins its slow restoration when husband and wife reunite as a social and mythic unit.

Meditation:

Do you sense a way in which perhaps a warring presence in your home, a signal of reality's discord, may find a way to align with the love that Aphrodite brings?

December 10: Book XXIII

"Come tell me of the trial, since hereafter I think,
I too shall hear of it and it is no worse for me to learn of it at
once...."
"Strange woman, why do you strongly urge me and bid me to speak?
Well, I will tell it myself and shall not conceal it
But your heart shall not rejoice, nor do I myself
Rejoice, since he ordered me to visit many towns
Of mortals, holding in my hands a well-fitted oar,
Till the time I come unto those who do not know
The sea and do not eat a food that has been mixed with salt,
And where they do not know about ships with purple cheeks.
Or about well-fitted oars that are the wings for ships" (XXIII. 261-62; 264-72).

The sad truth is that Odysseus' wanderings are not complete. His home in Ithaka is yet another temporary dwelling, like so many were before. He is fated to continue his voyages until he arrives at a place where the world of seas and ships is unknown. The oar will be the symbol of such a world as the sword was the object of war. Only when he has entered such a foreign world will he rest. Strange to the sea, these people he meets will allow him to complete his fated travels. He is also not finished telling his story, revealing what he has concealed until now. Coming home seems to indict a long process of pealing back his secret life, the one untold, until his wife knows the full terms of his homecoming.

Cedric Whitman writes of the ending of the *Odyssey* that the hero relays what Tiresias prophesied in Hades, that he "will meet death from the sea, that shifting and chaotic substratum of boundless possibility which gives the whole poem its atmosphere of haunting and unfathomable romance" ("The *Odyssey* and Change" 290). Even when we think we are finally home, our wished-for dwelling, there remain forces in the world that may push us out the front door again on another adventure to fulfill our fated franchise. We can go home again but only to visit. Perhaps all of our fates are to be in motion, with occasional respites, breaks and recovery periods, until we finally come to rest in the cushion of death.

Meditation:

Are the journeys you have taken in your life actually respites from the final resting place of death? Are they pauses that comfort until your journey comes to a close?

December 11: Book XXIII

"When another wayfarer has confronted me
And said I had a winnowing fan on my gleaming shoulder,
He bade me fix my oar then into the earth
And offer fine sacrifices to lord Poseidon,
A ram, a bull, and a boar, the mounter of sows,
Then to go back home and sacrifice sacred hecatombs
To the immortal gods who possess broad heaven,
To all of them in order. Far from the sea will death come
Ever so gently, to my person, and slay me
Worn out with sleek old age" (XXIII. 274-83).

Not wishing to spoil his homecoming at this joyous hour, Odysseus nonetheless tells Penelope what the shade of Tiresias has revealed to him: he is to die old in a strange land among people who know nothing of the sea or ships. It is a painful prophecy to share with her at his moment of return, but it is absolutely necessary to uncover this last part of his life for her. His instructions are very clear and pointed. Turn to the gods, for his fate is not to grow old in the house of Ithaca. As a traveler he will not enjoy the comfort of dying at home, among his family and with his own people. For finally life is not to be lived according to one's own terms but in accord with what the gods have led him to, along with the powerful force of his own fate.

Death itself is the ultimate journey, even if it occurs in one's own bedroom. One takes nothing with them but what they have done in life. It is a time to turn more fully to the divine dimensions in us, to ponder their presence and to yield to their eternal nature, which is reflected in us as well. The final journey is lived into differently by each of us. We can spend our whole life preparing for it or running to escape it. In this light Homer's epic may be the richest and most complex work in showing us that our life journeys are always preparing us for the time when we become still in eternity when we enter the realm of mystery. Andrew Dalby informs us that "the *Iliad* and the *Odyssey* tell us about our relation with the gods in a way that makes sense to us whatever our religion" ("Reading the *Iliad* and the *Odyssey* Afresh" 199). Mortality and immortality are their great themes.

Meditation:

What images or feelings do you harbor about your own death? What can or have you done to prepare for what cannot be altered or avoided?

December 12: Book XXIII

And Eurynome, servant of the chamber, conducted them
With a torch in her hand as they went on to bed.
She led to the bedroom and went away again. They then
Arrived happily at the site of their old bed. . . .
The two, when they had taken their pleasure of delightful love,
Enjoyed themselves with stories, talking to one another:
She, the godly woman, told how much she endured in the halls
To look upon the destructive throng of the suitors
Who on her account had slaughtered oxen and goodly sheep
In numbers, and much wine had been drawn off from the jars (XXIII. 293-96; 300-05).

Now the couple so long separated is home in their own bed in love making, followed by storytelling. The latter carries within itself its own erotic energy. Each in turn shares body and soul with the other, who listen closely to the other's suffering and loss. Penelope recounts having to tolerate the violations of the suitors for years as they pirated their home, drained the wine jars and killed the cattle to satisfy their appetites without resistance. Odysseus in turn tells his tales of wandering as he struggled for home in various stages of battle and hardships in captivity and loss of his men. Both share their own heroic quality of endurance, of holding on, of being patient and craftily bringing the reign of the suitors to an end.

Once home, the person returning, especially after ordeals suffered in the world, is present physically but not narratively, psychologically and emotionally. One arrives home in part by recounting stories of their time away from the household. Now their past has a chance to catch up to them, to join the present through the past's reclamation via narratives that remember and shape their history. "Epic," Fred Turner offers, "consciously bestrides the boundary between prehistory and history, situating itself imaginatively where we as a species first began to speak" ("A New Medium of Communication" 287). The thrust of epics resides in their story-telling prowess. Stories told to loved ones and heard from those we love has in this process healing qualities that benefit everyone.

Meditation:

Recall a situation or a life condition when you did not feel at home, wherever you were, until you told your story and heard the narratives relayed by others.

December 13: Book XXIII

He told them all, and she enjoyed hearing, nor did sleep
Fall upon her eyelids before he had told it all.
He began how first he had conquered the Cicones and then
Had gone to the fertile land of the Lotus-eating men,
And all the Cyclops did, and how he made him pay the penalty
For the valiant companions he ate and did not pity. . . .
And he told about Circe's wiles and resourcefulness,
And how he went down to the dank dwelling of Hades
So he might consult the soul of Theban Tiresias
In a ship with many oarlocks and saw all his companions
And the mother who bore him and reared him when he was small, . . .
(XXIII. 308-13; 321-25).

It is crucial that Penelope hears Odysseus' adventures and threats to his life in detail. While her recounting reveals the relentless repetition of the suitors' behavior, Odysseus' story is more varied and complex. Both of their narratives complement one another to create a rich unity in diversity. He needs to recount to her the particulars of his exploits, all in the service of reuniting with her and their son. Narratives knit them together as much, if not more, than love making. Both forms of expression bring them closer to mending the wounded home and so heal itself from its constant violation. Homecoming includes healing the home.

Wounding in whatever form can alter the objects and persons permanently. By reclaiming one's past and sharing it with others, not only are their souls healed but the *oikos* itself is mended. Not only are there physical wounds that can damage lives, but also "moral woundings," according to Larry Kent Graham: "We constantly need to reset our compasses to take us toward healing of the injuries that have been inflicted upon us as well as those we have brought about because our compasses have been set wrong or we did not follow them" (*Moral Injury* 4). Often these moral wounds are much deeper and more debilitating than physical afflictions and may require a new way of dealing with their healing. For veterans returning from combat, one way of healing is through story-telling.

Meditation:

Think of a time when telling a particular story to another or listening to their story of being wounded was the first step in healing and/or reconciling.

December 14: Book XXIII

>   Odysseus
> Rose from his soft bed and laid a charge on his wife:
> "My wife, we are already glutted, the two of us,
> With many trials. Here you wept for my troublesome return.
> But, while I was wanting to go, Zeus and the other gods
> Held me back in pains from my fatherland.
> Now since we have arrived at the bed of much desire,
> Give heed to the goods which are mine in the halls.
> As for the sheep of mine the presumptuous suitors pillaged,
> Many others I shall myself plunder back; still others the Achaians
> Shall give me until they have filled up all the folds" (XXIII. 348-58).

Odysseus speaks to Penelope about his "troublesome return," alluding to the meaning of his name. He knows that trouble is far from over. Now that the gods' restraints have been lifted and he is home among family and property, he desires to retrieve all that the suitors have cost his absence. He seeks more trouble as a consequence. It seems that no rest or peace will visit his household until he once again takes up arms to exact vengeance and retribution through reclaiming what he has lost to the suitors' excessive appetites. Odysseus seems to have no other options than warring his way to justice.

Returning home is only a part of a warrior's project after combat. If one returns to a lawless home or one that has been unfaithful or been shattered, then restoring a previous balance is essential to right the home to its earlier order and virtue. Otherwise, the home remains tainted, out of joint and disordered. Chaos is a human/divine order and structure. Chaos brings disorder. Violence righting the house may be inevitable in restoring the *oikos*. But is this the only alternative--to fall back into the very patterns that arranged the disorder initially? Homer has another avenue that he suggests one can pursue. Larry Graham advises that "moral dissonance most often arises from the moral climate in which history and culture have embedded us" (*Moral Injury* 13), which includes the moral values that may have fallen into jeopardy.

Meditation:

When your life was thrown out of balance, what alternatives did you choose from in order to restore a sense of order, serenity and harmony to it?

December 15: Book XXIII

"And then I shall go on myself to the well-wooded land
To see my noble father, who is heavily grieved for me.
And, my wife, I charge you this, prudent as you are:
At once at the rising of the sun the report will travel
About the suitors, whom I slaughtered in the halls. . . ."
He spoke, and put the lovely armor about his shoulders.
He roused Telemachos, the oxherd and the swineherd
And ordered them all to take the war gear in their hands.
They did not disobey, but armed themselves in bronze. . . .
Light was on the earth already, and Athene hid them
In night and led them rapidly out of the city (XXIII. 359-63; 366-69; 371-72).

Once again, strife, battle, all-out war are on the horizon for Odysseus and his household, aided by the warrior Athene. Word of the massacre in his home will be met with rage for retribution. The homes of the young men who died at Odysseus' hands will also seek justice and balance. Restraint will not be part of their calculus. Troy's conflict will once again visit Ithaca in replicating the desire to retrieve what has been lost over time and by unruly appetites. Odysseus seems to know only one way to exact justice in protecting what he has left of his household. It is the only recourse available to him at this level of development. As a warring culture, its options for justice seem limited to strife and conquering one's enemies. In the past, however, he has engaged oath-taking as a way to avoid destruction.

We may remember the biblical injunction, "An eye for an eye, a tooth for a tooth" as a form of retributive justice. Yet is this to be the format for a continuation of bloodshed, with no escape from its literal form of payment? Might there exist another manner of balancing two equal forces, both with claims to justice? The *Odyssey* will move to an alternative in Book XXIV, the last installment of this classic homecoming. Jonathan Shay writes that "Homeric heroes inflict trauma, but it is just as true to say that trauma creates heroes" (*Odysseus in America* 243). The wounds inflicted on continually warring parties keeps its people in a constant state of trauma and paralysis, no matter the victor.

Meditation:

Have you found an alternative to a sense of justice that demands an exact literal payment? Can you describe any other options you deployed to achieve an equitable settlement through some form of mediation?

December 16: Book XXIV

And Hermes of Cyllene summoned forth the souls
Of the suitors, and he held in his hand the lovely gold wand
With which he enchants the eyes of those men he wishes,
And others he wakens even when they are asleep.
He stirred them with it and drove them. They followed squeaking,
As when bats in the corner of a prodigious cave
Squeak as they fly when one of them falls away
From the cluster on the rock where they cling to one another;
So they squeaked as they went together. And Hermes,
The deliverer, led them on along the dank ways (XXIV.1-10).

The final book opens with one of those rare moments when the narration moves away from mortals to let us glimpse into the other world, the underworld, as Hermes, guide of the shades of the suitors, delivers their souls to lord Hades. The rich metaphor of squeaking bats reveals no great stature of these souls, but rather a cluster of bats resounding in hollow caves when they respond to one of their kind falling away. It is a scene behind the scene to reveal the afterlife of those dead who continue to inhabit a region of creation, as we saw when Odysseus and his men visited Hades earlier, to be seen no longer. It is a scene terrifying and sad at once.

The gods play a major role in human life and death in most world cultures. They can seem omnipotent, guiding, delivering, protecting, favoring and moving one's fate along its ordained path. We may in this passage consider the way divine presences move in and through us in life and how we may imagine their influence in death. Hades here is the final home, the alternate *oikos* where one may rest and inhabit the afterlife forever. But they arrive there, as Jane Ellen Harrison notes, by way of the guide Hermes Chthonios who is appeased in a Greek ritual called "the holy Pot-Feast," in which "Hermes is appeased on behalf of the dead" (*Prolegomena To the Study of Greek Religion* 36-37). Hermes as soul guide is a major divine presence in ushering the dead to their right place after life. He is the god of fitting or fittingness in matters pertaining to the dead. Even in Hades there exists a cosmos, a right-ordering and a sense of justice deployed to all souls.

Meditation:

What relation do you have to the dead, specifically to those who are now your ancestors? Do you perform any rituals in remembering and honoring them?

December 17: Book XXIV

They came upon the soul of Achilles, son of Peleus,
The soul of Patroclos, and of excellent Antilochos,
And of Ajax, who was the finest in body and form
Of all the Danaans, after the excellent son of Peleus.
So they thronged around that man, and right close to them
The soul of Agamemnon came on, the son of Atreus,
Grieving. And the others drew in together, all those
Who had died with him and met their fate in Aigisthos' house.
The soul of the son of Peleus spoke out to him first:
"Son of Atreus, we thought you were dear beyond other heroes
To Zeus who hurls the thunderbolt, for all your days, . . ." (XXIV. 15-25).

Still in the underworld, the narrative asks us to remember those who died at Troy, and in the case of Agamemnon, when he returned from Troy with the prophetess Cassandra. Some of the great heroes from the *Iliad* converse in this land of the shades, many of whom Odysseus communicated with earlier. Achilles addresses Agamemnon, King of Mycenae, who led the Greeks into the Trojan War that lasted a decade. Now we witness them in war's backwash. The descriptions are of excellence, renown, *kleos*, or glory, and finally, death. The descriptions of the heroic follow immediately after the suitors' description; they are the antithesis of the warriors mentioned here who gave everything to the battle. The underworld is, among others things, the place of memory, of the past and of a greatness that will not be forgotten. Achilles stands alone as the one most mourned at Troy.

Remembering the dead may be part of any warrior's homecoming. While war is not celebrated, heroism within the horrors of conflict is. Remembering heroism is a necessary part of the warrior's narrative as s/he struggles to come fully home. Edward Tick makes a profound observation about the warrior's homecoming: "Warriors, their families, and communities confess through storytelling. Stories release emotion, reveal secrets, educate, organize our lives into coherent narratives, and point toward meaning" (*Warrior's Return* 211). They must be able to tell their stories to one another, as happens in the above quote and following. Tick adds to the above: "Individual warrior's stories become their culture's warrior mythology" (211).

Meditation:

In what ways do you remember and ritualize the dead heroes in your own life?

December 18: Book XXIV

Then the soul of the son of Atreus spoke to him:
"Blessed are you, son of Peleus, godlike Achilles,
You who died in Troy far from Argos. Around you, others,
The best sons of the Achaians and of the Trojans were killed
Contending over you. . . .
But when we had brought you up on the ships out of battle,
We set you down upon a bier and cleaned off your lovely
skin
With warm water and oil, and the Danaans shed
Many hot tears over you and sheared off their hair.
Your mother came from the sea with the deathless girls of the sea
When she heard the report" (XXIV. 35-39; 43-48).

Agamemnon, king of the Greek soldiers, steps up to remember Achilles in battle and his subsequent, and chosen, death—the consequence of choosing a short life of glory (*kleos*) over a long life of hiddenness. Agamemnon offers a glimpse of Achilles' death and immolation as heroic guardian of the Greeks. He recounts how Achilles' immortal mother came out of the sea to grieve for her son; she is accompanied by other feminine cohorts of the ocean. Death reveals itself here as a reminder of life's imminent end. The memory is nostalgic of lost glory and renown and reveals an underworld understanding. What happens here in remembrance on a broader scale is the structure and content of the *Odyssey*.

Without the continual reminder of death surrounding our lives that haunt our everyday world, we can easily think that what is right in front of us will continue forever. The dead remind the living that life is temporary and unpredictable in its ending. Thomas Laqueur's excellent study of the place of the dead in our lives is helpful here: "The book begins with and is supported by a cosmic claim: the dead make civilization on a grand and intimate scale, everywhere and always. Their historical, philosophical, and anthropological weight is enormous and almost without limit and compare" (*The Work of the Dead* 11). The dead serve us as we serve them; the boundary between us and them is so thin as to be almost nonexistent. They wish to be remembered in stories.

Meditation:

Who among the dead do you converse with? What comfort or value does addressing the dead serve in your life?

December 19: Book XXIV

A prodigious cry arose
Over the ocean, and a trembling seized all the Achaians,
And they would have sprung up and gone to the hollow ships
If a man had not restrained them who knew many ancient matters,
Nestor, whose advice had also before seemed best.
With good intent he spoke out to them and addressed them:
"Hold back, Argives; do not flee, young Achaians. His mother
This is, here from the sea with the deathless girls of the sea;
She has come to be beside her son who has died."
So he said, and the great-hearted Achaians were held back
from flight (XXIV. 48-57).

Nestor appeared at the beginning of the epic to counsel Telemachos when he visited the elder at Pylos. Now he offers in his wisdom to those grieving by the body of Achilles at Troy a major theme guiding the entirety of the *Odyssey*: restraint, along with moderation and control when another impulse threatens to bring chaos into the moment. As the soldiers prepare to bolt from Achilles' mother's appearance, accompanied by the eternal feminine presences in the sea, Nestor calls for caution, explaining to them the wondrous presence of eternal Thetis and her consort. Leadership here calls for restraint, not aggression. Leaders must have the wisdom to determine what response is most affirming.

Often our first impulse in a perceived crisis is to flee or to fight without allowing what intrudes an opportunity to fully reveal itself. The voice of wisdom, if present, can curtail and modulate what might otherwise prove harmful or disarming, the consequence of too hasty action. Prudence is the word we use today. It is important to be able to hear and to heed wisdom's voice when we are present to it and willing to be open to more than our fear or impulse for aggression. Part of this more reasoned response is to be attuned to the wisdom of elders who have earned the right to be heard and heeded. We may on occasion turn to our ancestors more than those living, to be guided.

Meditation:

Have you served or been served by the voice of wisdom in a moment of crisis? Was the voice that of an ancestor?

December 20: Book XXIV

"But when the flame of Hephaistos had made an end of you,
At the dawn, Achilles, we gathered your white bones
In unmixed wine and in oil. And your mother gave
A golden two-handled jar. She said it was a gift
Of Dionysos, the work of highly renowned Hephaistos.
So in it, glorious Achilles, your white bones lie,
Mingled with those of dead Patroklos, Menoitios' son;
Apart are those of Antilochos, whom you honored
Above all your other companions after the dead Patroklos. . . .
       You were very dear to the gods.
So you did not lose your name. even when you died, Achilles" (XXIV. 71-79; 92-93).

Agamemnon continues his praise of Achilles and finishes the story not given in the *Iliad*: his death and honor. Here the gods mingle with the lives of mortals; Achilles' half-mortal, half-divine nature bridges the two. His mother, Thetis, the gods Hephaistos and Dionysos all gather in name and press around the corpse of Achilles to give him an honorable burial, one befitting a great hero. This scene forces us to remember the origin and return of Odysseus who battled bravely in Troy and has now returned to fight again to restore the spirit of hospitality in the home. The heroic image of Achilles is a lodestar to show the magnificence of the heroic which can be lost within the mediocrity and acquisitiveness of the suitors.

All of our experiences have a memory, a history which we should not lose in the present. Our memory contextualizes the past into a form we can both comprehend and share, if not occasionally alter. Then the fuller outlines of the plot of our lives and those of others can be revealed; without these memories like the one above, we live in a half-realized story. Stories told can be even more potent than stories lived. The psychiatrist Robert Coles writes in *The Call of Stories* that "the beauty of a good story is its openness—the way you or I or anyone reading it can take it in, and use if for ourselves" (qtd. in Slattery, *Our Daily Breach* 11). Stories are portable mirrors for self-reflection, inspiration and guidance on how to live authentically.

Meditation:

Have you considered writing a memoir to leave for others a legacy of your full story, as you remember it? Leaving such a legacy can be a treasure to others.

December 21: Book XXIV

And then the soul of Amphimedon addressed him:
"Glorious son of Atreus, Zeus-nourished Agamemnon,
Lord of men, I do remember all the things you say,
And I shall tell you everything truthfully and well,
The evil end of our death, the way it came about.
We wooed the wife of Odysseus, who was gone so long;
She neither refused the hateful wedding nor carried it out,
Contriving for us death and black destiny; . . .
She set a great loom in the halls, and on it she wove
A large and delicate fabric. . . .
And in the nights she undid it, when she had the torches set up.
So three years she fooled the Achaians and persuaded them" (XXIV. 120-27; 129-30; 140-41).

One of the suitors steps forward to pick up the memory of another narrative and weave it into the one just recounted, that of the heroic performance of Penelope who had her own war at home and to which she found a disguise to conceal her true intentions. As Odysseus had has spear, bow and shield, Penelope had her great loom as a weapon of deception through disguise. Without her courage and *metis* there would be no home for Odysseus to return to. Her making/unmaking in a constant rhythm, aligned with the natural cycle of day and night, allowed her deception to be believed long enough for Odysseus to struggle home and use his own *metis* to disguise himself, and with Athene's agency, to devise a plan to defeat his adversaries.

So many of our life's challenges become possible to overcome when we are assisted by another. When the labor is distributed, allowing each to exercise their respective talents, success becomes more possible. The *Odyssey* is an epic about the power of cooperation and a shared vision of what conspires within shared values. Being mortal and limited, we often need the assistance of both gods and other mortals. Penelope's oath or promise that she will marry one of the suitors when the garment, the *pharos,* (*The Craft of Zeus* 68), is completed, adds another layer of persuasion to her deception.

Meditation:

Recall a life circumstance wherein only with the help of another or others could you make your way through it to achieve a goal you set out to realize.

December 22: Book XXIV

Then the soul of the son of Atreus spoke out to him:
"Blessed son of Laertes, Odysseus of many wiles,
Truly you have won a wife of great excellence.
How good was the mind of blameless Penelope,
Daughter of Icarios, who remembered Odysseus well,
Her wedded husband! And so the fame of her excellence
Shall never die. The immortals shall make for men on the earth
A delightful song about constant Penelope.
Not so did the daughter of Tyndareus devise her evil deeds,
Who killed her wedded husband; and a hateful song shall there be
Among men, and she will bestow a harsh reputation
On womankind, even on one who is good in what she does" (XXIV. 191-202).

The soul of Agamemnon praises Penelope above all others to her husband. She is to be as renowned as Odysseus; together they will share in *kleos*. She achieved her own heroic epic challenge. Her memory of him is woven into the fabric of her funeral shroud for Laertes, her husband's father. Penelope has achieved glory equal to her husband such that songs will be sung of her, as Homer does here in the epic. She is praised in dramatic contrast to the infidelity of Clytemnestra who murders her husband Agamemnon shortly after he arrives home from Troy. Her reputation will now be sullied in song for eternity.

We cannot or should not self-praise. The code above is that one performs right heroic action and then leaves it to others to sing of one's achievements. It is a form of immortality. To perform one's life well, with skill, humility and in accord with the divine, will bring its own rewards. Fame in this way is a form of immortality and one's life is perpetuated through song and story as a model for others to emulate. Here the dead are at work in the lives of the living, conferring on them rewards and shame from the realm of Hades. Homer reveals repeatedly that neither the gods nor the dead are separate from those still alive. A constant porous membrane is all that separates Olympus, earth and Hades. If these exempla of excellence are lost, then incidents of heroism will disappear from our memories.

Meditation:

Who do you praise? Who do you help confer immortality on through your remembrance of their achievements?

December 23: Book XXIV

He found his father alone in the well-laid vineyard,
Digging around a plant. He had a dirty tunic on,
A sorry patched one. And greaves of oxhide were bound
In patches on his calves to keep him from getting scratched.
He had gloves on his hands on account of brambles. . . .
With this in mind, Odysseus went directly to him.
The man was holding his head down and digging around the plant.
Standing beside him, his illustrious son spoke out:
"Old man, no lack of skill is yours as you tend
The orchard, but good care is yours. . . .
Your person is not well cared for, but along with woeful old age
You have a foul squalor and are wearing sorry clothes" (XXIV. 226-30; 241-45; 249-50).

The moment connecting Odysseus to his father is a crucial event in the former's homecoming. Not just to the fatherland of Ithaca but to the father, person of his origins. The old man digging in the earth seems to have despaired of his son ever returning to him, so he has ceased caring for himself. He digs in the earth to ward off his sorrow. His son addresses him with respect but also acknowledges how the old man has allowed squalor to overtake him unchecked. He wears "sorry clothes" as Odysseus did to disguise himself in his own home. It is a gentle rebuke to his father, but just underneath it is a sadness over the fact that Odysseus' absence has contributed to his father's condition of despair and degradation. Connecting with his origins contributes to his ritual of homecoming.

Homer points to the suffering family members who also endure exceptional loss over time as their family member, as warrior, and wanderer, was gone for a long time; the pain of abuse and the human cost of war cannot be adequately measured. Its many forms of suffering are too excessive and too unbelievable. Many may never speak of it or calibrate its effects on family and friends. Many, like Laertes, would prefer to die than to endure the pain of loss much longer. Trauma from war is not confined to those who actually do battle on the field.

Meditation:

What loss of a family member or close friend brought you to the edge of despair or extreme grief at their loss?

December 24: Book XXIV

"Here I am, father, the very man you ask about:
I have come in the twentieth year to my fatherland.
But hold off from weeping and tearful lamentation.
I shall tell you right out; nevertheless, we must hurry.
I have slain the suitors within our own halls,
Punishing their heart-hurting injury and evil deeds."
And then Laertes answered and spoke out to him:
"If you are my son Odysseus who have arrived here,
Tell me now some very plain sign, so I may be convinced . . . ."
"First of all, take notice with your eyes of this scar
That a boar inflicted on me with shining tusk on Parnassos
When I had gone there" (321-29; 331-33).

Revelation rather than concealment guides this scene as Odysseus presents himself to his father, who stands in disbelief that the warrior before him is his son. But before he can question Odysseus' identity, the latter urgently confirms that slaughtering the suitors will incite a backlash by their families that Odysseus must prepare for. But he pauses when his father asks for some documentation as to his son's identity. The scar is the memory of the wound inflicted on him by the wild boar when he was young, and he was named by his grandfather in infancy. His father Laertes knows of the scar's history and the story surrounding its rim. Homer reveals, as he does throughout the epic, of the intimacy between history and myth, between time and autobiography and between wounding and identity.

Perhaps the most famous scar in literature asks us to reflect on how the body is marked with memories of previous encounters and carries our identity deep within them. Tattoos, birth marks, surgical scars, wounds from battles past, dismemberments all point to the textual nature of the body, which is continually marked by the world. I have written elsewhere on the *Odyssey* and scars: "If the body is always an emblem of our history, then its wounded markings are the permanent witnesses to that same body's identity. In the markings of the body are the tracings of that person's mythology" ("Nature and Narratives" 27).

Meditation:

Describe a mark or scar on your body and relate its history within your life's broader narrative. Was the marking a signal moment in your development?

December 25: Book XXIV

Now the messenger Rumor went everywhere fast through the town
Declaring the suitors' hateful death and destiny.
When all had heard it, they strayed in from every side
With murmur and groaning in front of Odysseus' halls.
They carried their corpses, each from his house and buried them. . . .
Then they went in a body to the places of assembly, grieving in heart. . . .
"Let us go. Or else hereafter we shall always be disgraced."
These deeds are a shame to learn about, even for future men;
Unless we avenge us on the murderers of our kinsmen and sons.
To my mind at least it would not then be sweet to live" (XXIV: 413-17; 419-20; 432-35).

Rumor is a powerful psychic and emotional force in society; it can create great dissension among those who seek an outlet for their agony and frustration. Rumor can breed and cultivate false stories to rile up an individual or a people. The news of the slaughter seeps into all corners of Ithacan life and galvanizes the grieving families who have come to bury their sons and daughters. The father of the suitors' leader, Antinoos, speaks out of his pain. Eupeithes calls to arms those suffering losses. More warfare is needed to avenge Odysseus' massacre in order to reclaim his home. Shame is the motivator to save face and avenge their children's deaths; shame is also a motivating force in Homer's world, as E.R. Dodds describes it ("From Shame Culture to Guilt Culture" 17).

When a society becomes ensnared in violence as the first way to solve a complex problem, then the imagination has once again surrendered to its easiest impulse—to war with the other. Nothing more nuanced or thoughtful will allow for a more permanent compromise. In this case, hospitality (*xenia*) has been violated in the families of the suitors. Violence in the service of preserving one's dignity will deliver the same result: more violence. Such is the way of an addiction on an individual or on a collective scale. The fact that life itself has been violated transcends the violation of their individual families.

Meditation:

In what situation did you call on violence, either in thought, word or deed, as a solution? Was the result what you intended?

December 26: Book XXIV

Then Athene spoke out to Zeus, the son of Cronos:
"Our father, son of Cronos, highest of all rulers,
Tell me when I ask, what plan of yours is concealed here?
Will you fashion further an evil war and dread battle,
Or will you establish friendship between both sides?"
And cloud-gathering Zeus addressed her in answer:
"My child, why do you ask me and question me about this?
Why did you not think out this idea by yourself,
That Odysseus might indeed take vengeance on them when
He came?
Do as you wish, but I will tell you what seems fitting" (XXIV. 472-81).

It sounds as if the current unrest has gotten out of hand as Athene, in a quandary over more fighting, cannot grasp mortals' propensity to solve everything through violence. She turns to her father in bewilderment, wondering what grand design *he* might possess. He questions her on why *she* did not think through to the end the return of Odysseus and his certain wrath toward the suitors. She feels check-mated by the preparation of both Odysseus as well as the family and friends of the suitors to clash once more in yet another version of the Trojan conflict that rested on the insult against the Achaians because of Helen's abduction. *Bie* without *metis* in conjunction or cooperation, leads to more of the same solutions that are, finally, not satisfactory because they do not explore the nature of conflict itself deeply enough in order to imagine a more peaceful resolution.

Individuals, tribes, and nations seem most often to follow a blind instinct to create war as a solution so that who is mightiest and most forceful is the victor. Often open diplomacy can deflect catastrophic damage and loss of life, but so often we see beautiful and irreplaceable cities leveled and whole populations forced on to the highway, escaping often with only a few bags of possessions. With this destruction history is left with a hole or gap in it. The adamant sense of both sides believing they are absolutely right and thus having the authority to obliterate their opponent often levels both adversaries. The price tag can be beyond belief.

Meditation:

Do you have a method for engaging conflict and even diffusing it? Does the conflict itself take over and dictate the terms of its growth?

December 27: Book XXIV

"Since godly Odysseus has done vengeance on the suitors,
Let them solemnize an oath that he may always reign.
And let us bring about oblivion for the murder
Of their sons and kinsmen. Let them love one another
As before, and let there be abundant wealth and peace."
When he said this, he aroused Athene, who was eager before.
She went down in a rush from the summits of Olympos. . . .
"Here they are nearby. Let us quickly arm ourselves!"
So he said. They rose up and got their armor on,
Four including Odysseus, and the six sons of Dolios,
And among them Laertes and Dolios put armor on,
Gray though they were, warriors by necessity (XXIV. 481-87; 495-99).

Zeus speaks first here in laying out a plan that will require both warring parties to concede their wrath and compulsion to get even. His solution is words, not war, a mutual compromise, not escalating conflict, a contract to agree on, not chaos to feed on. His solution pleases Athene, goddess of war and words, so she moves quickly to implement it. The second speaker is Odysseus, who falls back into the impulse for war to defend his *oikos* and to reclaim goods lost to the suitors. Old and young don armor to recreate on a smaller scale the Trojan conflict. The future then promises more bloodshed and loss for both sides, as well as the attendant suffering it will perpetuate.

Two solutions: come to an agreement through the restraint of an oath or push into bloodshed that will create further resentment and civil uncertainty. One requires sacrificing resentment and beginning again; the other is to further the violence and loss that war guarantees. The first moves human consciousness forward while the latter perpetuates the same destruction and loss. The first advances humankind; the latter encourages the same futile pattern of waste. I have suggested "an oath is a woven marriage between contrary tensions into a fabricated whole even as it contains the scar tissue of the conflict" ("Oath-Taking as Scar-Making" 82). Zeus' wisdom suggests, "Let them love one another as before."

Meditation:

Where in your life situations did you discover the value of oath-taking, or compromise agreed upon by both parties, as a valued response to an intractable conflict?

December 28: Book XXIV

At once he spoke out to his dear son Telemachos:
"Telemachos, you will soon learn, now you have come yourself
To where men are fighting and the best ones are judged,
Not to disgrace the family of your fathers, who before
Were distinguished for strength and prowess on the whole earth."
The sound-minded Telemachos said to him in answer:
"In my present spirit, dear father, you will see, if you wish,
That, as you say, I shall not at all disgrace your family."
So he said, and Laertes rejoiced and spoke a word:
"What a day is this for me, dear gods! I greatly rejoice
That my son and my grandson contend over excellence" (XXIV. 505-15).

For the first time in the epic, father, son and grandson form a trio in the service of more warfare, traditionally the horrific ground for individuals to show excellence (*arete*) in character and deeds; from this they may gain *kleos*, or renown. In so doing, it perpetuates war as a field for fame and glory. There seems to be no other option. But Zeus' suggestion of oath-taking makes restraint, yielding and compromise the new heroic code. It will, however, require a yielding of the will on both sides in order to be secured. A new form of heroism, one based on restraint and moderation rather than warfare, may be birthed. Dodds relates how *ate* is a form of the irrational (38) and "a temporary clouding or bewildering of the normal consciousness" ("Shame" 5). Further war at this stage seems to be a consequence of *ate*. Both old and young fear disgrace, a form of dishonor.

Yielding, compromising, restraining can be spun as being soft or lacking moral fortitude that battle seems to offer. But interpreted along the lines of psychic and emotional growth, it is a signal of strength in new garments. "An oath allows a different imagination to intervene (puer energy) through an oral or written oath; it then codifies this imaginal form (senex energy). . . ("Oath-Taking" 83). A new form of consciousness emerges as a new world view revisioned, a less warring *habitus*, one that preserves the past rather than scatters it in warfare. Less physical fighting to reveal *bie*, more a *metis*-driven solution through language's power to restrain. Oath-making may then replace life-taking.

Meditation:

Do you believe there is power in compromise? In what way?

December 29: Book XXIV

He made a crash as he fell, and his armor clattered upon him.
Odysseus and his glorious son fell upon the fighters in the front
And struck at them with their swords and their two-edged spears.
Now they would have destroyed all and made them without return,
If Athene, the daughter of aegis-bearing Zeus, had not
Shouted with her voice and restrained the whole host:
"Ithacans, hold off from war, which is disastrous,
So you may separate without bloodshed as soon as you can."
So did Athene say. And sallow fear got hold of them (XXIV. 525-33).

We are to remember the horror of Homer's poetic language to reveal war's soaring costs and horrific blood bath both in the *Iliad* and here. Now is time for a change of heart. But for the present, Odysseus and his men are fully engaged in the slaughter of those who grieve and wish to avenge the death of their sons and kin and so deflect shame and dishonor. Athene's intervention ushers in a new consciousness, based on "holding off." Her entrance is replete with both force and craft as she insists on restraint from both sides. Their separation will preserve the city; her speech in her unmediated voice strikes terror in her audience wherein they show immediate restraint.

So often in history one or the other side in a conflict affirms that God or a god spoke directly to them to go to battle in righteousness. A divinity or deity is often crafted to justify any horrible or self-serving interests. Not often does a divinity cry out for war's cessation, which makes the *Odyssey* a revelatory poem of compromise to preserve something larger than either sides' claim to rightness and justice. An oath forms a community out of differences and oppositions, not sameness. "An oath offers both sides of a conflict an occasion to imagine themselves through the oath's image in a newly-formatted consciousness" ("Oath-Taking" 84). Then the tension that develops in both sides compromising by giving up something of value thwarts shame, dishonor and guilt. It creates a third world, one in which energy exists in the compromise. The essence of that tension exists in honoring the terms of the truce. Language prevails as a force for peace.

Meditation:

What might you add to the value of a contract or oath-taking that preserves both history and the future?

December 30: Book XXIV

Godly Odysseus, who had endured much, shouted dreadfully.
He bunched himself up and swooped down like a high-flying eagle.
Then the son of Cronos shot a smoldering thunderbolt.
It fell before the bright-eyed daughter of the mighty father.
Then bright-eyed Athene spoke out to Odysseus:
"Zeus-born son of Laertes, Odysseus of many wiles,
Hold off and cease from the strife of impartial war,
Lest Zeus, the broad-seeing son of Cronos, in some way get angry" (XXIV. 537-44).

Odysseus' response is like that of a god. He swoops down like an eagle amid his powerful shouts. Zeus joins him by sending a thunderbolt to the earth, a signal of his power and perhaps his growing impatience, to awaken the mortals. Mortal and immortal meet in such a terrifying and potent moment. Fear and a sense of panic pervade the scene. Close to her father's lightning bolt, Athene speaks words of restraint to Odysseus and cautions against rousing her father's wrath. She calls war "impartial" to suggest it will delete men on both sides without favoritism. Together, father and daughter seem to drain the appetite for further violence from both adversaries. Athene is clear that once Zeus' own wrath is unleashed, there will be far worse consequences for both sides.

The language of restraint, holding back, pausing in moments of crisis may spare destruction and death that need not happen unless all fetters are lifted. Pedro Lain Entralgo has written that the presence of "Logotherapy is as ancient as Western culture itself," but "the curative word—by this I mean the use of the spoken word to achieve the cure of a patient" was part of the Homeric world (*The Therapy of the Word* 32). The power and wisdom of the right words can forestall greater and often senseless destruction. But it seems to need some divine intervention and assistance; so often it happens that calling on the gods is a way to begin a war, not end it. As the *Odyssey* began with an invocation to the muses to aid the poet in telling the story, so it ends with the invocation of the gods to bring the narrative to a new conclusion.

Meditation:

When have you been able to check yourself from going into battle, which includes with one's self? Did language in the form of persuasion play a role?

December 31: Book XXIV

So Athene said. He obeyed, and rejoiced in his heart.
Then Pallas Athene, daughter of aegis-bearing Zeus,
Established oaths for the future between both sides,
Likening herself to Mentor in form and in voice (XXIV. 545-48).

In these final lines of the epic, the city of Ithaca is spared duplicating the fate of Troy. Odysseus is not just relieved by the intrusion of an alternative to war, he rejoices in its presence. The divine feminine who embodies as well the masculine wisdom of the father, crafts the language of the oaths for the future by restoring in a healing way, the past. She performs this civilizing task by likening herself to mentor, teacher, shaman, as she aided the journey of Telemachos in Book I in the disguise of Mentes. So the epic opens with a disguise and closes with one. Failure to be instructed leaves no room for the space of mediation that oaths insist on and promote. She assumes both voice and form of the teacher who seeks in her students the desire for compromise. This is the great achievement of Homer's epic that uses Odysseus and Penelope and the young Telemachos, but then goes beyond them to a new template for marriage, one between opposing forces that requires a third presence in order to achieve a higher level of consciousness: the oath itself, fashioned into language by Athene's wisdom.

Jean Pierre Vernant offers an insightful comment on the place of memory in the Greek imagination: "Memory has a deep ordering principle at its core. It [she] has the capacity to return us to origins, the beginnings of things. To reach the very foundation of being, to discover what is original—makes it possible to understand the whole process of becoming" (*Myth and Thought Among the Greeks* 78). An oath, therefore, is a memory of an agreement, fixed in words to be recalled regularly. Through Athene "Words now have warrior energy in a new form" ("Oath-Taking" 85). Oaths mediate irreconcilable differences not by destroying one or favoring another, but by creating an atmosphere so both attitudes can exist in a peaceful tension with one another. Mediation marries difference through the ritual act of oath-creating and oath-remembering. It is, as Vernant says of memory, an ordering principle that holds order in tension with the always-possible disorder, in a mutual marriage.

Meditation:
You might ask where in your own life would an oath or some language compromise relieve tension and suffering by allowing contrary forces to coexist?

EPILOGUE

A word on the poems that follow. As I developed this project I had the good fortune to meet Dr. Edward Tick, founder of www.soldiersheart.org, a nonprofit organization that assists American veterans in healing from both physical and moral wounds from Viet Nam and other deployments in various wars we continue to wage in the world.

That meeting led me to pay more attention to Odysseus as a traumatized war veteran seeking asylum in his own home that he struggles for a decade after the war to reclaim. Tick's work, *Warrior's Return: Restoring the Soul After War* (2014) was particularly influential in understanding this complex dimension of Odysseus and his men as they struggled for stability after the Trojan War. In our conversations and sharing our poetry, Ed sent me four poems that he had written when using Homer's epic to aid veterans as they sought to reclaim their own souls by returning to Vietnam or sought counseling within Ed's organization.

I include them here with Ed's permission as a tribute to his and his organization's work over decades, serving those veterans who struggle to complete their homecoming in both body and soul. For many, coming home could happen only after returning to Viet Nam to recover their souls and make peace with the conflicts still roiling within them. I hope you enjoy these "Homeric" poems as much as I have. They are an excellent Epilogue to the story you have just journeyed through. I hope the journey revealed delicious mysteries of your own myth.

AND LIKE ACHILLES...

And like Achilles enraged
at the slight of commanders
lesser at leadership or arms,
at the loss of my beloved,
my friends, my golden armor,

I assault the staunch, stubborn
walls that shield another love
and, maelstrom against cliff-face,

waste myself in slaughter
of the man most noble, kind, true,

and finally fall, temples throbbing,
eyes, hands, legs runnels of red,
until ire and insult lift
and I see not the hated city

but the high one, loved, deserving,
where honor lived above pride,
service above greed. At my hands gone.
And I turn my heels toward Paris. . . .

NAUSIKAA

> Nausikaa was the Phaeacian princess who found Odysseus washed up on her island, then succored and protected him during his last stop on his long journey home from the Trojan War. *Odyssey,* Book VI.

Gentle princess of this sea-bleached isle,
the gift you have prayed for
lies washed up on your shore.
A storm-slashed hulk,
he sleeps on your gleaming sands.

Gaze upon his strong still form
as Helios' golden fingers
swath his salt-stained skin.
Gently - O do not rouse him! -
wash then oil his limbs and hair.

Step back. He stirs awake.
His battles with thunder, sea and men
still wrinkle and beat his broad brow.
Meet his dark gaze with the liquid eyes
that anoint and melt the muscles of war.

Wrap him in the soft white robes
that caressed your dove-filled shoulders.
Guide him to the king your father
imploring the rites of strangers.
Feast him. Gift him. Hear his tales.

How many years have you cried, Princess,
before the Mother's altar.
Your thighs, your arms, your heart
have ached to wrap him round.
Now like seafoam the gift has come.

Your heart trills, but his dark eyes
stare toward a sea-flung hearth.
Is the gift yours? Or do we lose the beloved
forever at the moment of arrival?
Is the smile of the goddess her curse?

When your father's strong oars
lance him through the cutting waves
you must let him go. Throw your empty arms
wide across the great carved altar,
your hot tears the only oil of offering.

THE BAG OF WINDS

> When in return I asked his leave to sail
> and asked provisioning, he stinted nothing,
> adding a bull's hide sewn from neck to tail
> into a mighty bag, bottling storm winds....
> *Odyssey,* X, 19-22

Mere wind, I cried
against their fear that turned a bag of breeze
into gold filling only my pockets.
My men, I cried
against the god whose breath battered
my skiff from native shores toward oblivion.
How could they? I tore my cloak but knew.
It is our hunger weaves a fiend of breath.
It is our terror makes the powers that glide us home
exile us the very moment
we betray the trust of the wind.

ODYSSEUS' PRAYER

Your supplicant here
stomping the shores of sea-girdled Ithaca
pacing his palace with lion's thighs
till the very stones shake.

Your priestess there
on her azure breasted isle
skin forever smooth as olive oil
longing forever maiden.

And my wife still waiting on the portico
gazing across the frothing sea
eyes glazed with cataracts
fingers arthritic from weaving.

You play great tricks
on your chosen ones, O Goddess,
to hear their prayers
and grant them.

WORKS CITED

Arbery, Glenn. "Homer: The *Iliad* and the *Odyssey*." *Invitation to the Classics: A Guide to You've Always Wanted to Read*. Ed. Louise Cowan and Os Guinness, The Trinity Forum, Baker Books, 1998, pp. 29-33.
Armstrong, Robert Plant. *Wellsprings: On the Myth and Source of Culture*. U of California P, 1975.
---. *The Powers of Presence: Consciousness, Myth, and Affecting Presence*. U of Pennsylvania P, 1981.
Austin, Norman. "Nausikaa and the Word that Must Not Be Spoken: A Reading of Homer's *Odyssey*, Book Six." *Arion*, 25. 1, 2017.
Bond, D. Stephenson. "Play: Where Two Worlds Touch." *Living Myth: Personal Meaning as a Way of Life*. Shambhala, 1993, pp. 99-126.
Bowra, C.M. *Ancient Greek Literature*. Oxford UP, 1960.
Brann, Eva. *Homeric Moments: Clues to Delight in Reading the Odyssey*. Paul Dry Books, 2002.
Bradt, Kevin, S.J. "Rejecting Story: Modern Psychotherapy." *Story as a Way of Knowing*. Sheed and Ward, 1997, pp. 63-87.
Campbell, Joseph. "Departure." *The Hero With a Thousand Faces*. Bollingen Series XVII. Princeton UP, 1973, pp. 49-96.
---. *Thou Art That: Transforming Religious Metaphor*. Ed. Eugene Kennedy. New World Library, 2001.
---. "The Vitality of Myth." *Mythology and the Individual*, tape 5. The Joseph Campbell Foundation, 1996.
---. *The Inner Reaches of Outer Space: Metaphor as Myth and as Religion*. New World Library, 1986.
---. "*Iliad* and *Odyssey*: Return to the Goddess." *Goddesses: Mysteries of the Feminine Divine*. Safron Rossi, editor, New World Publishing, 2013, pp. 143-79.
---. "Mythologies of War and Peace." *Myths to Live By*. Penguin Group, 1972, pp. 169-200.
---. *Correspondence: 1927-1987*. Evans Lansing Smith and Dennis Patrick Slattery, editors, New World Library, 2019.
Casey, Edward S. *The World at a Glance*. Bloomington: Indiana UP, 2007.
---. *Getting Back into Place: Toward A Renewed Understanding of the Place World*. Indiana UP, 1993.

Coupe, Laurence. "Part II: Mythic Reading." *Myth: The New Critical Idiom*. Second edition. Routledge, 2009, pp. 83-214.

Cowan, Donald. "The Stages of Learning." *Classic Texts and the Nature of Authority: An Account of a Principals' Institute Conducted by The Dallas Institute of Humanities and Culture*. Donald and Louise Cowan, editors, The Dallas Institute Publications, 1993, pp. 69-75.

---. "The Uses of Defeat." Classic Texts and the Nature of Authority, pp. 50-56.

Cowan, Louise. "Epic as Cosmopoiesis." *The Epic Cosmos*. Larry Allums, editor, The Dallas Institute Publications, 1992, pp. 1-26.

---. "Poetic Knowledge and Poetic Form." Lecture at The University of Dallas, Irving Texas, Nd.

---. "The Literary Mode of Knowing." *Classic Texts and the Nature of Authority: An Account of a Principals' Institute Conducted by The Dallas Institute of Humanities and Culture*. Donald and Louise Cowan, editors, The Dallas Institute Publications, 1993, pp. 14-22.

---. "The Joy of Learning." Lecture Delivered at The Dallas Institute of Humanities and Culture, Dallas, Texas, December 14, 1983.

---. "*The Odyssey* and the Efficacy of Imagination." *Classic Texts and the Nature of Authority: An Account of a Principals' Institute Conducted by The Dallas Institute of Humanities and Culture*. Donald and Louise Cowan, editors, The Dallas Institute Publications, 1993, pp. 57-68.

Dalby, Andrew. "Reading the *Iliad* and the *Odyssey* Afresh." *Rediscovering Homer: Inside the Origins of the Epic*. Norton, 2006, pp. 196-204.

Denby, David. "Homer II." *Great Books: My Adventures with Homer, Rousseau, Woolf, and Other Indestructible Writers of the Western World*. Simon and Schuster, 1996, pp. 76-87.

DeSalvo, Louise. *Writing as a Way of Healing*. Beacon P, 2000.

Detienne, Marcel. *The Masters of Truth in Ancient Greece*. Janet Lloyd, translator, Zone Books, 1999.

Dimock, G.E. Jr. "The Name of Odysseus." *The Odyssey*. Albert Cook, translator and editor, Norton, 1974, pp. 406-424.

Dodds, E.R. "From Shame Culture to Guild Culture." *The Greeks and the Irrational*. U of California P, 1951, pp. 28-63.

Downing, Christine. *Gods in Our Midst: Mythological Images of the Masculine: A Woman's View*. Crossroads, 1993.

Dreyfus, Hubert and Sean Dorrance Kelly. "Homer's Polytheism." *All Things Shining: Reading the Western Classics to Find Meaning in a Secular Age*. Free Press, 2011, pp. 58-87.

Eakin, John Paul. *How Our Lives Become Stories: Making Selves*. Cornell UP, 1999.

Easter, Sandra. *Jung and the Ancestors: Beyond Biography, Mending the Ancestral Web*. Muswell Hill Press, 2016.

Eliot, T.S. "The Love Song of J. Alfred Prufrock." *The Complete Poems and Plays, 1909-1950*. Harcourt, Brace & World, 1971, pp. 3-7.

Entralgo, Pedro Lain. "The Therapeutic Word in the Homeric Epic." *The Therapy of the Word In Classical Antiquity*. L.J. Rather and John M. Sharp, translators and editors, Yale UP, 1990, pp. 1-31.

Faivre, Antoine. "Chapter One. Hermes in the Western Imagination." *The Eternal Hermes: From Greek God to Alchemical Magus*. Joscelyn Godwin, translator, Phanes Press, 1995.

Felson-Ruben, Nancy. "Penelope's Perspective." *Folktales in Homer's Odyssey*. Denys Paige, editor, Harvard UP, 1973, pp. 163-79.

Fischer, Norman. *Sailing Home: Using the Wisdom of Homer's Odyssey to Navigate Life's Perils and Pitfalls*. Free Press, 2008.

Fisher, Philip. *Wonder, the Rainbow, and the Aesthetics of Rare Experiences*. Cambridge: Harvard UP, 1998.

Foley, Helen. "Penelope as Moral Agent." *The Distaff Side: Representing the Female in Homer's Odyssey*. Beth Cohen, editor, Oxford UP, 1995, pp. 93-115.

Frank, Arthur W. *The Wounded Storyteller: Body, Illness, and Ethics*. U of Chicago P, 1995.

Frank, Jaffa Vernon. *Eyes of the Gorgon: Endometriosis, Mythic Embodiment and Freedom*. Mandorla Books, 2019.

Frye, Northrop. *The Great Code: The Bible and Literature*. Harcourt Brace, 1982.

---. "Myth, Fiction, and Displacement." *Fables of Identity: Studies in Poetic Mythology*. Harcourt Brace, 1961, pp. 21-38.

Giroux, Henry A. *The Violence of Organized Forgetting: Thinking Beyond America's Disimagination Machine*. City Lights Books, 2014.

Graham, Larry Kent. *Moral Injury: Restoring Wounded Souls*. Abingdon Press, 2017.

Hall, Edith. *The Return of Ulysses: A Cultural History of Homer's Odyssey*. The Johns Hopkins UP, 2008.

Harrison, Jane Ellen. *Prolegomena to the Study of Greek Religion*. Princeton UP, 1991.

Harrison, Robert Pogue. *The Dominion of the Dead*. U of Chicago P, 2003.

Hatab, Lawrence. *Myth and Philosophy: A Contest of Truths*. Open Court, 1992.

Havelock, Christine Mitchell. "The Intimate Act of Footwashing: *Odyssey* 19." *The Distaff Side: Representing the Female in Homer's Odyssey*. Beth Cohn, editor, Oxford University Press, 1995, pp. 185-199.

Hawley, Jack. *The Bhagavad Gita: A Walkthrough for Westerners*. New World Library, 2001.

Heidegger, Martin. "Building, Dwelling, Thinking." *Poetry, Language, Thought*. Albert Hofstadter, translator, HarperCollins, 2001, pp. 141-60.

Hillman, James. *Healing Fiction*. Spring Publications, Inc., 1983.

---. "An Inquiry into Image." *Spring: An Annual of Archetypal Psychology and Jungian Thought*. Spring Publications, 1977, pp. 62-88.

---. "On the Necessity of Abnormal Psychology." *Facing the Gods*. Spring Publications, 1980, pp. 1-38.

---. *The Dream and the Underworld*. HarperCollins Publishers, 1979.

---. *Animal Presences. Uniform Edition of the Writings of James Hillman*, vol. 9. Spring Publications, 2008.

---. "Puer Wounds and Ulysseus' Scar." *Senex and Puer*, Glen Slater, editor. Volume 3 of *The Uniform Edition of the Writings of James Hillman*, Spring Publications, 2005, pp. 214-47.

---. "War is Sublime." *A Terrible Love of War*. Penguin, 2004, pp. 104-177.

Holscher, Uvo. "Penelope and the Suitors." *Reading the Odyssey: Selected Interpretive Essays*. Seth L. Schein, editor, Princeton UP, 1996, pp. 133-40.

Houston, Jean. *The Hero and the Goddess: The Odyssey as Mystery and Initiation*. HarperCollins, 1992.

Hoyle, Mary Lou. "From Comedy to Tragedy: The Shift in Perspective." *Classic Texts and the Nature of Authority: Essays From a Principals' Institute*. Donald and Louise Cowan, editors, The Dallas Institute, 1993, pp. 123-37.

---. "The Sword, the Plow, and the Song: Odysseus' Great Wanderings." *The Epic Cosmos*. Ed. Larry Allums, The Dallas Institute Publications, 2000, pp. 59-88.

Jabr, Ferris. "The Story of Storytelling." *Harper's Magazine*/March 2019. 36-41.

Jung, C.G. *The Red Book. Liber Novus. A Reader's Edition.* Introduction by Sonu Shamdasani, editor. Mark Kyburz, John Peck et al. Philomon Series, Norton, 2009.

---. The Archetypes and the Collective Unconscious. Vol.9i. *The Collected Works of C.G. Jung*. R.F.C. Hull and Gerhard Adler, editors and translators. 2nd. Edition, Princeton U P, 1959/1971.

---. *Mysterium Coniunctionis: An Inquiry into the Separation and Synthesis of Psychic Opposites in Alchemy*. Vol. 14. *The Collected Works of C.G. Jung*. Ed. Herbert Read, Michael Fordham, et. al., translators. R.F.C. Hull, Princeton UP, 1963/1977.

Kearney, Richard. "Narrative Matters." *On Stories*. Routledge, 2002, pp. 129-56.

Kerenyi, Carl. *Athene: Virgin and Mother. A Study of Pallas Athene*. Murray Stein, translator, Spring Publications, 1978.

---. *The Gods of the Greeks*. Norman Cameron, translator, Thames and Hudson, 1961.

Laqueur, Thomas W. *The Work of the Dead: A Cultural History of Mortal Remains*. Princeton UP, 2015.

Loy, David R. *The World is Made of Stories*. Wisdom Publications, 2010.

Maritain, Jacques. *The Range of Reason*. Charles Scribner's Sons, 1952.

McAdams, Dan P. "The Meaning of Stories." *The Stories We Live By: Personal Myths and the Making of the Self.* The Guilford P, 1993, pp. 19-38.

Melville, Herman. *Moby-Dick; or, The Whale.* Introduction by Clifton Fadiman. Illustrated by Boardman Robinson. Collector's Edition. The Easton Press, 1971.

Mendelsohn, Daniel. *An Odyssey: A Father, A Son and an Epic.* William Collins, 2018.

Murnaghan, Sheila. "The Plan of Athena." *The Distaff Side: Representing the Female in Homer's Odyssey.* Beth Cohen, editor, Oxford UP, 1995, pp. 61-80.

Nagy, Gregory. "Part I. Demodokos, *Odyssey, Iliad.*" *The Best of the Achaeans: Concepts of the Hero in Archaic Greek Poetry.* The Johns Hopkins UP, 1981, pp. 13-66.

O'Brien, Tim. *The Things They Carried.* Houghton Mifflin, 1990.

Onians. R.B. "Some Processes of Consciousness." *The Origins of European Thought: About the Body, the Mind, the Soul, the World, Time, and Fate.* Cambridge UP, 1994, pp. 13-22.

Otto, Walter F. *Dionysus: Myth and Cult.* Robert B. Palmer, translator, Indiana UP, 1965.

Otto, Walter F. "Religion and Myth in High Antiquity." *The Homeric Gods: The Spiritual Significance of Greek Religion.* Random House, 1954, pp. 13-40.

Pearson, Carol S. *The Hero Within: Six Archetypes We Live By.* Third Edition. HarperCollins Publishers, 1998.

Quibell, Deborah Anne, Jennifer Leigh Selig and Dennis Patrick Slattery. *Deep Creativity: Seven Ways to Spark Your Creative Spirit.* Shambhala Publications, 2019.

Reinhardt, Karl. "The Adventures in the *Odyssey.*" *Reading the Odyssey: Selected Interpretive Essays.* Seth L. Schein, editor, Princeton UP, 1996, pp. 63-132.

Rosenblatt, Louise. *The Reader, the Text, the Poem: The Transactional Theory of the Literary Work.* Southern Illinois UP, 1978.

Ross, Lena B. "Transitional Phenomena in Clinical Practice: The Toad is Always Real." *Liminality and Transitional Phenomena.* Nathan Schwartz-Salant and Murray Stein, editors, *The Chiron Clinical Series,* Chiron Publications, 1991, pp. 89-98.

Rowland, Susan. *Jungian Literary Criticism: The Essential Guide.* In the series: *Jung: The Essential Guides.* Luke Hockley, editor, Routledge, 2019.

Rumi, Jelaluddin. *The Essential Rumi.* Coleman Barks, editor and translator, Castle Books, 1997.

Sanford, W.B. *The Ulysses Theme: A Study in the Adaptability of a Traditional Hero.* Spring Publications, 1992.

Schacter, Daniel L. *Searching for Memory: The Brain, the Mind, and the Past.* Basic Books, 1996.

Scheid, John and Jesper Svenbro, et al. *The Craft of Zeus: Myths of Weaving and Fabric.* Carol Volk, translator. *Revealing Antiquity*, vol. 9. General Editor, G.W. Bowersock, Harvard UP, 1996.

Shay, Jonathan. *Odysseus in America: Combat Trauma and the Trials of Homecoming.* Scribner, 2002.

Shlain, Leonard. *The Alphabet and the Goddess: The Conflict Between Word and Image.* Penguin, 1998.

Skafte, Dianne. *Listening to the Oracle: The Ancient Art of Finding Guidance in the Signs and Symbols All Around Us.* Harper SanFrancisco, 1997.

Slattery, Dennis Patrick. "Hestia: Goddess of the Heart(h)." *Bridge Work: Essays on Mythology, Literature and Psychology.* Mandorla Books, 2015, pp. 93-102.

---. "The Narrative Play of Memory in Epic." *The Epic Cosmos.* Larry Allums, editor, Louise Cowan, Series editor, The Dallas Institute Publications, 2000, pp. 331-52.

---. "Nature and Narratives: Feeding the Fictions of the Body in Homer's *Odyssey.*" *The Wounded Body: Remembering the Markings of Flesh.* State U of New York P, 2000, pp. 21-50.

---. *A Pilgrimage Beyond Belief: Spiritual Journeys through Christian and Buddhist Monasteries of the American West.* Angelico P, 2017.

---. *Riting Myth, Mythic Writing: Plotting Your Personal Story.* Fisher King Press, 2012.

---. Review of Edward Tick's *Warrior's Return: Restoring the Soul After War.* "Depth Insights." Depth Psychology Alliance, Bonnie Bright, editor, Issue 9, Summer, 2016.

---. "Oath-Taking as Scar-Making:Remembering the Original Wound." *Conversing With James Hillman. Puer and Senex.* Robert Sardello, editor, Joanne H. Stroud, Series editor, Dallas Institute Publications, 2016, pp. 81-86.

Snell, Bruno. "Homer's View of Man." *The Discovery of the Mind: The Greek Origins of European Thought.* T. G. Rosenmeyer, translator, Harper and Brothers, 1953, pp. 1-22.

Spence, Donald P. *Narrative Truth and Historical Truth: Meaning and Interpretation in Psychology.* Norton, 1982.

Stern, Donnel B. *Partners in Thought: Working with Unformulated Experience, Dissociation, and Enactment. Psychoanalysis in a New Key* Book Series, volume 12, Routledge, 2010.

Stewart, Marilyn. "Imagination and Mapping in the *Odyssey.*" *Classic Texts and the Nature of Authority: An Account of a Principals' Institute Conducted by The Dallas Institute of Humanities and Culture.* Donald and Louise Cowan, editors, The Dallas Institute Publications, 1993, pp. 76-89.

Tick, Edward. *Warrior's Return: Restoring the Soul After War.* Sounds True, 2014.

---. *War and the Soul: Healing Our Nation's Veterans from Post-Traumatic Stress Disorder*. Quest Books, 2005.

Turner, Frederick. "A New Medium of Communication." *Epic: Form, Content, and History*. Transaction Publishers, 2012, pp. 287-322.

Turner, Victor. *The Ritual Process: Structure and Anti-Structure*. Transaction Publishers, 2008.

Vaihinger, H. *The Philosophy of 'As-If': A System of the Theoretical, Practical, and Religious Fictions of Mankind*. C.K. Ogden, translator, Routledge and Kegan Paul Ltd., 1968.

Vernant, Jean-Pierre. "Death with Two Faces." *Reading the Odyssey: Selected Interpretive Essays*. Seth L. Schein, editor, Princeton UP, 1996, pp. 55-61.

---. *Myth and Thought Among the Greeks*. Janet Lloyd and Jeff Fort, translators, Zone Books, 2006.

Whitman, Cedric H. "The Odyssey and Change." *Homer and the Heroic Tradition*. Norton, 1958, pp. 285-312.

Whitmont, Edward C. *The Alchemy of Healing Psyche and Soma*. North Atlantic Books, 1993.

Wilson, Emily, translator. *Homer: The Odyssey*. Norton, 2018.

Wood, David. *What Have We Done? The Moral Injury of Our Longest Wars*. Little Brown, 2016.

Zeitlin, Froma I. "Figuring Fidelity in Homer's *Odyssey*." *The Distaff Side: Representing the Female in Homer's Odyssey*. Beth Cohen, editor, Oxford UP, 1995, pp. 117-52.

FURTHER READINGS ON THE *ODYSSEY*

Armitage, Simon. *The Odyssey: A Dramatic Retelling of Homer's Epic.* Norton, 2006.
Austin, Norman. *Archery at the Dark of the Moon: Poetic Problems in Homer's "Odyssey."* U of California P, 1983.
---. "Odysseus/Ulysses: The Protean Myth." *The Odyssey and Ancient Art.* The Edith C. Blum Art Institute, Bard College, 1992, pp. 201-07.
Bergson, Henri. *Matter and Memory.* N.M Paul and W.S. Palmer, translators, Zone Books, 1988.
Bierlein, J.F. *Parallel Myths.* Ballantine Publishing Group, 1994.
Bittlestone, Robert. With James Diggle and John Underhill. *Odysseus Unbound: The Search for Homer's Ithaca.* Cambridge UP, 2005.
Brann, Eva. "Coda: The Life of the Imagination." *The World of the Imagination.* Rowman and Littlefield, 1991, pp. 787-98.
Brooks, Peter. *Reading for the Plot: Design and Intention in Narrative.* Alfred A. Knopf, 1984.
Burkert, Walter. "The Organization of Myth. Structure and History in Greek Mythology and Ritual." *Volume Forty-Seven of the Sather Classical Lectures.* U of California P, 1979, pp. 1-34.
Burns, Ken, and Lyn Novick. *The Vietnam War.* 10 episodes. PBS, 2017.
Calasso, Roberto. *Literature and the Gods.* Tim Parks, translator, Random House, 2001.
---. *The Mythic Dimension: Selected Essays 1959-1987.* Antony Van Couvering, editor, New World Library, 2007.
---. *The Mythic Image.* MJF Books, 1974.
---. *An Open Life: Joseph Campbell in Conversation with Michael Toms.* Larsen Publications, 1988.
---. *The Inner Reaches of Outer Space: Metaphor as Myth and as Religion.* New World Library, 1986.
---. "The Vitality of Myth." *Mythology and the Individual,* tape 5. The Joseph Campbell Foundation, 1996.
Casson, Lionel. *Travel in the Ancient World.* The Johns Hopkins UP, 1994.
Clark, Lindsay. *The Return from Troy.* HarperCollins, 2006.
Cobley, Paul. *Narrative. The New Critical Idiom.* Routledge, 2001.
Conforti, Michael. *Field, Form, and Fate: Patterns in Mind, Nature, and Psyche.* Revised Edition. Spring Journal, 1999.

Cohen, Beth, editor. *The Distaff Side: Representing the Female in Homer's Odyssey.* Oxford UP, 1995.

Cook, Albert. "The Man of Many Turns." *The Odyssey.* Albert Cook, translator and editor, Norton, 1974, pp. 444-58.

Cook, Erwin F. "In the Cave of the Encloser." *The Odyssey in Athens: Myths of Cultural Origins.* Cornell UP, 1995, pp. 93-110.

Corbin, Henri. "Mundus Imaginalis Or The Imaginary and the Imaginal." Ruth Horine, translator. https://www.amiscorbin.com/en/bibliography/mundusimaginalis-or-the-imaginary-and-the-imaginal/

Coupe, Laurence. "Part II: Mythic Reading." *Myth: The New Critical Idiom.* Second edition. Routledge, 2009, pp. 83-214.

Cousineau, Phil. *Once and Future Myths: The Power of Ancient Stories in Our Lives.* Conari Press, 2001.

Cowan, Donald. "The Uses of Defeat." *Classic Texts and the Nature of Authority: An Account of a Principals' Institute Conducted by the Dallas Institute of Humanities and Culture.* Donald and Louise Cowan, editors, The Dallas Institute Publications, 1993, pp. 50-56.

---. "The Stages of Learning." *Classic Texts and the Nature of Authority. An Account of a Principals' Institute Conducted by The Dallas Institute of Humanities and Culture.* Donald and Louise Cowan, editors, The Dallas Institute Publications, 1993, pp. 69-75.

---. "The Literary Mode of Knowing." *Classic Texts and the Nature of Authority: An Account of a Principals' Institute Conducted by The Dallas Institute of Humanities and Culture.* Donald and Louise Cowan, editors. The Dallas Institute Publications, 1993, pp. 14-22.

---. "Epic as Cosmopoiesis." *The Epic Cosmos.* Larry Allums,, editor. Louise Cowan, Series editor, The Dallas Institute Publications, 1992, pp. 1-26.

Davenport, Guy. *Every Force Evolves a Form. Twenty Essays.* North Point Press, 1987.

Denby, David. "Homer II." *Great Books: My Adventures with Homer, Rousseau, Woolf, and other Indestructible Writers of the Western World.* Simon and Schuster, 1996, pp. 76-87.

Detienne, Marcel. *The Masters of Truth in Ancient Greece.* Janet Lloyd, translator, Zone Books, 1999.

Doll, Mary Aswell. "Introduction: Moreness, Myth and the Pedagogy of Diversion." *The More of Myth: A Pedagogy of Diversion.* Sense Publishers, 2011, pp. xv-xviii.

Doty, William G. *The Study of Myths and Rituals.* Second edition. Alabama P, 2000.

Downing, Christine. *The Goddess.* iUniverse. 2007.

Feinstein, David and Stanley Krippner. *The Mythic Path: Discovering the Guiding Stories of Your Past—Creating a Vision For Your Future*. Introduction by Jean Houston, G.P. Putnam's Sons, 1997.

---. "Penelope's Perspective." *Folktales in Homer's Odyssey*. Denys Paige, editor, Harvard UP, 1973, pp. 163-79.

---. "Penelope's Perspective: Character from Plot." *Reading the Odyssey: Selected Interpretive Essays*. Seth L. Schein, editor, Princeton UP, 1969, pp. 163-83.

Ford, Andrew. *Homer: The Poet of the Past*. Cornell UP, 1992.

Frye, Northrop. *Words With Power: Being a Second Study of The Bible and Literature*. Harcourt, Brace, 1990.

Goldstein, Rebecca Newberger. "*The Odyssey* and the Other." *The Atlantic*, vol. 320, No. 5. December 2017, pp. 41-43.

Griffin, Jasper. "Greek Epic." *The Cambridge Companion to The Epic*. Catherine Bates, editor, Cambridge UP, 2010, pp. 13-30.

Gebauer, Gunter and Christoph Wulf. *Mimesis: Culture, Art, Society*. Don Reneau, translator, U of California P, 1992.

Gower, Dona. "Athena and the Paradigm of the Teacher." *Classic Texts and the Nature of Authority: An Account of a Principals' Institute Conducted by the Dallas Institute of Humanities and Culture*. Donald and Louise Cowan, editors, The Dallas Institute Publications, 1993, pp. 36-49.

Halliwell, Stephen. *The Aesthetics of Mimesis: Ancient Texts and Modern Problems*. Princeton UP, 2002.

Hanson, Victor Davis and John Heath. *Who Killed Homer? The Demise of Education and the Recovery of Wisdom*. Basic Books, 2001.

Hawkins, David R. *Power vs. Force: The Hidden Determinants of Human Behavior*. Hay House, Inc., 2002.

Hedges, Chris. *War is a Force That Gives Us Meaning*. Random House, 2002.

Hillman, James. "Further Notes on Images." *Spring: An Annual of Archetypal Psychology and Jungian Thought*. Spring Publications, 1978, pp. 152-182.

---. *The Soul's Code: In Search of Character and Calling*. Random House, 1996.

Hofstadter, Douglas and Emmanuel Sander. *Surfaces and Essences: Analogy as the Fuel and Fire of Thinking*. Basic Books, 2013.

Hollis, James. *The Archetypal Imagination. Number 8 of the Carolyn and Ernest Fay Series in Analytical Psychology*. David Rosen, General Editor, A&M U P, 2000.

Homer. *The Odyssey*. Edward McCrorie, translator. Introduction and Notes by Richard P. Martin, The Johns Hopkins UP, 2004, pp. 13-89.

Hoyle, Mary Lou. "The Sword, the Plow, and the Song: Odysseus' Great Wanderings." *The Epic Cosmos*. Larry Allums, editor, Louise Cowan, Series editon, The Dallas Institute Publications, 2000, pp. 59-88.

Illich, Ivan. *In the Vineyard of the Text: A Commentary to Hugh's Didascalicon*. U of Chicago P, 1993.

Jackson, Guida. *Traditional Epics: A Literary Companion*. Oxford UP, 1994.

Jung, C.G. "Psychology and Literature." *The Spirit in Man, Art, and Literature.* . R.F.C. Hull, translator. *The Collected Works of C.G. Jung,* volume 15. Bollingen Series XX. Princeton UP, 1978, pp. 84-105.

---. *The Wake of Imagination: Toward a Postmodern Culture.* U of Minnesota P, 1988.

Keleman, Stanley. *Myth and the Body: A Colloquy with Joseph Campbell.* Center Press, 1999.

Kovecses, Zoltan. "Metaphor in Literature." *Metaphor: A Practical Introduction.* Oxford UP, 2002, pp. 43-55.

Lattimore, Richmond, translator. *The Odyssey of Homer.* HarperPerennial Modern Classics, 2007.

Leeming, David Adams. *The World of Myth: An Anthology.* Oxford UP, 1990.

Levin, Harry. "Some Meanings of Myth." *Myth and Mythmaking.* Henry A Murray, editor, Beacon P, 1968, pp. 103-14.

Lockhart, Russel Arthur. *Psyche Speaks: A Jungian Approach to Self and World.* Chiron Publications, 1987.

Lombardo, Stanley. "On *The Odyssey.*" *The Epic Voice.* Alan D. and Robert E. Meagher, editors, Praeger Publishers, 2002, pp. 75-99.

Lord, Albert. *The Singer of Tales.* Harvard UP, 1973.

Maritain, Jacques. *Creative Intuition in Art and Poetry.* The A.W. Mellon Lectures in the Fine Arts. Bollingen Series XXXV.1. Pantheon Books, 1955.

Meletinsky, Eleazar M. "Part II: The Classic Forms of Myth and Their Expression in Narrative Folklore." *The Poetics of Myth.* Guy Lanoue and Alexandre Sadetsky, translators, Routledge, 1998, pp. 152-258.

Miller, J. Hillis. *Ariadne's Thread: Story Lines.* Yale UP, 1992.

McConkey, James, editor. *The Anatomy of Memory: An Anthology.* Oxford UP, 1996, pp. 13-66.

Nagy, Gregory. "Poetry of Praise, Poetry of Blame." *The Best of the Achaians.* John Hopkins UP, 1998, pp. 222-42.

Paz, Octavio. "Poetry and History." *The Bow and the Lyre: The Poem, The Poetic Revelation, Poetry and History.* Ruth L.C. Simms, translator, U of Texas P, 1956, pp. 167-229.

Potolsky, Matthew. "Part Two: Three Versions of Mimesis." *Mimesis: The New Critical Idiom.* Routledge, 2006, pp. 47-111.

Pozzi, Dora C and John M. Wickersham, editors. *Myth and the Polis.* Myth and Poetics Series. Series editor Gregory Nagy, Cornell UP, 1991.

Price, Simon and Emily Kearns, editors. *The Oxford Dictionary of Classical Myth and Religion.* Oxford UP, 2003.

Richards, I.A. *Coleridge on Imagination.* Indiana UP, 1965.

Richards, Mary Caroline. *Centering in Pottery, Poetry and the Person.* Wesleyan UP, 1964.

Sebeok, Thomas, editor. *Myth: A Symposium.* Indiana UP, 1968.

Segal, Charles. "Kleos and Its Ironies." *Reading the Odyssey: Selected Interpretive Essays*. Seth L. Schein, editor, Princeton UP, 1996, pp. 201-22.

Shay, Jonathan. *Achilles in Vietnam: Combat Trauma and the Undoing of Character*. Scribner's, 2003.

Slattery, Dennis Patrick. *Creases in Culture: Essays Toward a Poetics of Depth*. Fisher King Press, 2014.

---. "Poetry as Frame and as Form." *Bridge Work: Essays on Mythology, Literature and Psychology*. Mandorla Books, 2015.

---. "Mythopoiesis: The Shared Ground of Psyche's Dreaming and Poetic Impulse." *Creases in Culture: Essays Toward a Poetics of Depth*. Fisher King Press, 2014.

---. "Literary Classics and Personal Mythology." *Our Daily Breach: Exploring Your Personal Myth through Herman Melville's Moby-Dick*. Fisher King Press, 2015, pp. 1-19.

Slochower, Harry. "Introduction: Myth and Reality." *Mythopoesis: Mythic Patterns in the Literary Classics*. Wayne State UP, 1970, pp. 19-46.

Snodgrass, Mary Ellen. *Voyages in Classical Mythology*. ABC-Clio, Inc., 1994.

Some, Malidoma Patrice. *Ritual: Power, Healing and Community*. Swan/Raven and Company, 1993.

Stein, Murray, editor. *The Interactive Field in Analysis*. Volume One. Chiron Publications, 1995.

Tarnas, Richard. "The Evolution of the Greek Mind from Homer to Plato." *The Passion of the Western Mind: Understanding the Ideas That Have Shaped Our World View*. Harmony Books, 1991, pp. 16-40.

---. "VII. Awakenings of Spirit and Soul." *Cosmos and Psyche: Intimations of a New World Order*. Viking, 2006, pp. 353-451.

Trzaskoma, Stephen M., R. Scott Smith and Stephen Brunet, editors and translators. *Classical Greek Myth: Primary Sources in Translation*. Hackett Publishing Company, Inc., 2004.

Vernant, Jean-Pierre. "II. City-State Warfare." *Myth and Society in Ancient Greece*. Trans. Janet Lloyd, Zone Books, 1988, pp. 29-53.

---. *Myth and Thought Among the Greeks*. Janet Lloyd and Jeff Fort, translators, Zone Books, 2006.

Veyne, Paul. *Did the Greeks Believe in Their Gods? An Essay on the Constitutive Imagination*. Paula Wissing, translator, Chicago UP, 1988.

Walker, Steven F. *Jung and the Jungians On Myth: An Introduction*. Routledge, 2002.

Watts, Alan W. "Western Mythology: Its Dissolution and Transformation." *Myths, Dreams, and Religion*. Joseph Campbell, editor. E.P. Dutton and Co., Inc., 1970, pp. 9-25.

Weinrich, Harald. "VII. On the Poetry of Forgetting." *Lethe: The Art and Critique of Forgetting*. Steven Rendall, translator, Cornell UP, 2004, pp. 137-51.

Zolla, Elemire. *Archetypes: The Persistence of Unifying Patterns.* Harcourt Brace Jovanovich Publishers, 1981.

Zunshine, Lisa. *Why We Read Fiction: Theory of Mind and the Novel.* Ohio State UP, 2006.

ABOUT THE AUTHOR

Dennis Patrick Slattery, Ph.D., has been teaching for fifty-one years, the last twenty-six in the Mythological Studies Program at Pacifica Graduate Institute in Carpinteria, California. He is the author, co-author, editor, or co-editor of twenty-eight volumes, including seven volumes of poetry: *Casting the Shadows: Selected Poems; Just Below the Water Line: Selected Poems; Twisted Sky: Selected Poems; The Beauty Between Words: Selected Poems of Dennis Patrick Slattery and Chris Paris; Feathered Ladder: Selected Poems* with Brian Landis; *Road, Frame Window: A Poetics of Seeing. Selected Poetry of Timothy J. Donohue, Donald Carlson and Dennis Patrick Slattery;* and *Leaves from the World Tree: Selected Poems of Craig Deininger and Dennis Patrick Slattery.* He has co-authored one novel, *Simon's Crossing,* with Charles Asher. Other titles include *The Idiot: Dostoevsky's Fantastic Prince. A Phenomenological Approach; The Wounded Body: Remembering the Markings of Flesh; Creases in Culture: Essays Toward a Poetics of Depth;* and *Bridge Work: Essays on Mythology, Literature and Psychology.* With Lionel Corbett he has co-edited and contributed to *Psychology at the Threshold* and *Depth Psychology: Meditations in the Field;* with Glen Slater he has co-edited and contributed to *Varieties of Mythic Experience: Essays on Religion, Psyche and Culture;* and *A Limbo of Shards: Essays on Memory, Myth and Metaphor.* His more recent books include *Our Daily Breach: Exploring Your Personal Myth through Herman Melville's* Moby-Dick; *Day-to-Day Dante: Exploring Personal Myth Through the Divine Comedy;* and *Riting Myth, Mythic Writing: Plotting Your Personal Story.* With Jennifer Leigh Selig, he has coedited and contributed to *Re-Ensouling Education: Essays on the Importance of the Humanities in Schooling the Soul,* and *Reimagining Education: Essays on Reviving the Soul of Learning.* With Deborah Anne Quibell and Jennifer Leigh Selig he has co-authored *Deep Creativity: Seven Ways to Spark Your Creative Spirit;* with Evans Lansing Smith he has co-edited *Correspondence: 1927-1987* on the letters of Joseph Campbell. He has also authored over 200 essays and reviews in books, magazines, newspapers, and on-line journals.

He offers riting retreats in the United States and Europe on exploring one's personal myth through the works of Joseph Campbell and C.G. Jung's *The Red Book.*

For recreation he takes classes painting mythic themes in both water color and acrylic. He also enjoys riding his Harley-Davidson motorcycle with his two sons, Matt and Steve, through the Hill Country roads of Texas.

Made in the USA
Coppell, TX
07 November 2024